GRADES 2–3

The Education Center®

The IDEA MAGAZINE FOR TEACHERS® MAILBOX®

2005–2006 YEARBOOK

The Education Center, Inc.
Greensboro, North Carolina

The Mailbox® 2005–2006 Grades 2–3 Yearbook

Managing Editor, *The Mailbox* Magazine: Lauren E. Cox

Editorial Team: Becky S. Andrews, Kimberley Bruck, Karen P. Shelton, Diane Badden, Thad H. McLaurin, Debra Liverman, Karen A. Brudnak, Hope Rodgers, Dorothy C. McKinney

Production Team: Lori Z. Henry, Margaret Freed (COVER ARTIST), Pam Crane, Rebecca Saunders, Jennifer Tipton Cappoen, Chris Curry, Sarah Foreman, Theresa Lewis Goode, Clint Moore, Greg D. Rieves, Barry Slate, Donna K. Teal, Zane Williard, Tazmen Carlisle, Marsha Heim, Lynette Dickerson, Mark Rainey

ISBN10 1-56234-725-X
ISBN13 978-156234-725-3
ISSN 1088-5544

Printed in the United States of America.

The Education Center, Inc.
P.O. Box 9753
Greensboro, NC 27429-0753

Contents

Departments

Features

Arts & Crafts

Arts
&
Crafts

FOR A SOUPER GRANDMA!

Happy Grandparents Day! I love you a lot! Thanks for playing games with me and baking me chocolate chip cookies. They're my favorite!
Love,
Jeremy

"Soup-er" Grandparents Day Greetings

Showing grandparents or other special adults how much students care is as easy as A, B, C! Have each child make a greeting card by first folding a 9" x 12" light-colored sheet of construction paper in half. Then instruct him to draw a bowl of soup on the front of the card and to add desired decorations. Next, have him glue alphabet pasta into the soup bowl to spell a message like the one shown. On the inside of the card, direct him to write a short message along with his signature.

Lydia Hess, Chambersburg, PA

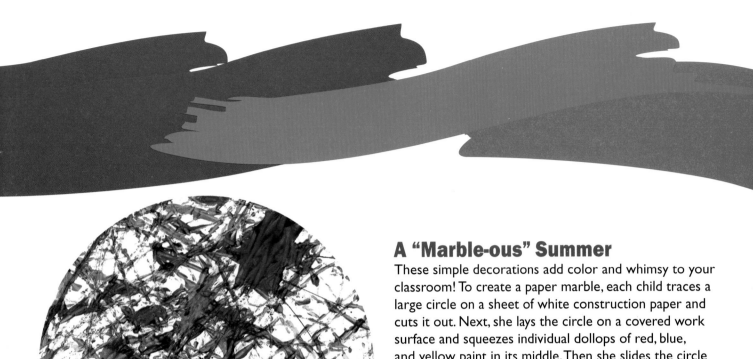

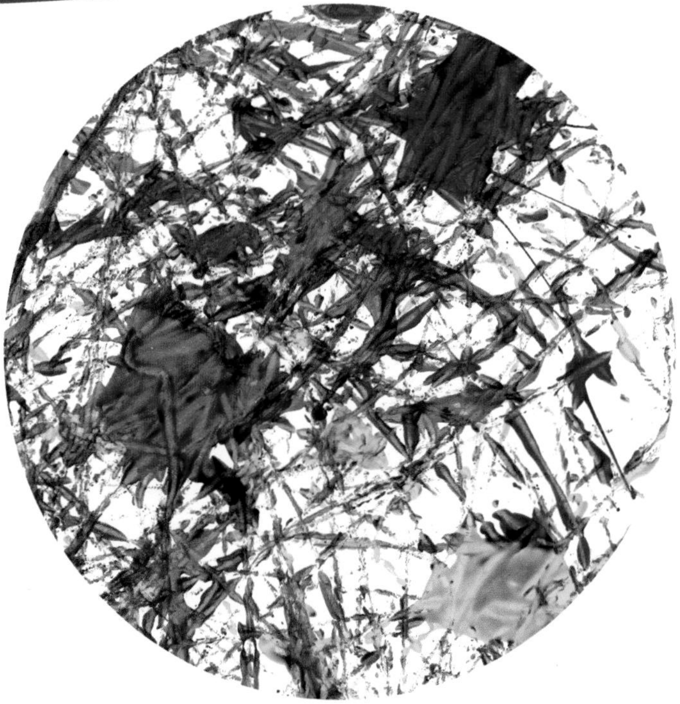

A "Marble-ous" Summer

These simple decorations add color and whimsy to your classroom! To create a paper marble, each child traces a large circle on a sheet of white construction paper and cuts it out. Next, she lays the circle on a covered work surface and squeezes individual dollops of red, blue, and yellow paint in its middle. Then she slides the circle inside a cereal box, along with four marbles. The student shakes the box, rolling the marbles back and forth, until the desired amount of paint is smeared. After the paint dries, invite each child to share her marble and a favorite memory from her summer vacation. Post the marbles on a display titled "We Had a 'Marble-ous' Summer."

Kari L. Seifert, Battle Creek Elementary, Battle Creek, NE

Alphabet Disguise

Create a one-of-a-kind display that's also a fun word puzzle! Have each child draw and color a picture that contains the letters in his name (or his initials) like the one shown. Next, instruct him to add any desired details to complete the scene. Then invite each child to share his picture with the class and challenge his classmates to find the disguised letters. Finally, display the pictures in the hall and invite students from other classes to find the hidden letters in each drawing.

Cindy Barber, Fredonia, WI

by Mario

Arts & Crafts

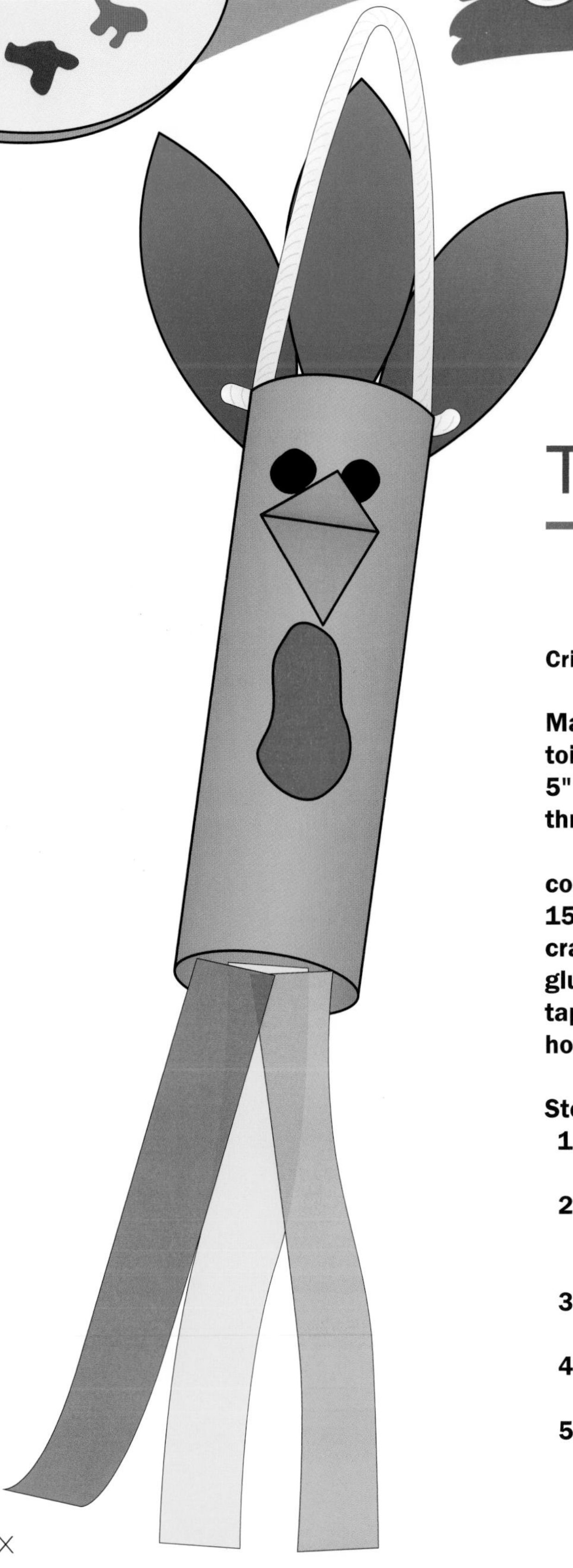

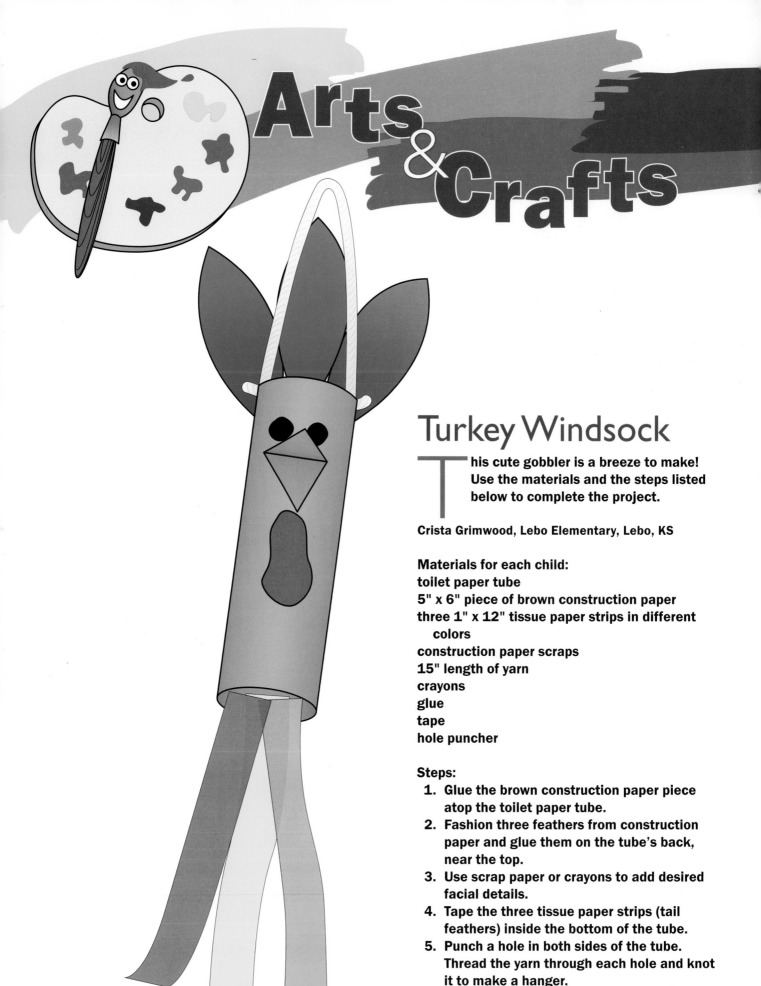

Turkey Windsock

This cute gobbler is a breeze to make! Use the materials and the steps listed below to complete the project.

Crista Grimwood, Lebo Elementary, Lebo, KS

Materials for each child:
toilet paper tube
5" x 6" piece of brown construction paper
three 1" x 12" tissue paper strips in different colors
construction paper scraps
15" length of yarn
crayons
glue
tape
hole puncher

Steps:

1. **Glue the brown construction paper piece atop the toilet paper tube.**
2. **Fashion three feathers from construction paper and glue them on the tube's back, near the top.**
3. **Use scrap paper or crayons to add desired facial details.**
4. **Tape the three tissue paper strips (tail feathers) inside the bottom of the tube.**
5. **Punch a hole in both sides of the tube. Thread the yarn through each hole and knot it to make a hanger.**

Scarecrow Glyphs

Welcome fall with these one-of-a-kind characters! Make a class supply of the scarecrow pattern on page 11 and the glyph form on page 10 and distribute them to students. Have each child follow the directions to make a scarecrow glyph. When she is finished, have her cut out her glyph. Display students' completed glyphs along with a code for easy reading. Invite students to examine the glyphs and guess who created each one.

Geoff Mihalenko, DeFino Central School, Marlboro, NJ

Spooky Spiders

Set the scene for the season with colorful creepy critters! To make a spider, use fabric glue to affix a large pom-pom to a smaller one. Next, center the large pom-pom over four pipe cleaners and secure them with fabric glue. Bend each pipe cleaner into segments to form the spider's legs as shown. Then glue wiggle eyes to the smaller pom-pom. To display each spider, loop a length of fishing line around the body and hang it from the ceiling. Spooky!

Julia Ring Alarie, Williston, VT

Scarecrow Glyph Form

Use with "Scarecrow Glyphs" on page 9.

Statements	Directions
1. I am a ________________.	Color the scarecrow's eyes
boy	blue
girl	green
2. I write with my ____________ hand.	Draw a patch on the scarecrow's
right	shirt
left	jeans
3. ___________ is my favorite season.	Color the scarecrow's shirt
Fall	orange
Winter	blue
Spring	green
Summer	red
4. My favorite subject is __________.	Draw a nose shaped like a
reading	○
math	△
5. I ____________ visited a farm.	Color the hat
have	brown
haven't	black
6. I have _____ people in my family.	On the shirt, draw that number of buttons shaped like a
two	○
three	□
four	△
five or more	▭
7. My favorite fall food is __________.	Color the scarecrow's jeans
an apple	red
pumpkin pie	orange

Scarecrow Pattern

Use with "Scarecrow Glyphs" on page 9.

TEC43021

Arts & Crafts

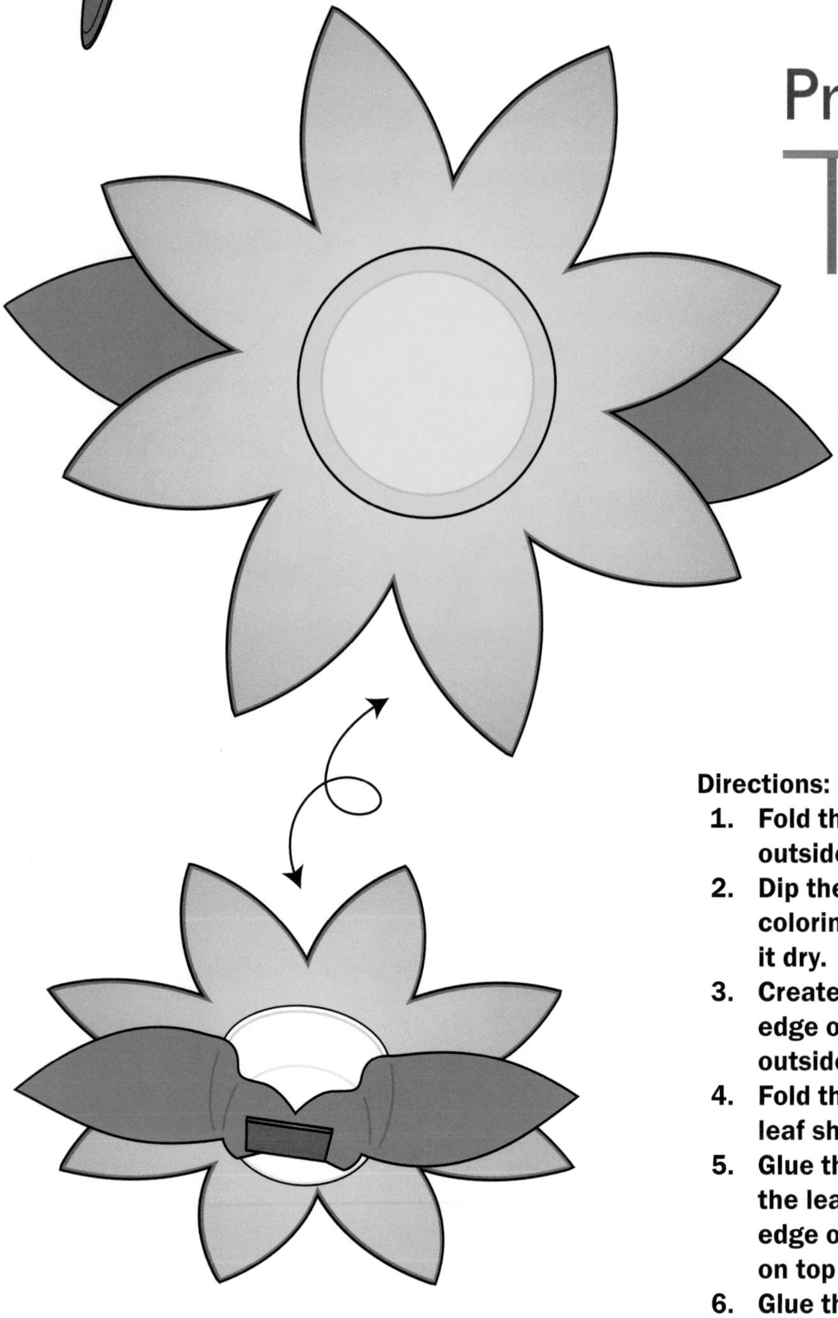

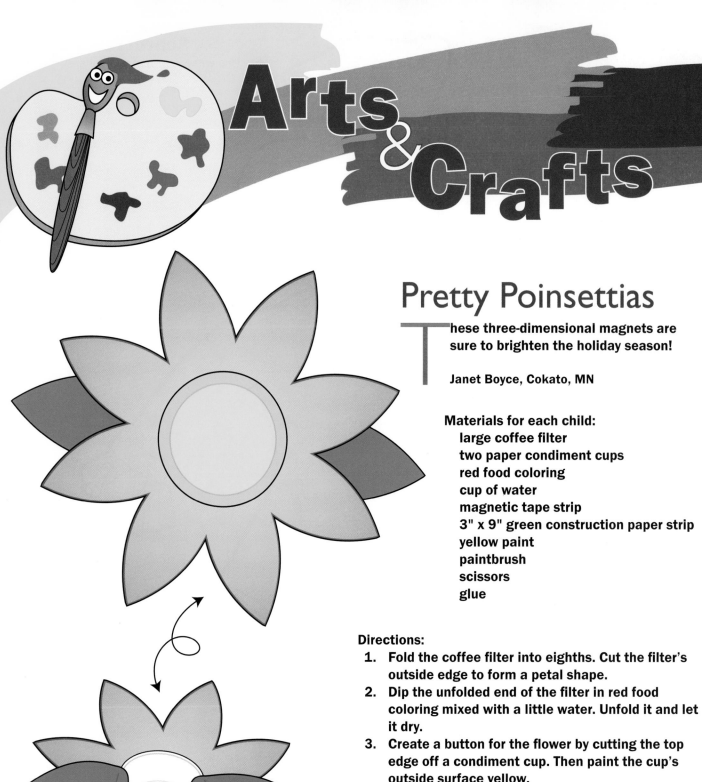

Pretty Poinsettias

These three-dimensional magnets are sure to brighten the holiday season!

Janet Boyce, Cokato, MN

Materials for each child:
- large coffee filter
- two paper condiment cups
- red food coloring
- cup of water
- magnetic tape strip
- 3" x 9" green construction paper strip
- yellow paint
- paintbrush
- scissors
- glue

Directions:
1. Fold the coffee filter into eighths. Cut the filter's outside edge to form a petal shape.
2. Dip the unfolded end of the filter in red food coloring mixed with a little water. Unfold it and let it dry.
3. Create a button for the flower by cutting the top edge off a condiment cup. Then paint the cup's outside surface yellow.
4. Fold the construction paper strip in half and cut a leaf shape. Unfold.
5. Glue the uncut condiment cup to the middle of the leaves. When it's dry, glue the filter to the top edge of the condiment cup; then glue the button on top of the filter.
6. Glue the leaves to the sides of the bottom condiment cup. Then affix a piece of magnetic tape to the back of the leaves.

CD Angel

This simple ornament adds beauty to any tree! In advance, gather a promotional CD (like those found in discount stores or junk mail) and two pipe cleaner halves for each child. To create the angel, cut out a large construction paper triangle and a small circle like the ones shown. Use crayons to add details to the angel's face and body; then glue the circle to the triangle's top. Center a pipe cleaner piece horizontally behind the triangle and secure it with fabric glue. After drying, bend the ends forward to create the angel's hands. Shape the remaining pipe cleaner piece into a halo and use fabric glue to attach it to the angel's head. Then glue the angel to the unprinted side of a CD. Add a ribbon loop for hanging, and cover the CD's back with construction paper if desired.

Barb Stefaniuk, Kerrobert, Canada

Don't Let the Sun Melt Me!

Celebrate winter with these sweet snowmen! Glue together three jumbo marshmallows as shown. Insert half a colored toothpick for a nose, and use a black permanent marker to create desired facial details. Then attach a cocktail umbrella to one side of the snowman.

Pat Biancardi, Homan Elementary, Schererville, IN

Arts & Crafts

become a
pitcher on the
baseball team
ake
all As

Lucky Four-Leaf Clovers

These 3-D clovers are the perfect classroom decoration! Have each child trace and cut out four four-leaf clovers. Then the student labels each with one thing he would use his new-found good luck for. He folds each cutout in half and then he glues the first cutout's right half to the second cutout's left half. He glues the second cutout's right half to the third cutout's left half. Finally, he attaches the fourth cutout to the remaining halves of the first and third cutouts. Finish the project by attaching a few strands of curling ribbon to the bottom. To hang the clovers, punch a hole in the top of each one and thread a length of yarn through the hole.

Conversation Heart Pencil Toppers

Invite students to send sweet messages with this quick activity! Give each child a piece of red, white, or pink craft foam and a pipe cleaner. Also provide markers, glue, and glitter. To make a pencil topper, each student traces and cuts out a foam heart. She writes a message on her heart, similar to the ones shown, and then uses markers, glitter, and glue to decorate the heart as desired. Next, she uses the pipe cleaner to punch a hole in the bottom of the heart. The child pushes the pipe cleaner's end through the hole, bends it, and twists it together. Finally, she wraps the remainder of the pipe cleaner around a pencil. Sweet!

BE MINE
YOU'RE COOL
CUTIE PIE

Stained Glass Sketches

Salute spring with this simple idea! Give each child a sheet of white paper and colored pencils. Have the student illustrate a spring scene like the one shown, making sure that his marks are heavy and dark. After he completes his drawing, give him a cotton ball with baby oil on it. The child rubs the cotton ball over his sketch to create a stained glass effect, covering the drawing completely. Allow the sketches to dry; then hang them on the windows in your classroom.

Amber Baker, Martinsville, IN

Arts & Crafts

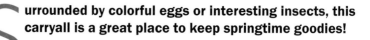

Beautiful Basket

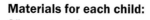

Surrounded by colorful eggs or interesting insects, this carryall is a great place to keep springtime goodies!

Deborah Lockhart, Scotia, NY

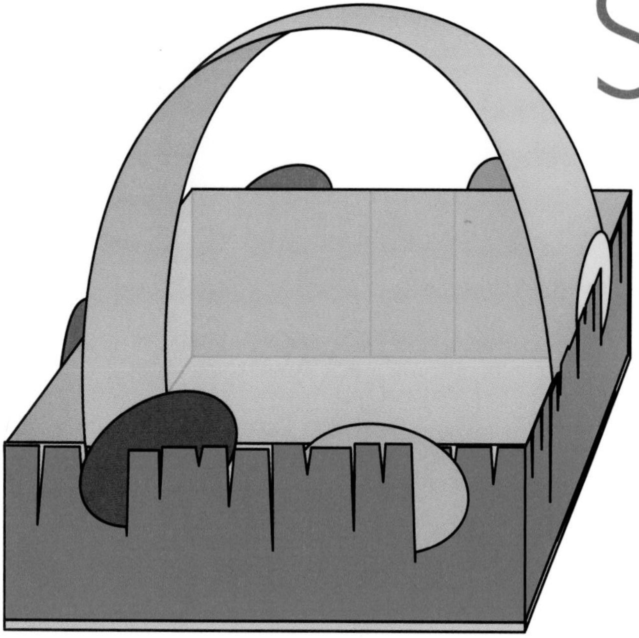

Materials for each child:
9" construction paper square
2" x 12" construction paper strip
2" x 20" green construction paper strip
construction paper scraps in a variety of spring colors
glue
scissors
ruler

Directions:

1. **Measure and mark two inches from each side of the nine-inch square. Cut two-inch slits on opposite sides of the square as shown. Use the marks as guides to make four folds.**
2. **Fold the middle pieces up; then fold the two adjacent pieces up and inward. Glue the pieces together to form the basket's base.**
3. **Cut one-inch slits a half inch apart in the green strip to make blades of grass. Glue the uncut part of the strip around the outside of the basket's base.**
4. **Glue the 2" x 12" strip to the inside of the base (handle).**
5. **Draw several ovals (eggs) on construction paper scraps and cut them out. Glue the eggs behind or between the blades of grass. Or, if desired, cut out construction paper insects and glue them in place of the eggs.**

Step 1

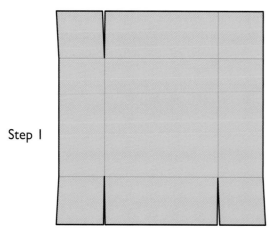

Step 2

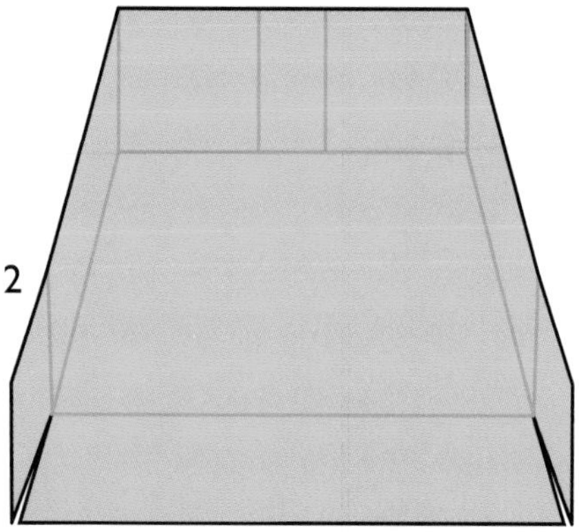

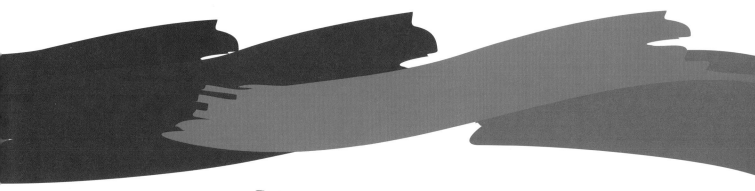

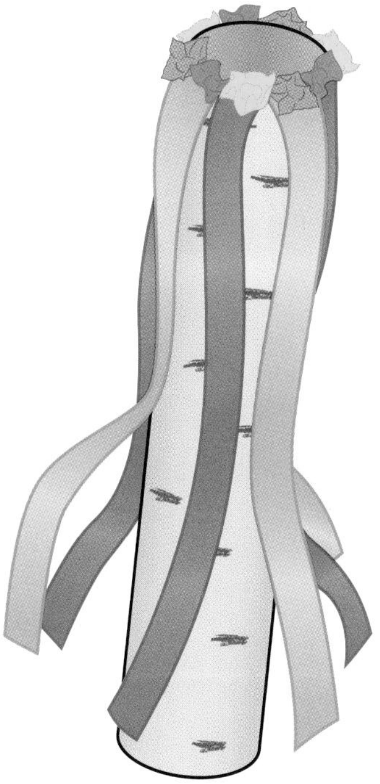

Springtime Symbol

Celebrate the first of May with this festive maypole! In advance, gather a class supply of paper towel tubes. Each student will also need a 6" x 12" piece of white tissue paper, three 12-inch streamers, and several one-inch squares of colorful tissue paper. To make a maypole, spread a thin layer of glue on the tube and cover it with the large tissue paper piece. Allow the glue to dry; then use a brown marker to add lines to resemble birch bark. Next, cut each streamer in half lengthwise. Glue one end of each streamer to the top of the tube. Finally, wrap each tissue paper square around the eraser end of a pencil and glue the square to the top rim of the tube.

Kathleen N. Kopp, Lecanto Primary School, Lecanto, FL

Mirror for Mom

This Mother's Day card is a true reflection of love! Before starting the activity, make a class supply of the mirror pattern on page 18 on white construction paper. Begin by asking each child to name an adjective that describes his mom or a loved one. List students' ideas on the board; then give each child a copy of the pattern. To complete the activity, the child cuts out the mirror and folds it in half. He writes around the circle adjectives that describe his loved one, referring to the board as needed. Next, he draws a picture of his mom inside the circle. Then he opens the card and copies the poem shown before adding his own Mother's Day message. Finally, he personalizes the card to his liking.

Dawn Marie Maucieri
Davison Avenue Elementary
Lynbrook, NY

Mom
helpful
kind
fun
smart
talented
pretty
neat

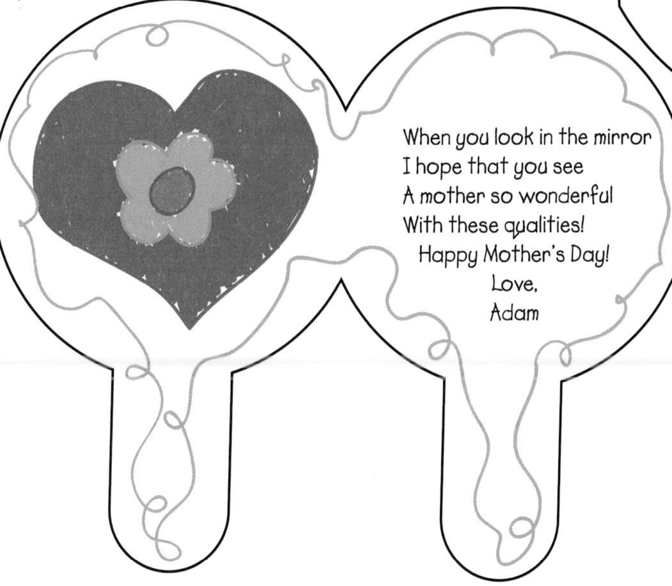
When you look in the mirror
I hope that you see
A mother so wonderful
With these qualities!
Happy Mother's Day!
Love,
Adam

Mirror Pattern

Use with “Mirror for Mom” on page 17.

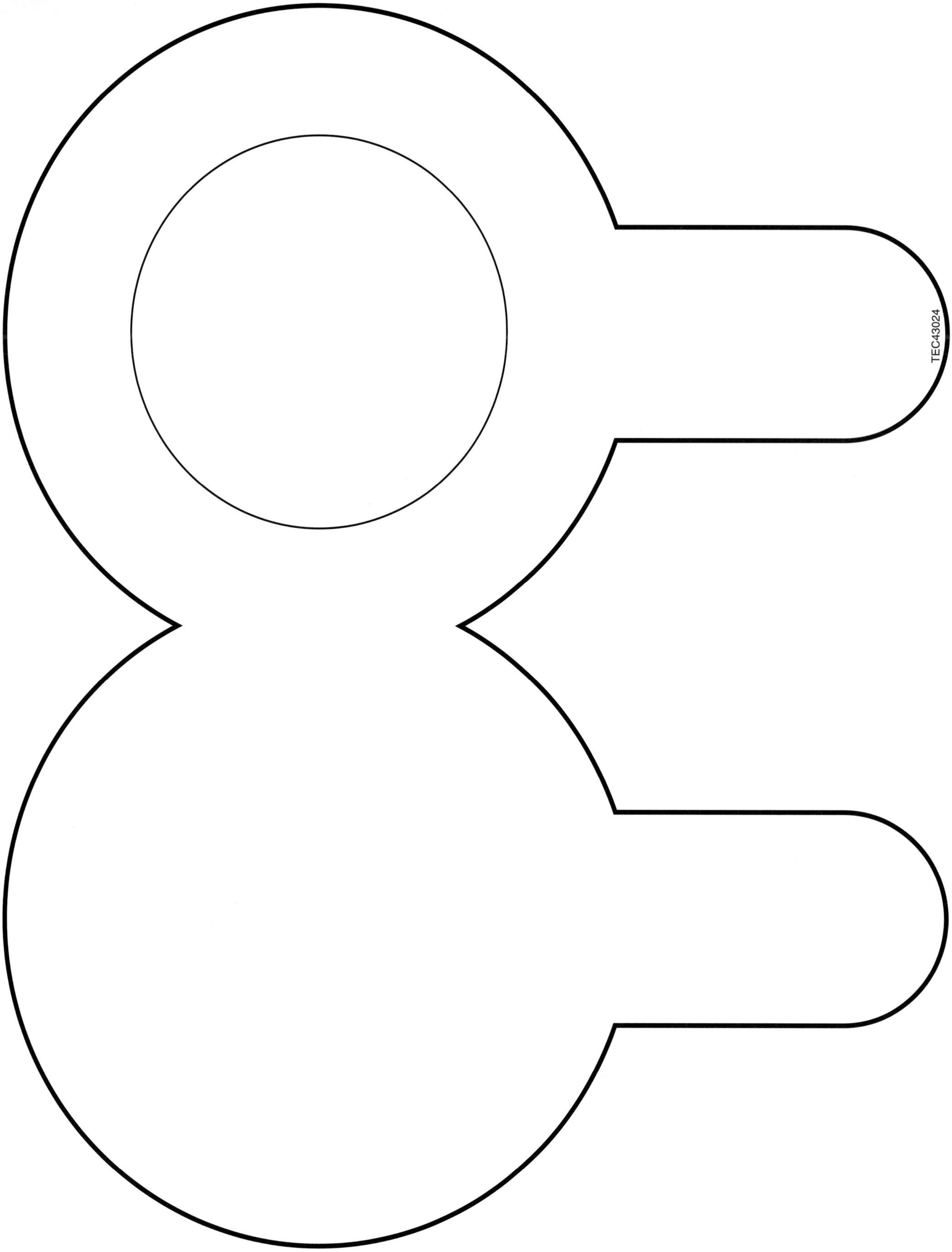
TEC43024

Arts & Crafts

Josh
2nd Grade
I remember how we observed real butterflies.
End
I remember learning about teeth at the health center.
Middle
I remember playing People Bingo on the first day of school.
Do you have a dog?
Beginning

Time Travels

Have students cruise down memory lane with this end-of-the-year project! Give each child a 6" x 18" piece of black construction paper, three $3^1/_2$" x 5" pieces of white paper, and a copy of the car and sign patterns on page 21. Have the student fold the black paper into fourths and then diagonally cut the sides of the top section as shown. He draws dotted lines down the paper's center with a yellow crayon. Next, he writes a favorite memory from the school year on each piece of white paper. He illustrates the sentences and glues the pieces of paper in order from earliest to latest, starting at the bottom section. Then he colors and cuts out the road signs and glues each one next to its matching sentence. Finally, he personalizes the car pattern, cuts it out, and glues it to the top of the black paper.

adapted from an idea by
Julie Douglas
St. Louis, MO

Brilliant Bugs

Brighten up summer days with these lovable lightning bugs! Give each student a copy of the lightning bug patterns on page 22 and a 16-inch length of black curling ribbon. Have her use crayons to personalize the thorax, head, and wing. She colors the abdomen with a yellow highlighter. Next, she cuts out each pattern and glues the three main body parts together as shown. She pokes a hole through the thorax's top and attaches the wing with a brass fastener. Finally, she measures and cuts eight two-inch ribbon lengths. She curls two pieces and tapes them to the back of the head and tapes the remaining pieces to the back of the thorax.

adapted from an idea by
Darcy Brown, Ward Elementary, Winston-Salem, NC

Name Flag

Students claim their personal space with these colorful desk flags. Give each student a 3" x 4" blue paper rectangle, a 2" x 3" white paper rectangle, and one individually wrapped red licorice stick. Also provide glitter glue, star stickers, and glue. To make a flag, each student writes his name on the white rectangle in pencil and then traces over it with glitter glue. After the glue dries, he glues the white rectangle atop the blue rectangle. Next, he decorates the flag with star stickers and glues the flag to the licorice stick. Finally, he presses the bottom of the licorice stick into a ball of clay and stands the flag on his desktop.

Carl

Laurie Heather Ginsberg, Milbrook Elementary, Baltimore, MD

Car and Sign Patterns

Use with "Time Travels" on page 19.

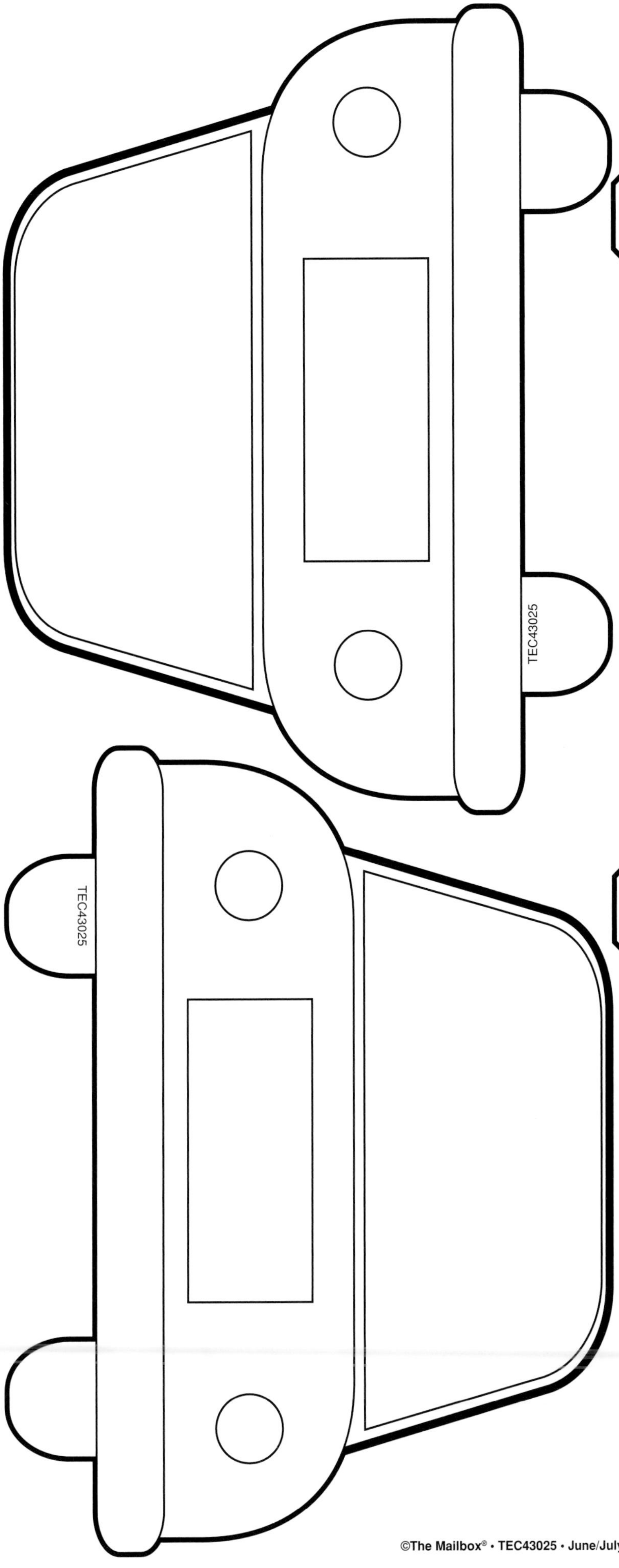

TEC43025
TEC43025

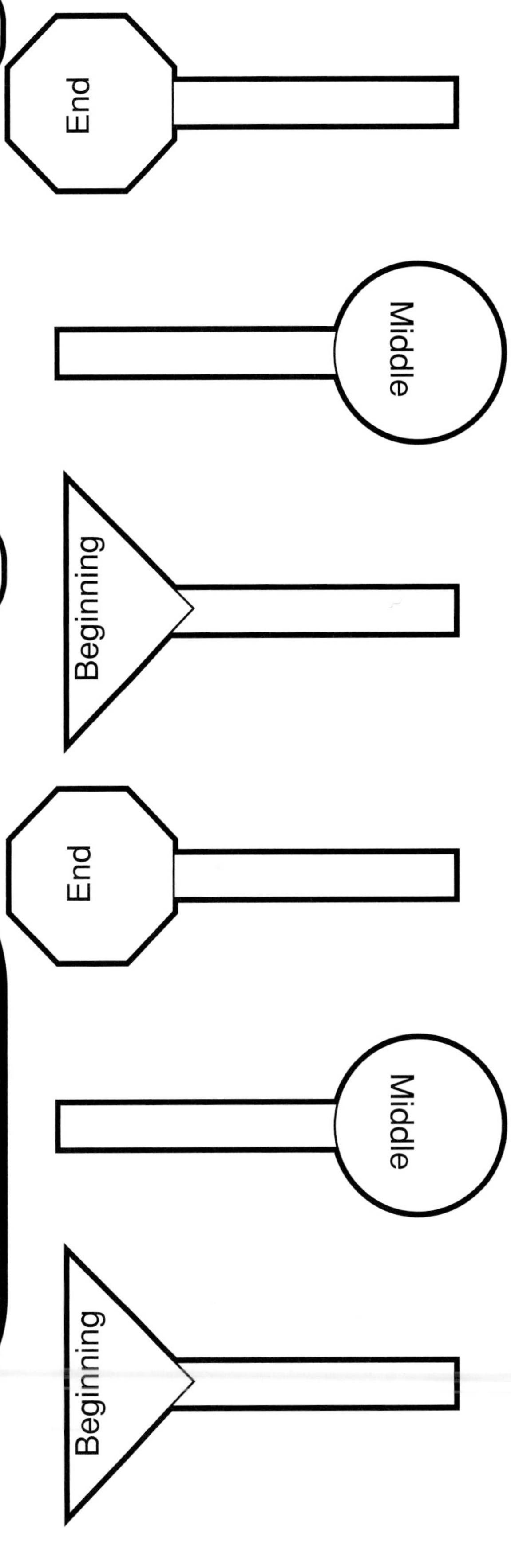

End
Middle
Beginning
End
Middle
Beginning

Lightning Bug Patterns

Use with "Brilliant Bugs" on page 20.

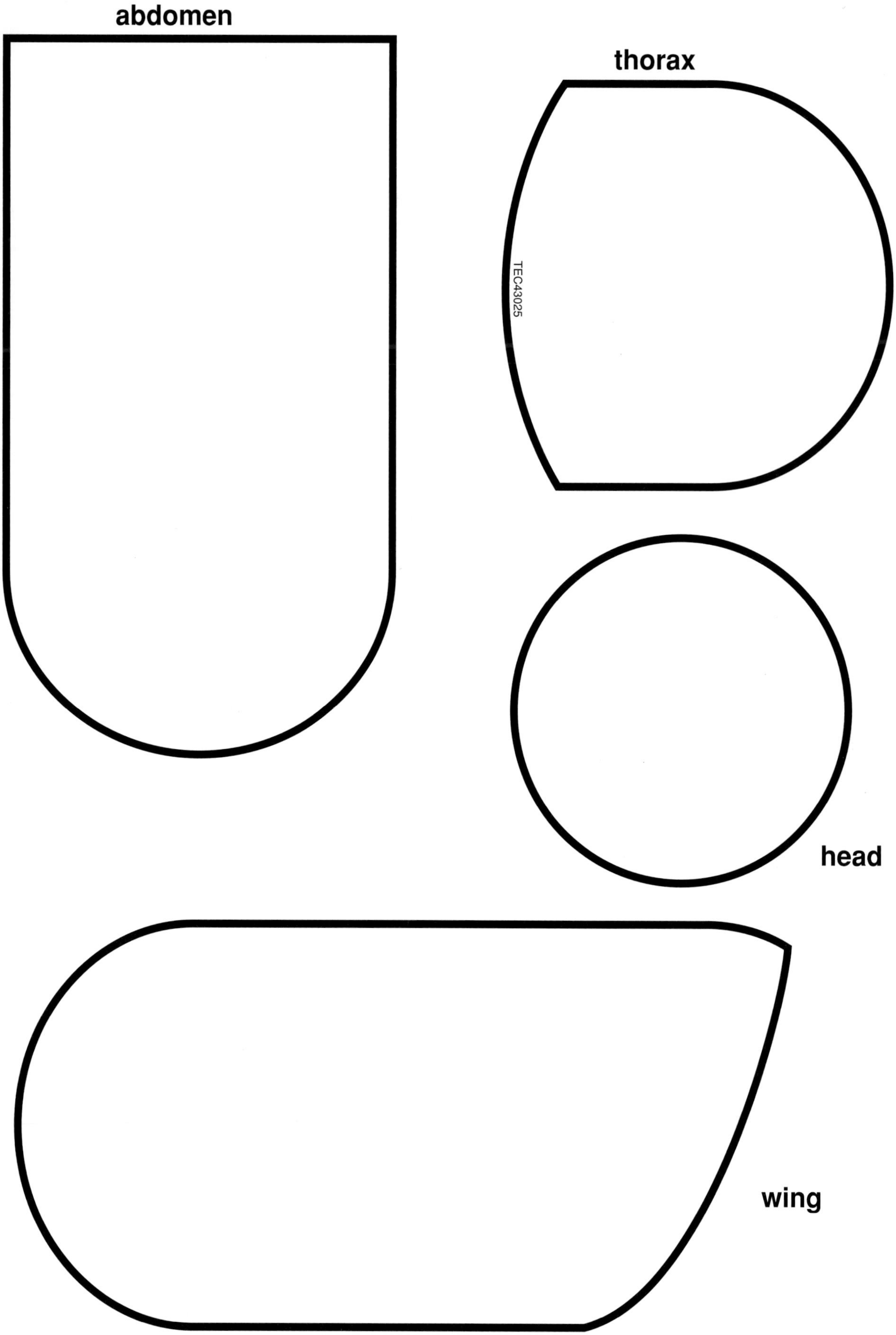
abdomen
thorax
TEC43025
head
wing

Classroom Displays

CLASSROOM

A Handful of Clues

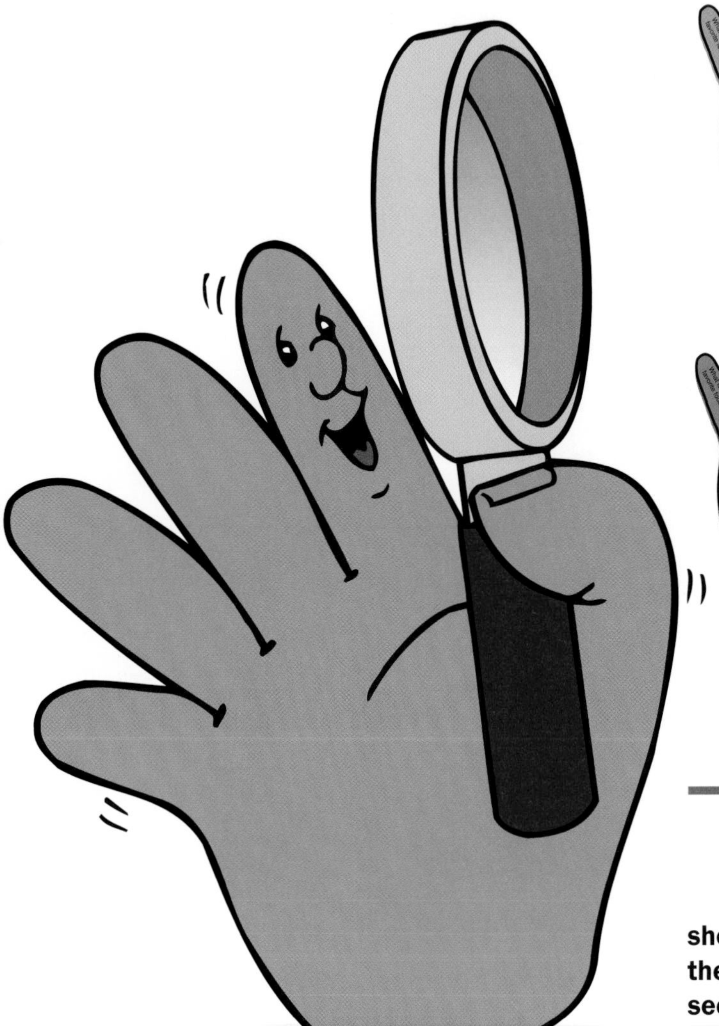

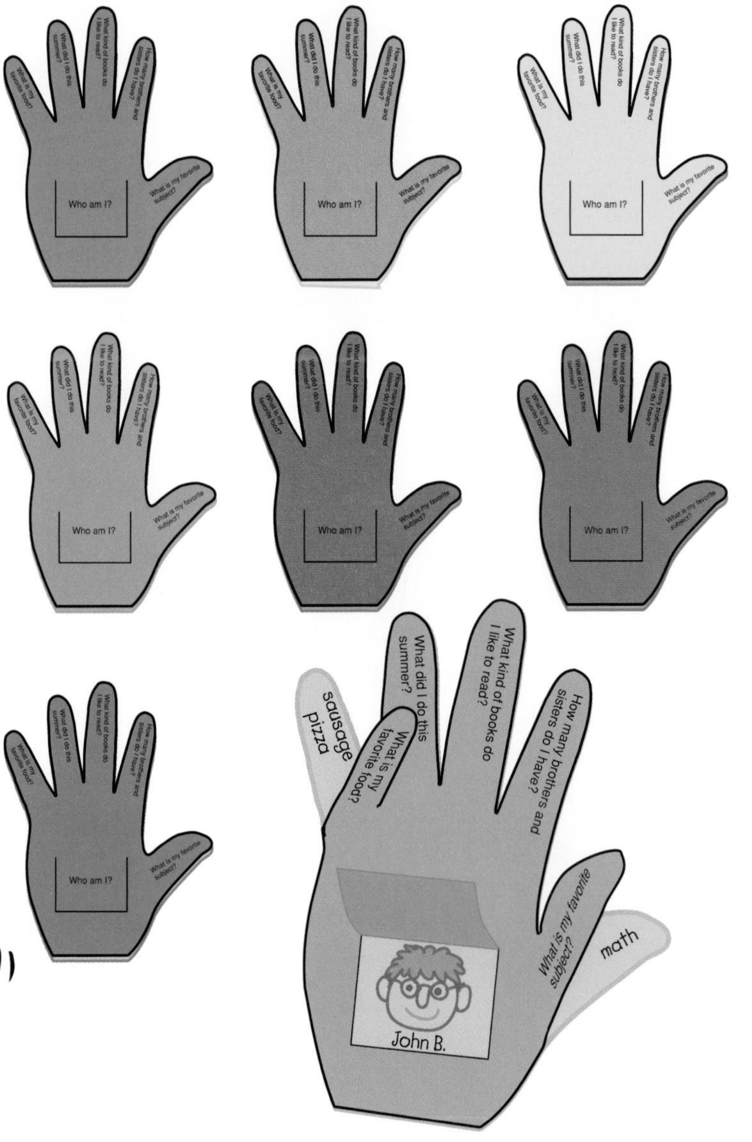

Who am I?
What is my favorite food?
What did I do this summer?
What kind of books do I like to read?
How many brothers and sisters do I have?
What is my favorite subject?
sausage pizza
math
John B.

This getting-acquainted display will get a high five from students! Each child cuts out a construction paper copy of page 26 and then traces and cuts out a second hand pattern from a different-colored sheet of construction paper. Next, he cuts out the flap in the middle of the pattern and glues the palm only to the second hand cutout, being careful not to glue down the flap. Then the child answers each question, writing his response behind the appropriate finger as shown. Finally, he draws and labels a self-portrait under the flap. Display the finished hands; then provide time for students to visit the board and learn more about their classmates.

Kristin Lane, Dolvin Elementary, Roswell, GA

DISPLAYS

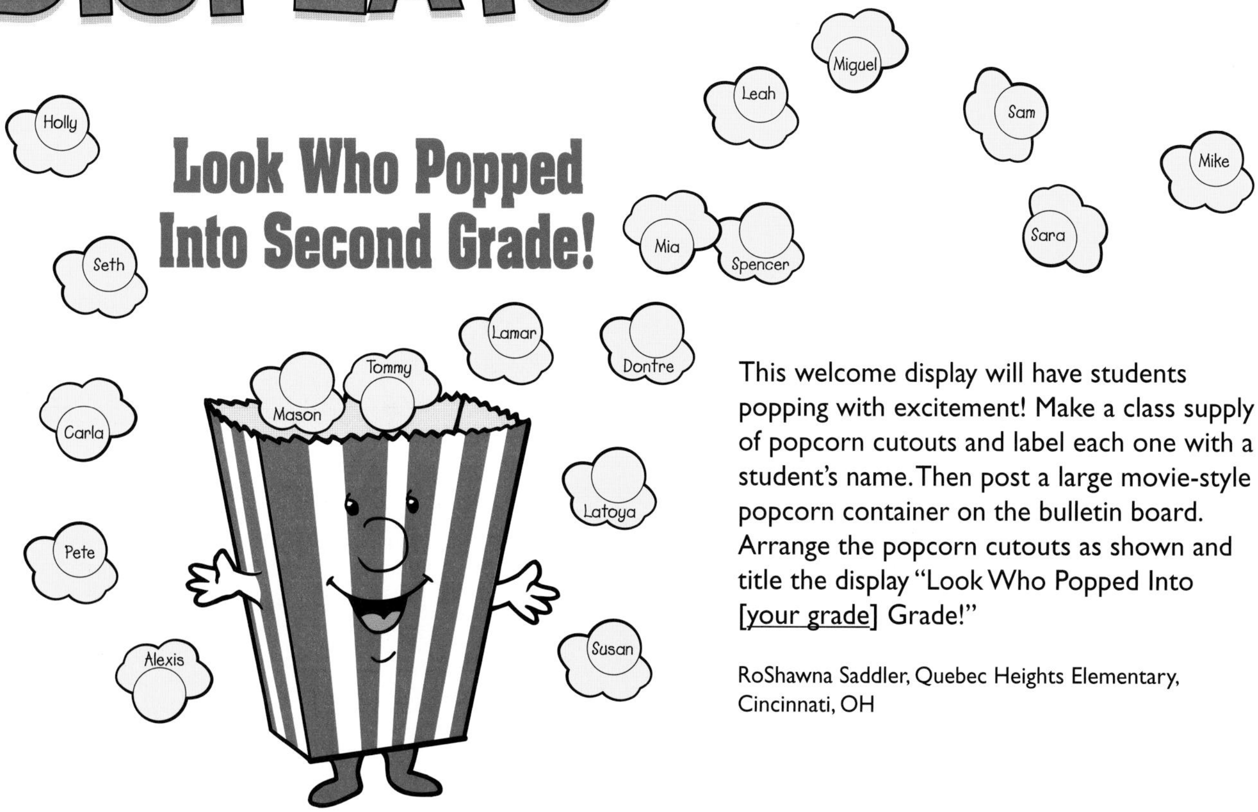

Look Who Popped Into Second Grade!
Holly
Seth
Carla
Pete
Alexis
Mason
Tommy
Lamar
Dontre
Mia
Spencer
Leah
Miguel
Sam
Sara
Mike
Latoya
Susan

This welcome display will have students popping with excitement! Make a class supply of popcorn cutouts and label each one with a student's name. Then post a large movie-style popcorn container on the bulletin board. Arrange the popcorn cutouts as shown and title the display "Look Who Popped Into [your grade] Grade!"

RoShawna Saddler, Quebec Heights Elementary, Cincinnati, OH

Our Staff Line-Up
Coach Farris
Mrs. Jones
Principal Davis
Ms. Smith
Ms. Winston
Assistant Principal Stevens
Ms. Kizer
Ms. Fields
My favorite color is red.
I love Italian food.
I have a cat named Henry.
Ms. Thomas

This is a perfect way to introduce faculty members to students and their families! Give each faculty member a copy of the T-shirt pattern on page 27. Have her write on the pattern her name and information she would like students to know, such as her favorite color, favorite food, and what kind of pet she has. Then create two T-shaped poles and post them on a centrally located wall in your school. Hang a length of clothesline between the poles and attach the T-shirt cutouts with small clothespins. What a "T-rrific" idea!

Roberta Fields, Seaford Christian Academy, Seaford, DE

Hand Pattern

Use with "A Handful of Clues" on page 24.

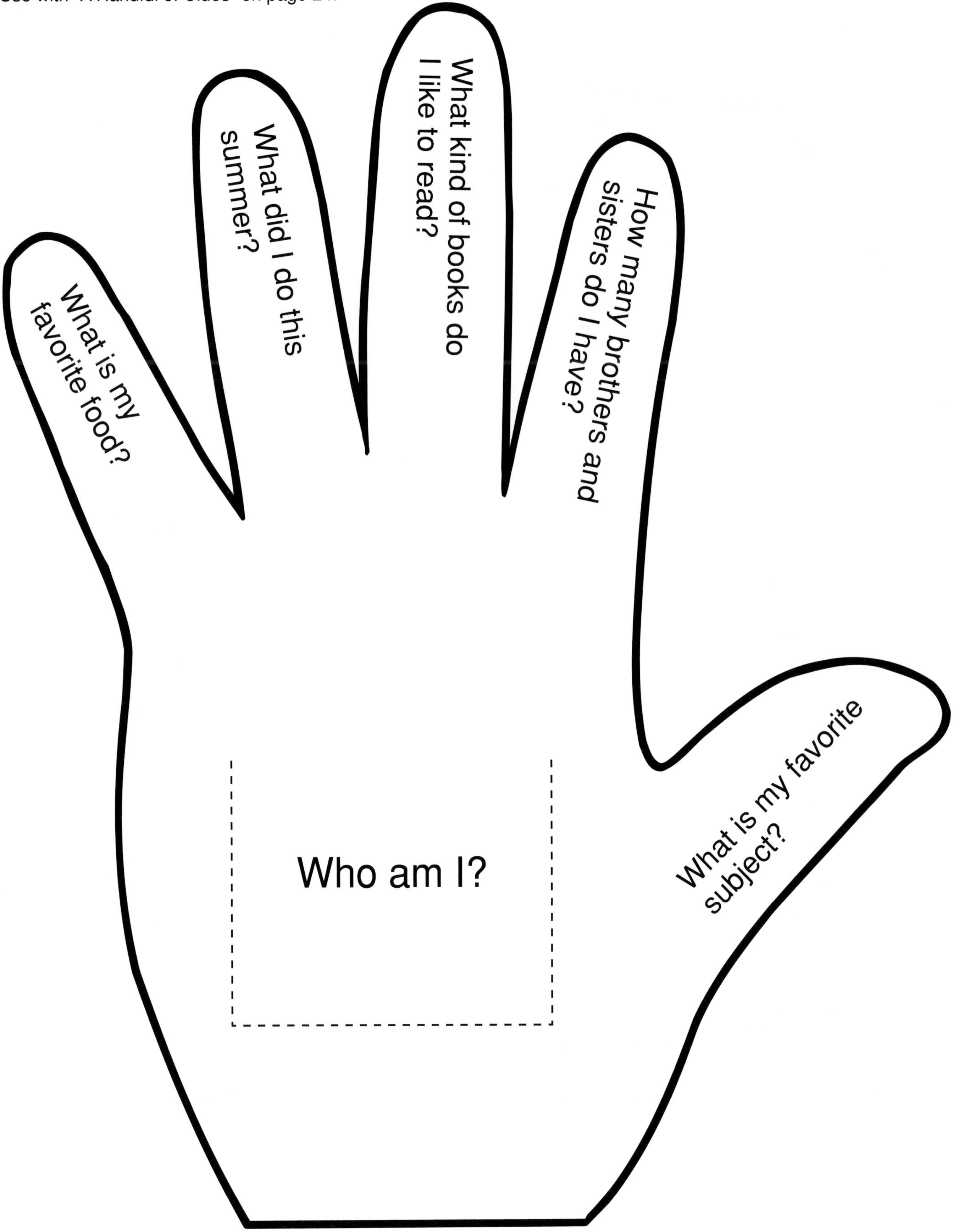
What is my favorite food?
What did I do this summer?
What kind of books do I like to read?
How many brothers and sisters do I have?
What is my favorite subject?
Who am I?

T-Shirt Pattern

Use with "Our Staff Line-Up" on page 25.

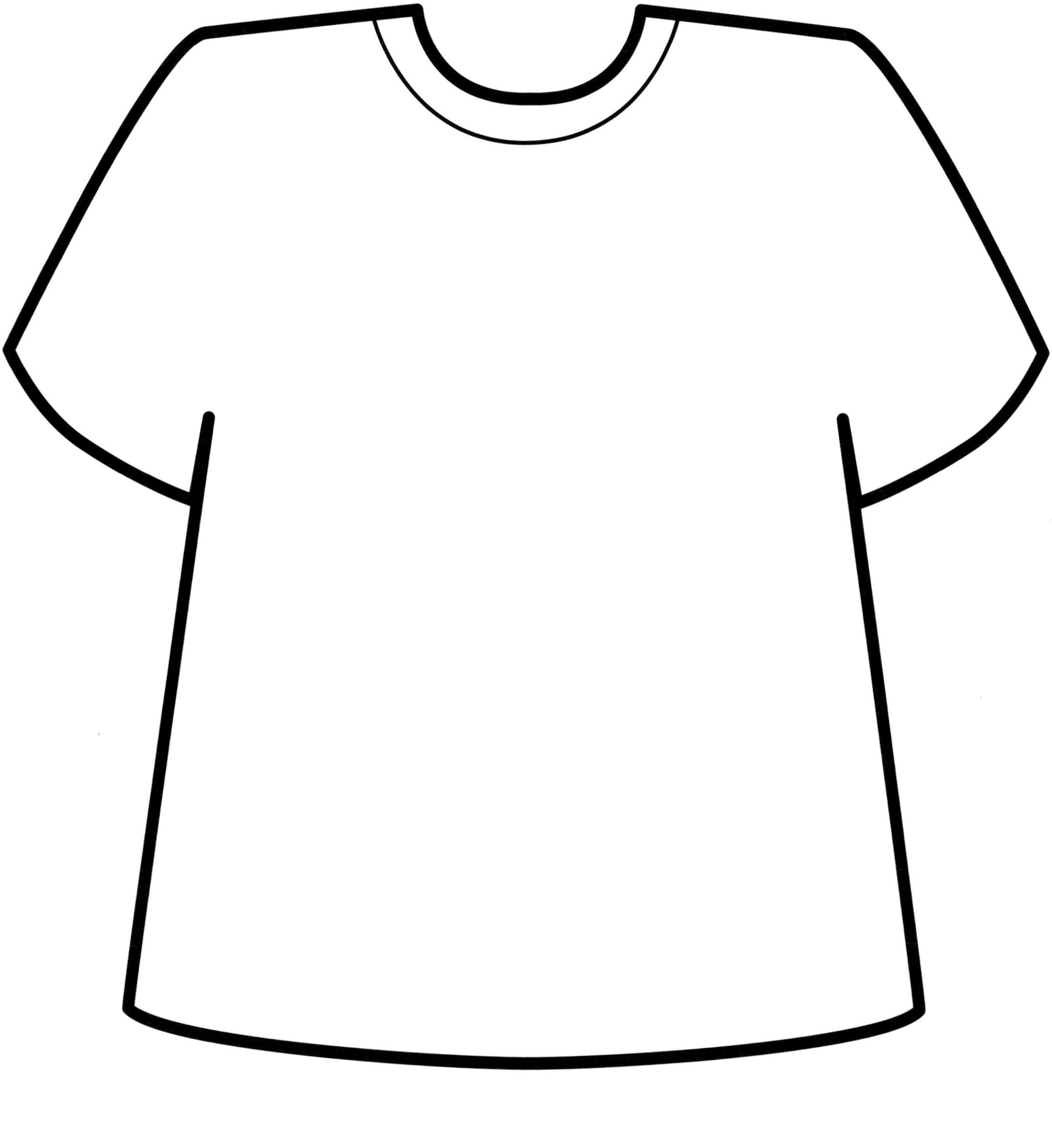

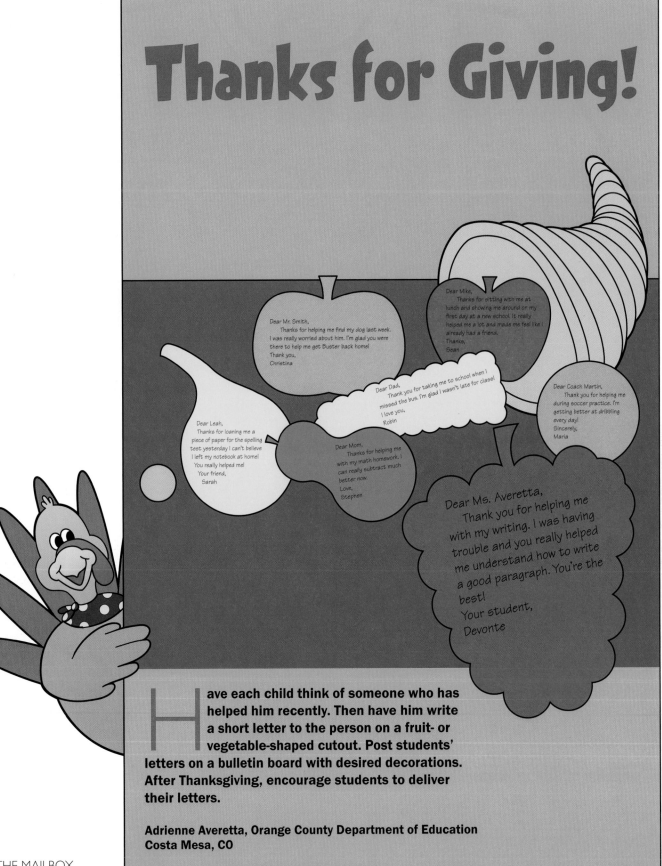

Thanks for Giving!
Dear Mr. Smith,
Thanks for helping me find my dog last week. I was really worried about him. I'm glad you were there to help me get Buster back home!
Thank you,
Christina
Dear Mike,
Thanks for sitting with me at lunch and showing me around on my first day at a new school. It really helped me a lot and made me feel like I already had a friend.
Thanks,
Sean
Dear Dad,
Thank you for taking me to school when I missed the bus. I'm glad I wasn't late for class!
I love you,
Robin
Dear Coach Martin,
Thank you for helping me during soccer practice. I'm getting better at dribbling every day!
Sincerely,
Maria
Dear Leah,
Thanks for loaning me a piece of paper for the spelling test yesterday. I can't believe I left my notebook at home! You really helped me!
Your friend,
Sarah
Dear Mom,
Thanks for helping me with my math homework. I can really subtract much better now.
Love,
Stephen
Dear Ms. Averetta,
Thank you for helping me with my writing. I was having trouble and you really helped me understand how to write a good paragraph. You're the best!
Your student,
Devonte

Have each child think of someone who has helped him recently. Then have him write a short letter to the person on a fruit- or vegetable-shaped cutout. Post students' letters on a bulletin board with desired decorations. After Thanksgiving, encourage students to deliver their letters.

Adrienne Averetta, Orange County Department of Education
Costa Mesa, CO

DISPLAYS

You Can Count on Us
I'm going to stay drug free so I can play soccer.
Natalie
to Stay Drug Free!

To create this say-no-to-drugs display, have each child pose in a black cape, pulling one end of the cape to her chin. Snap her picture and then post the developed photos with the title shown and a few spooky decorations. Finally, invite each child to write a graffiti-style message on the board explaining how or why she will stay drug free.

Becky Thurlkill, Junction City Elementary, Junction City, AR

Treats for Our School!
respect
homework
hard work
support
trust
laughter
kindness

Brainstorm with students a list of characteristics of a successful school. List each characteristic on a candy-shaped cutout. Then post the cutouts along with a construction paper bag, pictures of students and staff, and a title like the one shown.

Robin Brooks, Webster Elementary, Yankton, SD

We're Reading to Build a Snowman
Eliza Gray
Dion Smith
Lee Wong
Derrick Jones
Thomas Stevens
Bobby Martinez
Sara Best
Will Thayer
Lakia Thomas
Arjean Polis
Tia Ashton
Carlos Diaz
Stella Fisher
Derrick Jones
Amber Rivera
Seth Owens
Eliza Gray
Eliza Gray
Bobby Martinez
Eva Martin
Dion Smith

Dion Smith

This motivational bulletin board celebrates students' reading achievements! Draw a large snowman outline on a bulletin board. Each time a child completes his assigned reading, give him a copy of a snowflake pattern on page 32. Have him use a colored pencil to write his name on the snowflake and then attach it to the bulletin board. Repeat the process until the snowman is complete. Then, if desired, reward students with a treat.

Heather Volkman
Messiah Lutheran School
St. Louis, MO

Short-Vowel Stockings

a
e
i
o
u

Make the most of stocking stuffers with this interactive bulletin board! Create five paper stockings, as shown, and attach them to a paper fireplace. Attach a plastic resealable bag to the back of each stocking. Also cut out a variety of pictures of objects whose names have a short-vowel sound. Place the pictures in an envelope and post it on the bulletin board. Then invite each child to visit the board and place each picture in its correct stocking based on its vowel sound.

Patricia Frano, Meadville, PA

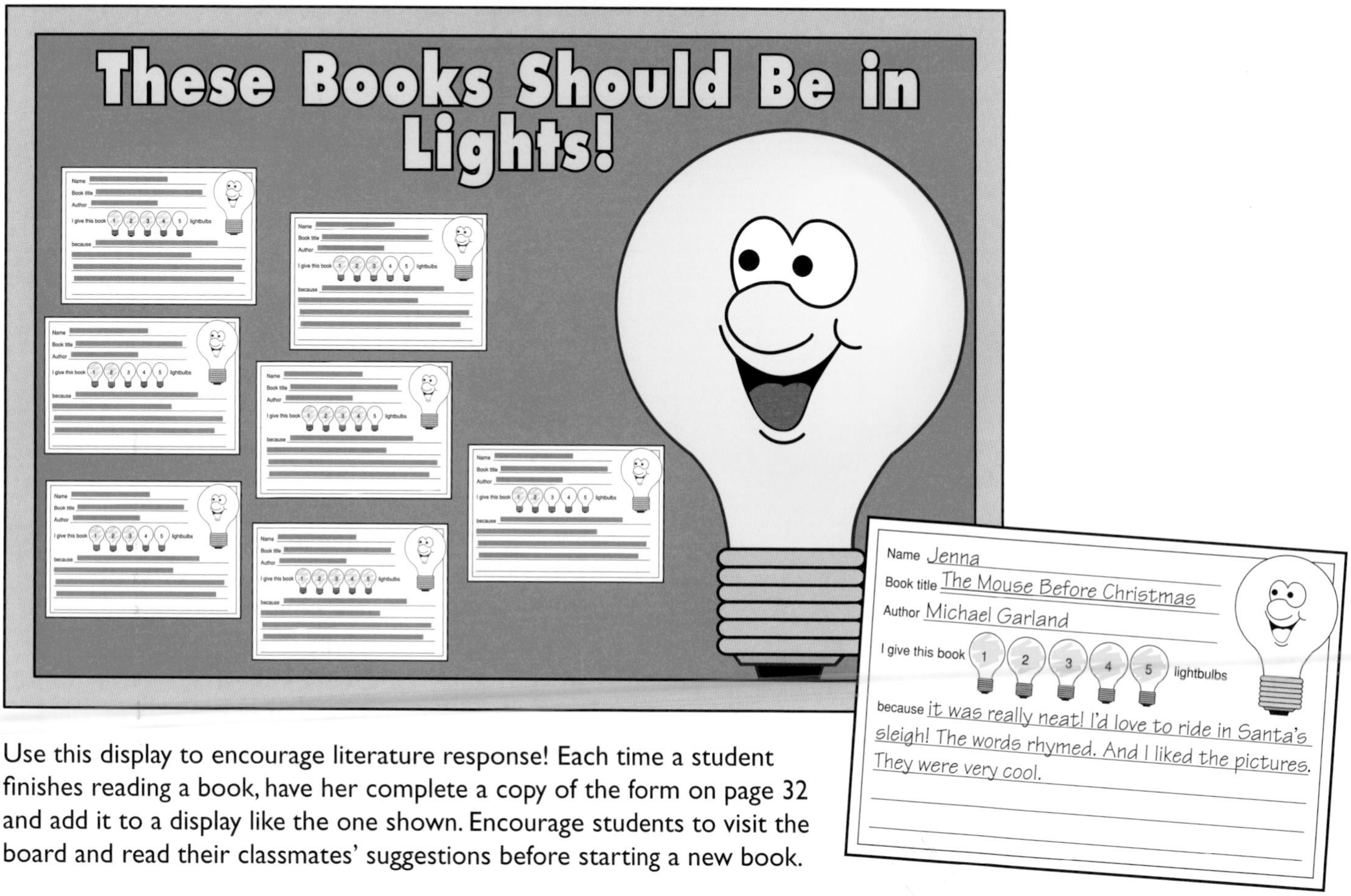
These Books Should Be in Lights!
Name Jenna
Book title The Mouse Before Christmas
Author Michael Garland
I give this book 1 2 3 4 5 lightbulbs
because it was really neat! I'd love to ride in Santa's sleigh! The words rhymed. And I liked the pictures. They were very cool.

Use this display to encourage literature response! Each time a student finishes reading a book, have her complete a copy of the form on page 32 and add it to a display like the one shown. Encourage students to visit the board and read their classmates' suggestions before starting a new book.

Stephanie Affinito, Glens Falls, NY

Snowflake Patterns

Use with "We're Reading to Build a Snowman" on page 30.

TEC43022

TEC43022

Book Response Form

Use with "These Books Should Be in Lights!" on page 31.

Name ________________________________

Book title ________________________________

Author ________________________________

I give this book 1 2 3 4 5 lightbulbs

because ________________________________

____

____

____

____

Coin Patterns

Use with "Antonyms Are Priceless" on page 34.

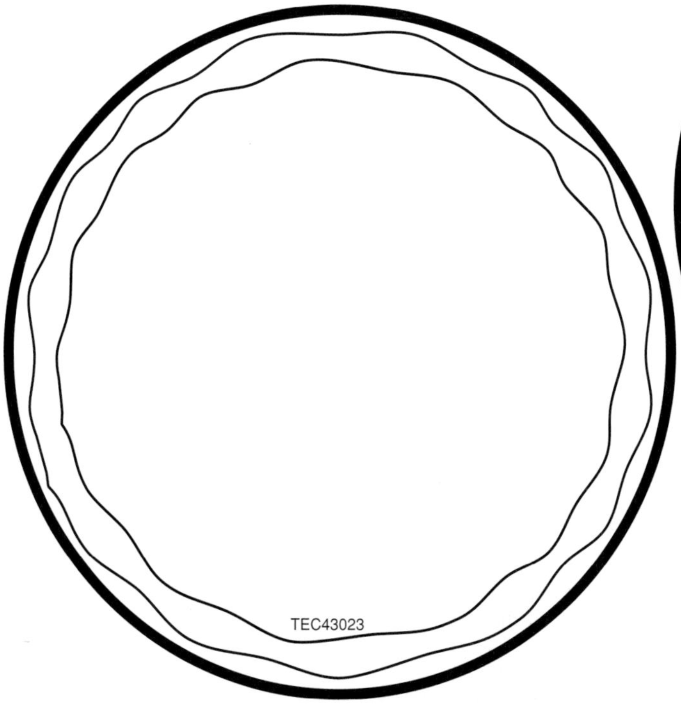
TEC43023

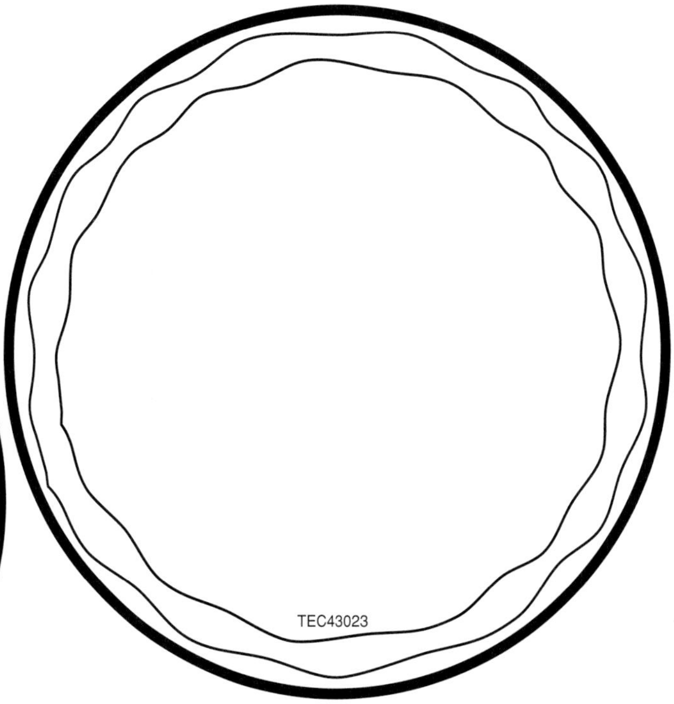
TEC43023

Candy Patterns

Use with "We're Sweet on Super Work!" on page 35.

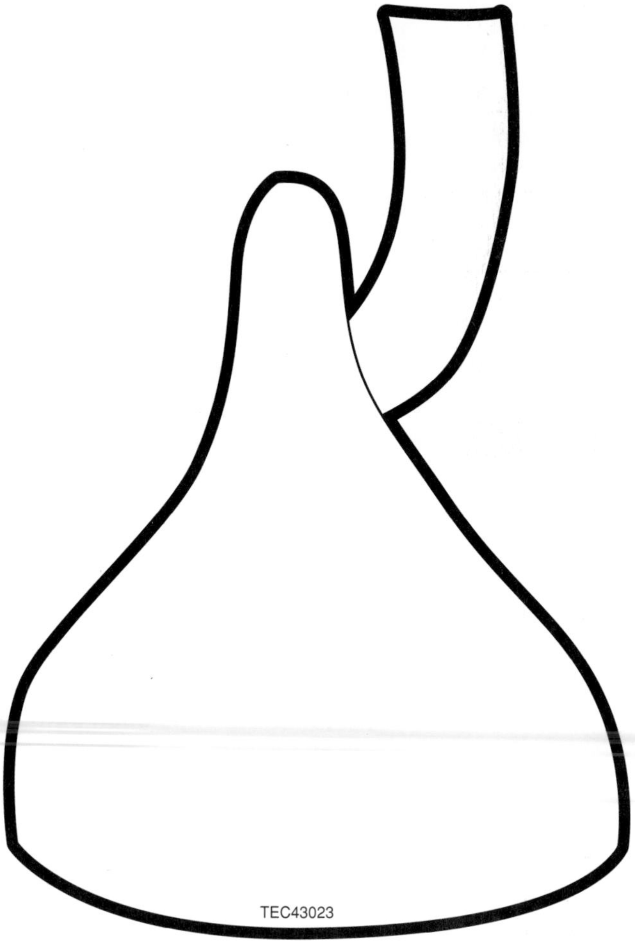
TEC43023

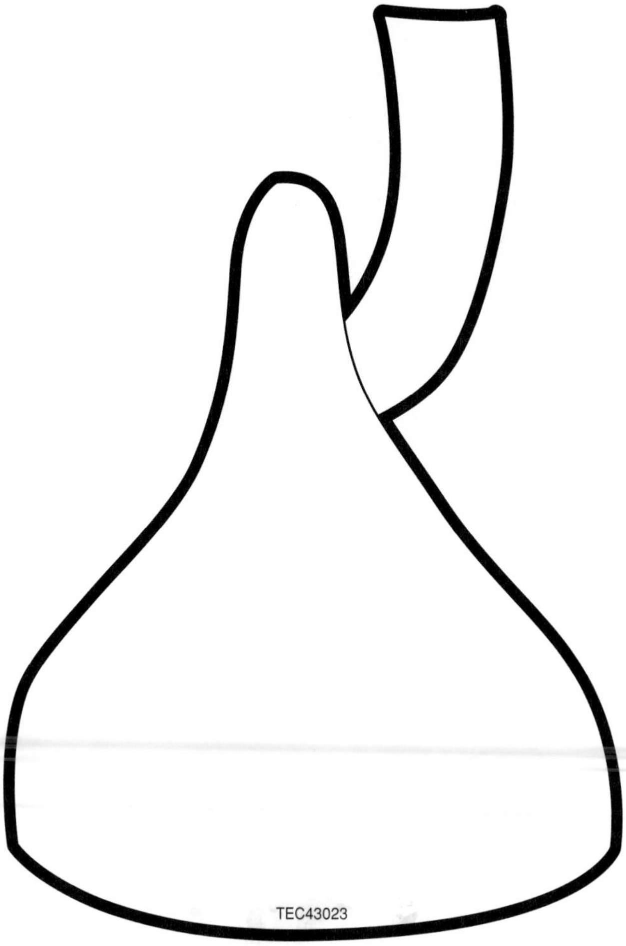
TEC43023

CLASSROOM

day
night
open
rough
stop
little
light
old
hard
close
take
give
smooth
dark
new
big
go
soft

Antonyms Are Priceless

hot
cold

Antonym practice is golden with this interactive bulletin board! Make a supply of the coin patterns on page 33 on yellow construction paper. Label each pattern with one word from an antonym pair, as shown, and program its back for self-checking. Next, post a bulletin board paper pot and rainbow on the display. Affix the loop side of a Velcro fastener to each coin's back and attach the hook side to the board near the top of the pot. Also place a small pot and a supply of paper clips on the floor below the display. A child visits the board and finds matching antonym pairs. He clips each pair together and places it in the small pot. After matching all of the pairs, he turns them over to check his work. Then he reattaches the coins to the display for the next student.

adapted from an idea by
Traci Mayfield, O'Fallon, IL

DISPLAYS

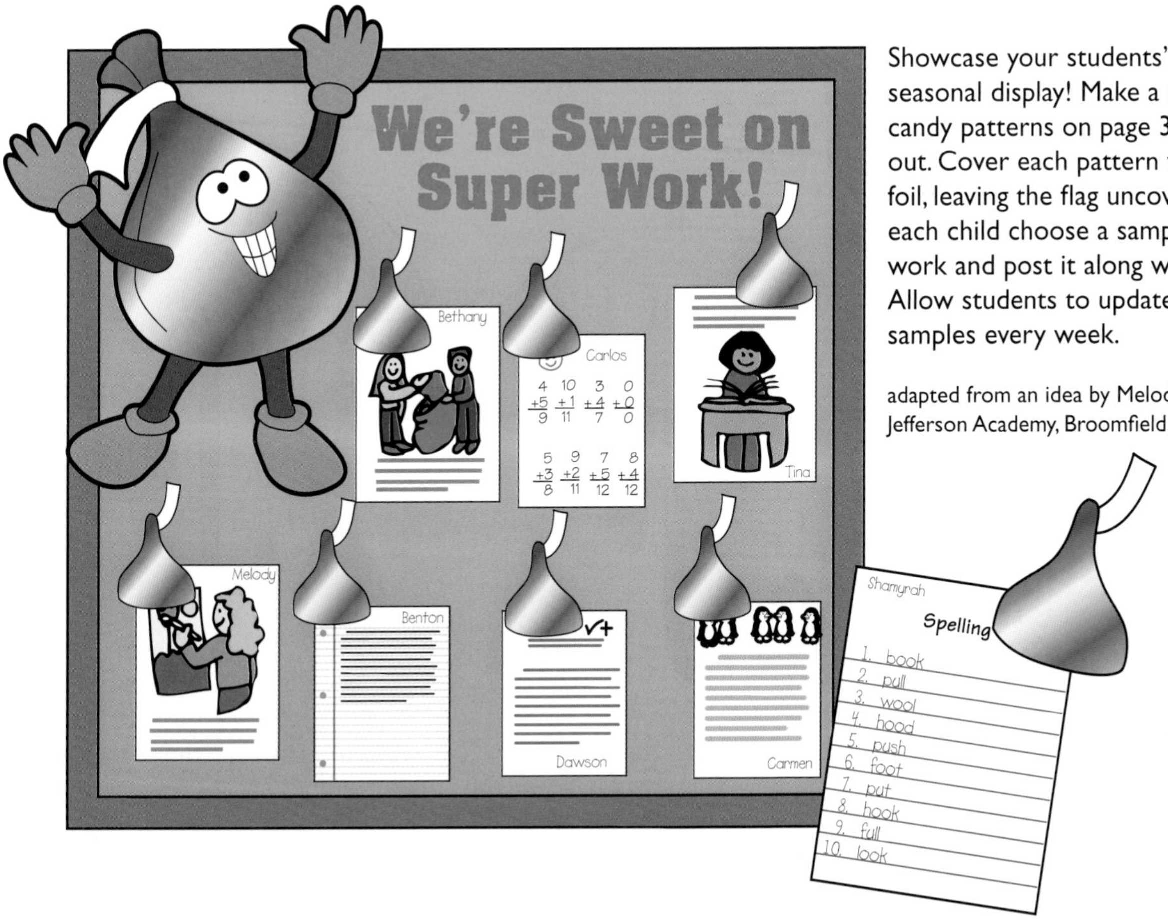
We're Sweet on Super Work!
Bethany
Carlos
Tina
Melody
Benton
Dawson
Carmen
Shamyrah
Spelling
1. book
2. pull
3. wool
4. hood
5. push
6. foot
7. put
8. hook
9. full
10. look

Showcase your students' work with this seasonal display! Make a supply of the candy patterns on page 33 and cut them out. Cover each pattern with aluminum foil, leaving the flag uncovered. Then have each child choose a sample of her best work and post it along with a candy kiss. Allow students to update their work samples every week.

adapted from an idea by Melody Landaiche, Jefferson Academy, Broomfield, CO

Challenge students to think about their futures! Have each child write a paragraph describing his personal lifetime goals. Then pair students and give each twosome two sheets of black construction paper and a white crayon. Have the pair take turns drawing each other's profile on the black paper. Afterward, each child cuts out his profile and mounts it on red construction paper. He posts his silhouette and paragraph on a bulletin board titled like the one shown.

Dawn Dawson
Benton Lake Elementary
Floweree, MT

Future Famous Americans
When I grow up, I want to be a doctor. I want to find cures that help people who are sick. I will help people feel better and live longer.
José

A Shower of Vivid Verbs

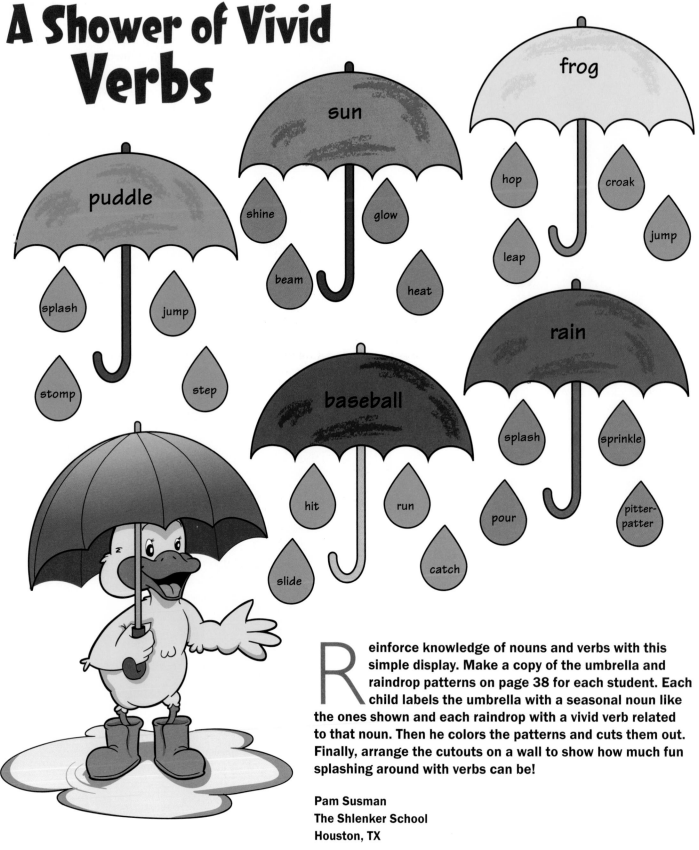

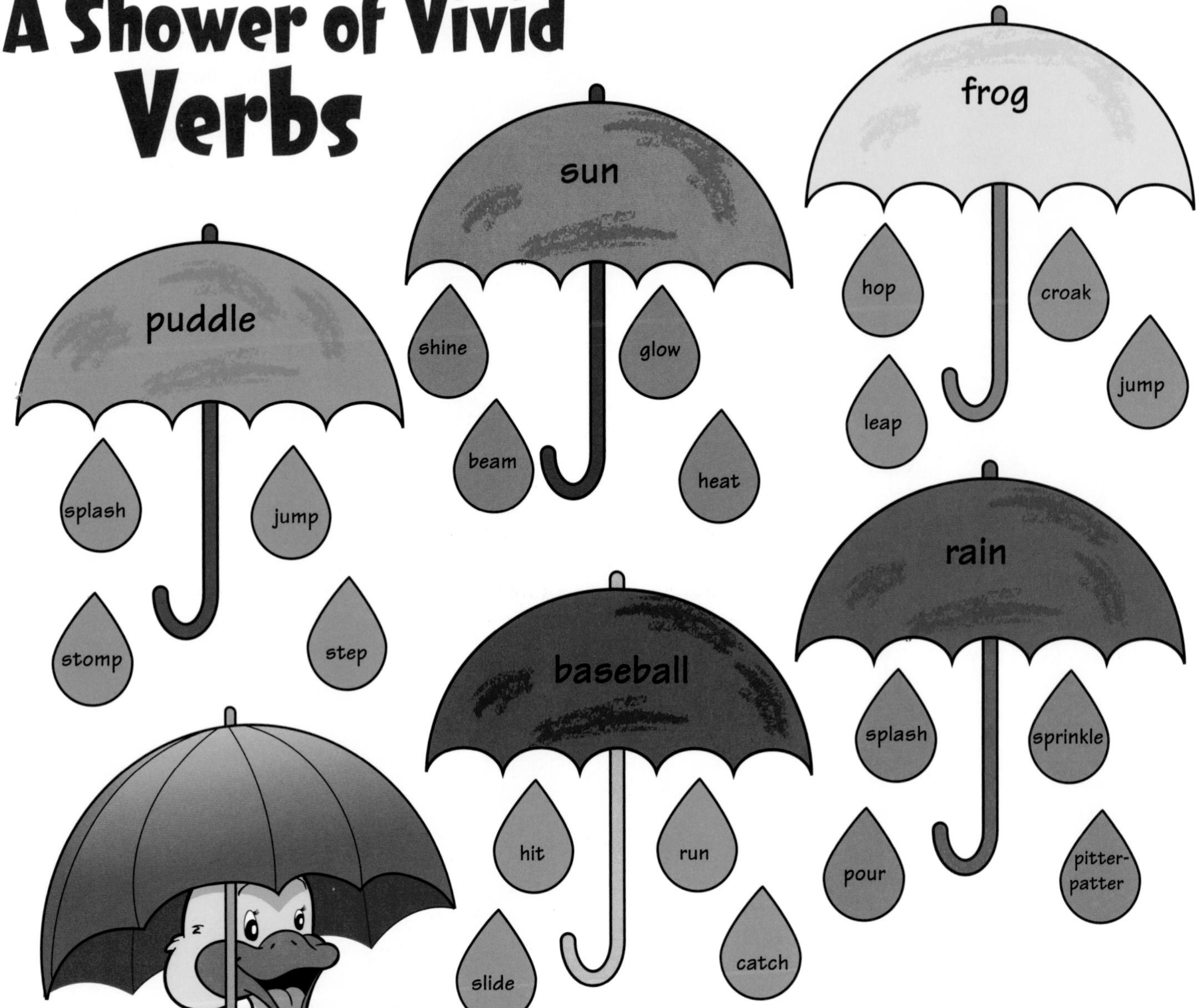
frog
hop
croak
leap
jump
sun
shine
glow
beam
heat
puddle
splash
jump
stomp
step
rain
splash
sprinkle
pour
pitter-
patter
baseball
hit
run
slide
catch

Reinforce knowledge of nouns and verbs with this simple display. Make a copy of the umbrella and raindrop patterns on page 38 for each student. Each child labels the umbrella with a seasonal noun like the ones shown and each raindrop with a vivid verb related to that noun. Then he colors the patterns and cuts them out. Finally, arrange the cutouts on a wall to show how much fun splashing around with verbs can be!

Pam Susman
The Shlenker School
Houston, TX

DISPLAYS

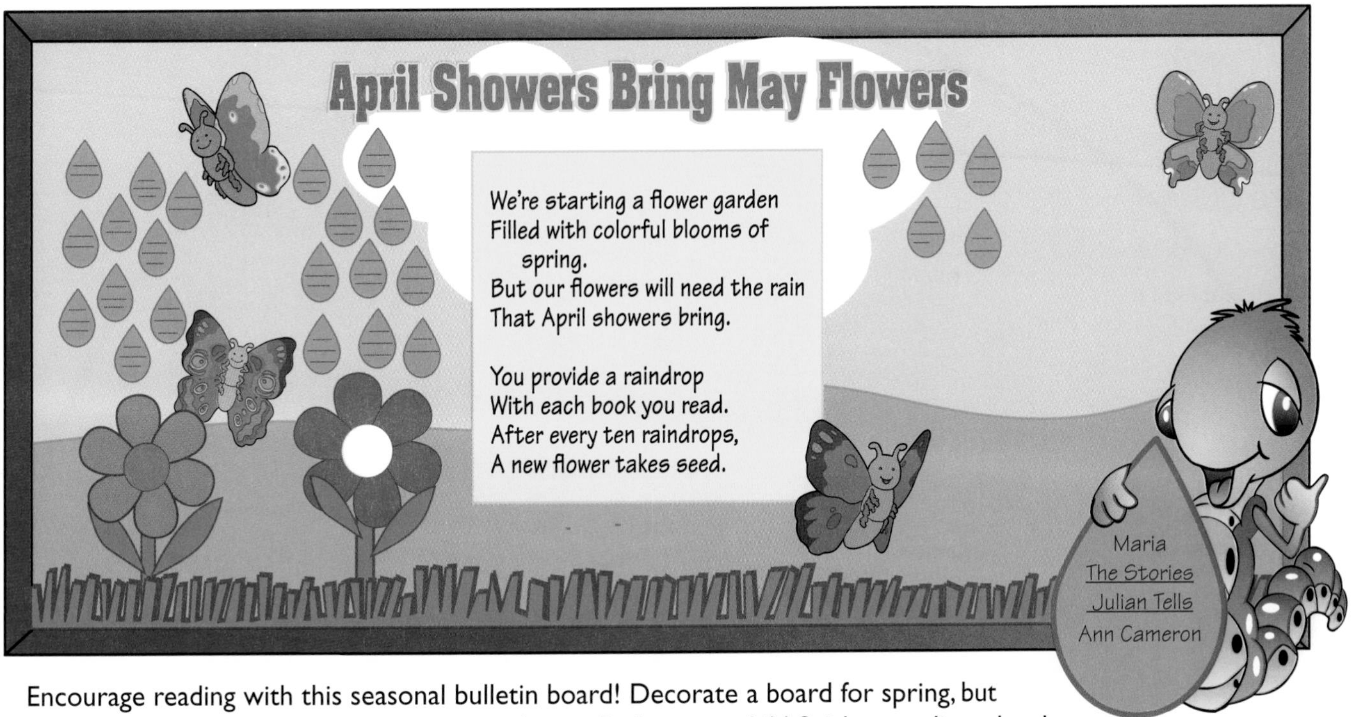
April Showers Bring May Flowers
We're starting a flower garden
Filled with colorful blooms of
spring.
But our flowers will need the rain
That April showers bring.
You provide a raindrop
With each book you read.
After every ten raindrops,
A new flower takes seed.
Maria
The Stories
Julian Tells
Ann Cameron

Encourage reading with this seasonal bulletin board! Decorate a board for spring, but don't include flowers. Also post the poem shown. Each time a child finishes reading a book, have her write her name and the book's title and author on a raindrop cutout. Post the raindrop on the board. Then, after ten raindrops have been added to the display, post a construction paper flower. Continue adding raindrops and flowers as needed.

Jennifer Mack
Phoenixville, PA

Start Time
10:00
End Time
10:40
It's Time for Spring!

To provide interactive practice with elapsed time, make a large clockface with movable hands as shown. Also copy the leaves on page 39 on green construction paper and laminate them. Post the clock, the leaves, and a stem on a board as shown. Before beginning an activity, use a dry-erase marker to write the start time on the corresponding leaf. When the activity ends, have a child record the end time on the matching leaf. Then invite another student to show the start time on the clock. He slowly moves the clock's hands to show the end time while his classmates use the clock's petals to calculate the elapsed time. Repeat the activity several times for a few days; then allow students to visit the board on their own to practice finding elapsed time.

Cindy Barber, Fredonia, WI

Umbrella and Raindrop Patterns

Use with “A Shower of Vivid Verbs” on page 36.

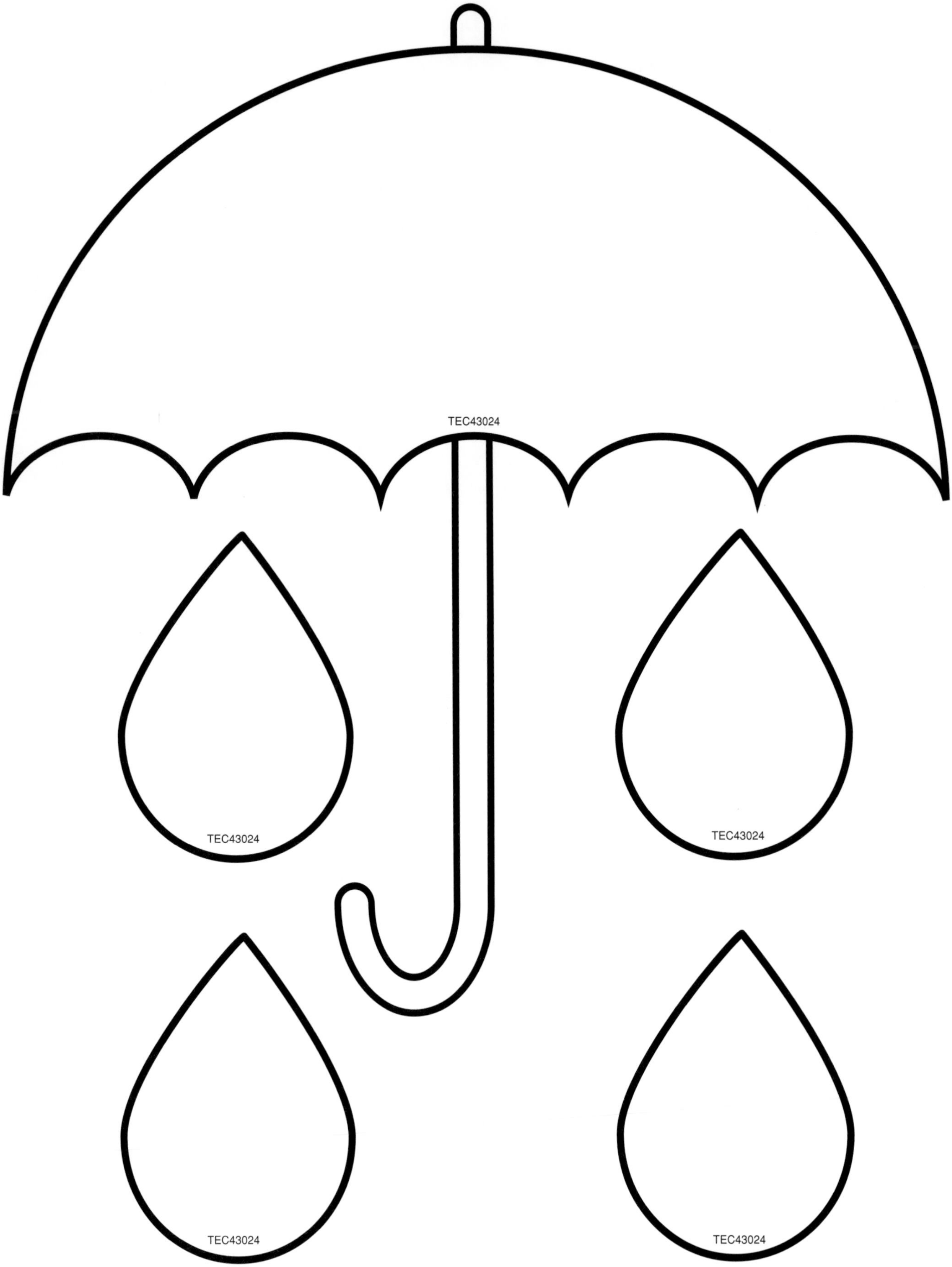
TEC43024
TEC43024
TEC43024
TEC43024
TEC43024

Leaf Patterns

Use with "It's Time for Spring!" on page 37.

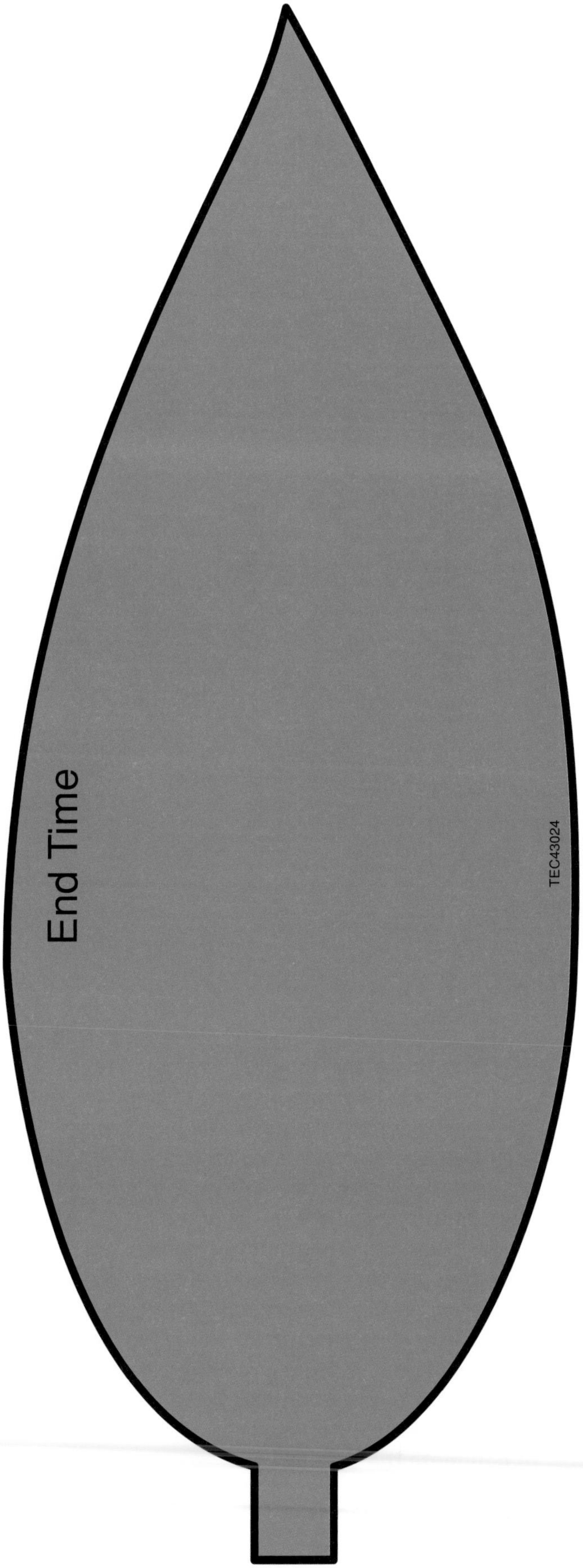
End Time
TEC43024

Start Time
TEC43024

CLASSROOM

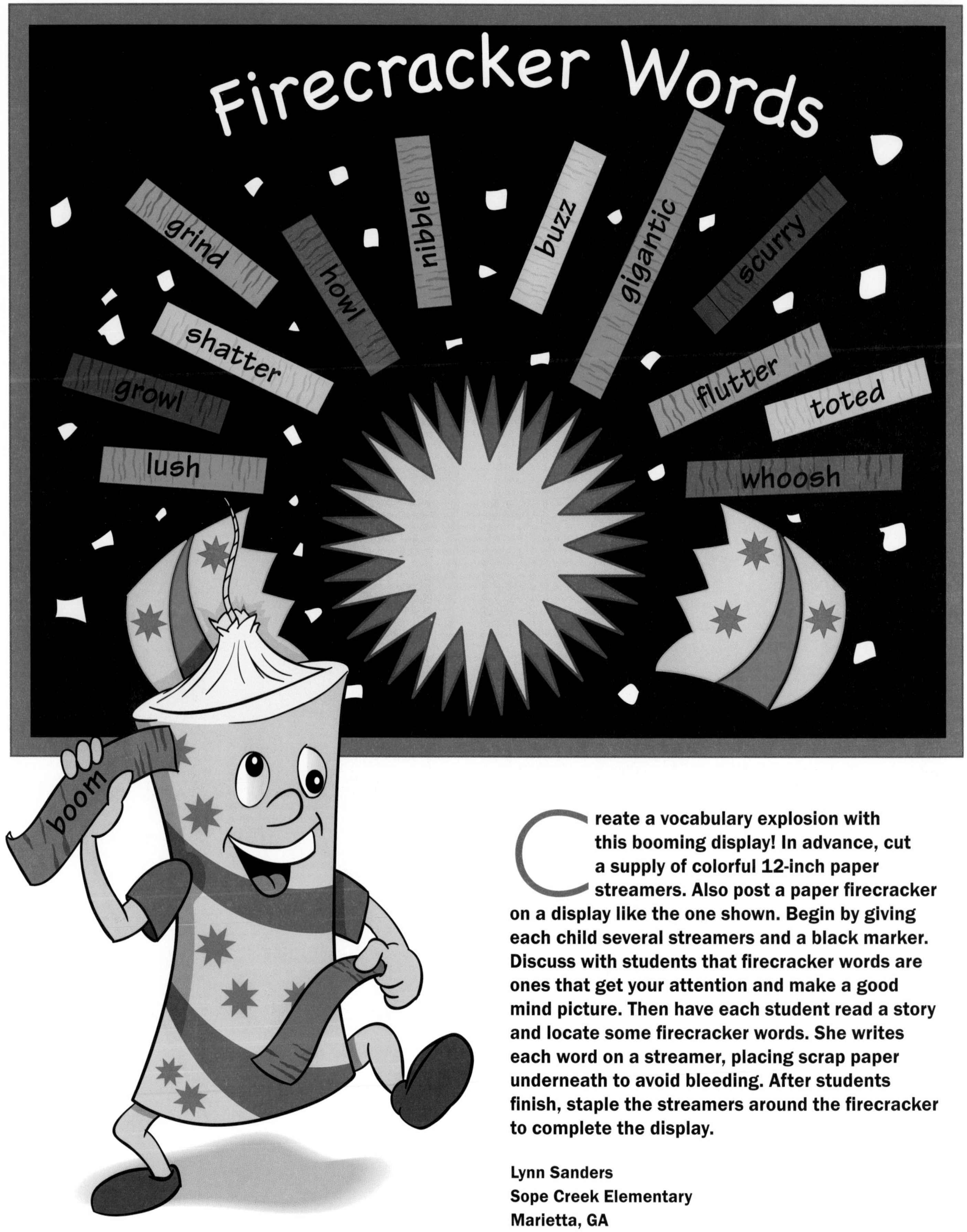

Firecracker Words
grind
howl
nibble
buzz
gigantic
scurry
shatter
growl
lush
flutter
toted
whoosh
boom

Create a vocabulary explosion with this booming display! In advance, cut a supply of colorful 12-inch paper streamers. Also post a paper firecracker on a display like the one shown. Begin by giving each child several streamers and a black marker. Discuss with students that firecracker words are ones that get your attention and make a good mind picture. Then have each student read a story and locate some firecracker words. She writes each word on a streamer, placing scrap paper underneath to avoid bleeding. After students finish, staple the streamers around the firecracker to complete the display.

Lynn Sanders
Sope Creek Elementary
Marietta, GA

DISPLAYS

Slices of Third Grade
David
Mike
Latoya
Denise
Max
Mario
Grey
My favorite memory of third grade is when we went to the planetarium. It was cool!

Show off favorite memories of the school year! Give each student a copy of the watermelon and knife patterns on page 42. He records his favorite memory from the school year on the watermelon and writes his name across the knife. Next, he lightly colors the watermelon and cuts out both patterns. He glues the cutouts to a paper plate before sharing his memory aloud. Title the display and post the memories as shown.

Jaima Hess
Providence School
Waynesboro, PA

Students will flip for this great work display! Copy a class supply of the dolphin pattern on page 42 and give one to each student. She writes her name across the dolphin, personalizes it to her liking, and cuts it out. Then she chooses a sample of her best work and posts it along with the dolphin. Add a title and update the work samples periodically.

Brooke Shaw
Columbia, SC

Work to Flip Over
Mark
Ally
A Perfect Example
Diego
1820
1913
Harriet Tubman
Harriet Tubman was important to our country. She was a slave but she escaped. Harriet Tubman helped many other slaves find freedom. She was a big part of our history.
Neha
South Carolina
New York
Virginia
Tennessee
North Carolina
Ohio

Knife and Watermelon Patterns
Use with "Slices of Third Grade" on page 41.

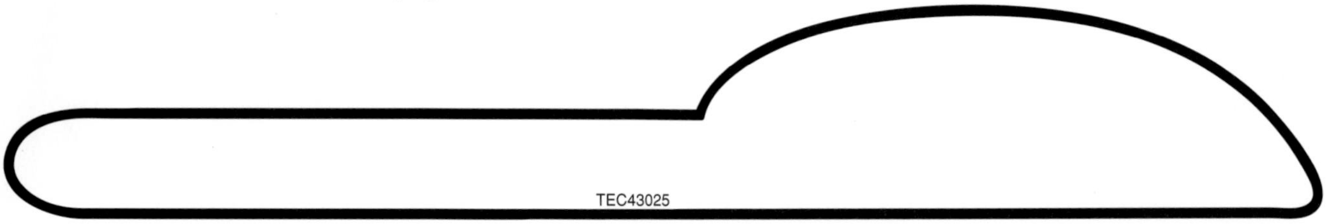
TEC43025

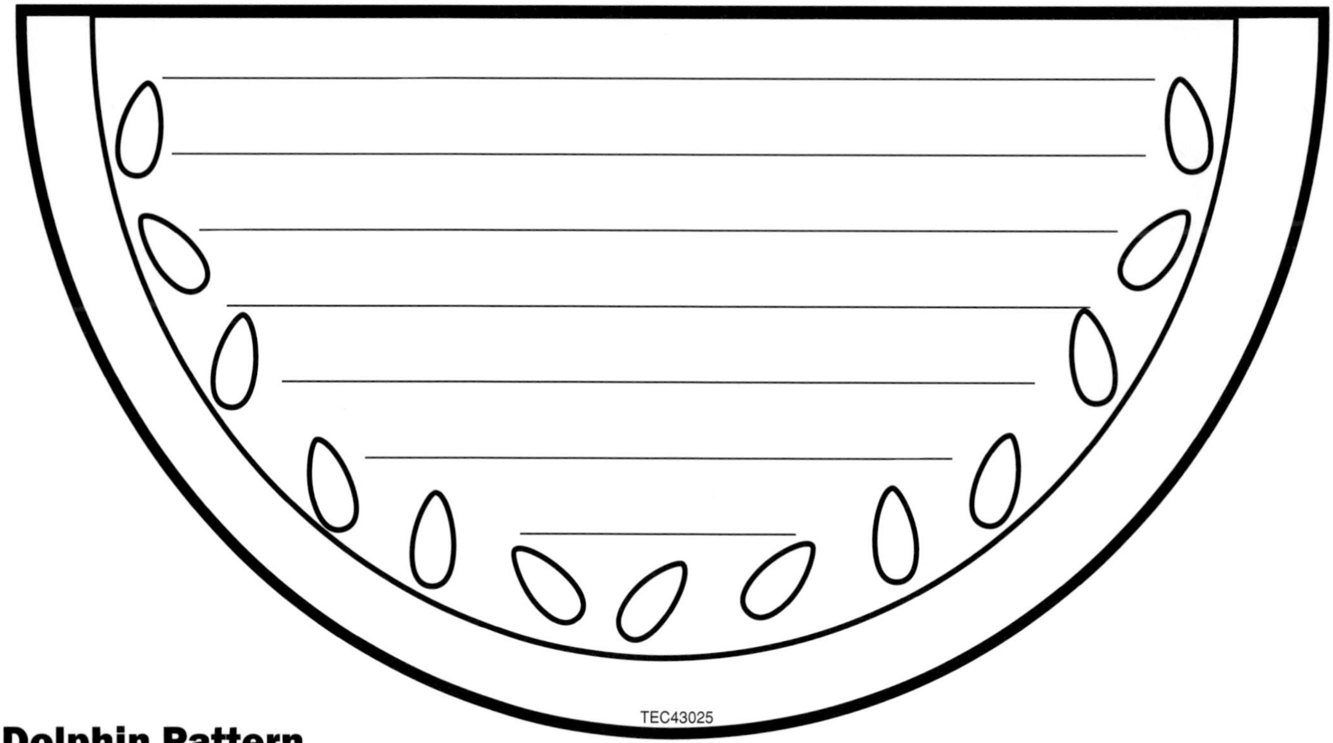
TEC43025

Dolphin Pattern
Use with "Work to Flip Over" on page 41.

TEC43025

Learning Centers

blaze
chose
coal

Tackling the Alphabet

What's the catch of the day at this center? Improved alphabetizing skills! Label a supply of fish cutouts with spelling or vocabulary words. Laminate the fish and cut them out. Store the fish and a supply of clothespins in a small tackle or pencil box. Also hang a length of fishing line along a wall or under a bulletin board. Place the tackle box near the fishing line along with paper and pencils. A student uses the clothespins to attach the fish to the line in alphabetical order. After he finishes arranging the words, he writes them in alphabetical order on his paper.

froze
goal
mail
play
spoke
stain
away
blaze
chose
coal
fail
flame

Sondra Alexander
Mobile County Public Schools
Mobile, AL

Crayon

Money Match

Use this center to sharpen coin skills! Make a copy of the money cards on page 46. Color the cards, cut them out, and mount them on construction paper. Code the backs of the cards for self-checking; then place them at a center. A student selects a card and then finds the card that shows the same amount. Quick and easy money practice!

Gayle Benjamin, Lincoln Elementary, Escondido, CA

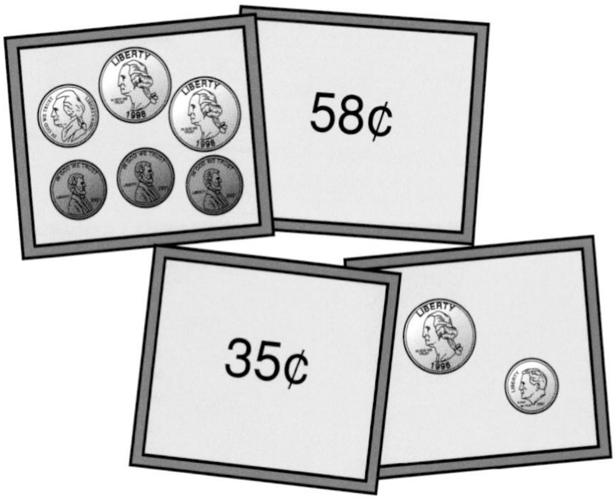
58¢
35¢

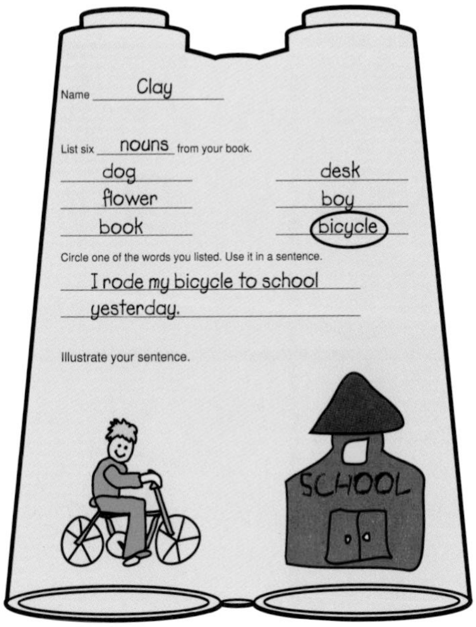
Name Clay
List six nouns from your book.
dog
desk
flower
boy
book
bicycle
Circle one of the words you listed. Use it in a sentence.
I rode my bicycle to school yesterday.
Illustrate your sentence.
SCHOOL

Word Search

Parts of speech are the focus of this center! Program the pattern on page 47 for the part of speech your students are practicing; then copy a supply of the pattern onto colored construction paper. Place the patterns at a center along with a variety of short reading selections, paper, pencils, and scissors. Each child chooses and reads a selection. Then he completes the activities on the pattern. After he finishes, he cuts out the pattern and stores it in his writing folder for quick reference.

adapted from an idea by Rita Skavinsky
Minersville Elementary Center
Minersville, PA

Ten Up!

Improved addition skills are in the cards with this partner game! Place at a center a deck of cards with the jokers and face cards removed. The object of the game is for the student to collect as many ten cards, or pairs of cards whose face values add up to ten, as she can. Explain that aces are equal to 1. To play, four cards are dealt to each player and the remaining cards are placed facedown in a pile. Player 1 checks her cards for a ten or for two cards whose added face value is ten. If she has ten, she lays the card or cards faceup on the table and draws replacement cards from the deck. If she does not have ten, the child places one of her cards at the bottom of the card pile and draws one from the top. Player 2 takes a turn in the same manner. Play continues until no cards are left. The student with more cards that add up to ten at the end of the game wins.

Anna Walsh, M. B. Garvin Microsociety School, East Orange, NJ

Money Cards

Use with "Money Match" on page 45.

	26¢		65¢
	32¢		70¢
	76¢		58¢
	35¢		47¢
	78¢		60¢
	18¢		62¢

Binoculars Pattern

Use with "Word Search" on page 45.

Name ______________________

List six ____________ from your book.

______________________ ______________________

______________________ ______________________

______________________ ______________________

Circle one of the words you listed. Use it in a sentence.

____

____

Illustrate your sentence.

Learning Centers

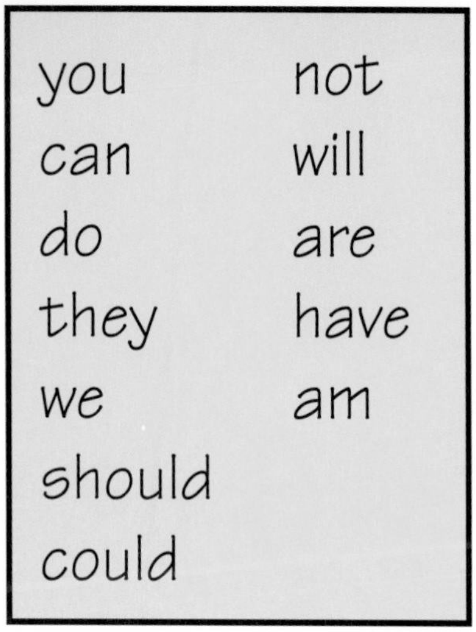
you
can
do
they
we
should
could
not
will
are
have
am

I
have
've
could
not
n't
you
'll

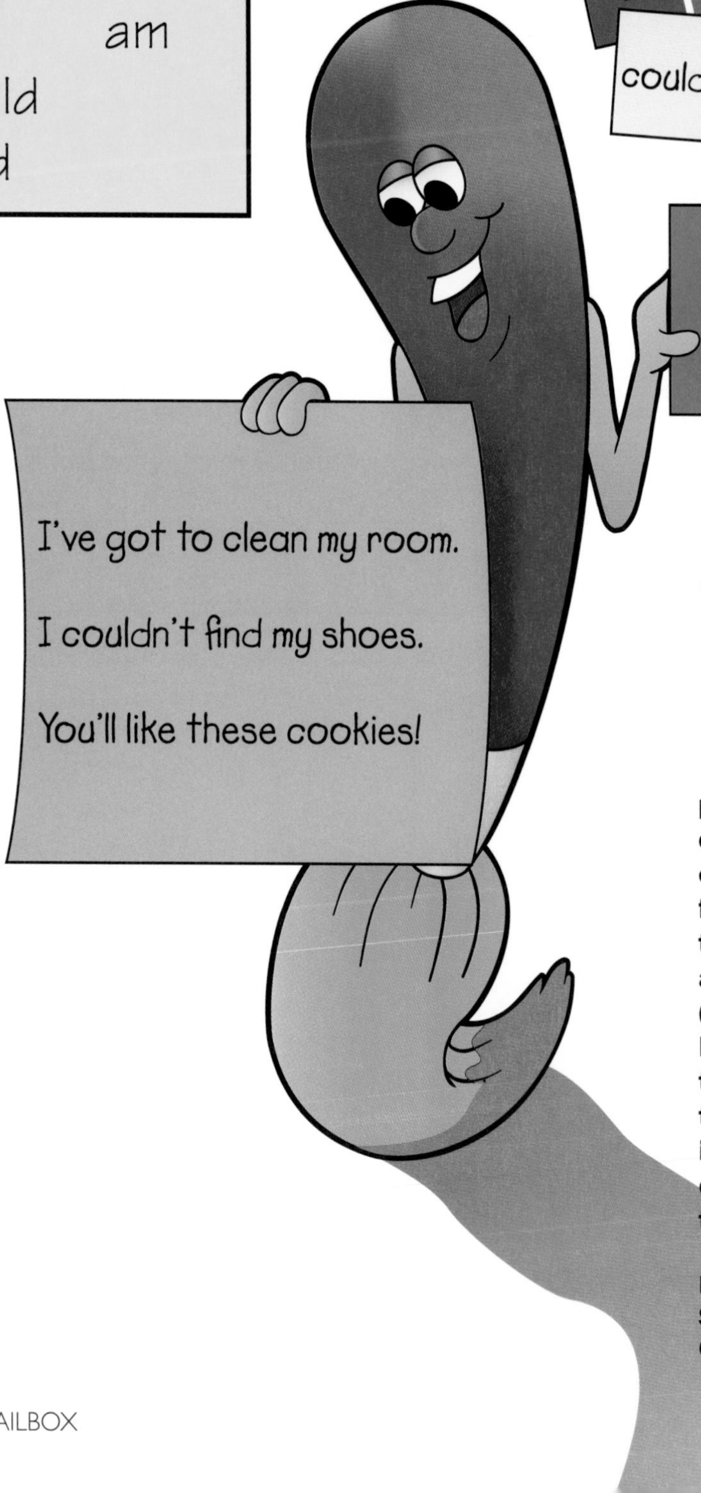
I've got to clean my room.
I couldn't find my shoes.
You'll like these cookies!

Paint Chip Contractions

Here's a colorful way for students to practice forming contractions! Make a chart containing words that make up contractions and place it at a center. Also provide a variety of four-color paint chips, paper, and pens. A child selects a paint chip and writes in the first two boxes two words from the chart that when combined form a contraction as shown. Next, he writes the new ending (including the apostrophe) in the fourth box. He accordion-folds the last two squares so that the ending replaces the second word to form the contraction. Then he copies the information from the paint chip onto a sheet of paper. He repeats the process twice and then uses each contraction in a sentence.

Renee Campbell
Saint Patrick's School
Charlotte, NC

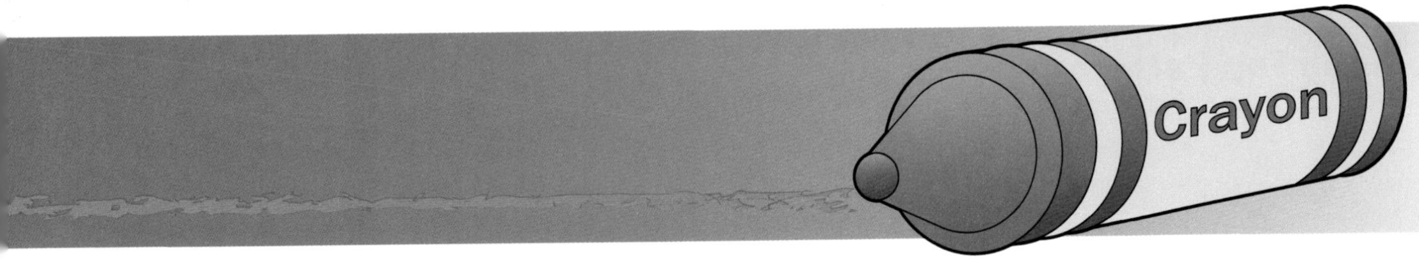
Crayon

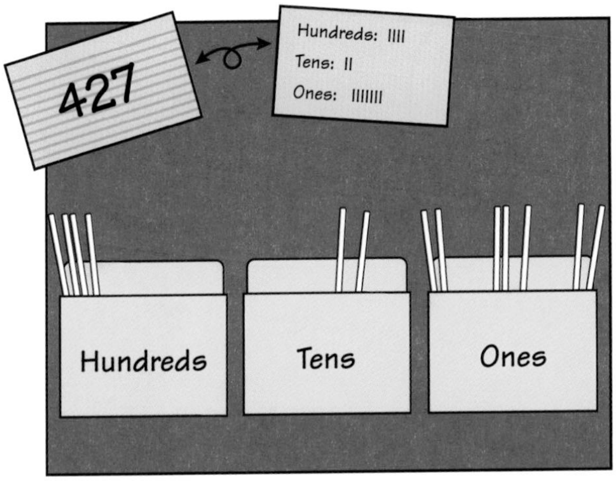
427
Hundreds: IIII
Tens: II
Ones: IIIIIII
Hundreds
Tens
Ones

Number Pockets

Stir up place-value practice at this center! Label three library pockets as shown, and glue them to a sheet of construction paper. Next, program index cards each with a different two- or three-digit number. For self-checking, label the back of each card as shown. Place the pocket mat, the cards, and a supply of coffee stirrers at a center. A child chooses a card, places the matching number of stirrers in each pocket to show the number's value, and then turns over the card to check her work.

Christine Fischer, Edward S. Rhodes School, Cranston, RI

Opposites Attract

Matching antonyms has never been sweeter! Laminate and cut out a construction paper copy of the lollipop top patterns on page 50. Also label a supply of craft sticks each with an antonym from the box on this page. Next, attach a piece of magnetic tape to the back of each lollipop top and a piece to the top of each stick as shown. Then use a permanent marker to program the back of each lollipop for self-checking. Store the lollipop tops and sticks in a resealable plastic bag and place the bag at a center. A child matches all the antonym pairs and then turns them over to check his work.

Amy Barsanti, Pines Elementary, Plymouth, NC

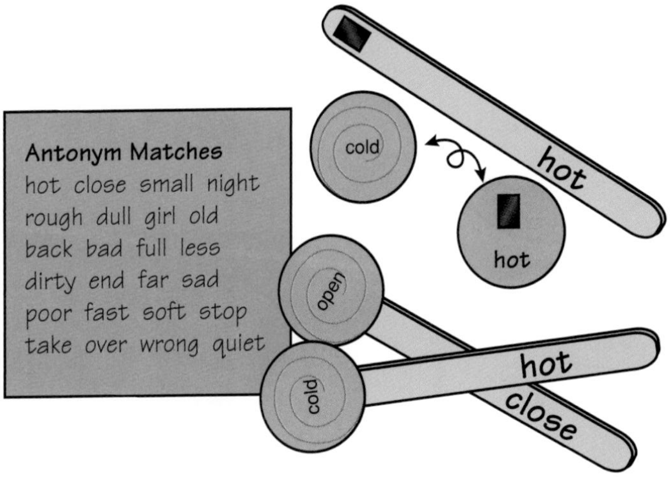
Antonym Matches
hot close small night
rough dull girl old
back bad full less
dirty end far sad
poor fast soft stop
take over wrong quiet
cold
hot
hot
open
cold
hot
close

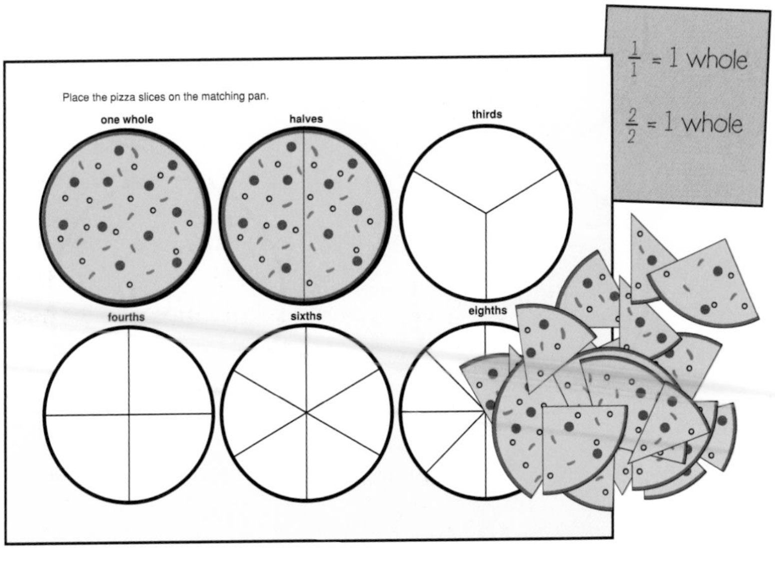
Place the pizza slices on the matching pan.
one whole
halves
thirds
fourths
sixths
eighths
$\frac{1}{1}$ = 1 whole
$\frac{2}{2}$ = 1 whole

Pizza Pies

Anyway you slice it, strengthening fraction skills at this center is a tasty treat! Copy the pizzas on page 51, color them, and cut them apart. Store them in a resealable plastic bag. Place the bag, student copies of the mat on page 52, paper, and pencils at a center. A child practices creating a whole pizza by matching corresponding slices. After he finishes, he writes a fraction to represent the whole part of each pizza. To further practice fractions, use the pizzas and the mat to help students recognize equivalent fractions.

adapted from an idea by Laura Hess, Providence School Waynesboro, PA

Lollipop Top Patterns

Use with "Opposites Attract" on page 49.

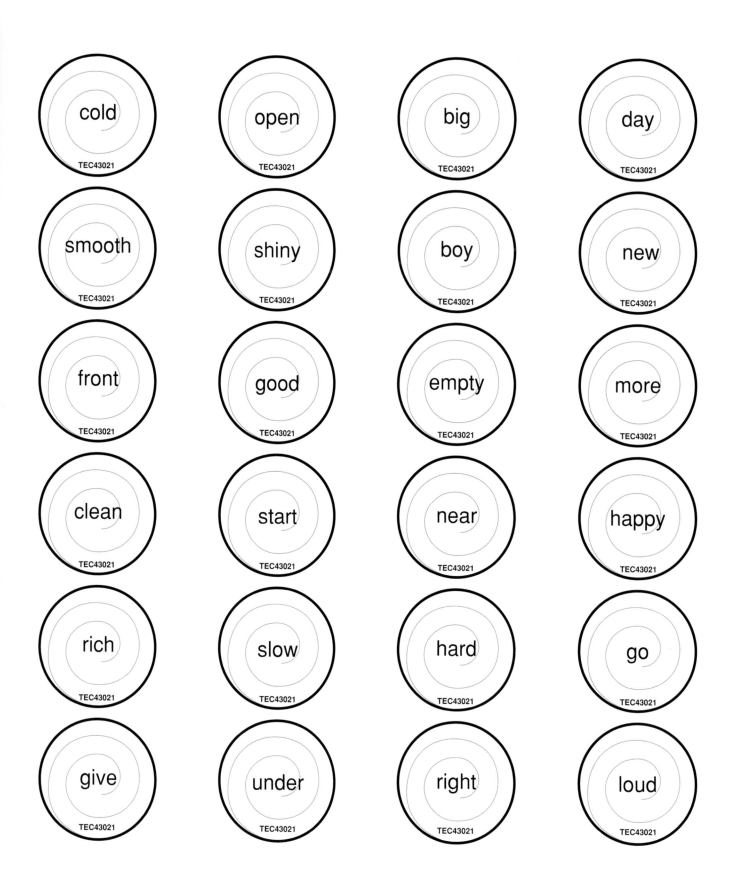

cold TEC43021	open TEC43021	big TEC43021	day TEC43021
smooth TEC43021	shiny TEC43021	boy TEC43021	new TEC43021
front TEC43021	good TEC43021	empty TEC43021	more TEC43021
clean TEC43021	start TEC43021	near TEC43021	happy TEC43021
rich TEC43021	slow TEC43021	hard TEC43021	go TEC43021
give TEC43021	under TEC43021	right TEC43021	loud TEC43021

Fraction Pizzas

Use with "Pizza Pies" on page 49.

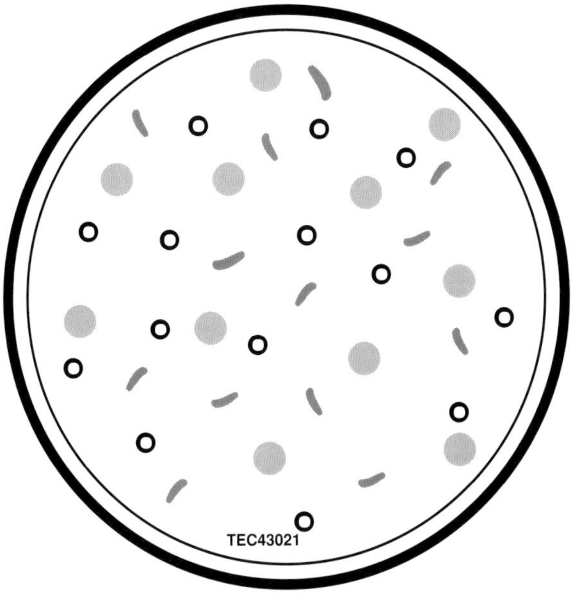
TEC43021

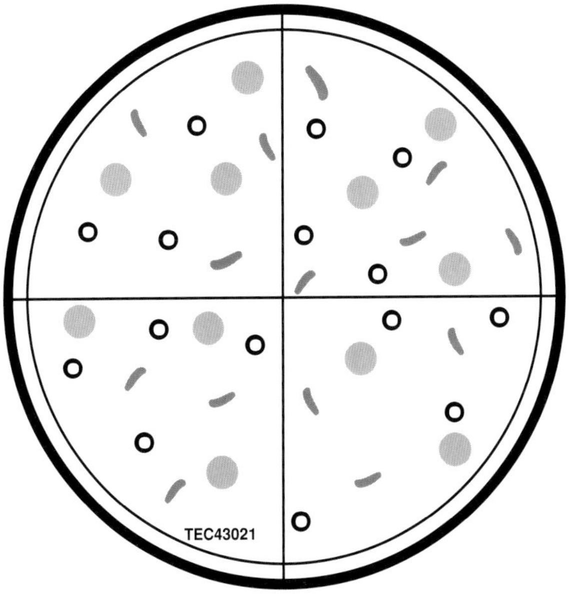
TEC43021

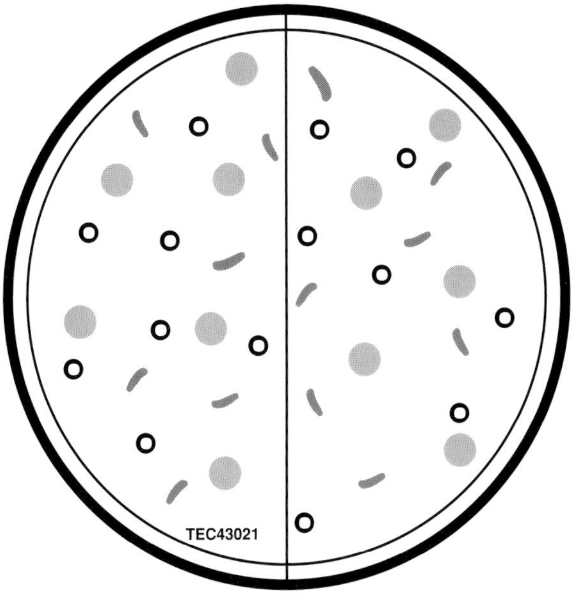
TEC43021

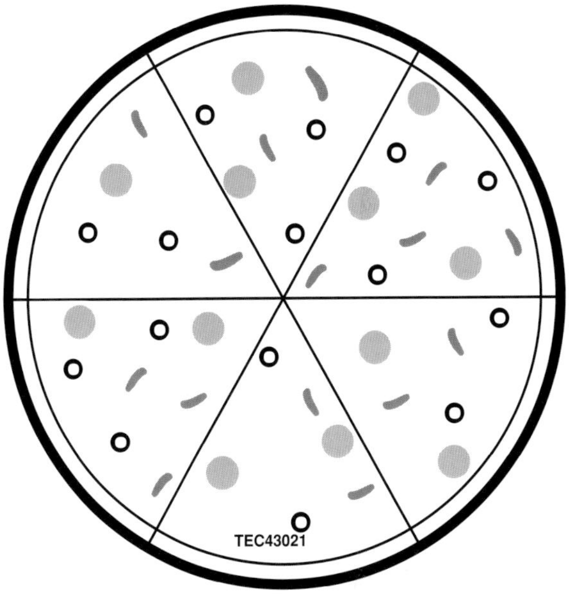
TEC43021

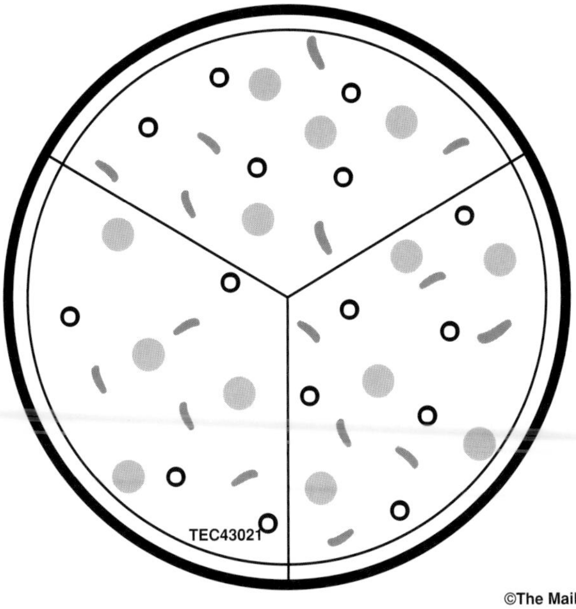
TEC43021

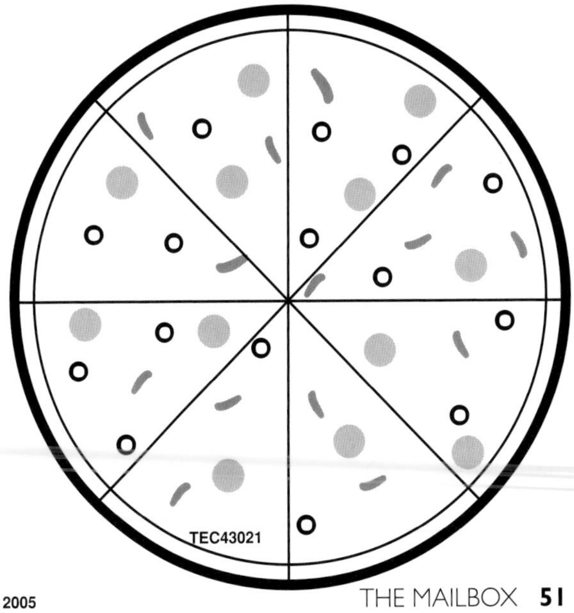
TEC43021

Sorting Mat

Use with “Pizza Pies” on page 49.

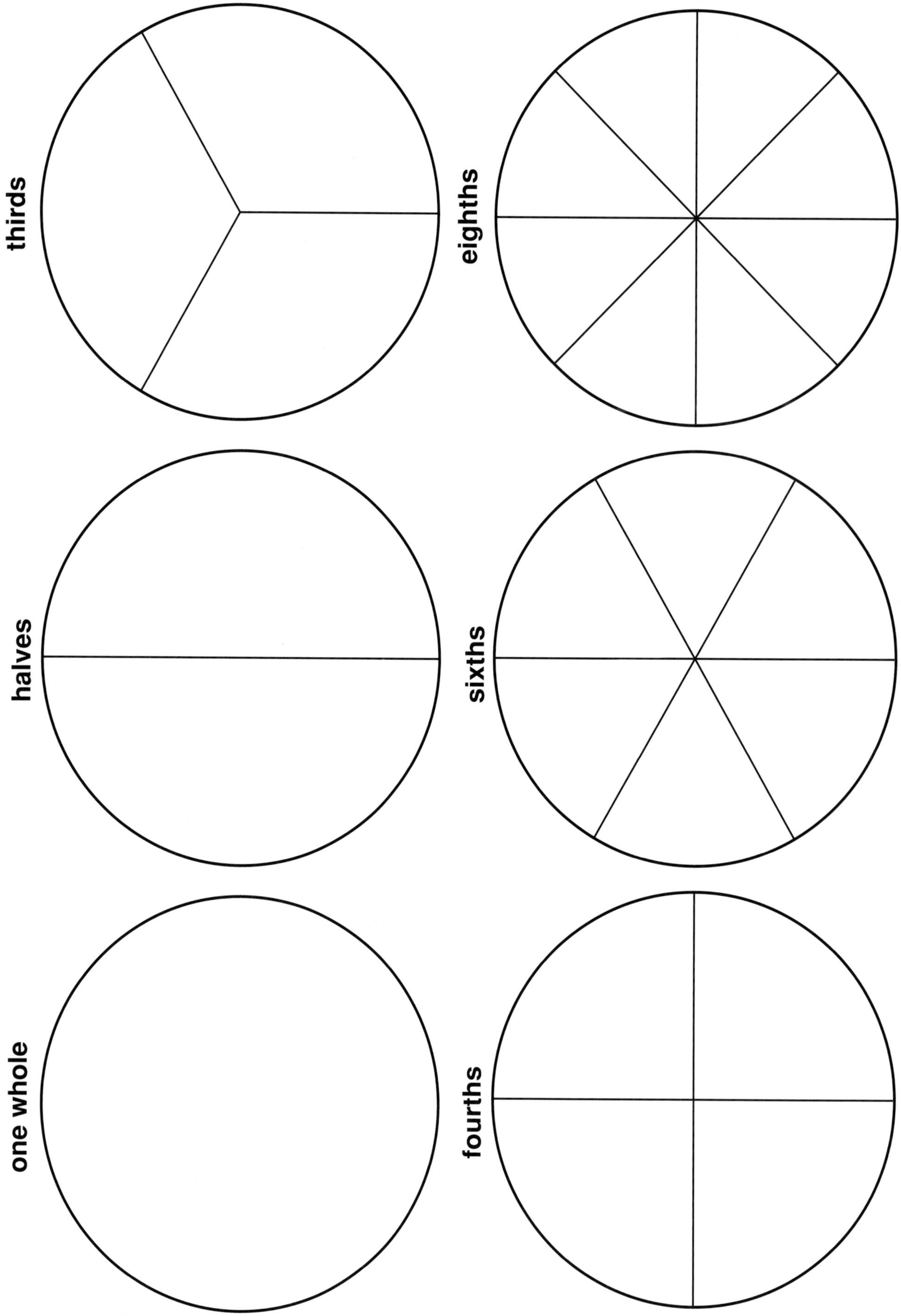
thirds
eighths
halves
sixths
one whole
fourths

Place the pizza slices on the matching pan.

Learning Centers

Incorrect
How are you.
Correct
to the park yesterday.
We finished our homework early.

Stoplight Sentences

Easy punctuation practice gets the green light with this sorting activity! Prepare the center by making a copy of the sentence cards on page 55. Program the back of each card with a green or red dot for easy self-checking. Then place at a center the cards and a colored copy of the sorting mat on page 56. A child reads each card and decides whether it is punctuated correctly. Then he places it in the corresponding space on the mat. After sorting the cards, he turns them over to check his work.

Jean Erickson
Grace Christian Academy
West Allis, WI

I'm so excited about our party!

Crayon

Snowball Math

Help students memorize basic facts with this exciting partner game! Make 20 copies of the snowball pattern on page 57. Program two snowballs with each digit from 0 to 9, resulting in two sets of matching snowballs. To play, each partner receives a set of snowballs and holds them facedown. The pair says, "One, two, three…go!" and both partners turn over their top card, revealing two numbers. The first student to say the sum wins both cards. Play continues in this manner until all the cards have been played. Extend the activity by having students find the difference or the product of the two numbers.

Cinthea Thurman, Dr. Charles R. Drew Elementary, Silver Spring, MD

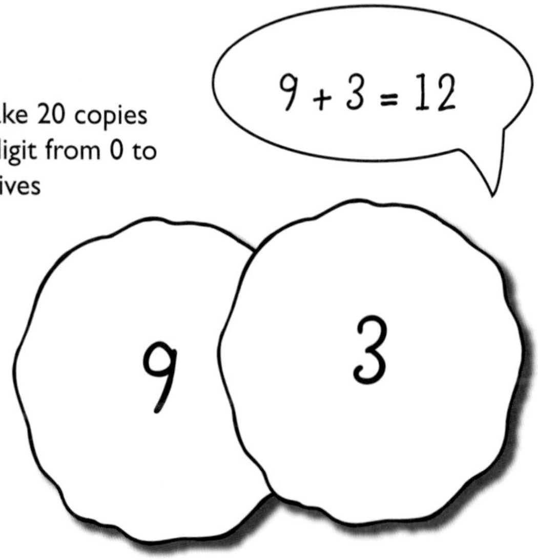
9 + 3 = 12
9
3

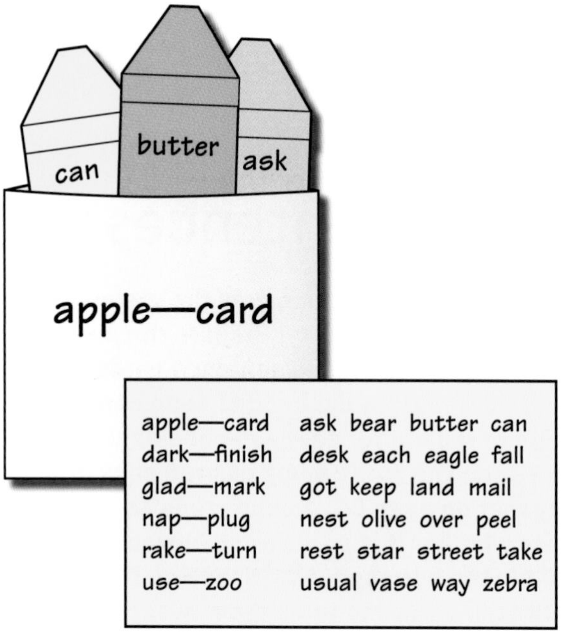
can
butter
ask
apple—card
apple—card ask bear butter can
dark—finish desk each eagle fall
glad—mark got keep land mail
nap—plug nest olive over peel
rake—turn rest star street take
use—zoo usual vase way zebra

Colorful Guide Words

Strengthening dictionary skills is the focus at this center! Seal three letter-size envelopes; then cut them in half, creating six pockets. Program each pocket with a set of guide words like the ones shown. Also make a supply of the crayon pattern on page 57 and program each one with a different word. Place the crayons, the pockets, and an answer key at a center. A child matches the word on each crayon to its correct guide words and then places the crayon in the corresponding pocket. After sorting the crayons, she checks her work with the answer key.

Laura E. Skrypczak, Ferber Elementary, Appleton, WI

May I Take Your Order, Please?

At this center, pairs work together to practice adding money! Gather a variety of restaurant menus and place them at a center along with a supply of the order pad pattern on page 57. One child chooses a menu, and names three or four things he would like to order. His partner writes down each item and uses the menu to find its price. Then he finds the total cost. Pairs take turns ordering and finding the total for as long as desired.

Gina Bittner, Hoff Elementary, Keenesburg, CO

Item
Price
fried rice $ 2.15
egg roll $ 0.75
wontons $ 2.50
chicken lo mein $ 5.75
$.
$.
Total: $ 11.15

Sentence Cards

Use with “Stoplight Sentences” on page 53.

Did your team win the game. TEC43022	We finished our homework early. TEC43022
I’m so excited about our party! TEC43022	When do you go home? TEC43022
Wow, those are neat. TEC43022	May I have dessert now! TEC43022
What time is it? TEC43022	I can’t believe I won? TEC43022
We went to the park yesterday. TEC43022	Why can’t I go. TEC43022
I love to eat candy. TEC43022	I want to be a better swimmer. TEC43022
How are you. TEC43022	The movie is starting. TEC43022
I don’t want to be late? TEC43022	I just saw him over there. TEC43022
What a catch! TEC43022	What will you order! TEC43022

Sorting Mat

Use with "Stoplight Sentences" on page 53.

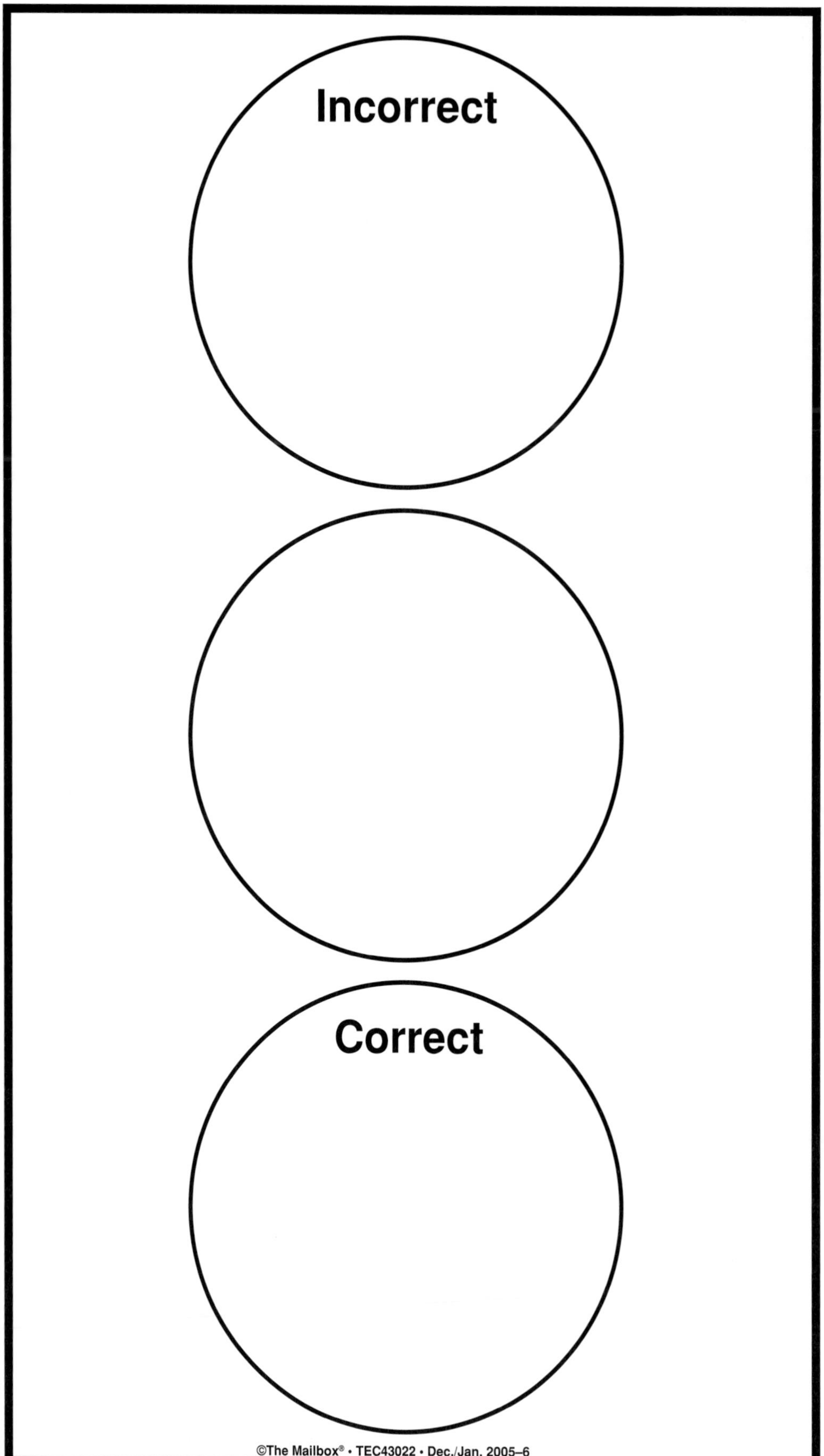
Incorrect
Correct

Snowball Pattern

Use with "Snowball Math" on page 54.

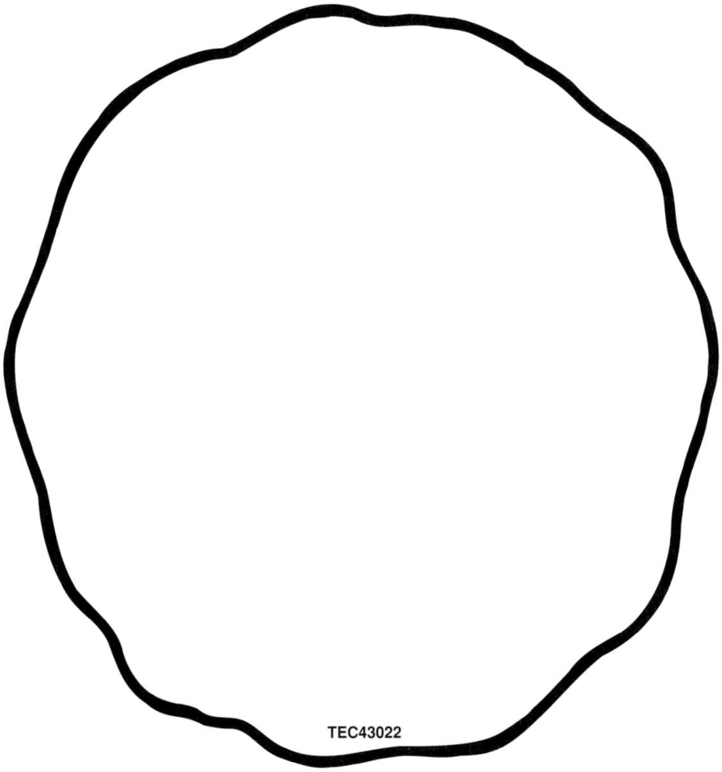
TEC43022

Crayon Pattern

Use with "Colorful Guide Words" on page 54.

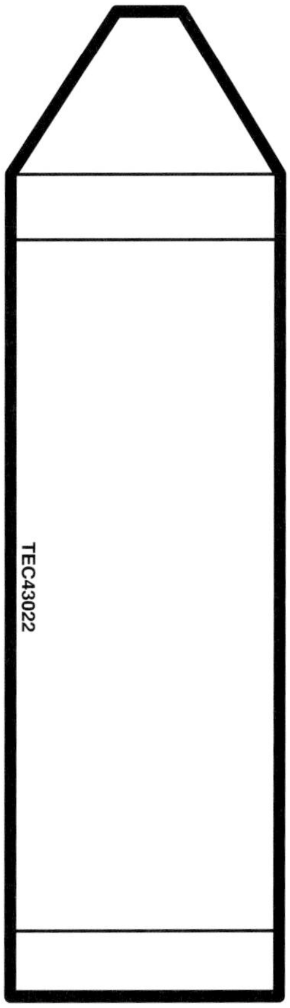
TEC43022

Order Pad Pattern

Use with "May I Take Your Order, Please?" on page 54.

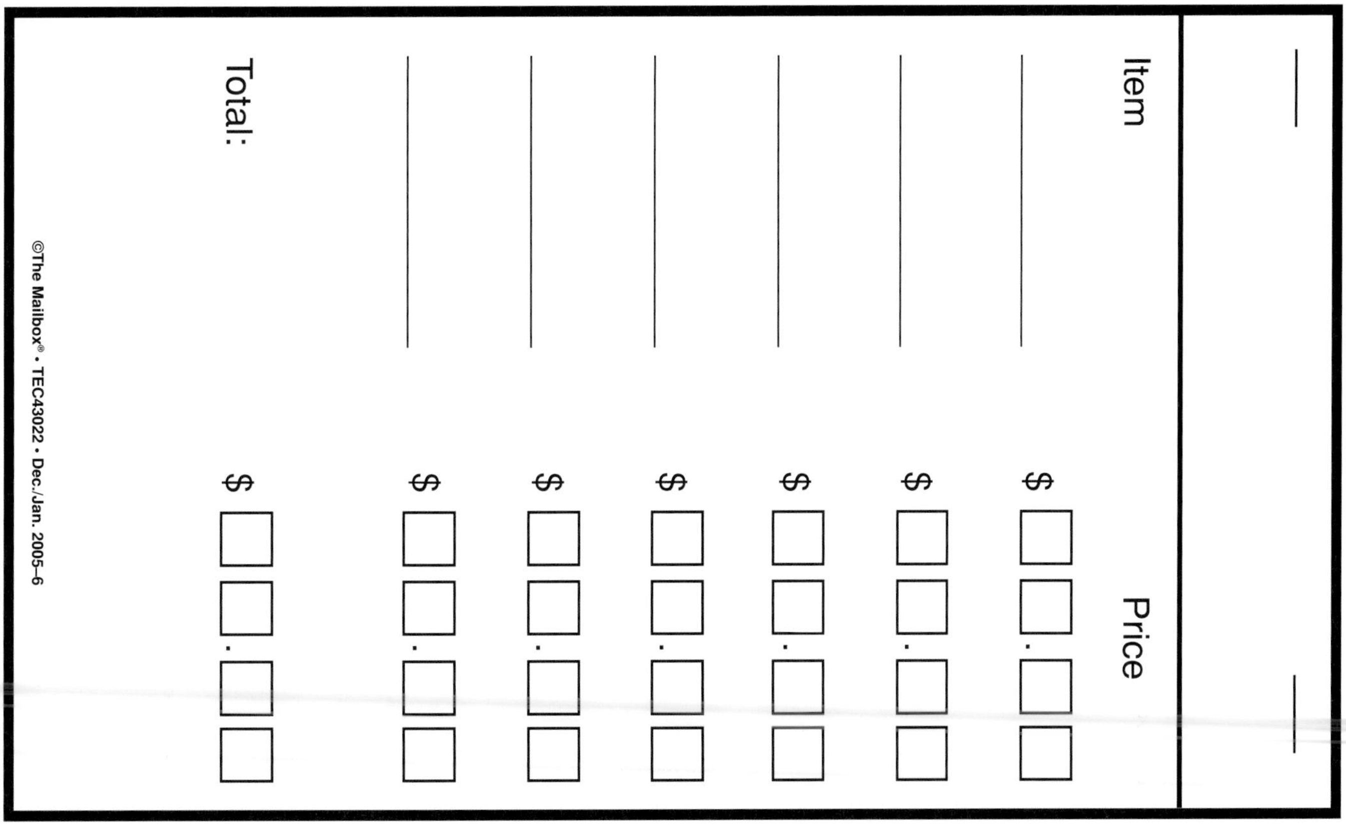
Item
Price
$.
$.
$.
$.
$.
$.
Total:
$.
©The Mailbox® • TEC43022 • Dec./Jan. 2005–6

Learning Centers

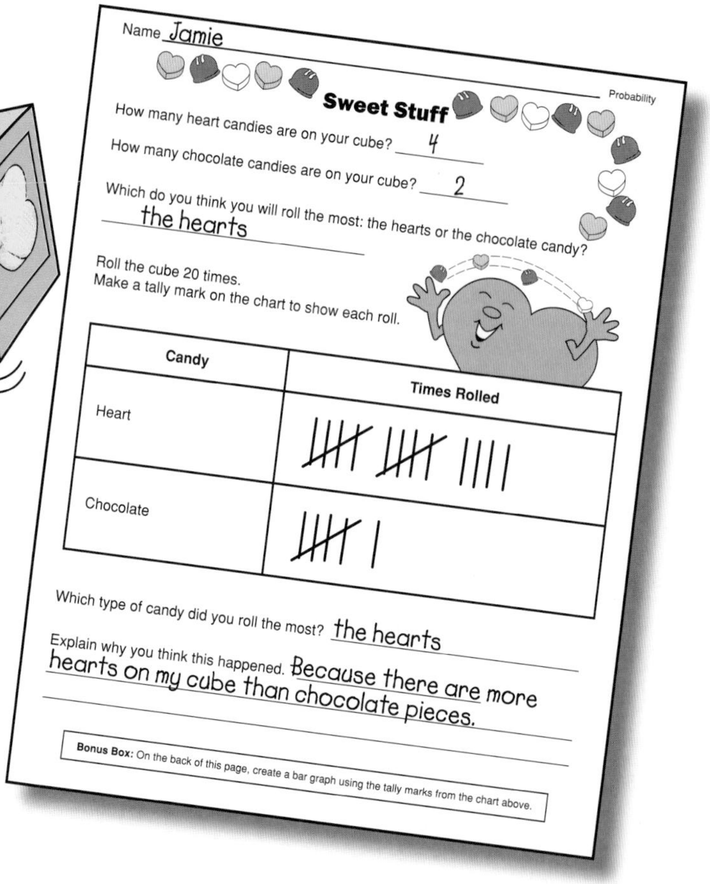

Name Jamie

Sweet Stuff Probability

How many heart candies are on your cube? 4

How many chocolate candies are on your cube? 2

Which do you think you will roll the most: the hearts or the chocolate candy?
the hearts

Roll the cube 20 times.
Make a tally mark on the chart to show each roll.

Candy	Times Rolled
Heart	~~IIII~~ ~~IIII~~ IIII
Chocolate	~~IIII~~ I

Which type of candy did you roll the most? the hearts

Explain why you think this happened. Because there are more hearts on my cube than chocolate pieces.

Bonus Box: On the back of this page, create a bar graph using the tally marks from the chart above.

Sweet Stuff

Students will be on a roll with this probability activity! In advance, make a class supply of pages 60 and 61. Place the copies at a center along with scissors, crayons, glue, and pencils. A child cuts out the candy pictures and the cube pattern on page 60. He selects six pictures, making sure he has both types of candy. Then he colors them and glues one on each side of the cube. He discards the remaining pictures and assembles the cube according to the directions on the page. Then the student uses his cube to complete the activity on page 61.

adapted from an idea by Stacie Stone Davis
Lima, NY

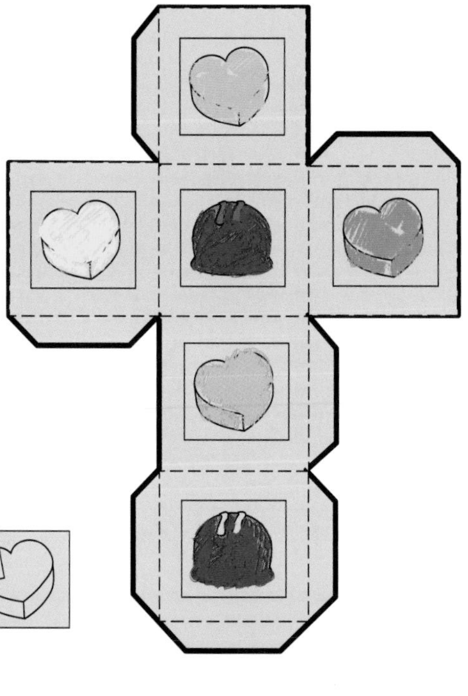

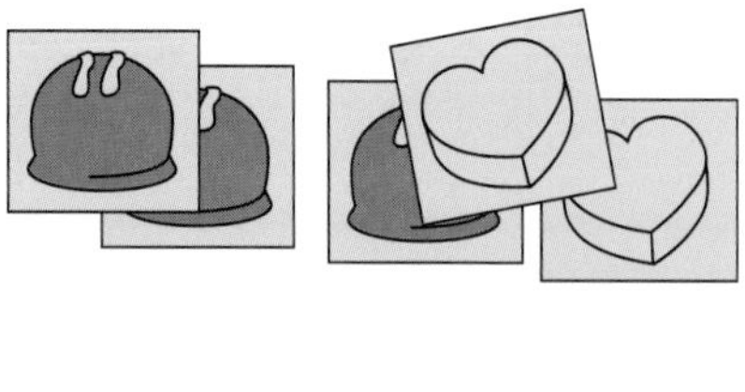

Crayon

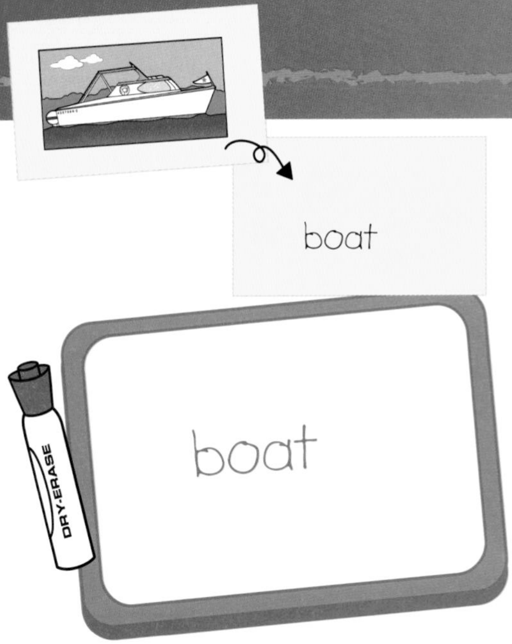
boat
boat
DRY-ERASE

Spelling Box

Help students practice sounding out and spelling words! In advance, cut out a variety of magazine pictures featuring objects whose names you want students to practice spelling. Glue each picture to one side of a blank index card and write the word on the opposite side. Store the cards in a box and place it at a center along with a small dry-erase board and a wipe-off marker. A student selects a card and looks at the picture. She sounds out the word and writes it on her board. Then she flips the card over to check her work. She continues drawing cards and spelling words for as long as desired.

Melinda Folson, St. James the Less School, Columbus, OH

Broken Hearts

Piece together division practice with this center! Copy page 62 and color the cards. Then cut out the cards and program the back of each for self-checking. Place the cards at a center. A child matches each division problem to its answer and then turns the cards over to check his work.

Amy Emmons, Enon Elementary, Franklinton, LA

21 ÷ 7 =
3
28 ÷ 4 =
7

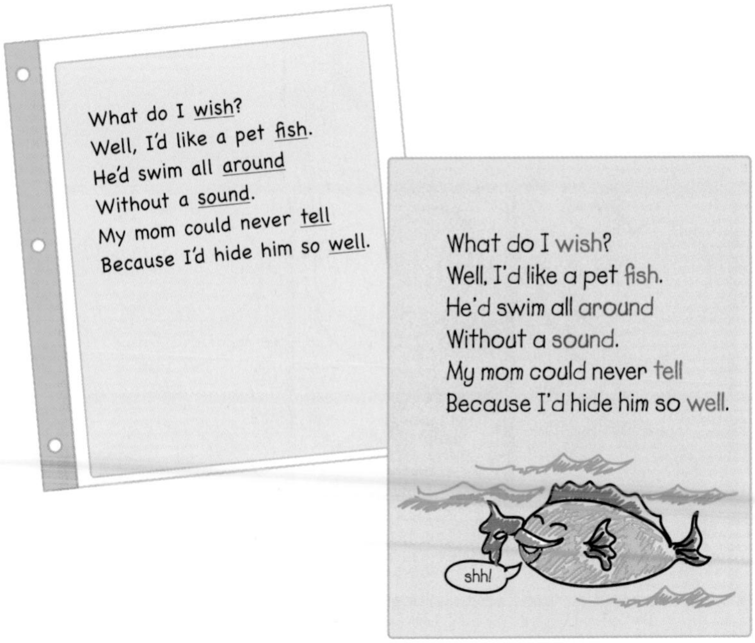
What do I wish?
Well, I'd like a pet fish.
He'd swim all around
Without a sound.
My mom could never tell
Because I'd hide him so well.
What do I wish?
Well, I'd like a pet fish.
He'd swim all around
Without a sound.
My mom could never tell
Because I'd hide him so well.
shh!

Poetry Place

Identifying rhyming words is a snap with this activity! At the beginning of each week, write a poem on a sheet of paper. Insert the poem into a plastic sheet protector and place it at a center along with a wipe-off marker, moistened paper towels, paper, and colored pencils. A child visits the center and reads the poem. She uses the marker to underline the words that rhyme. Then she copies the poem onto a sheet of paper, writing each set of rhyming words in the same color. Finally, she illustrates the poem and wipes the page protector clean so that it is ready for the next student.

April Lewis, Warsaw Elementary, Warsaw, NC

Candy Pictures and Cube Pattern

Use with "Sweet Stuff" on page 58.

Directions:

1. Cut out the pattern along the bold lines.
2. Color and cut out six pictures, making sure you have at least one of each type of candy.
3. Glue one picture in each square.
4. Fold the pattern on the dotted lines.
5. Tape or glue the sides together at the tabs to form a cube.

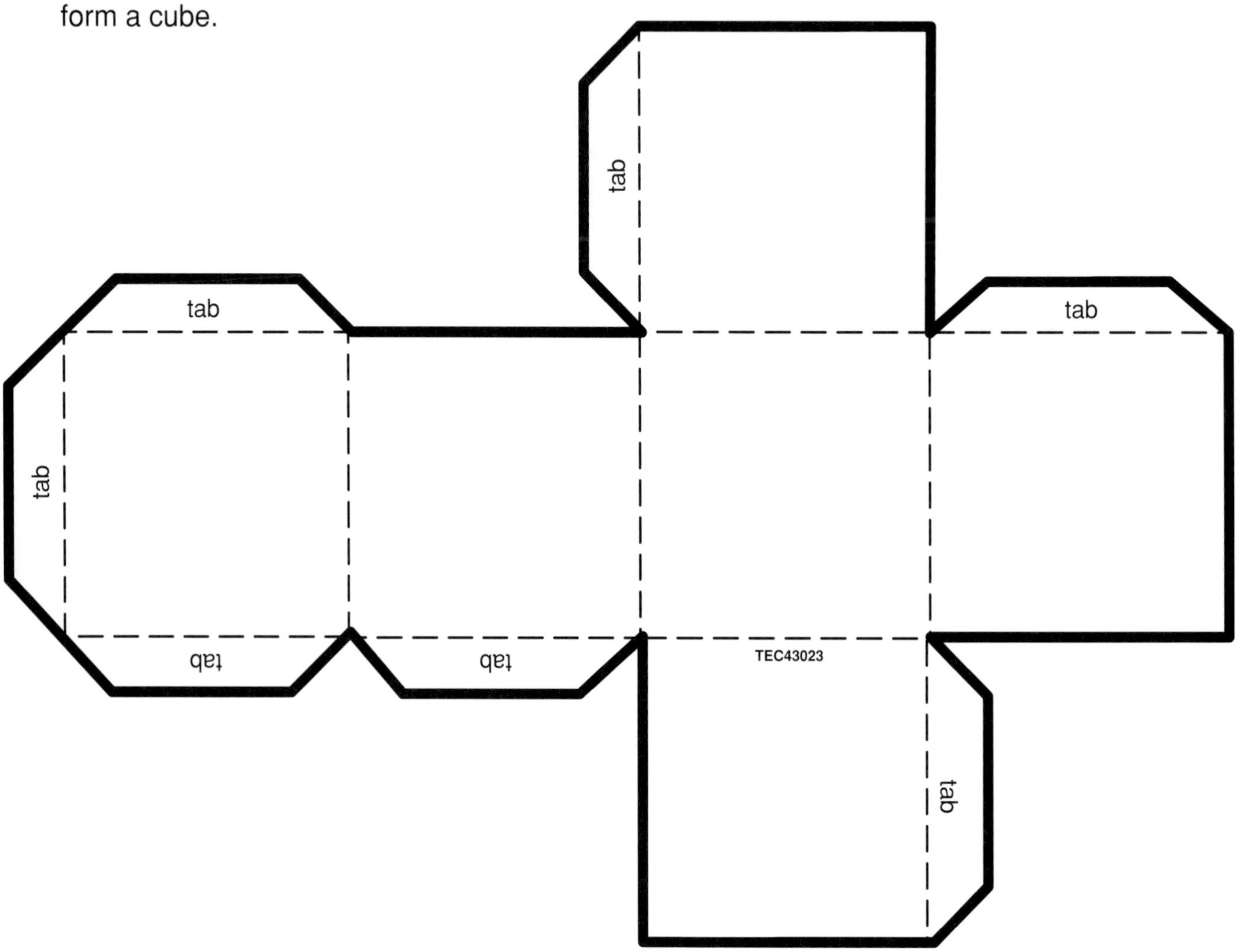
tab
tab
tab
tab
tab
tab
tab
TEC43023

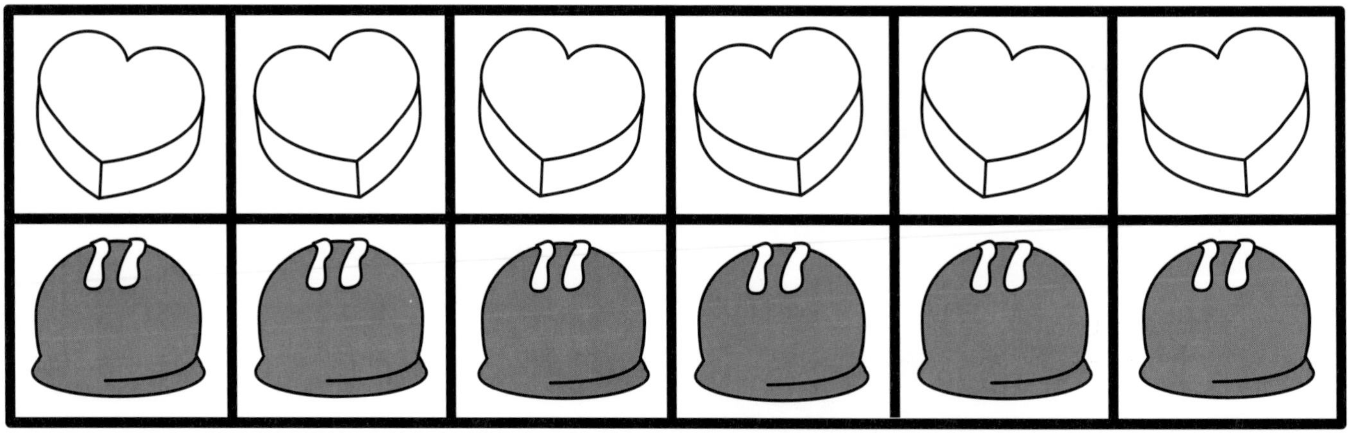

Name ____ Probability

Sweet Stuff

How many heart candies are on your cube? ____________

How many chocolate candies are on your cube? ____________

Which do you think you will roll the most: the heart or the chocolate candy?

____

Roll the cube 20 times.
Make a tally mark on the chart to show each roll.

Candy	Times Rolled
Heart	
Chocolate	

Which type of candy did you roll the most? ______________________________

Explain why you think this happened. ____________________________________

____

____

Bonus Box: On the back of this page, create a bar graph using the tally marks from the chart above.

Note to the teacher: Use with "Sweet Stuff" on page 58.

Center Cards

Use with "Broken Hearts" on page 59.

24 ÷ 4 = 6
TEC43023
15 ÷ 5 = 3
TEC43023
16 ÷ 4 = 4
TEC43023
10 ÷ 2 = 5
TEC43023
36 ÷ 6 = 6
TEC43023
28 ÷ 4 = 7
TEC43023
14 ÷ 2 = 7
TEC43023
18 ÷ 3 = 6
TEC43023
20 ÷ 5 = 4
TEC43023
21 ÷ 7 = 3
TEC43023
35 ÷ 7 = 5
TEC43023
24 ÷ 3 = 8
TEC43023

Learning Centers

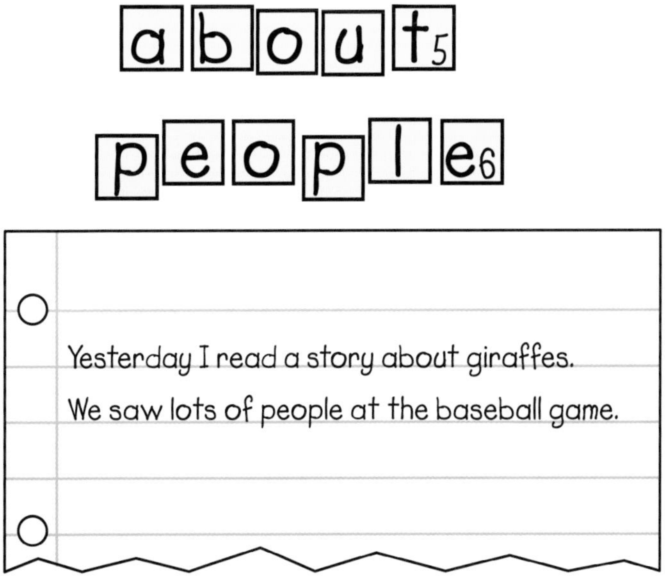
about5
people6
Yesterday I read a story about giraffes.
We saw lots of people at the baseball game.

Scrambled Eggs

This Grade A activity provides valuable practice with word wall words! In advance, gather a supply of plastic eggs and one-inch paper squares. Write one letter of a word wall word on each square. Also write the number of letters in the word on the last square. Next, place inside each egg the letters that make up two words. Store the eggs in a basket along with paper and pencils. A child selects an egg and opens it. He arranges the letters to form two words from the word wall. Then he uses each word in a different sentence and writes his sentences on a sheet of paper. He continues selecting eggs and forming words in this manner for as long as desired.

Pat Manker, Washington School, Jacksonville, IL

Crayon

Fraction Frogs

Finding a fraction of a set has never been so easy! Make a copy of page 66 and mount it on construction paper. Color the cards so that the frog cards match the fractions on the lily pads, and cut them out. Program the back of each card for self-checking, and place the cards at a center. A child matches each fraction card to its corresponding picture card. Then she turns the cards over to check her work.

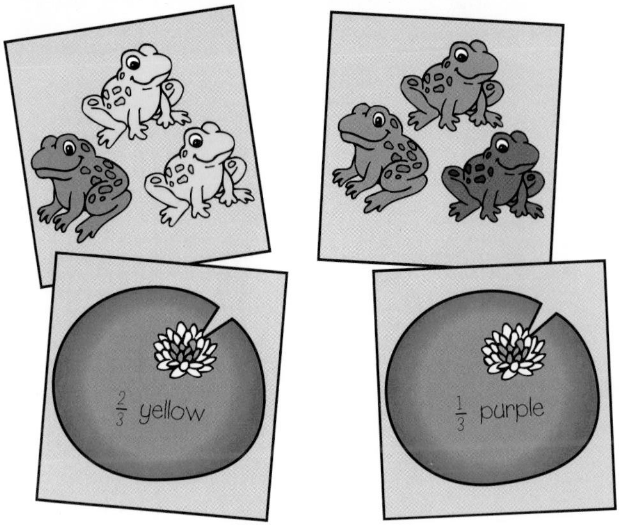
$\frac{2}{3}$ yellow
$\frac{1}{3}$ purple

it
it's
is
will
won't
not

Contraction Flowers

These colorful blooms are just the thing to help students identify words that form contractions! Make a supply of the leaf and flower patterns from page 65 on colored construction paper. Write a contraction on the center of each flower. Using Velcro fastener pieces, attach two leaves to opposite sides of each flower's back as shown. Label each leaf with one of the two words that combine to form the contraction on the flower. Separate the pieces and place them at a center with pencils and paper. A child matches two leaves to the corresponding flower. Then he records the two words and the contraction that they form.

Victoria DeOrnellis, Aberdeen Elementary, Aberdeen, MS

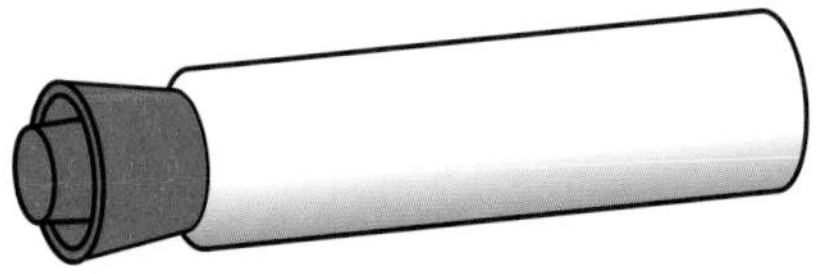

Symmetry Sort

Help students recognize symmetrical figures with this simple activity! Copy and laminate the cards on page 67. Cut out the cards; then program the back of each for self-checking. Place the cards at a center along with a dry-erase marker and two index cards: one labeled "Yes" and the other labeled "No." A student sorts the cards into two piles according to whether they are symmetrical. She uses the dry-erase marker as needed to check for lines of symmetry. Then she turns the cards over to check her work.

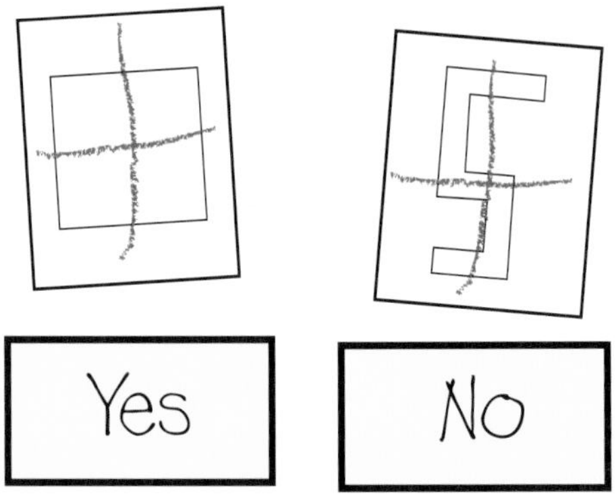
Yes
No

Flower and Leaf Patterns

Use with "Contraction Flowers" on page 64.

TEC43024
TEC43024
TEC43024
TEC43024
TEC43024
TEC43024
TEC43024
TEC43024
TEC43024
TEC43024
TEC43024
TEC43024

Center Cards

Use with "Fraction Frogs" on page 64.

TEC43024

TEC43024

TEC43024

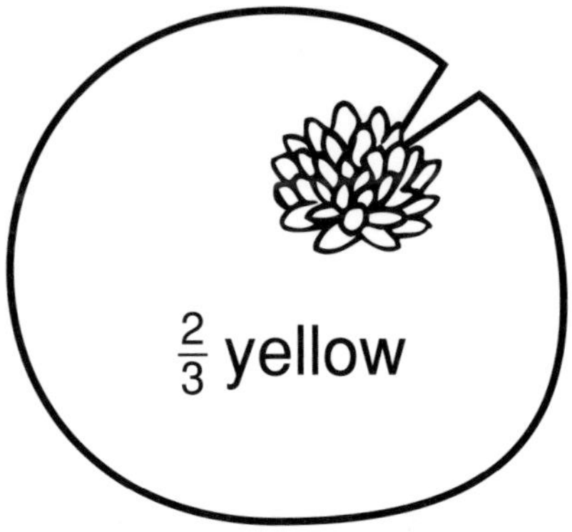
$\frac{2}{3}$ yellow

TEC43024

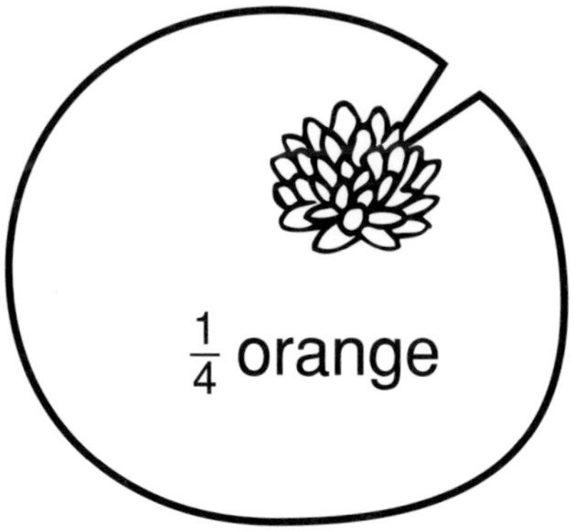
$\frac{1}{4}$ orange

TEC43024

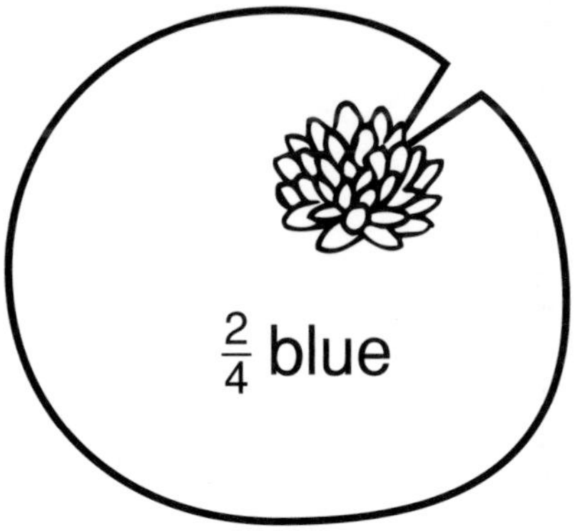
$\frac{2}{4}$ blue

TEC43024

TEC43024

TEC43024

TEC43024

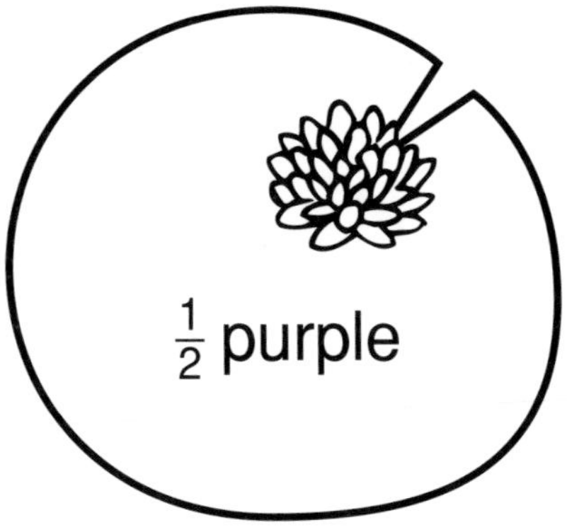
$\frac{1}{2}$ purple

TEC43024

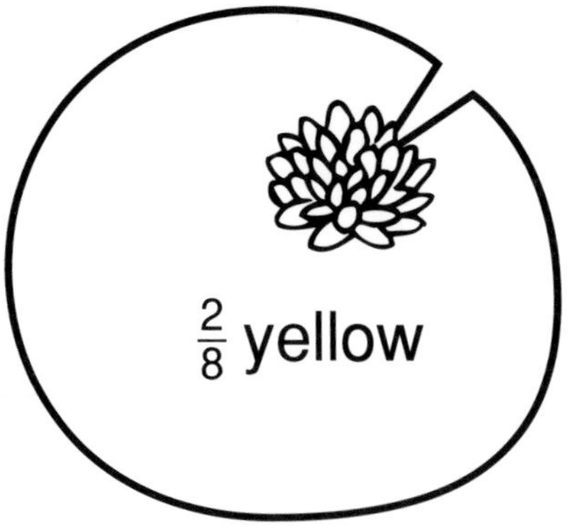
$\frac{2}{8}$ yellow

TEC43024

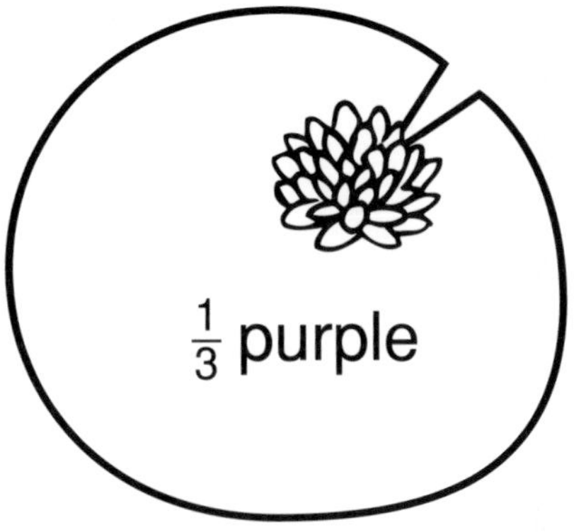
$\frac{1}{3}$ purple

TEC43024

Shape Cards

Use with "Symmetry Sort" on page 64.

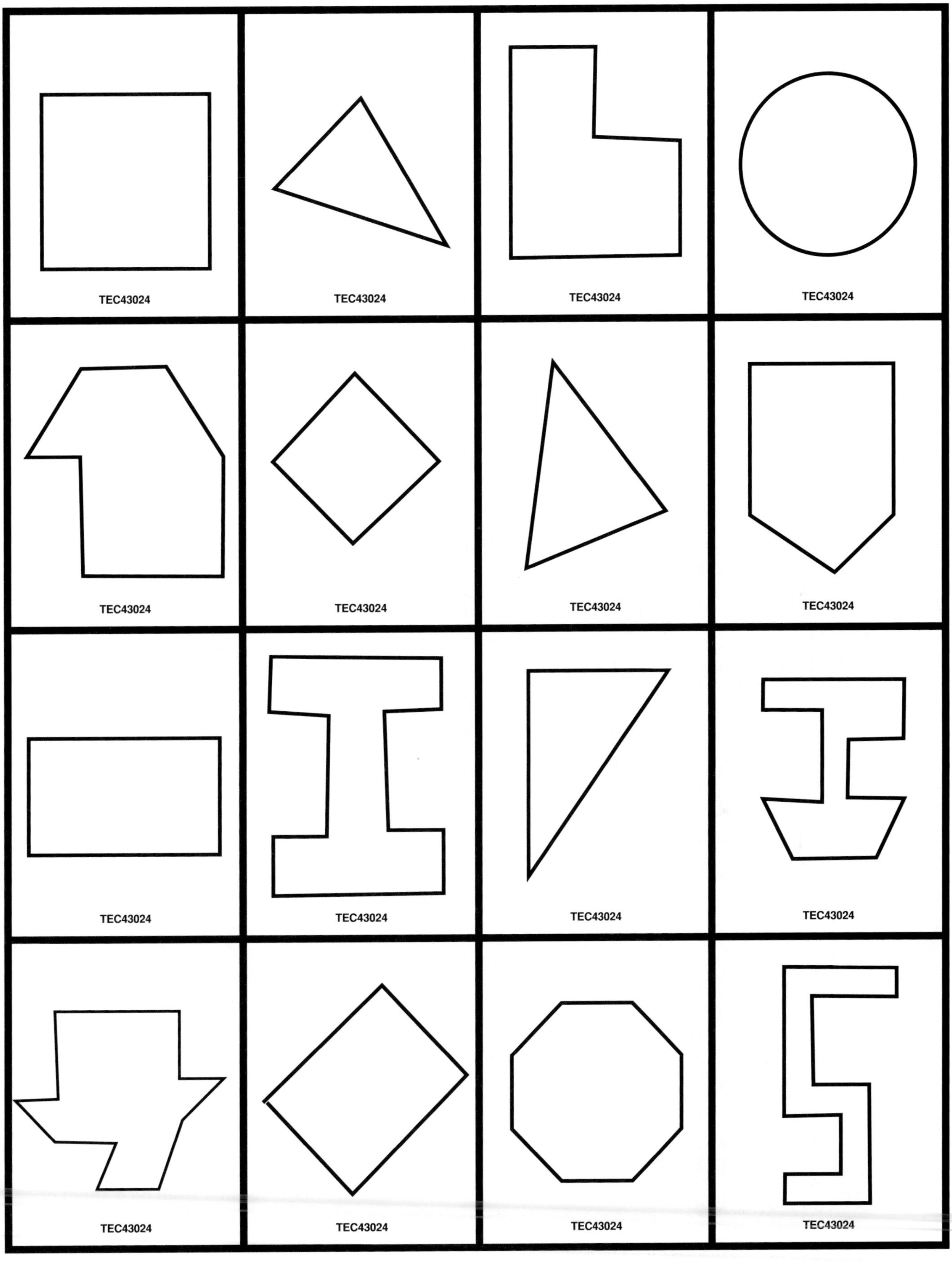
TEC43024
TEC43024
TEC43024
TEC43024
TEC43024
TEC43024
TEC43024
TEC43024
TEC43024
TEC43024
TEC43024
TEC43024
TEC43024
TEC43024
TEC43024
TEC43024

Learning Centers

re
un
kind
happy
place
able
cool
heat
copy
read

Chilly Challenge

Refresh students' prefix skills with this cool activity! In advance, gather several cotton balls, an ice cube tray, plastic cups, and plain sticker dots. Write a different prefix on each cup. Then write on each sticker dot a different root word that, when combined with one of the prefixes, forms a new word. Affix a sticker dot to each cotton ball and store it in a section of the ice cube tray. Make the center self-checking by writing the root words on the bottom of the matching cups. Then place the cups and the tray at a center along with paper and pencils. A child chooses a cotton ball and puts it in the correct cup to make a new word. He writes the newly formed word on a sheet of paper. When all of the cotton balls have been placed in a cup, he checks his work.

Lydia Hess, Chambersburg, PA

Crayon

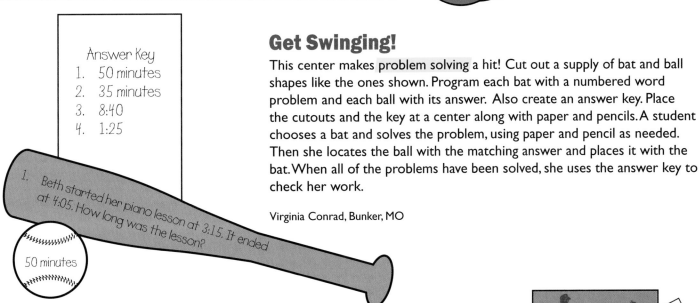

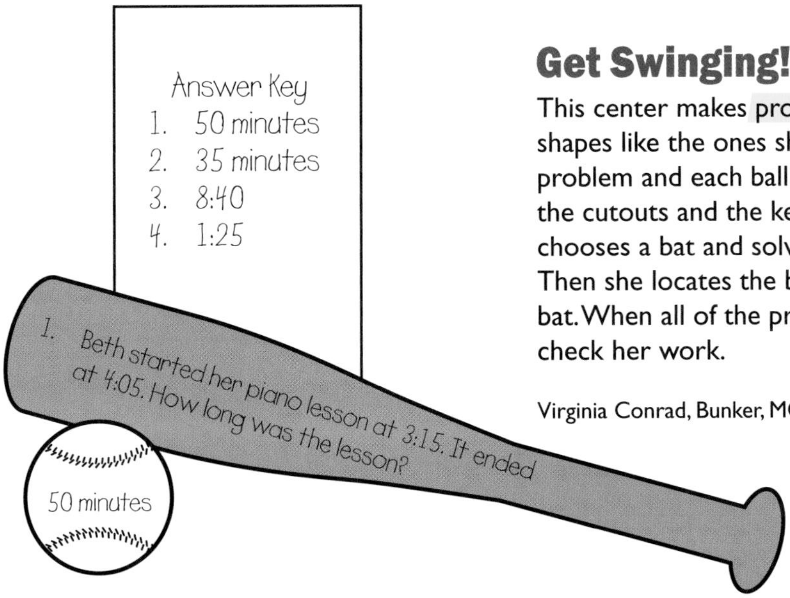
Answer Key
1. 50 minutes
2. 35 minutes
3. 8:40
4. 1:25
1. Beth started her piano lesson at 3:15. It ended at 4:05. How long was the lesson?
50 minutes

Get Swinging!

This center makes problem solving a hit! Cut out a supply of bat and ball shapes like the ones shown. Program each bat with a numbered word problem and each ball with its answer. Also create an answer key. Place the cutouts and the key at a center along with paper and pencils. A student chooses a bat and solves the problem, using paper and pencil as needed. Then she locates the ball with the matching answer and places it with the bat. When all of the problems have been solved, she uses the answer key to check her work.

Virginia Conrad, Bunker, MO

Dig In

Students will be eager to plow through this question-writing activity. Cut out seasonal pictures, like the ones shown, from newspapers and magazines. Store the pictures in a bucket and place it at a center with glue, paper, and pencils. A student selects a picture and glues it to his paper. Then he writes three questions about the picture. If time allows, he uses visual cues and his own prior experiences to provide possible answers.

Robbie
1. Why is the family leaving the beach?
2. How long were they there?
3. How do they feel?

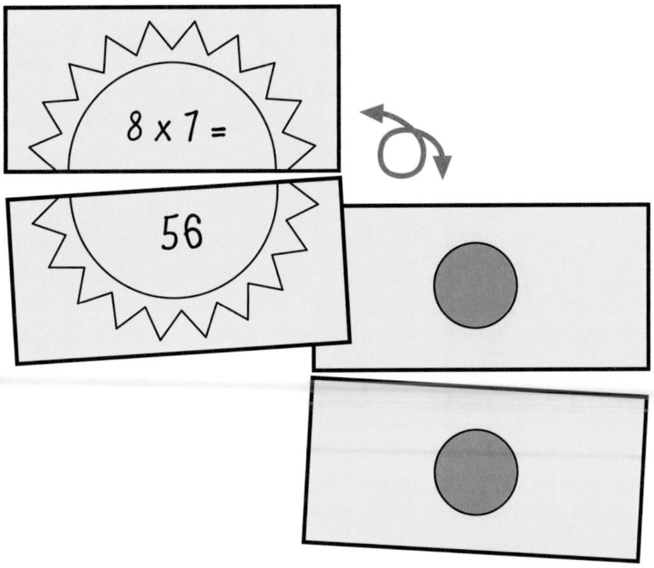
8 x 7 =
56

Sunny Facts

Multiplication skills shine at this center! Copy page 70 on yellow paper; then cut out the cards. Write a multiplication problem on the top of each sun and its answer on the bottom. Program the backs of matching cards with same-colored dots for self-checking and then place them at a center. A child matches each problem to its answer. Then she turns the cards over to check her work.

Patricia Frano, Meadville, PA

Sun Cards

Use with "Sunny Facts" on page 69.

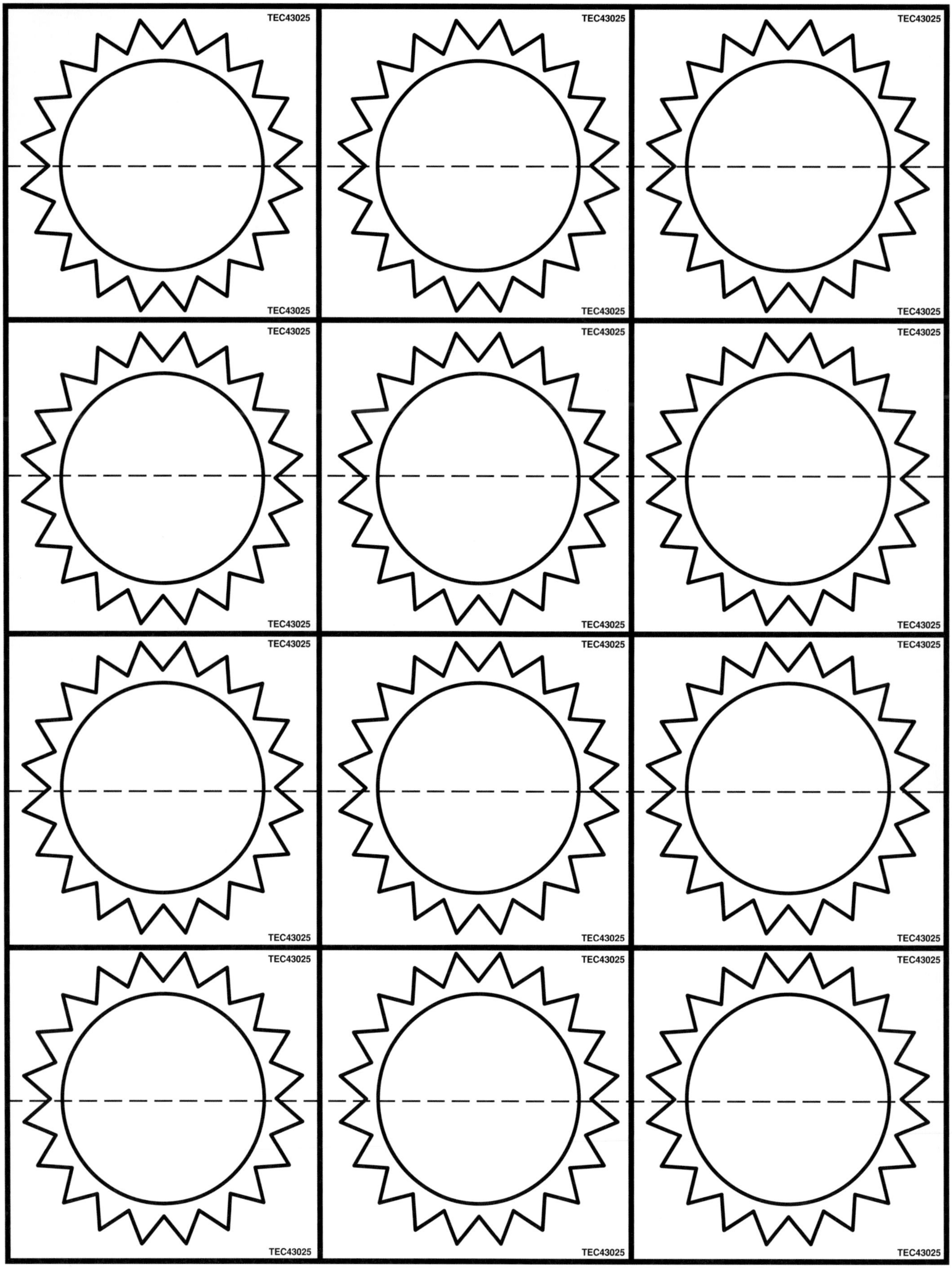
TEC43025
TEC43025
TEC43025
TEC43025
TEC43025
TEC43025
TEC43025
TEC43025
TEC43025
TEC43025
TEC43025
TEC43025
TEC43025
TEC43025
TEC43025
TEC43025
TEC43025
TEC43025
TEC43025
TEC43025
TEC43025
TEC43025
TEC43025
TEC43025

Management Tips & Timesavers

Management Tips & Timesavers

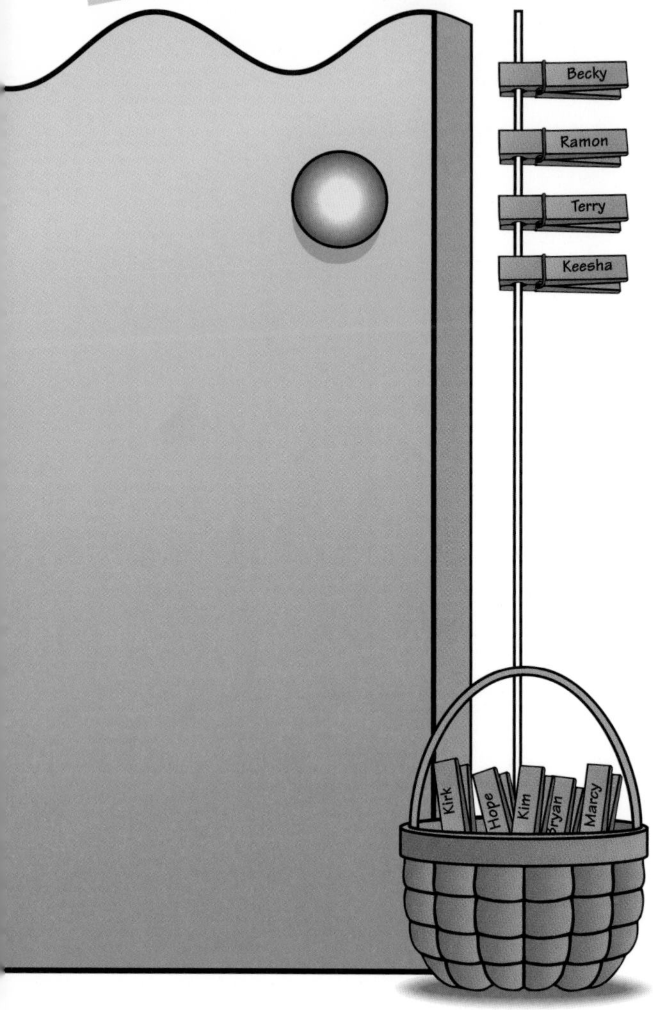
Becky
Ramon
Terry
Keesha
Kirk
Hope
Kim
Marcy

Clothespin Attendance

Taking attendance is a snap with this simple tip! Label each of a class supply of clothespins with a different child's name. Also hang a length of clothesline or decorative ribbon vertically by your classroom door. Clip the clothespins to the line and place a basket below it. To take attendance, have each child remove his clothespin and place it in the basket as he enters the classroom. Then quickly scan the clothespins still on the line to see which students are absent. At the end of the day, reclip the clothespins for the next day's attendance.

Shauna Aukerman, Woodland Elementary, Gages Lake, IL

Weekday Drawers

This organizational tip makes it easy to prepare for the days ahead! Label each drawer in a small six-drawer filing cabinet with a day of the school week. After completing your lesson plans, gather the needed reproducibles, transparencies, and other materials for each day's lessons and place them in the corresponding drawer. In the sixth drawer place miscellaneous materials or sponge activities. Then simply pull out the necessary materials each morning and you're ready to go!

Elizabeth Compton, Western Union Elementary, Waxhaw, NC

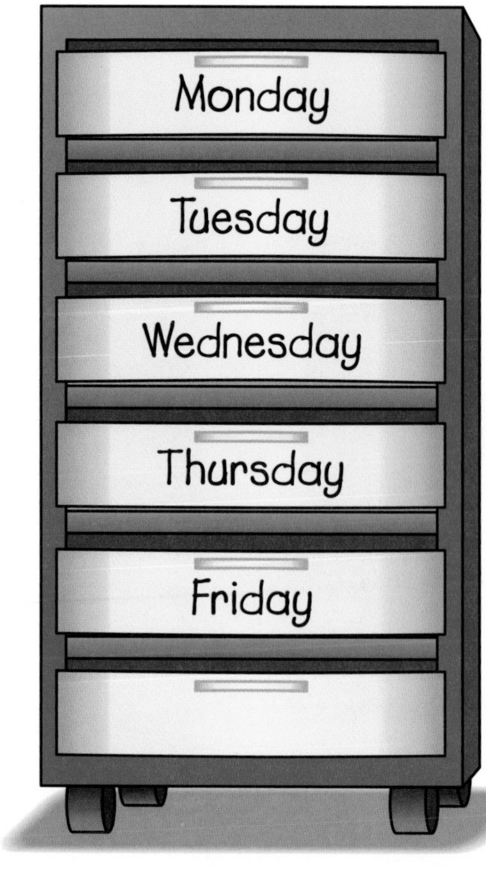
Monday
Tuesday
Wednesday
Thursday
Friday

Management Tips & Timesavers

Spelling List
Spelling

Extra Forms Board

This timesaver eliminates the need to copy extra forms for students at the end of the day. Label a supply of pocket file folders with different subject areas and attach the folders to a bulletin board. Inside the corresponding folders place extra copies of your weekly spelling list, math practice sheets, or reading recording sheets. When a student needs a replacement for a lost form, she simply locates the appropriate folder and takes one without having to ask for an extra copy.

Pamela Vadas, Eden Christian Academy, Pittsburgh, PA

Pajama Day
Favorite Stuffed Animal Day
Crazy Hair Day
Favorite Team Jersey Day

Compliment Chain

This teamwork incentive creates a chain reaction that leads to cooperation every time it's used! At the beginning of the year, brainstorm as a class a list of reward days like the ones shown. Explain that students can earn a reward day by working together. Then, each time the class receives a compliment for teamwork, add a link to a paper chain posted in the classroom. When the class has earned a predetermined number of compliments, allow students to vote for their favorite reward day choice.

Mary Lovelace, Jerome Harrison Elementary, North Branford, CT

Keep the Color

Never hand out the master copy of a reproducible to a student again! Whenever you make a class supply of a reproducible, make an extra copy on light-colored paper. Then place the color copy in your files and distribute only white copies to students. What a simple solution!

Tiffany Gosseen, Polo R-VII, Polo, MO

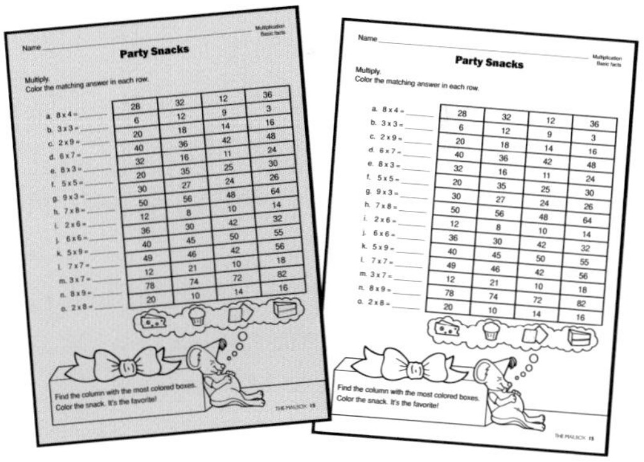
Party Snacks
Party Snacks

Ms. Smith
Josh
Ms. Smith

Special Delivery

Ensure that your morning routine runs smoothly with this useful tip! Place a mailbox or a box decorated to resemble one in a location accessible to students. Also place with it a supply of envelopes. When a child has a note or money to turn in, have him take an envelope and address it to you. Then have him write his own name in the return address spot, place the item(s) inside the envelope, seal it, and place it in the mailbox. You can check the mail and respond to it as you have time during the day.

Bridgette Smith, Kennedy Elementary, McComb, MS

Management Tips & Timesavers

Talking Card
• The person holding this card is the only one who should be talking.
• Each person can only keep the card for one minute.
• Each person must have a chance to talk.

Talking Cards

How can you help small groups run more efficiently? Label the fronts and backs of several large index cards as shown. Laminate the cards for durability. Then, each time students are working in small groups, give each group a Talking Card and have it follow the rules on the back. The cards help keep the noise level down and provide time for each group member to share his ideas.

Cassie Young, University Meadows, Rock Hill, SC

Give 110%

Improve hallway behavior with this simple tip! Each time your class leaves the room, challenge students to earn 110% by doing the following:

- walking in a straight line like the number 1
- keeping their hands at their sides like the number 1
- making sure there is zero talking

After several 110% performances, reward the class with a special treat.

Renee Kerstetter, Selinsgrove Intermediate School, Selinsgrove, PA

Management Tips & Timesavers

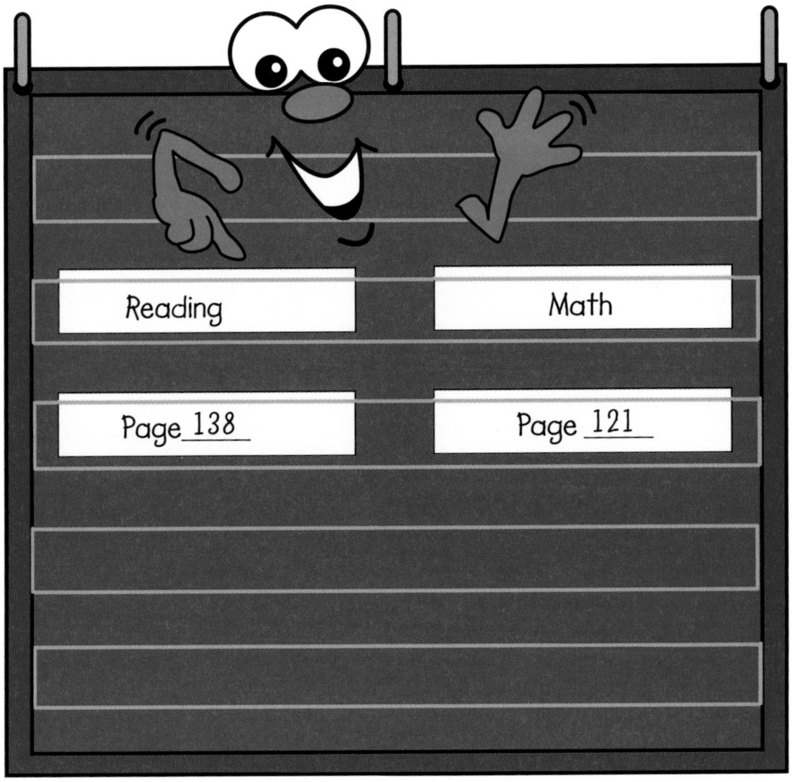

Reading
Math
Page 138
Page 121

On the Same Page

Eliminate questions about textbook page numbers with this simple tip! Cut a sentence strip into fourths. Label each section as shown and then laminate it. Before class, use a wipe-off marker to list each textbook's page number; then place the strips in a pocket chart. Now students who need reminders for the correct page number need only look at the chart!

Anna Parrish, Joseph Keels Elementary, Columbia, SC

Super Secret Agents of Kindness

Send students on a mission to promote kindness and respect! Write each child's name on a slip of paper, and place the slips in a bag. Every Monday, have each student draw a name from the bag without revealing it. Throughout the week, the child becomes a secret agent of kindness to his designated person (and to others so that his person cannot be identified) by sending happy notes or pictures, helping with problems, or inviting her to play at recess. At the end of the week, have each student reveal his chosen person. Invite the chosen student to share one thing her secret agent did that made her feel special.

Gail Romig, Park Forest Elementary, State College, PA

Your secret agent
Dear Angie,
I hope you have a great day!
Your secret agent

Management Tips & Timesavers

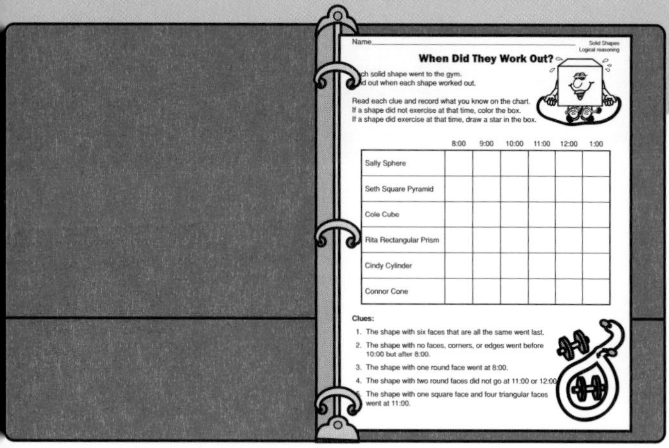

When Did They Work Out?
Solid Shapes
Logical reasoning
8:00 9:00 10:00 11:00 12:00 1:00
Sally Sphere
Seth Square Pyramid
Cole Cube
Rita Rectangular Prism
Cindy Cylinder
Connor Cone
Clues:

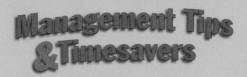

Notebook Files

Use this simple tip to keep resources at your fingertips! Look through your files and find the reproducibles and activities you are most likely to use during the year. Make a copy of each; then return the originals to your files. Place the copies in a three-ring binder, organizing them by subject or time of year. Keep the binder on your desk or bookshelf. Then, when you need a specific activity or reproducible, it's easy to locate. Plus, when you start a new unit, it's easy to view your frequently used files.

Abby Kail, Arie Crown Hebrew Day School, Skokie, IL

Kindness Catcher

Celebrate students' acts of kindness! Each week, assign one student to be the class Kindness Catcher and to observe her class-mates during the week. Each time she sees a fellow student being kind, she writes on a paper strip the child's name and what he did. Then she places the strip in a basket. At the end of the week, read aloud the paper strips and reward each child mentioned with a round of applause.

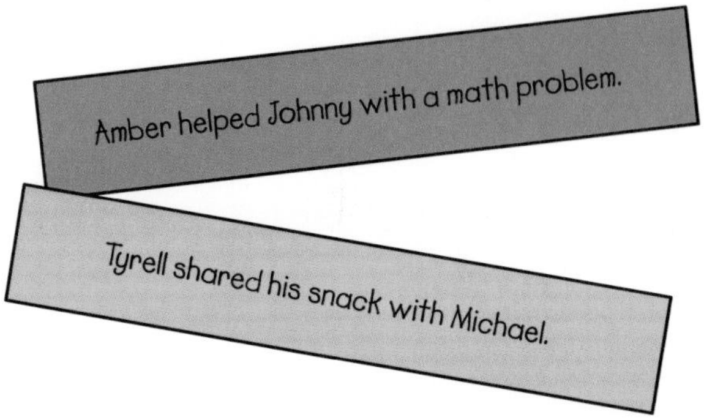

Amber helped Johnny with a math problem.
Tyrell shared his snack with Michael.

Christine Stavash, Van Zant Elementary, Marlton, NJ

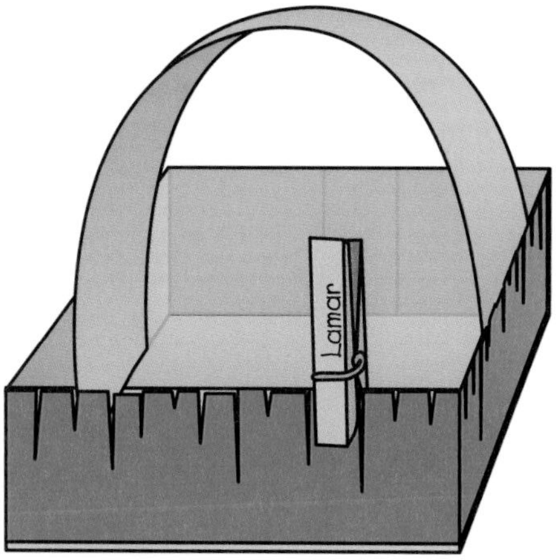

Lamar

Craft Clothespins

Avoid confusion when completing multistep arts-and-crafts projects! Program each of a class supply of clothespins with a different student's name. At the end of the class, attach each child's clothespin to his project. When the student is ready to continue working, he simply finds the clothespin with his name and retrieves his project.

Michelle Wolak, Columbia, NJ

Easy Cleanup

Use music to signal students that an activity is over! In advance, select a short song (about two to three minutes long). Before beginning an activity, tell students that when the song begins to play, they should put finishing touches on their work and clean up their materials. Also explain that by the time the song ends, they should be in their seats ready to start the next activity. Then, when time is up, play the song. Guide students to wrap up their assignments and straighten their areas.

Meghan Kelley, St. Christopher School, Rocky River, OH

Management Tips & Timesavers

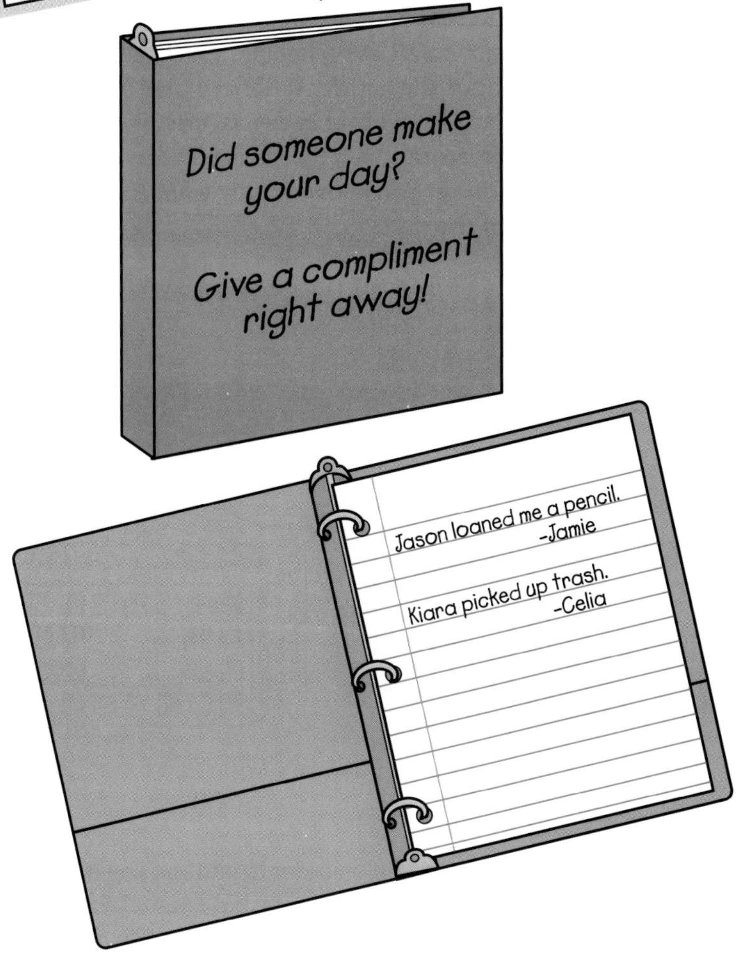
Did someone make your day?
Give a compliment right away!
Jason loaned me a pencil.
-Jamie
Kiara picked up trash.
-Celia

Compliment Book

Make your classroom atmosphere even more positive and caring with this notebook! To create one, place a supply of loose-leaf paper in a three-ring binder and label the front with the rhyme shown. Explain to students that whenever they see a classmate behaving well, doing a kind deed, or helping someone, they should write a compliment about that person in the notebook. Remind students to praise a child's actions or deeds instead of his appearance. When possible, share the compliments with the class, making sure that each student hears something positive about himself.

Lucille Iscaro, P.S. 11, Bronx, NY

Deck of Students

Use this simple tip to ensure that you call on different students throughout the day! Purchase a deck of blank playing cards (found in teacher supply stores) and label each card with a child's name and her photo. Keep the cards on your desk or in an easily accessible place. Then, when you want to call on a student, simply select a card from the deck. Also encourage substitute teachers to use the cards to help identify specific students.

Paulette M. Cesario, Fairfield Academy, Chicago, IL

Tyler Martinez
nna Mack

Management Tips & Timesavers

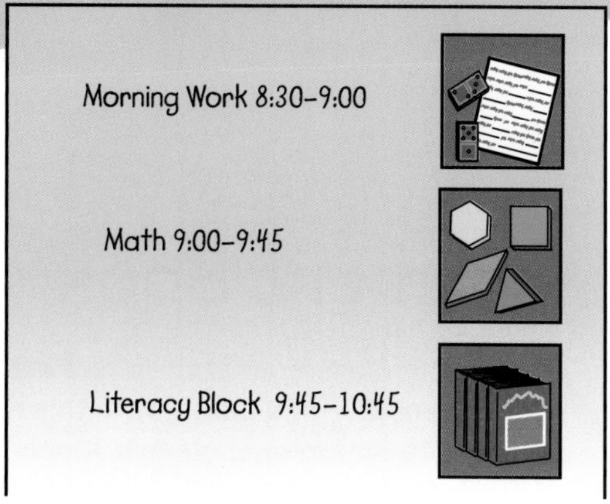
Morning Work 8:30–9:00
Math 9:00–9:45
Literacy Block 9:45–10:45

Photographic Lesson Plans

This helpful hint provides smooth sailing for substitute teachers! Take pictures of the materials you use on a regular basis. In the space beside each subject on a class schedule, attach the picture of the materials needed for the activity. If desired, also add pictures of students who are involved in special classes. After completing the schedule, store it in a three-ring binder with your daily lesson plans. Substitutes will know exactly what they need throughout each part of the day!

Gayla Hammer, West Elementary and South Elementary, Lander, WY

Baskets of Time

These handy tubs hold hands-on activities for early finishers! Purchase several small plastic baskets and label each with one of the following subjects: reading, math, science, and social studies. Then place inside each basket file folder games, books, and other materials that relate to a current unit of study for that topic. Store the baskets in an area that is accessible to students. Then, when a child finishes an assignment before time is called, encourage him to grab a basket and select from the materials inside.

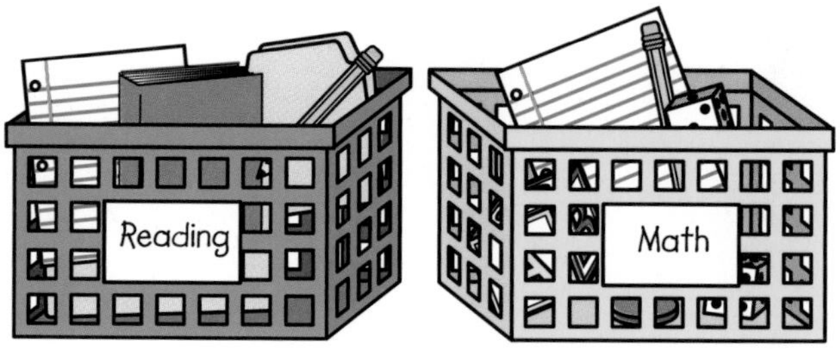
Reading
Math

Shannon Payne, Highland Oaks Elementary, Memphis, TN

Lost and Found

Lost and Found

Make your classroom neater and help students find missing items! Label a cubby or box in your classroom "Lost and Found." Each time a child finds an item that is out of place, have him place it inside. Then, when a student has misplaced an object, have him look in the designated area. Lost items will be much easier to locate, and your classroom will be much neater!

Heidi Gackenbach, Hebbville Elementary, Baltimore, MD

Coin Cups

This simple idea makes it easy to organize and store coin manipulatives! Gather a supply of wooden paint paddles and empty coffee cups and lids. Glue four cups to each paddle and then place coin manipulatives in the cups, storing denominations together. Place the coin cups at a center whenever students need the manipulatives to complete an activity, or give them to students to use during whole-class activities. When the activity is over, a child returns the coins to their proper cups and puts the lid on each one.

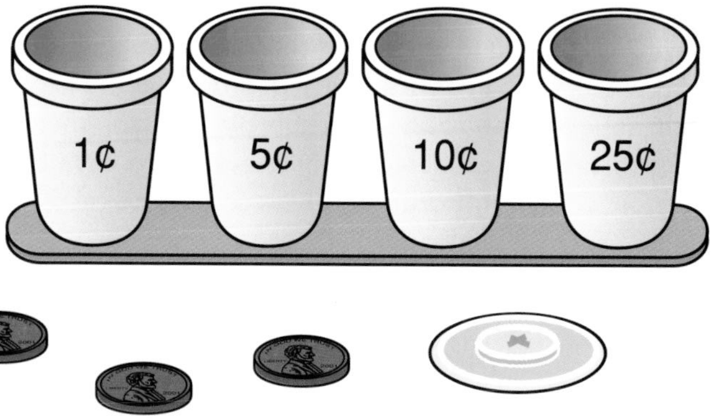
1¢
5¢
10¢
25¢

Jennifer Burwin, Lincoln Elementary, New Britain, CT

Math Mailbag

Math Mailbag

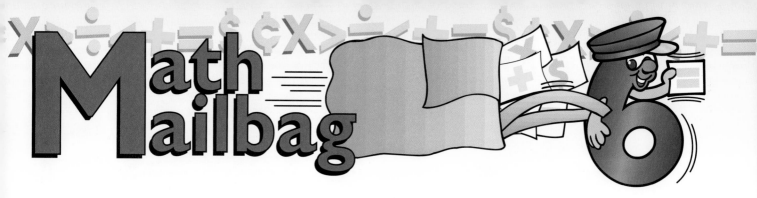

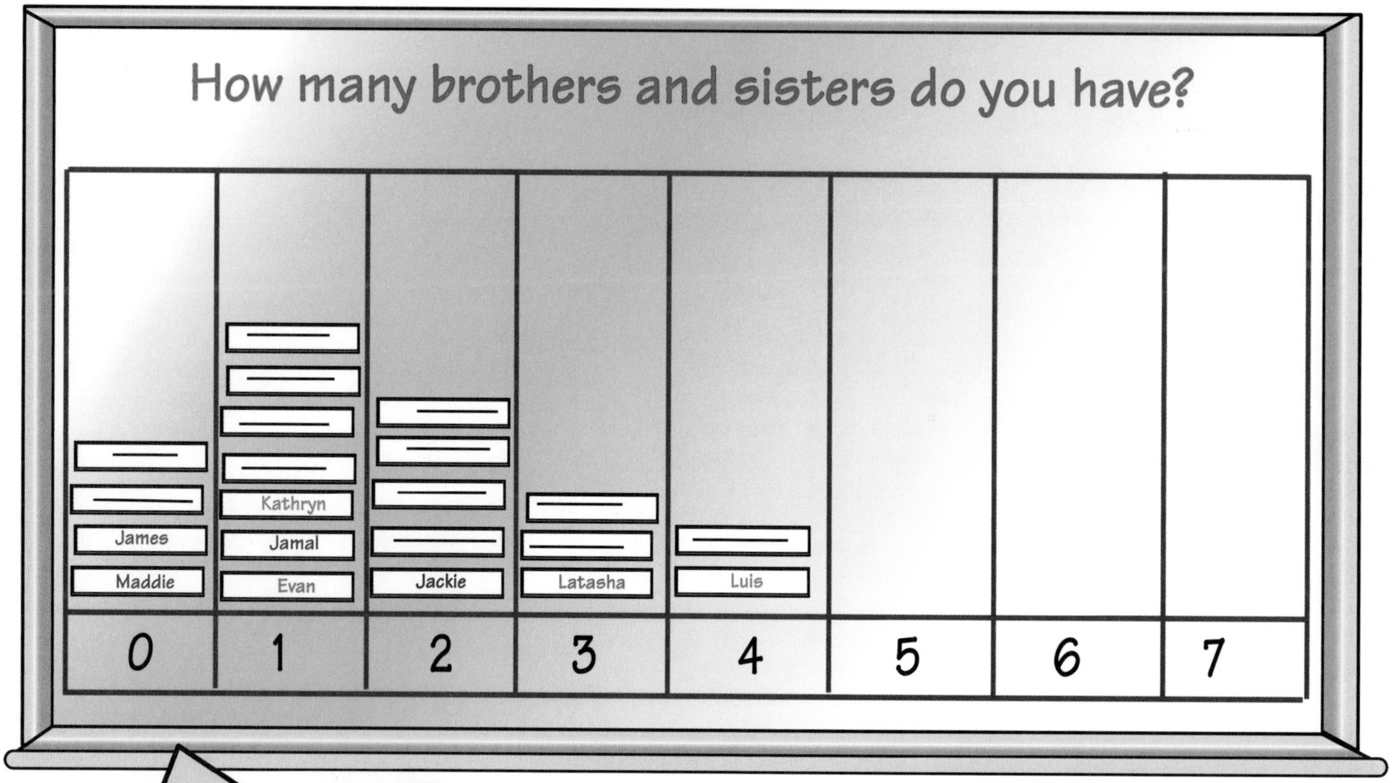
How many brothers and sisters do you have?
James
Maddie
Kathryn
Jamal
Evan
Jackie
Latasha
Luis
0
1
2
3
4
5
6
7

Forrest

Getting to Know You

Bar graphs

Students will love this get-acquainted activity, and you'll love how quick it is to complete! Prepare a magnetized nametag for each child and place the nametags on the board. Then, each morning for several days, choose a question for students to answer, such as one of the following:

- **How many family members do you have?**
- **What did you do during summer vacation?**
- **What kind of pet do you have or would you like to have?**

Then draw a bar graph outline on the board and label each column with a possible student response. Post the question on the board, and have each child answer it by placing his nametag in the appropriate column on the graph. After the graph is complete, discuss the results as a class.

Tiffany Nicely, Karns Intermediate School
Knoxville, TN

Moving On Up
Place value, regrouping

Take the confusion out of identifying ones, tens, and hundreds with this hands-on activity! Make a supply of the place-value mat on page 82 and laminate the mats for durability. Give each small group of students a mat along with ten unit cubes, ten rods, and one hundreds flat. Begin by having a member of each group place the unit cubes in the ones house. After he realizes only nine cubes will fit, explain that the tens need a bigger house. Guide students to see that ten unit cubes can be exchanged for a tens rod, which will fit in the tens house. Repeat the process, seeing how many tens will fit in the tens house; then exchange all the tens rods for the hundreds flat. Use the mats for continued place-value and regrouping practice.

Carolyn Hoople
Deer Run School
Calgary, Alberta, Canada

Hundreds
Tens
Ones

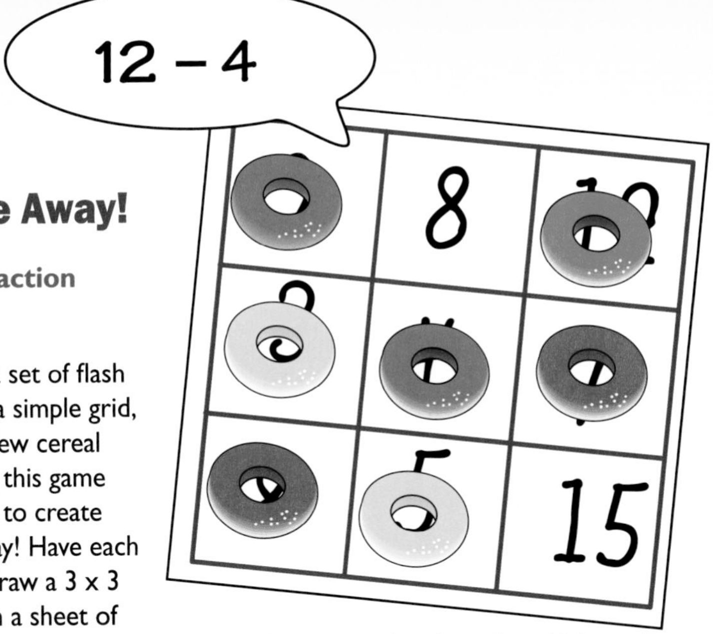
12 – 4
8
15

Take Away!
Basic subtraction facts

With a set of flash cards, a simple grid, and a few cereal pieces, this game is easy to create and play! Have each child draw a 3 x 3 grid on a sheet of scrap paper and then write a different number from 0 to 18 in each space. Next, have him cover each number with a cereal piece. To play, call out a basic subtraction fact. If the child has the answer on his grid, he removes the cereal piece from the square. Play continues in this manner until a student uncovers three squares in a row. He then says, "Take away!" and calls out his answers for the teacher to check. After a winner is declared, each student re-covers the numbers on his grid, and a new round of the game begins.

Bonnie Baumgras, Kirk L. Adams Elementary, Las Vegas, NV

What Comes Next?
Finding a pattern rule, extending a pattern

Get students actively involved in problem solving! Have several youngsters come to the front of the class, and assist them in modeling a pattern. (See the provided list.) Then ask the remaining students to find the pattern rule. Have students share their ideas with the class; then invite a child to come up and extend the pattern by performing the next step. Next, divide students into small groups. Have each group create a unique pattern using all of its members. Finally, invite each group to share its pattern with the class while the remaining students try to find the pattern rule.

Betty Silkunas, Lower Gwynedd Elementary, Ambler, PA

- student with arms raised, student with arms down, student with arms raised, student with arms down
- standing child, crouching child, crouching child, standing child, crouching child, crouching child
- forward-facing boy, backward-facing boy, forward-facing girl, backward-facing girl

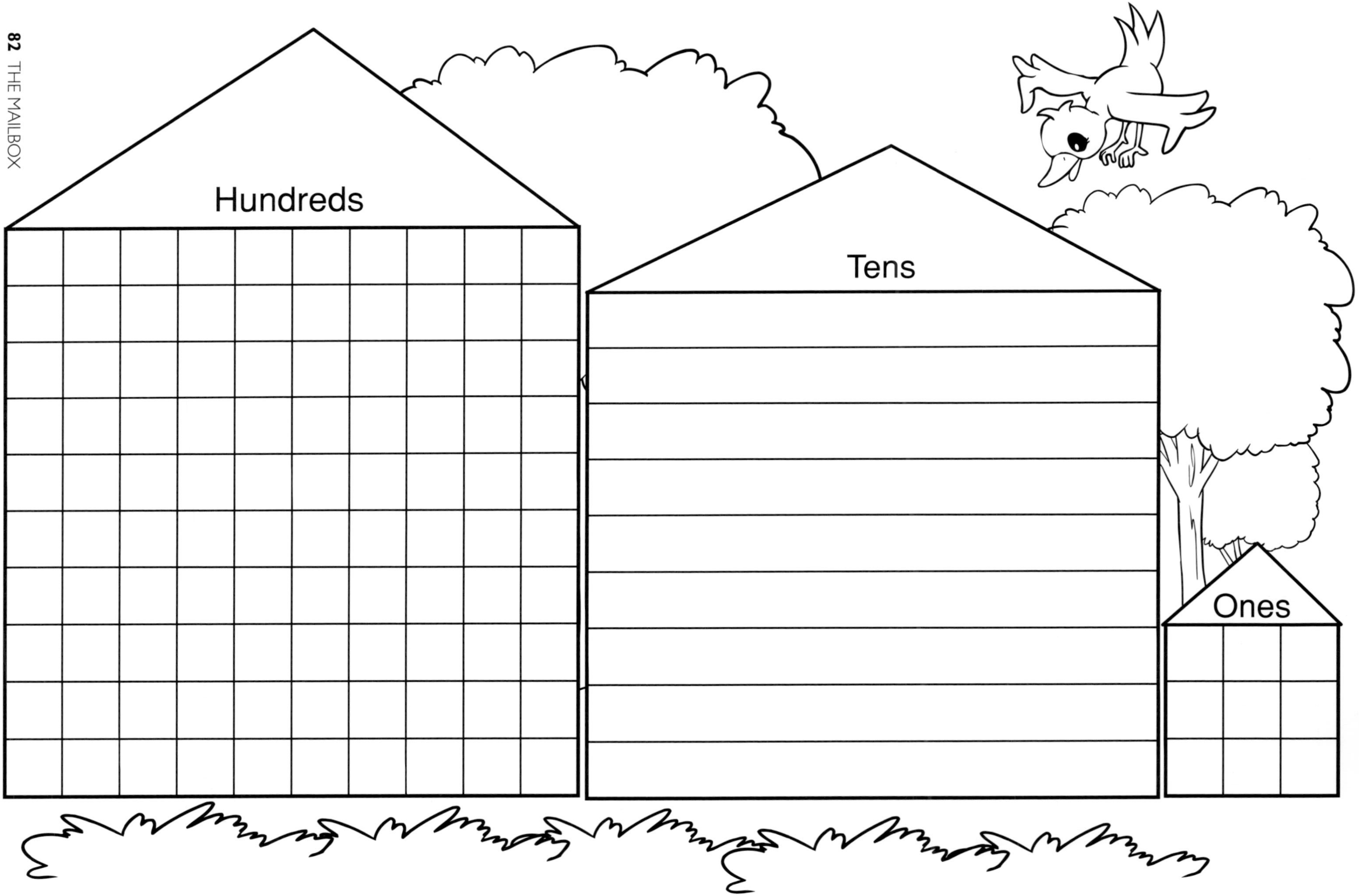
Hundreds
Tens
Ones

Note to the teacher: Use with “Moving On Up” on page 81.

Name____

Lunch Money

Complete each number pattern.

A. 3, 5, ____, 9, ____, ____, ____, ____, 19, ____
L (under the 6th blank...)

B. 85, 80, ____, ____, 65, ____, ____, ____, ____, 40

C. 18, 21, ____, ____, ____, 33, ____, 39, ____, ____

D. 56, 54, ____, ____, ____, 46, ____, ____, 40, ____

E. 18, 24, 30, ____, ____, ____, 54, ____, ____, 72

F. 22, 26, ____, ____, 38, ____, ____, 50, ____, ____

G. 100, 90, ____, ____, ____, 50, ____, ____, 20, ____

H. 37, 42, 47, ____, ____, ____, 67, ____, ____, 82

I. 46, 43, ____, ____, 34, ____, ____, 25, ____, ____

J. 61, 65, 69, ____, ____, ____, ____, 89, ____, 97

Orange Soda

How did the starfish pay for his lunch?

To solve the riddle, write the letters above on the matching numbered lines below.

____ ____   ____ ____ ____ ____   ____
60 36   72 40 75 21   42

____ ____ ____ ____   ____ ____ ____ ____ ____ ____!
48 57 54 10   34 77 93 15 80 24

Math Mailbag

Mystery Number Guidelines
Find the next blank page in the notebook.
Pick any two-digit number.
Write this mystery number at the top of the page.
Then write four clues for the number.
Clue 1: Tell whether the number is odd or even.
Clue 2: Tell the sum of its two digits.
Clue 3: Tell a number that is greater than (>) or less than (<) the mystery number.
Clue 4: Write one more clue!
My mystery number is even.
The sum of its digits is 12.

Clever Clues

Number sense

It's no mystery why students look forward to this homework assignment! Attach to the front inside cover of a spiral notebook a set of guidelines like the ones shown. Send the notebook home each afternoon with a different child. On the following school day, have the student read aloud the clues he wrote and challenge his classmates to identify his mystery number. Keep a number line or chart handy for a visual reference. After every child completes the assignment, begin Round 2!

Lisa Buchholz
Abraham Lincoln School
Glen Ellyn, IL

Math Mailbag

Pizza Preferences

Organizing data

Serve up a different version of page 86 for each of several mouthwatering reviews of a tally table! On a copy of the page, write what you'd like students to find out (a preferred pizza topping, a favorite time of day to eat pizza, a pizza crust preference). Then make student copies. A child labels her tally table with three choices before she surveys class-mates, family members, and friends. She uses tally marks to organize her data on the table and then uses the table to complete the activity.

Lisa Shulman, Sebastopol, CA

Name Kat — Making and interpreting a tally table

Pizza to Go

Find out a favorite pizza topping

Label the tally table with three different choices.
Ask 15 people.
Draw one tally mark to show each choice.

Pizza Choices	
pepperoni	𝍸 ||||
hamburger	|||
olives	|||

Remember: I stands for 1 and 𝍸 stands for 5.

COOL CAT PIZZA

Use the table to answer each question.

1. Is there a favorite choice? yes
2. Is there a least favorite choice? no
3. How many people made the favorite choice? 9
4. How many people did not make the favorite choice? 6
5. What is one thing the tally table shows you? Pepperoni is a very popular pizza topping!

Bonus Box: On the back of this paper, write one more question to ask about the tally table. Answer the question.

Crack the Safe

Coin sets of equal value

This large-group activity reminds students that different combinations of coins can equal the same amount of money. Place several plastic coins inside a play safe (or similar container) and post the amount of money that is inside. Tell the class that the safe cannot be opened until the exact coin combination is identified. Have students take turns suggesting different combinations of coins. Attempt to open the safe each time the suggested coins equal the value of the money in the safe, but only open the safe when the coin set is an exact match. Then replace the coins and repeat the activity.

Heather Schumacher
Coronado Village Elementary
Universal City, TX

65¢

Colorful Lineup

Two-digit addition

A touch of color is just what students need to keep addends aligned. When writing addends on the board or overhead, use blue for ones and green for tens. Remind students that the colors must line up before the numbers can be added. Have students use the same two colors on their math papers. This colorful solution also works well when regrouping. Need to carry a ten? Make it green and line it up!

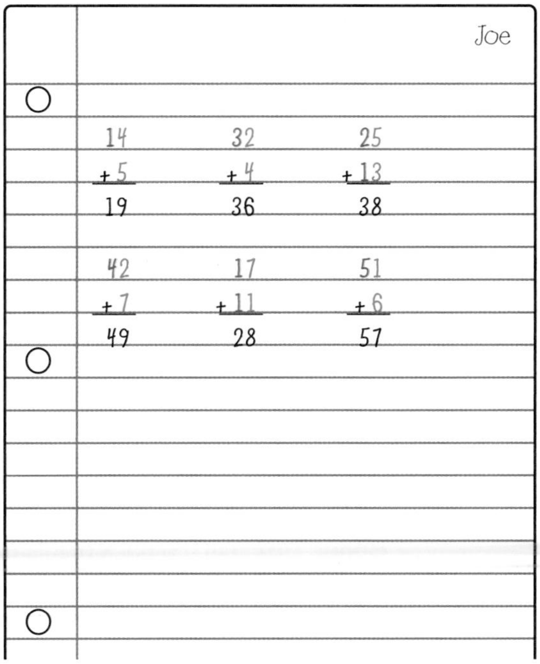
Joe
14
+5
19
32
+4
36
25
+13
38
42
+7
49
17
+11
28
51
+6
57

Anna Parrish
Joseph Keels Elementary,
Columbia, SC

Name____ Making and interpreting a tally table

Pizza to Go

Find out ____________________________________.

Label the tally table with three different choices.
Ask 15 people.
Draw one tally mark to show each choice.

Pizza Choices	

Remember:
I stands for 1 and
𝍸 stands for 5.
COOL CAT
PIZZA

Use the table to answer each question.

1. Is there a favorite choice? __________

2. Is there a least favorite choice? __________

3. How many people made the favorite choice? __________

4. How many people did not make the favorite choice? __________

5. What is one thing the tally table shows you? ____________

____

____

Bonus Box: On the back of this paper, write one more question to ask about the tally table. Answer the question.

Note to the teacher: Use with "Pizza Preferences" on page 85.

Name ______________________________ Number sense

Tricky Pumpkins

Write seven different numbers on each pumpkin.
Use the numbers in the box.
Be careful! Some numbers cannot be used!

Cross out the numbers you use!

61	11	95	50	66	22	58	94	48	5
42	65	43	16	12	64	74	21	10	32
73	47	35	77	39	27	89	19	90	63

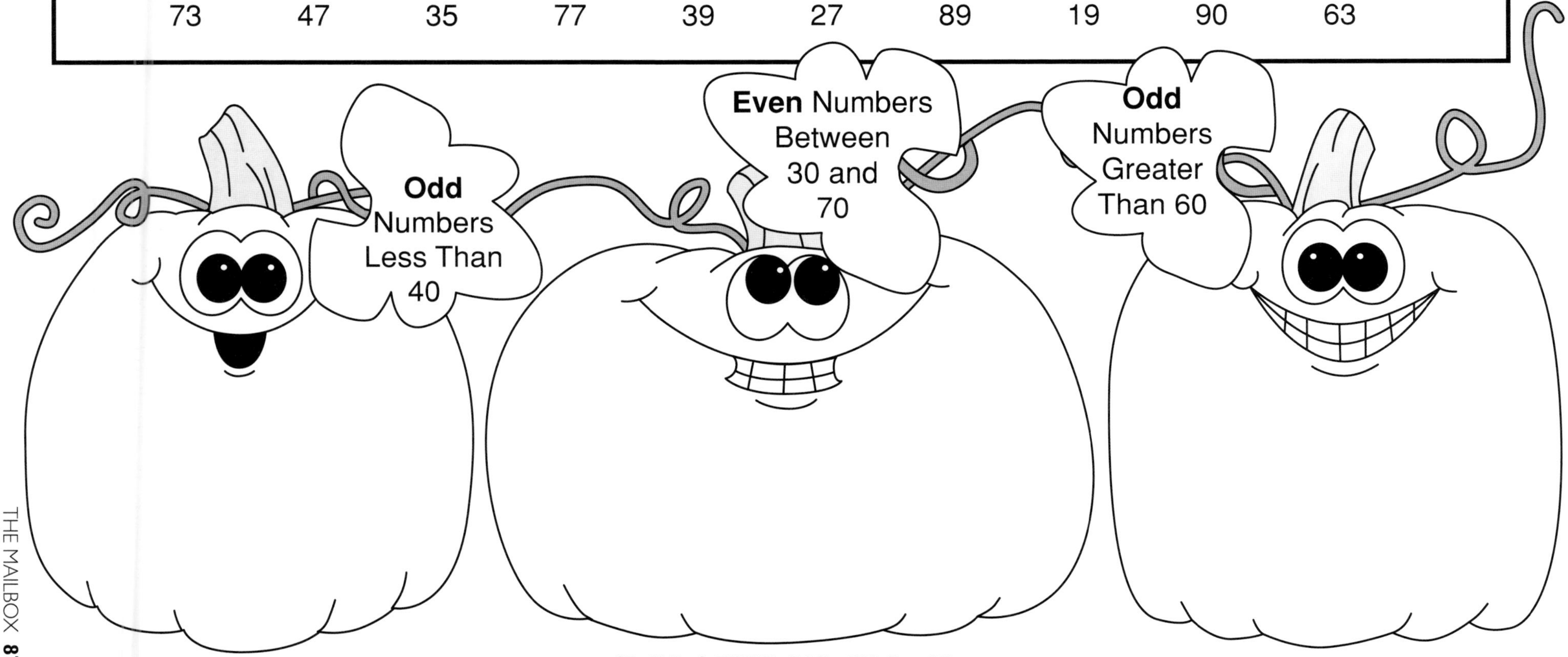
Odd Numbers Less Than 40
Even Numbers Between 30 and 70
Odd Numbers Greater Than 60

Math
Mailbag

It Takes Two
Roll Action
2 + 5 minutes
3 – 30 minutes
4 + 10 minutes
5 – 5 minutes
6 – 15 minutes
7 – 10 minutes
8 + 30 minutes
9 + 15 minutes
10 + 5 minutes
11 – 5 minutes
12 + 10 minutes

It Takes Two

Adding and subtracting time

First, copy and color the gameboard on page 90. Mount the gameboard on construction paper. Next, give a student pair the gameboard, a pair of dice, and 48 small game markers (small counters or paper squares). Explain to the twosome that each clock section equals five minutes and that each student is trying to fill both clocks on his side of the gameboard, equaling two hours. To start, each player places six markers adjacent to each other on one clock. Then Player 1 rolls the dice and uses the chart to add time to or take time from his clock. Player 2 takes a turn in the same manner. If a child has no markers on either clock and rolls a number that requires him to subtract time, he rolls until he gets a number to add. Play continues until one student calls out, "It takes two!" signaling that he has filled both of his clocks.

Meg Bowman
Lincoln School
Winchester, MA

How Many Snowmen Can You Make?

Possible outcomes, making organized lists

Bring the fun indoors with this build-a-snowman activity! Write on the board the information shown in the box below. Then pair students and have each twosome make a T chart like the one shown. Explain that students will use the chart to list all of the possible types of snowmen that could be created using one type of nose and one type of accessory (key on page 311). After students have completed their charts, discuss the results as a class. Extend the activity by adding choices to the existing list or by creating new categories, such as accessory colors or types of hats.

Brooke Beverly
Julia Bancroft School
Auburn, MA

Types of noses: coal, carrot, button, stick
Types of accessories: scarf, mitten, hat

Nose	Accessory
coal	scarf
coal	mitten
coal	hat

I Spy

Place value

In advance, prepare a gameboard like the one shown with a variety of two- and three-digit numbers. Make a copy for each student pair. Then give each twosome a gameboard and two different-colored crayons. One student secretly chooses a number from the board and gives her partner clues such as "I spy a number that has a seven in the ones place and a two in the tens place." Her partner looks at the numbers on the gameboard and makes a guess. If correct, she colors the box with a crayon. If she is incorrect, her partner continues to give her clues until she guesses the number. Play continues in this manner, with partners taking turns, until time is called or each number has been guessed.

Pam Temerowski
Green Acres Elementary
Warren, MI

28	56	412	89
871	404	230	651
92	327	143	84
101	55	784	219

The Magic Number

Basic facts, multiple addends

Improve students' math skills with a handful of Unifix cubes! Each week focus on a different number, such as eight. Give each child the corresponding number of Unifix cubes. Have the student divide the cubes into two different trains and use the number of cubes in each train as addends in a problem equaling eight. He repeats the process until he has listed all number pairs that equal eight when added. Then encourage him to divide the cubes into three trains and repeat the process.

Kelly Hanover
Vernon Elementary
Kenosha, WI

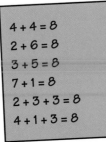

4 + 4 = 8
2 + 6 = 8
3 + 5 = 8
7 + 1 = 8
2 + 3 + 3 = 8
4 + 1 + 3 = 8

It Takes Two

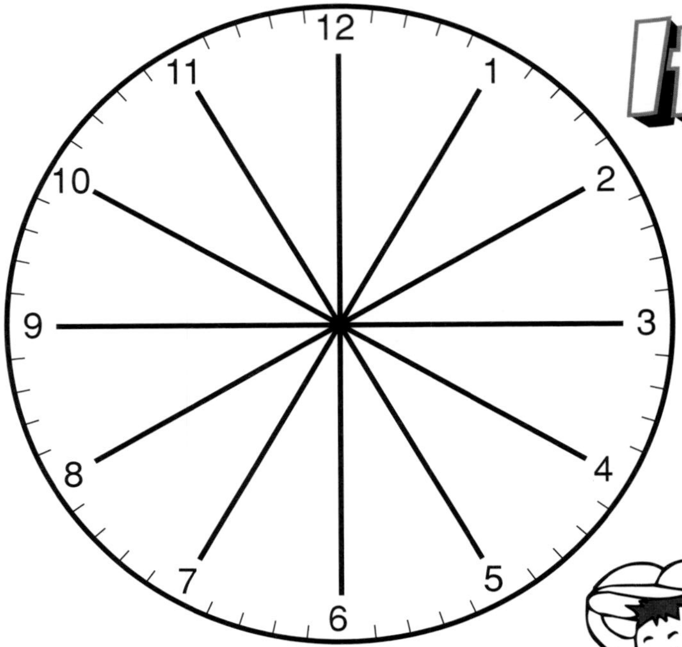

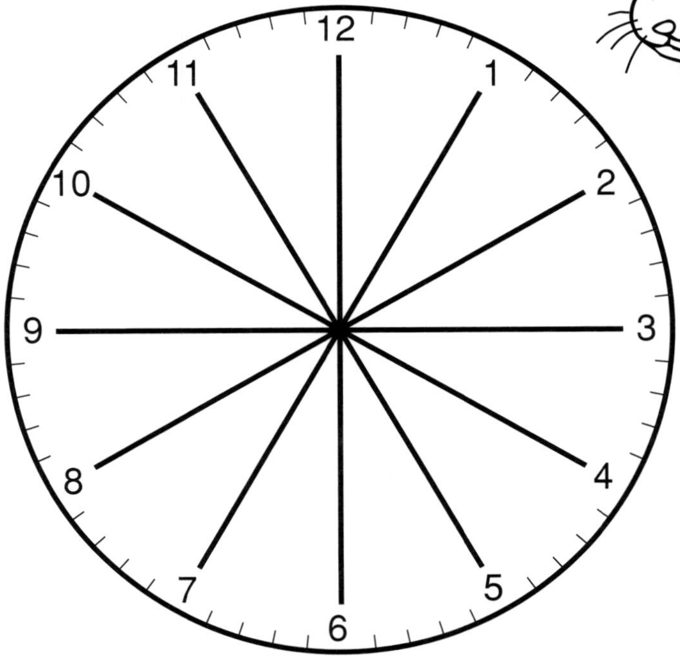

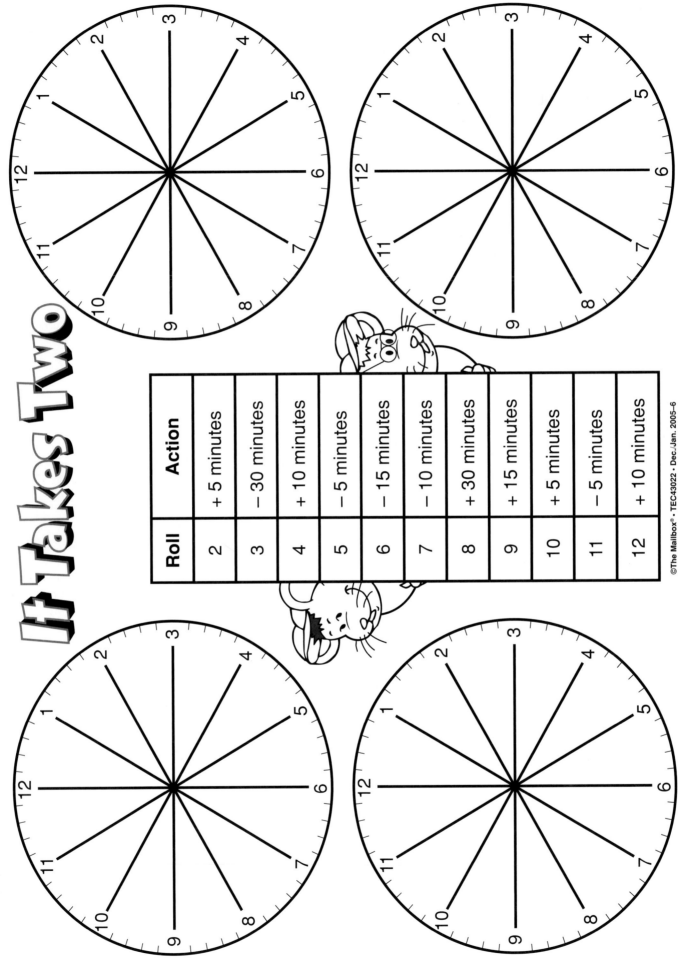

Roll	Action
2	+ 5 minutes
3	– 30 minutes
4	+ 10 minutes
5	– 5 minutes
6	– 15 minutes
7	– 10 minutes
8	+ 30 minutes
9	+ 15 minutes
10	+ 5 minutes
11	– 5 minutes
12	+ 10 minutes

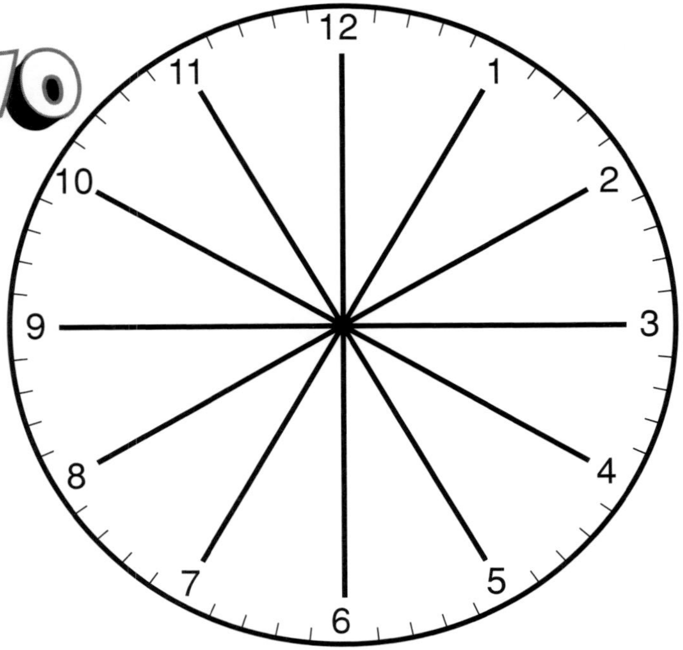

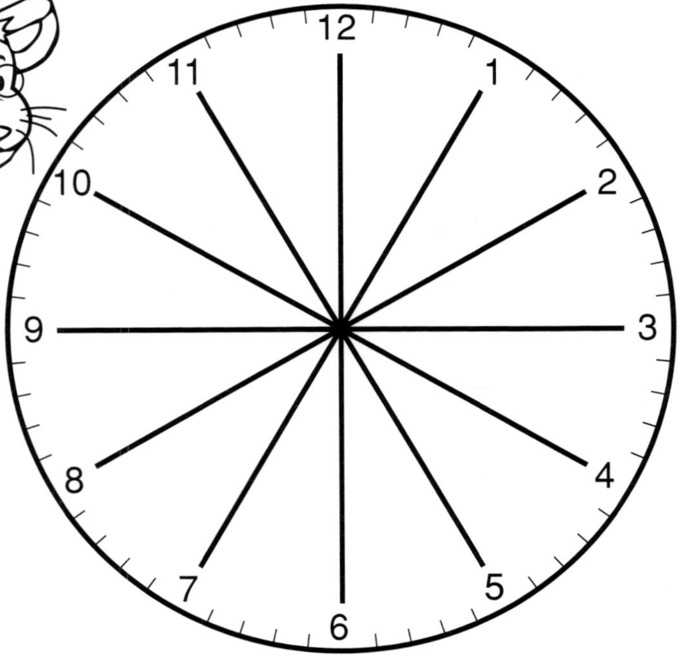

Name____

Getting Gelts

Estimate.
Color the gelt with the matching answer.
Not all gelts will be colored.

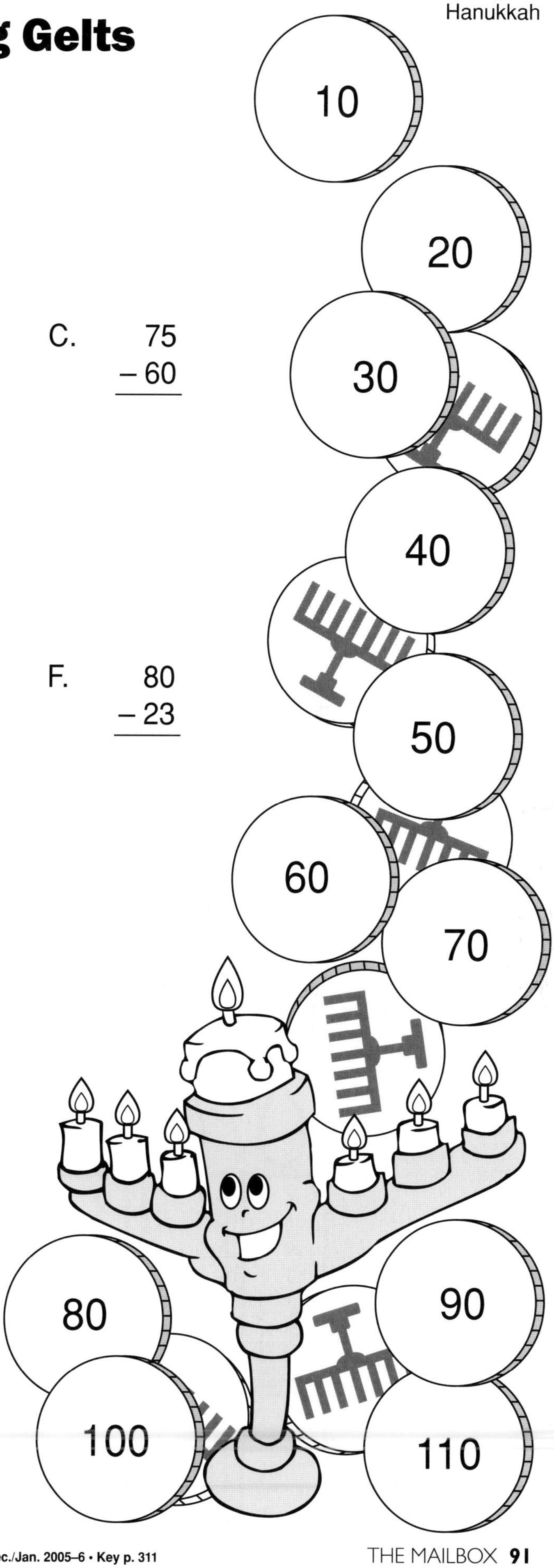
10
20
30
40
50
60
70
80
90
100
110

A. $\begin{array}{r} 64 \\ -\ 14 \\ \hline \end{array}$

B. $\begin{array}{r} 39 \\ +\ 38 \\ \hline \end{array}$

C. $\begin{array}{r} 75 \\ -\ 60 \\ \hline \end{array}$

D. $\begin{array}{r} 76 \\ +\ 19 \\ \hline \end{array}$

E. $\begin{array}{r} 45 \\ +\ 20 \\ \hline \end{array}$

F. $\begin{array}{r} 80 \\ -\ 23 \\ \hline \end{array}$

G. $\begin{array}{r} 58 \\ -\ 33 \\ \hline \end{array}$

H. $\begin{array}{r} 57 \\ -\ 45 \\ \hline \end{array}$

I. $\begin{array}{r} 67 \\ -\ 26 \\ \hline \end{array}$

J. $\begin{array}{r} 56 \\ +\ 34 \\ \hline \end{array}$

Name ______________________________

Logic
Kwanzaa

Light the Way

Lightly color each candle and cut it out.
Read each clue.
Then glue each candle in order.

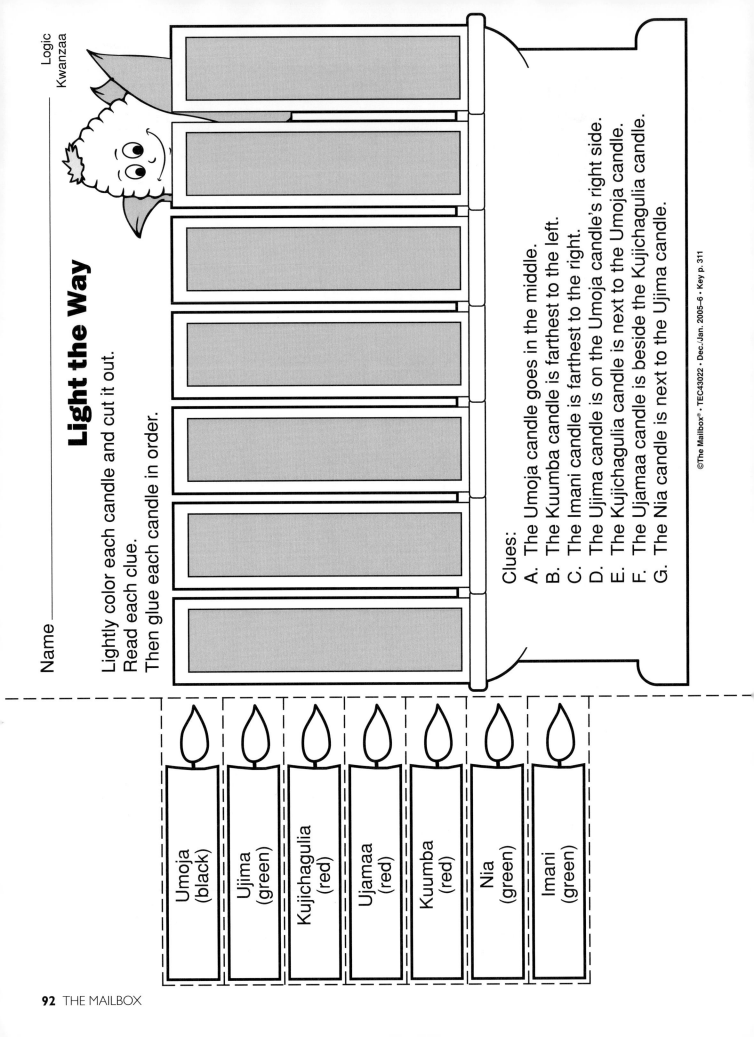

Clues:
A. The Umoja candle goes in the middle.
B. The Kuumba candle is farthest to the left.
C. The Imani candle is farthest to the right.
D. The Ujima candle is on the Umoja candle's right side.
E. The Kujichagulia candle is next to the Umoja candle.
F. The Ujamaa candle is beside the Kujichagulia candle.
G. The Nia candle is next to the Ujima candle.

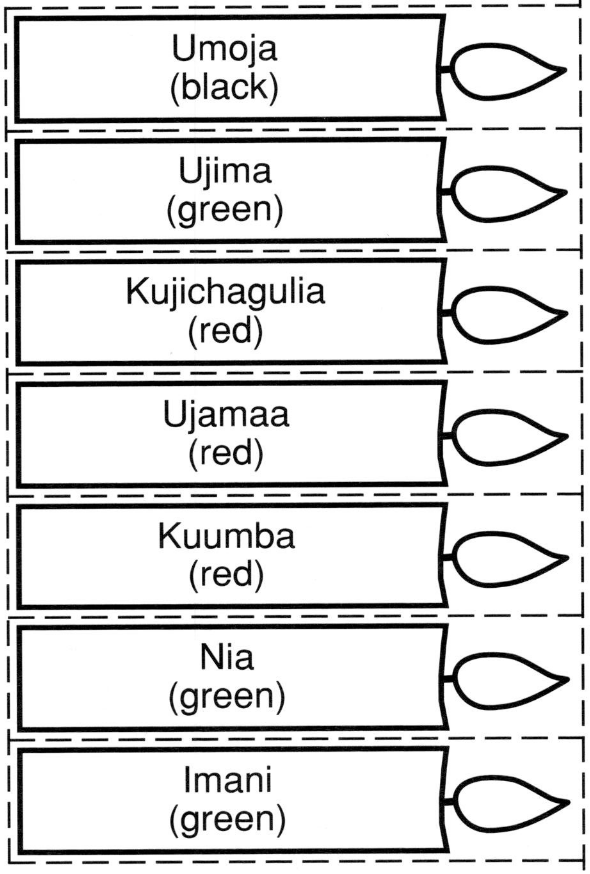
Umoja (black)
Ujima (green)
Kujichagulia (red)
Ujamaa (red)
Kuumba (red)
Nia (green)
Imani (green)

Math
Mailbag

2
÷
=
6
5
3
8
Four?

Take a Guess!

Multiplication, division, logical reasoning

Start this guessing game by writing a multiplication or division problem on a sheet of paper for your reference. Then draw on the board a blank for each digit in the equation and a box for the operation sign as shown. Next, invite one child at a time to guess a missing number between zero and nine or the missing operation sign. If his guess is correct, write it in the appropriate blank. (If it is a number, write it as many times as it appears in the problem.) Also list any incorrect guesses for student reference. Allow the child to guess the equation to finish his turn. If he is correct, invite him to choose a new equation and lead the next round of play. If he is incorrect, choose another student and continue playing in the same manner until the equation is identified. Play additional rounds for as long as desired.

Starin Lewis, Phoenix, AZ

Math Mailbag

Human Coordinate Grid
Plotting points on a graph

Tape and a simple phrase are all you need to explain coordinate graphs! Before the activity, use masking tape to create a life-size coordinate grid on your classroom floor. Label both axes with numbers as shown. Start the activity by writing on the board a pair of coordinates and the phrase shown. Tell the class that the numbers describe a certain place on the grid. Then show students how to find the place by starting at (0, 0) and, using the specific words in the phrase, moving across the grid and then up. Next, invite student volunteers to come forward. Assign each student a pair of coordinates, and have him use the phrase to find the corresponding place on the grid. Extend the activity by placing various objects on the grid. Have each child write the object's name and location on a sheet of paper.

Dana Johansen, Greenwich Academy, Greenwich, CT

Across the hall and **up** the stairs.
0
1
2
3
4
5
1
2
3
4
5

Capacity Stackers
Customary units of capacity

Strengthen students' understanding of liquid measures with this simple puzzle! Make a class supply of the capacity patterns on pages 95 and 96. Give each child a copy of both pages and have him cut out the patterns. To complete the activity, he places the gallon unit on his desk. Next, he places the four quart pieces atop the gallon, covering it completely. Then he stacks the pint pieces so they cover the four quarts. Finally, he places the cup pieces so they cover the pints. After the stackers are complete, have students use them to create equations for different measures, such as four quarts equal one gallon.

Jennifer Pick, Healy School, Chicago, IL

1 cup
1 cup
1 cup
1 cup
1 cup
1 cup
1 cup
1 cup
1 cup
1 cup
1 cup
1 cup
1 cup
1 cup
1 cup
1 cup

Easy Transformations
Slides, flips, and turns

This activity will have students flipping over geometric transformations! In advance, make two construction paper shamrocks for each child. Begin by reviewing with students how to slide, flip, or turn an object. Then have students use their shamrocks to make each type of transformation. Follow up the activity by having students complete the reproducible on page 97.

adapted from an idea by Amy Barsanti, Pines Elementary, Plymouth, NC

Capacity Patterns

Use with “Capacity Stackers” on page 94.

1 quart
TEC43023

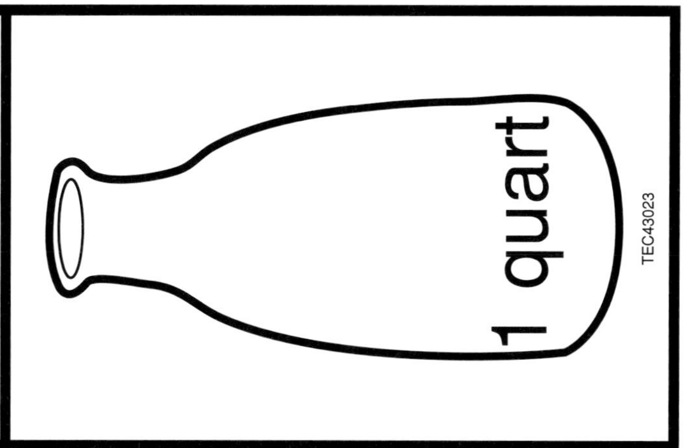
1 quart
TEC43023

1 quart
TEC43023

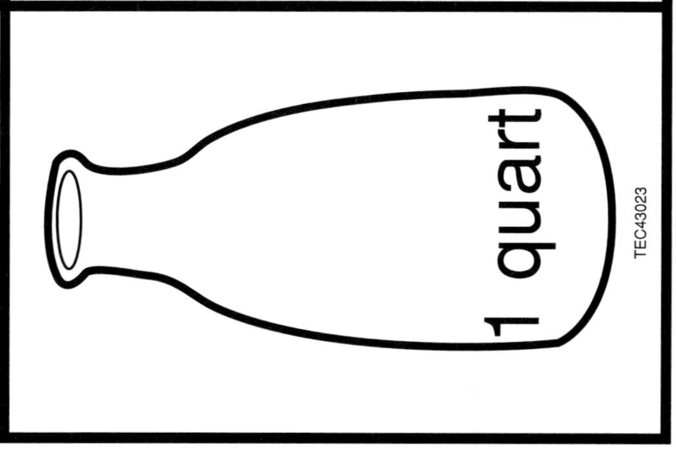
1 quart
TEC43023

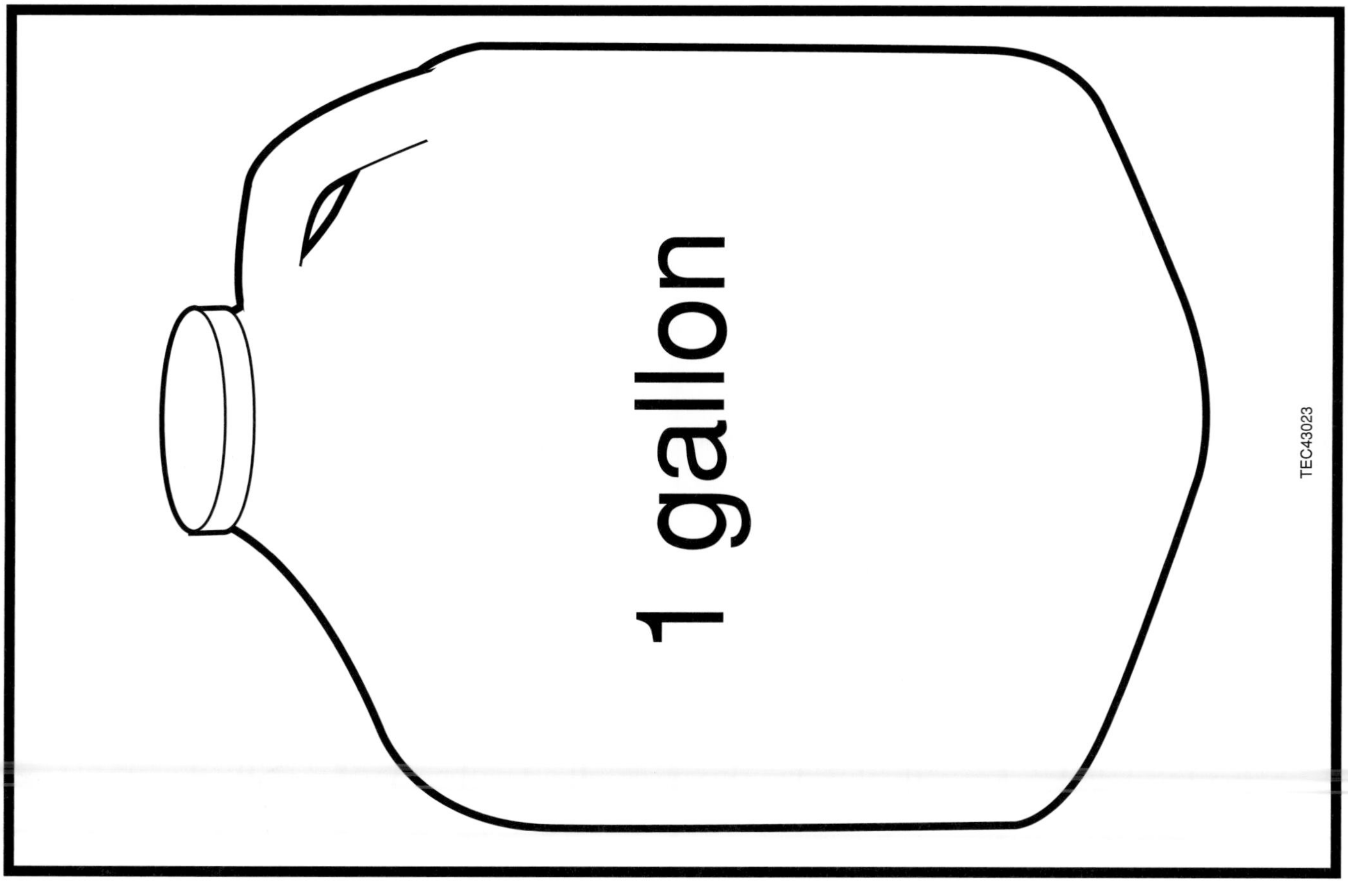
1 gallon
TEC43023

Capacity Patterns

Use with "Capacity Stackers" on page 94.

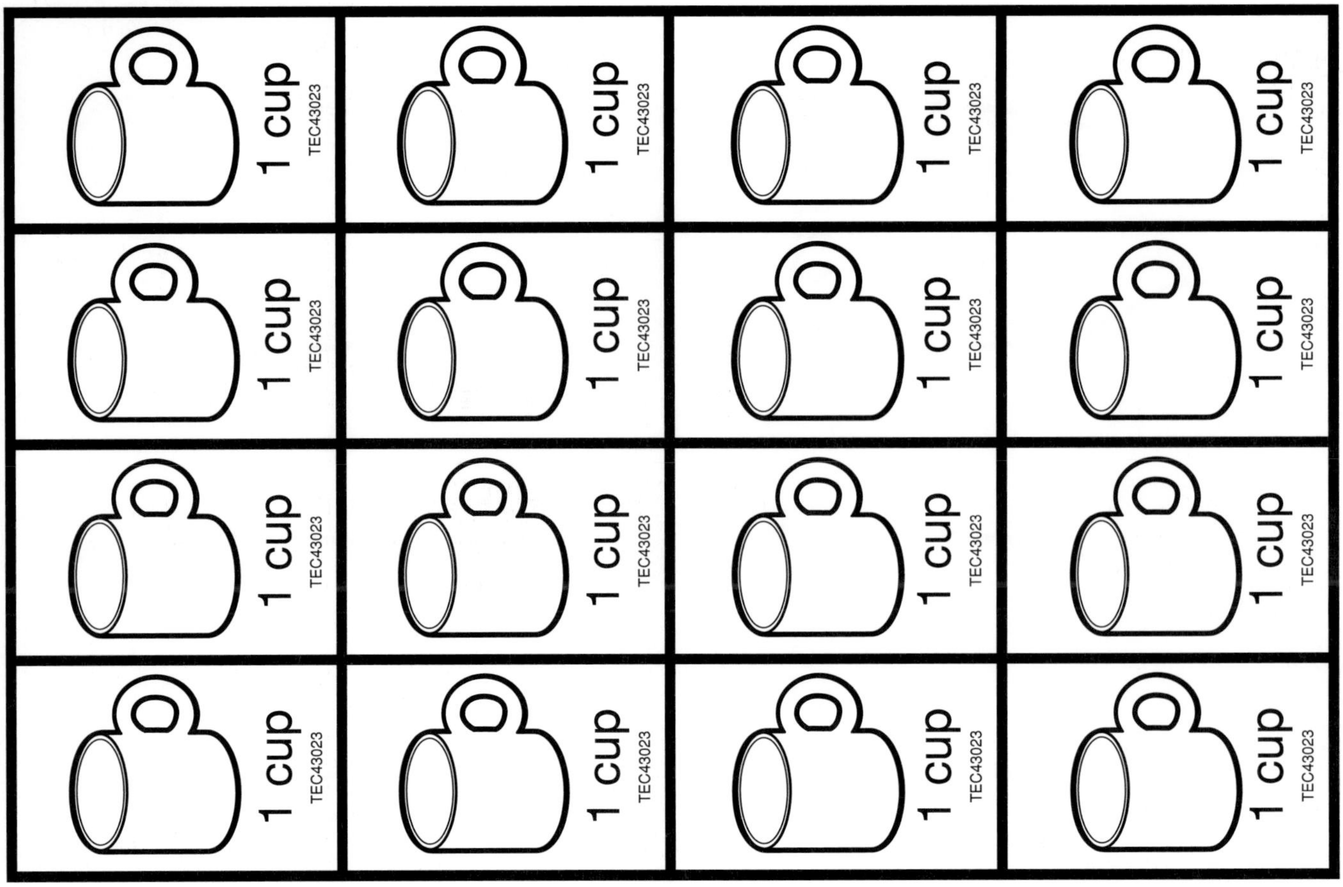
1 cup
TEC43023
1 cup
TEC43023
1 cup
TEC43023
1 cup
TEC43023
1 cup
TEC43023
1 cup
TEC43023
1 cup
TEC43023
1 cup
TEC43023
1 cup
TEC43023
1 cup
TEC43023
1 cup
TEC43023
1 cup
TEC43023
1 cup
TEC43023
1 cup
TEC43023
1 cup
TEC43023
1 cup
TEC43023

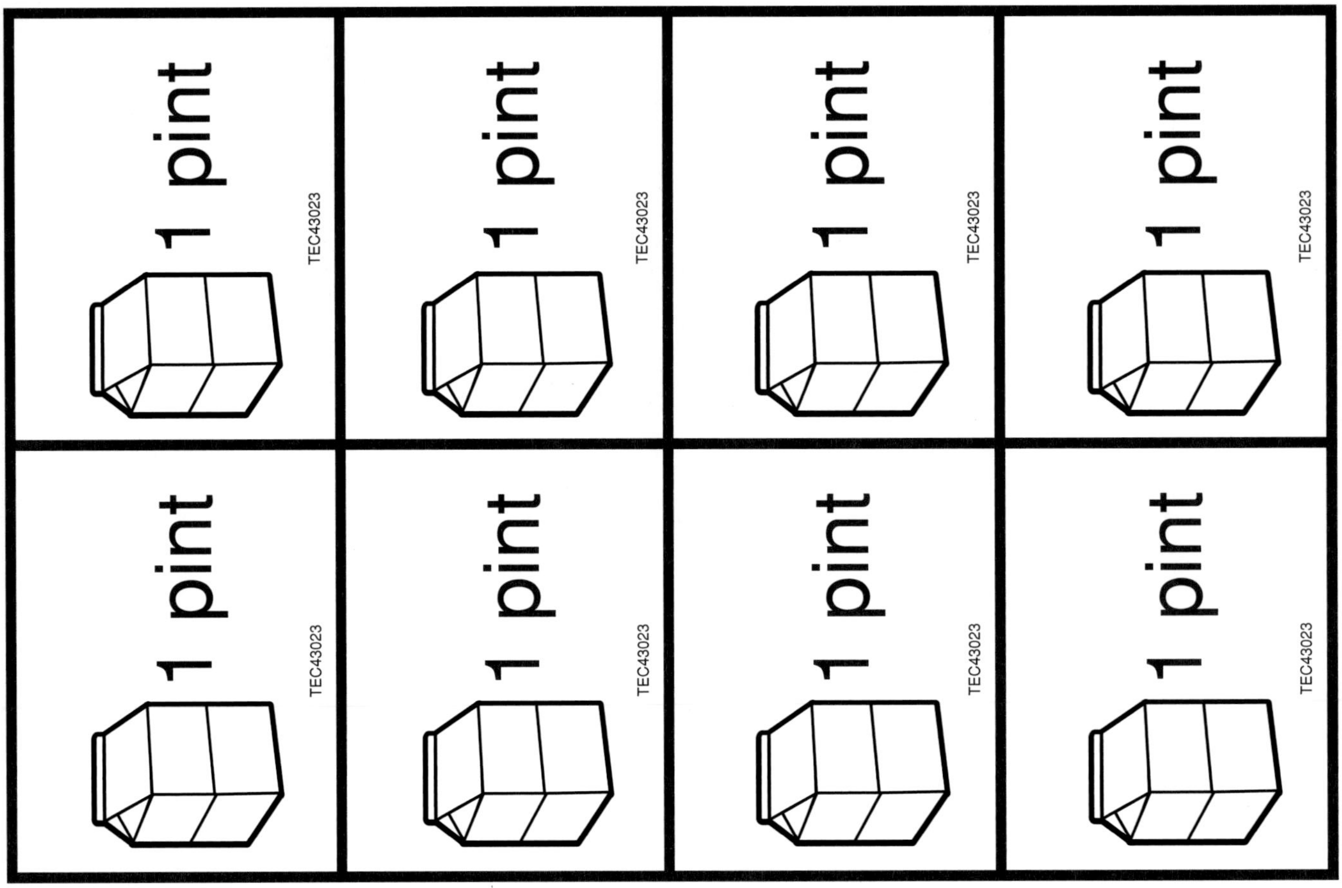
1 pint
TEC43023
1 pint
TEC43023
1 pint
TEC43023
1 pint
TEC43023
1 pint
TEC43023
1 pint
TEC43023
1 pint
TEC43023
1 pint
TEC43023

Name ______________________________ Slides, flips, and turns

Leprechaun Shuffle

Look at each pair of leprechauns.
Write the word *slide, flip,* or *turn* on the line below the pair.

1. ____________

2. ____________

3. ____________

4. ____________

5. ____________

6. ____________

7. ____________

8. ____________

9. ____________

Note to the teacher: Use alone or with "Easy Transformations" on page 94.

Math Mailbag

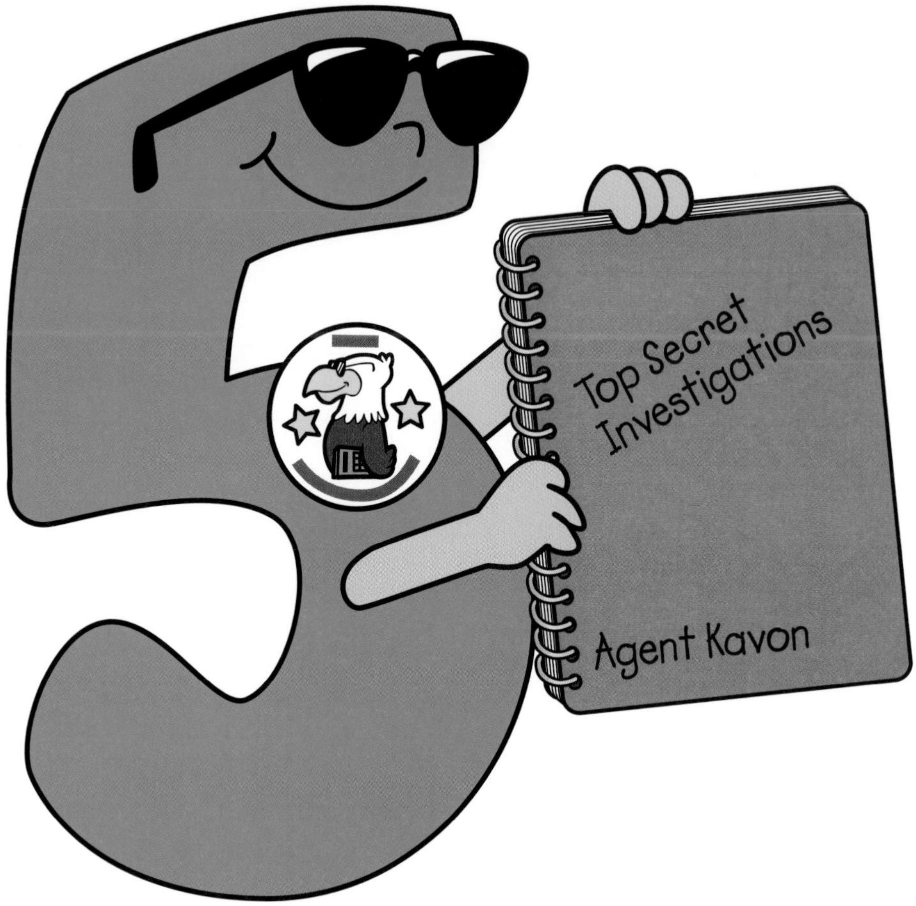
Top Secret
Investigations
Agent Kavon

Undercover Mathematicians

Motivation

Students are eager to start each day's math lesson when you recruit them as special agents! Give each child a copy of the Math Investigation Bureau (MIB) badge to personalize (patterns on page 100). Laminate the badges and have each child glue his badge to a clothespin. Also, label the child's math journal as shown. At the beginning of each day's math activities, have students clip on their badges. Then provide a challenge problem for agents to solve, and have them record their work in their "Top Secret Investigations" journals. Sending students on math missions has never been so rewarding!

Chrissy Sandifer, Keith L. Ware Elementary, Fort Riley, KS

Volcanic Cash
$1.00
Key
1 = 1¢
2 = 5¢
3 = 10¢
4 = 25¢
5 = 50¢
6 = coin of choice

Volcanic Cash
Coin values

Fun erupts with this easy partner game! In advance, make a class supply of the gameboard on page 102. Give each student pair two gameboards, transparent counters, and a die. To play, Player 1 rolls the die and uses the key to determine the cash value of the roll. Then she places a counter(s) over the coin(s) equal to that value. Player 2 continues in the same manner, covering the coins on his own board. At any point during the game, a player may forfeit her roll and trade up to the next row; for example, if she has five pennies covered, she can remove the counters and cover a nickel instead. The first player to reach the top wins.

Amy Barsanti, Pines Elementary, Plymouth, NC

Solar Spinners
Place value

Put a spin on place value practice with this small-group activity! Give each student a paper clip and a copy of page 101. Review with students how to use the paper clip and a pencil to spin the spinner. To complete the activity, each child looks at number 1 on her sheet. She spins the spinner and then decides where to place the digit to make the largest possible number. She records the digit on her sheet and continues spinning until each place is filled to make a number. Then she shares the results with her group to determine who has the largest number. The activity is repeated for each number on the recording sheet. If desired, have students use the same digits on their pages to create the smallest numbers possible.

Cynthia Holcomb, Mertzon, TX

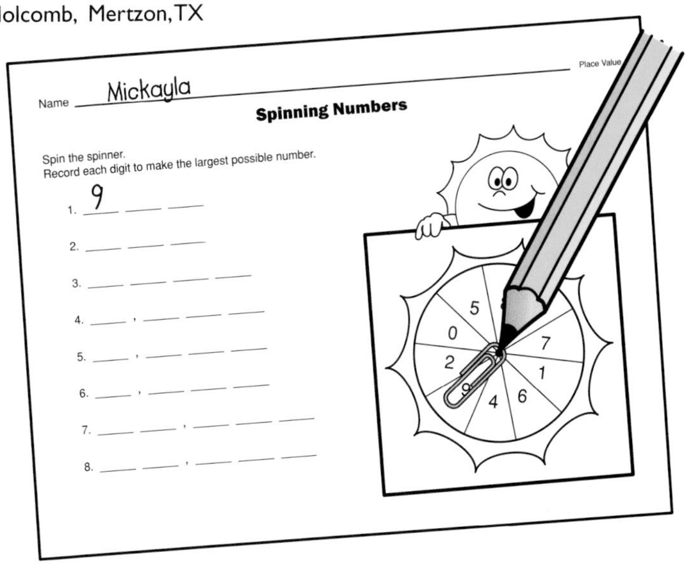
Place Value
Name Mickayla
Spinning Numbers
Spin the spinner.
Record each digit to make the largest possible number.
1. 9
2.
3.
4.
5.
6.
7.
8.
5
0
7
2
1
9
4
6

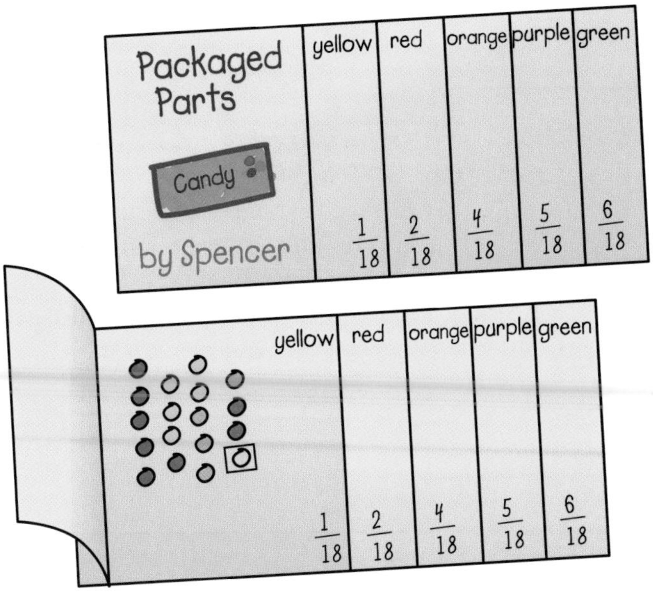
Packaged Parts
Candy
by Spencer
yellow
red
orange
purple
green
1/18
2/18
4/18
5/18
6/18

Packaged Parts
Naming and ordering fractions

In advance, make a copy of the recording sheet on page 100. Begin by giving each student a snack-size bag of colored candies, making sure each student has five different colors. Tell him to count the total number of candies in the bag and write the number on the sheet. Next, have him sort the candies by color and record the fractional part each color represents. To complete the activity, each child overlaps three $4\frac{1}{2}$" x 12" strips of construction paper, as shown, leaving a one-inch margin on the right. He staples the booklet and titles the first page. In the right margin of each page, he writes each candy's color and fraction, placing them in order from least to greatest. Finally he adds an illustration to represent each fraction and draws a box around the fractional part.

Laura Wagner, Raleigh, NC

MIB Badge Patterns

Use with "Undercover Mathematicians" on page 98.

Math
Investigations Bureau
TEC43024

Math
Investigations Bureau
TEC43024

Name ______________________________ Naming and ordering fractions

Comparing Candies

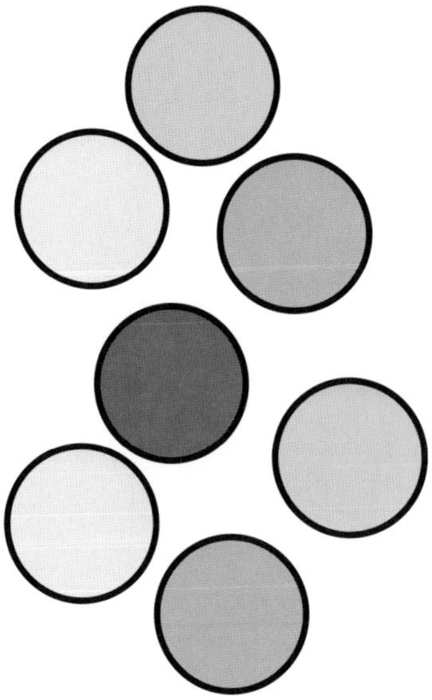

1. How many candies are in your bag? ________
2. What are the colors of the candies in your bag?

____

3. Write a fraction to show each candy's color.

red ________ yellow ________

green ________ orange ________

blue ________ brown ________

 Note to the teacher: Use with "Packaged Parts" on page 99.

Name ______________________________

Spinning Numbers

Spin the spinner.
Record each digit to make the largest possible number.

1. ____ ____ ____

2. ____ ____ ____

3. ____ ____ ____ ____

4. ____ , ____ ____ ____

5. ____ , ____ ____ ____

6. ____ , ____ ____ ____

7. ____ ____ , ____ ____ ____

8. ____ ____ , ____ ____ ____

8
3
7
1
6
4
9
2
0
5

Note to the teacher: Use with “Solar Spinners” on page 99.

Volcanic Cash

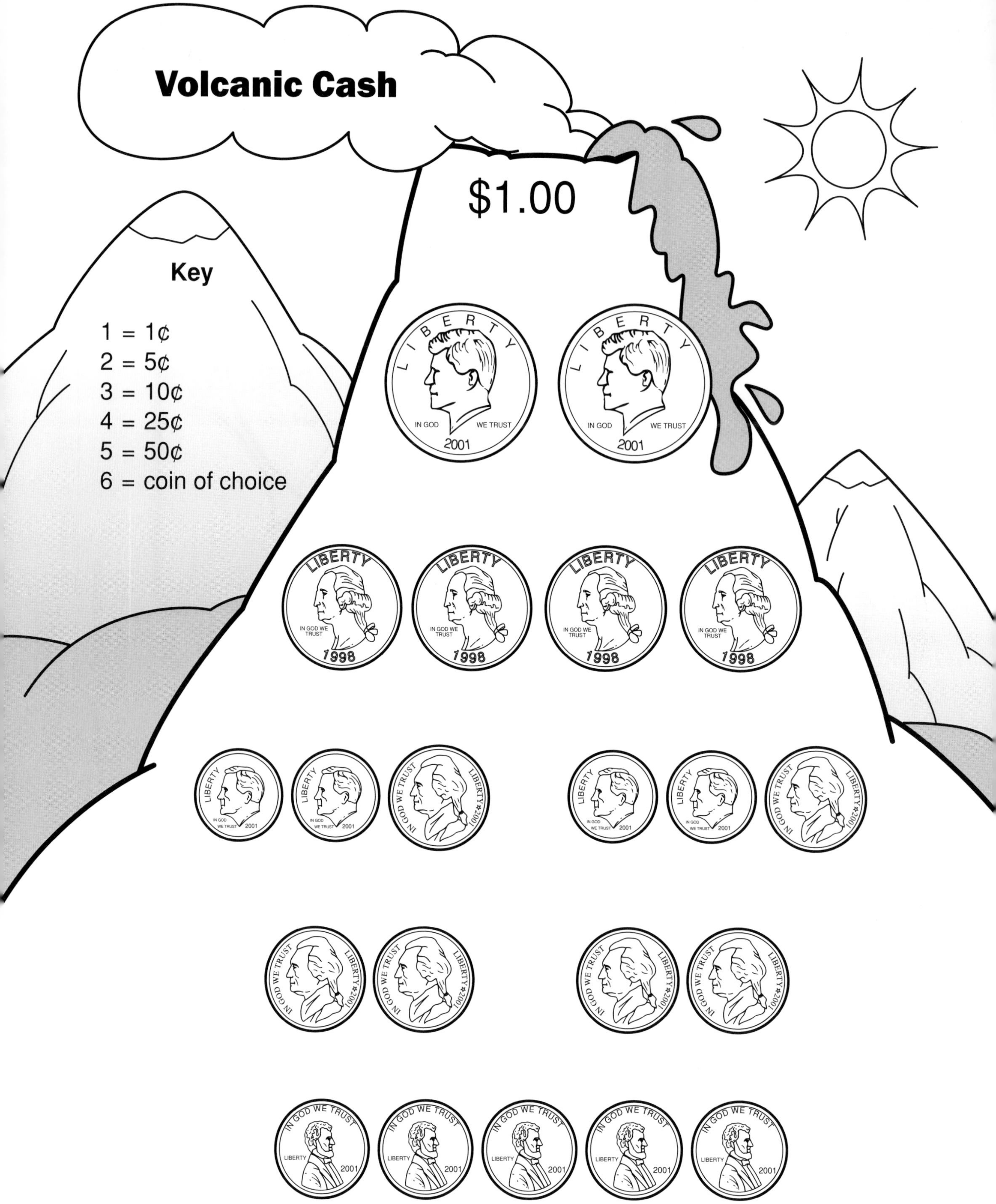
$1.00

Key

1 = 1¢
2 = 5¢
3 = 10¢
4 = 25¢
5 = 50¢
6 = coin of choice

 Note to the teacher: Use with "Volcanic Cash" on page 99.

Math
Mailbag

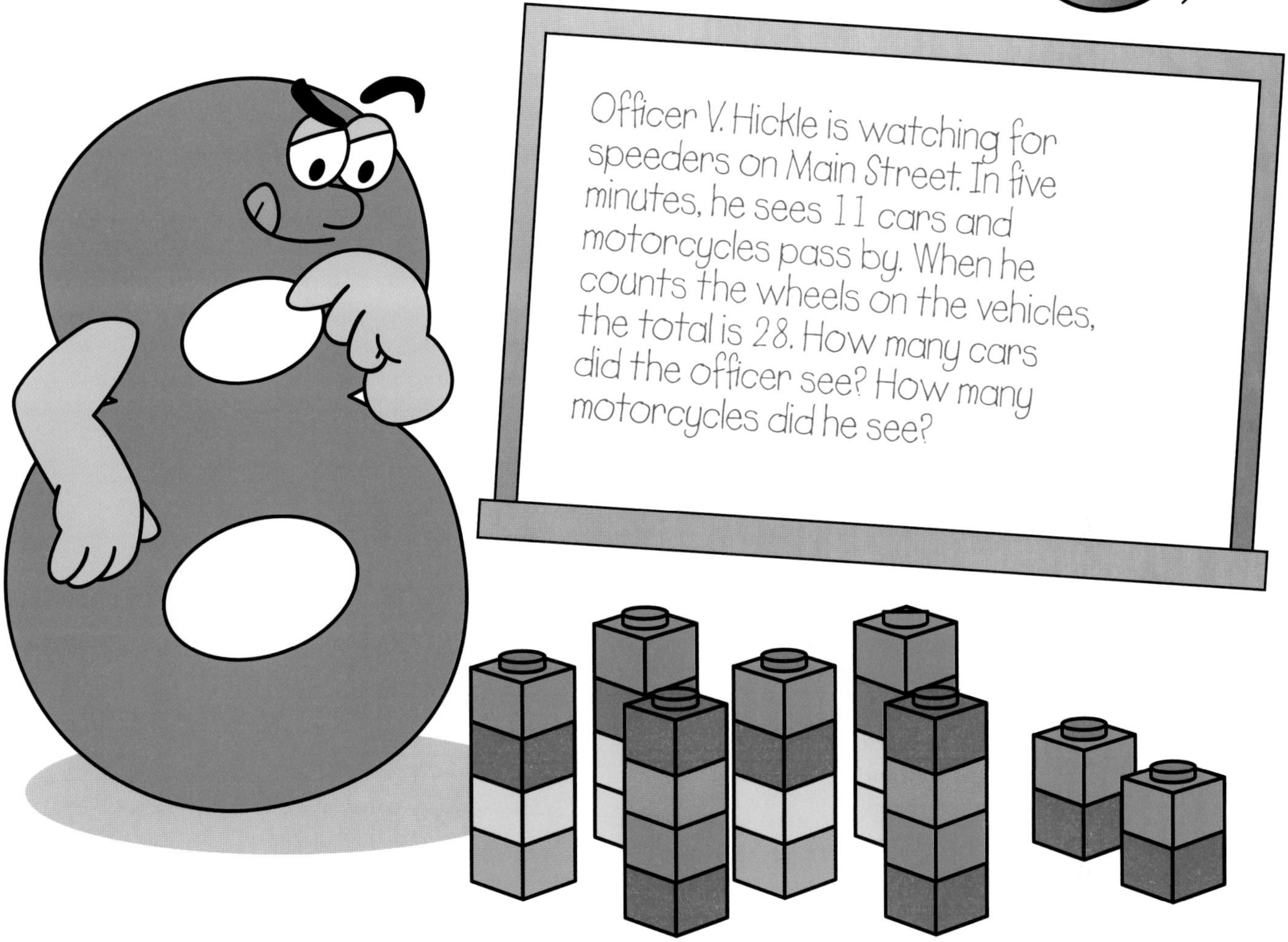
Officer V. Hickle is watching for speeders on Main Street. In five minutes, he sees 11 cars and motorcycles pass by. When he counts the wheels on the vehicles, the total is 28. How many cars did the officer see? How many motorcycles did he see?

Check Out Those Wheels!

Problem solving

Shift into the guess-and-check strategy with this simple idea! In advance, write on the board the problem shown. Begin by giving each child 28 Unifix cubes; then read the problem aloud. Challenge students to use the cubes to represent the number of wheels on each vehicle type by using four cubes for cars and two cubes for motorcycles. Have them use the guess-and-check strategy to change the total until they have three cars and eight motorcycles with 28 total wheels. Continue the problem solving by having students determine the number of cars and motorcycles the officer saw based the following:

- **8 vehicles with 28 wheels *(6 cars, 2 motorcycles)***
- **8 vehicles with 24 wheels *(4 cars, 4 motorcycles)***
- **7 vehicles with 24 wheels *(5 cars, 2 motorcycles)***
- **6 vehicles with 22 wheels *(5 cars, 1 motorcycle)***

David Green, North Shore Country Day School, Winnetka, IL

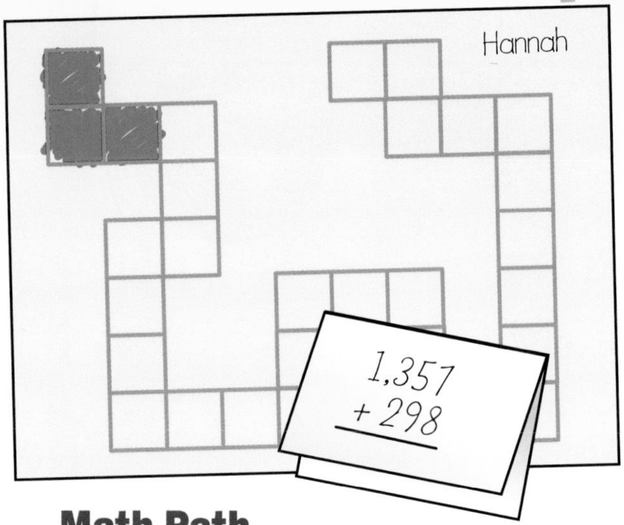
Hannah
1,357
+ 298

Math Path
Computation review, motivation

Students will love tracking their progress on this mathematical journey! Fold a supply of 5" x 8" blank index cards in half. Label each card's front with a math problem and write the answer inside. Post the problems in an area accessible to students, forming a path with them. Also create an identical path on a sheet of paper and duplicate it for each child. Then pair students. During the day, each child visits the Math Path, copies the first problem, and returns to her seat and solves it. Then she gives her paper to her partner to check her work. If correct, she colors the appropriate box on her path. If incorrect, she recopies the problem and tries again, asking for help as needed. The student repeats the process as time allows during the day. Set aside a portion of each day for students to work on their Math Paths.

Jeanne Lokar, Fairport, NY

Not the Same Old Guessing Jar
Estimating, fractions

In advance, gather a clear jar and make a mark to show where the jar would be one-fourth, one-half, three-fourths, and completely full (four-fourths). Also gather a supply of candy and fill the jar to the one-fourth mark. Begin by having each child estimate the number of candies needed to fill the jar to that mark, recording his guess on a chart like the one shown. Then count the items as a class and have students record the actual amount. On the following day, fill the jar to the one-half mark and repeat the process, this time telling students to use the data from the previous day to make their estimates. Continue in this manner to estimate and find the amount of candy needed to fill the jar three-quarters and completely full.

Jill Hamilton Lutz
Schoenecic Elementary
Stevens, PA

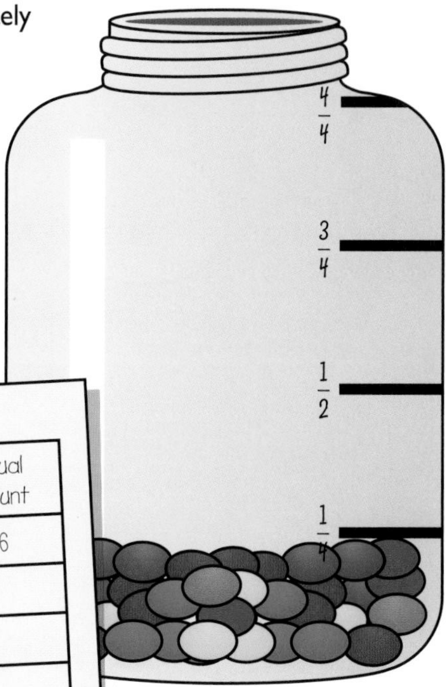
4/4
3/4
1/2
1/4

Lee

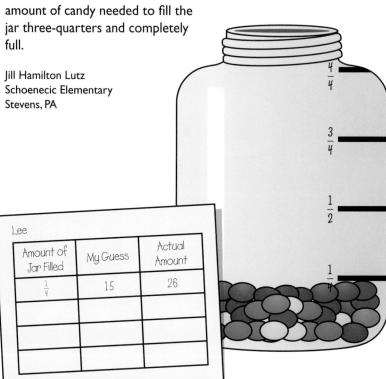

Amount of Jar Filled	My Guess	Actual Amount
1/4	15	26

Measurement Tunes
Area and perimeter

Use these simple songs to help students understand the difference between area and perimeter! Write each song on a sheet of chart paper and post them in the classroom for students to refer to as they practice finding area and perimeter.

Carol Webster, Whiting School, Whiting, NJ

Finding Area
(sung to the tune of "He's Got the Whole World in His Hands")

Length times width is area.
Length times width is area.
Length times width is area.
Area's the whole inside.

Use square units to measure it.
Use square units to measure it.
Use square units to measure it.
Area uses square units.

Perimeter Song
(sung to the tune of "The Farmer in the Dell")

Perimeter is around.
Perimeter is around.
Oh, oh, don't you know, perimeter is around.

You add up all the sides.
You add up all the sides.
Oh, oh, don't you know, you add up all the sides.

Our Readers Write

Our Readers Write

Class Quilt

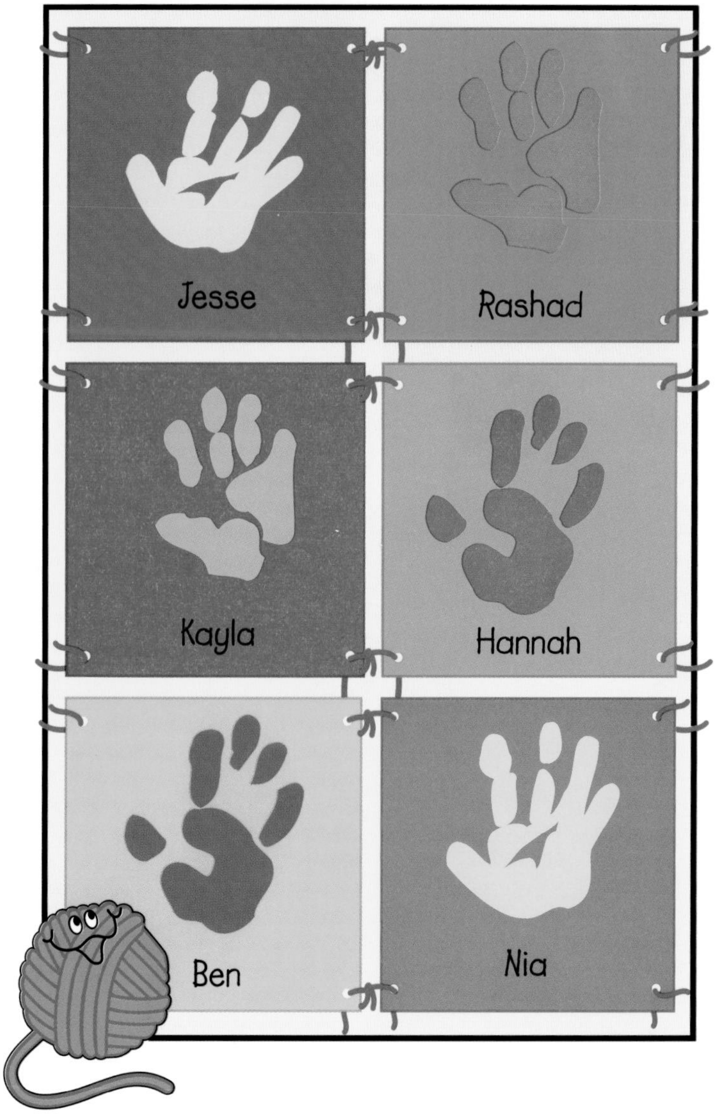

Jesse
Rashad
Kayla
Hannah
Ben
Nia

This art display reinforces the idea that although each member of our class is unique, we fit together perfectly. Each child lightly coats his hand with tempera paint. He makes a handprint on a construction paper square and signs his name below it. Then I punch a hole in each corner of each square and thread yarn through the holes to create a quilt. I hang the quilt in our classroom under the title "These Are the Hands That Shape the Future."

Nancy Richards, Bayview Community School, Mahone Bay, Nova Scotia, Canada

Apple-Picking Time

This sweet idea provides a warm welcome on the first day of school! I post the poem shown outside my classroom along with a supply of apple nametags labeled with students' names. Each child reads the poem, retrieves her nametag, and enters the room knowing that I'm happy to see her! It brings a smile to every face!

Nancy Hawkins, Brookville Elementary
Brookville, IN

Welcome back;
Come on in!
Now that you're here,
We can begin.
I'm so glad that
You have arrived!
Pick your name
And come inside.
Deanna

Notebook Paper Reminder

To help my students write on the correct side of notebook paper, I place three self-adhesive reinforcement labels on the far left-hand sides of their desks. I space the reinforcers so that they match the spacing between the holes on notebook paper. Then, before writing, each child checks his paper to see whether the holes are on the left, just like the ones on his desk!

Margaret Hinceman
Beulah Elementary
Chesterfield County, VA

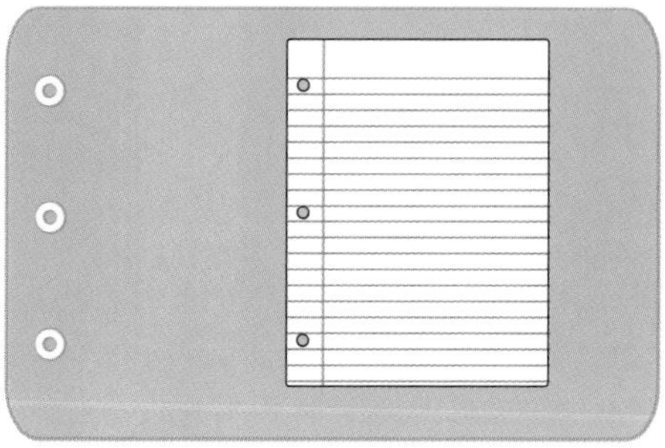

Personalized Pencils

To make sure students return the pencils they borrow, I purchase a set of brightly colored pencils with my name printed on them. I place the pencils at centers and loan extras to students who need one. Missing pencils are easy to track down because of their bright color, and they can never be mistaken for a student's!

Carol Williamson, Wilmington, DE

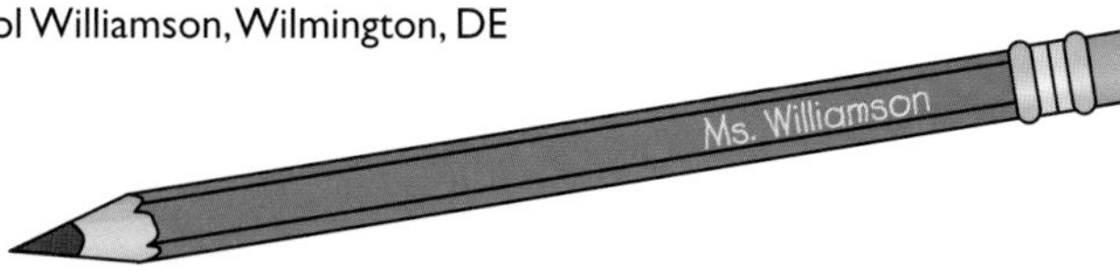

Ms. Williamson

Instant Wall Space

I use a pretaped drop cloth to create extra writing space on the walls and windows of my classroom! It's easy to use: I just cut off the amount I need, attach the tape to the wall, and unfold the plastic. Then I write on the plastic with a permanent marker. It can be moved easily and it's perfect for any area where writing space is needed.

Honora Pollard, Anthon School, Uvalde, TX

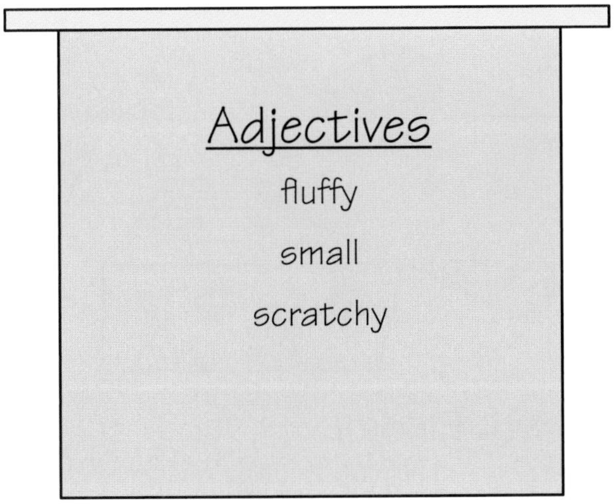
Adjectives
fluffy
small
scratchy

Small Glue Bottles

You'll love these easy-to-handle glue bottles! I purchased some small squeeze bottles at a craft store and filled them with glue. Now my students have bottles that are a better fit for their small hands!

Diane Compton, Howe Hall Elementary, Goose Creek, SC

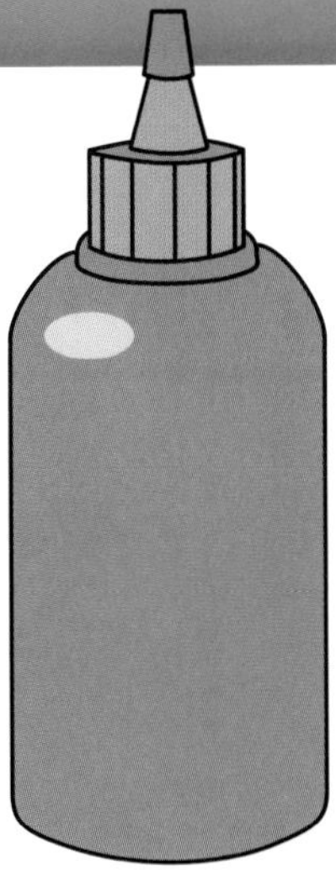

Ps of Perfect Penmanship

To help my students remember the steps to good handwriting, I post a reminder like the one shown. It really helps them stay focused!

Deb Brun
Orlo Avenue School
East Providence, RI

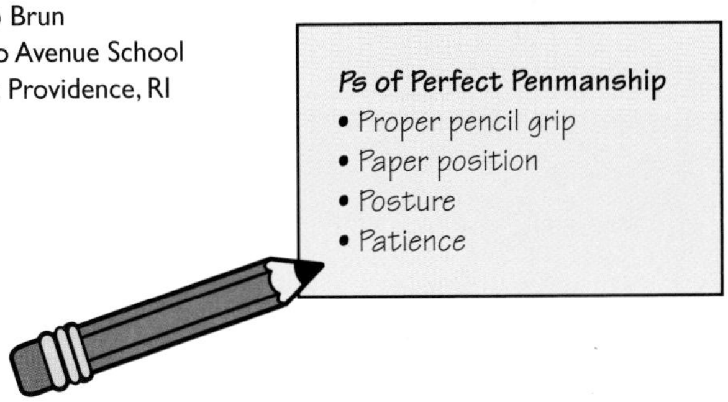
Ps of Perfect Penmanship
• Proper pencil grip
• Paper position
• Posture
• Patience

Titles in a Jiffy

I save time and paper by reusing letters for bulletin board titles! First, I laminate ten sheets of construction paper in each of several colors. Then I use my school's die-cut machine to make several cutouts of each letter per color. Afterward, I sort the letters and store them in an index card file box. When it's time to change bulletin boards, I pull out the letters I need and post them. Simple!

Valerie Wittkop
Coronado Village Elementary
Universal City, TX

Q
S
A
R

Special Thanks

To thank parents who chaperone field trips, I create a picture CD. I simply carry a digital camera on our trip and snap pictures throughout the day. Then I burn the pictures onto blank CDs and give them to parents who helped out on the trip. It's a thank-you that always brings a smile to their faces!

Karen Fouts, Honey Creek Elementary, Conyers, GA

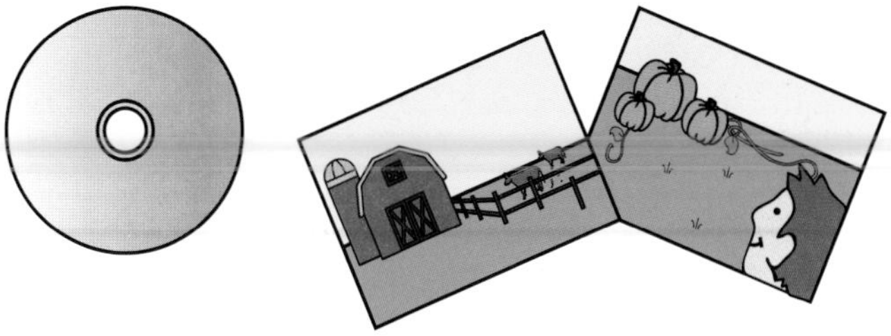

Our Readers Write

Reading Wand

I use a plastic light-up fairy wand to keep students focused during whole-class reading. I read first and hold the wand until I'm ready for a student to read. Then I pass it to a child, and he repeats the process. My students follow wand rules such as a boy must pass the wand to a girl and vice versa and the wand can only be passed to a student who isn't talking. It's an inexpensive way to add fun to our reading while keeping students engaged.

Elizabeth Compton, Western Union Elementary, Waxhaw, NC

Wipe-Off Marker Tip

I use baby wipes to clean transparencies and laminated materials after writing on them with wipe-off markers. I cut the wipes in half. Their small size makes cleanup a snap, and they're not as messy as a wet paper towel.

Jennifer Hart, Oak Ridge R-6
Oak Ridge, MO

Review Boxes

To create storage for review cards, I cover small boxes (like checkbook boxes) with old maps or wrapping paper, wrapping each piece separately. I put the review boxes at a center. Then, as students write facts about the topic we are studying, they place their cards inside. Students visit the center to read over the cards on their own, or pairs use the facts to quiz each other. Students can take the boxes home to study or to share with their parents at the end of the unit.

VaReane Heese, Springfield Elementary, Omaha, NE

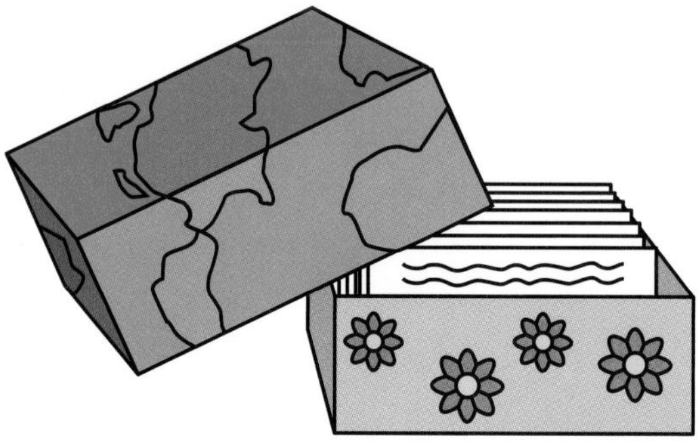

Homework Pledge

I wrote this poem to help my students remember to complete their homework. I copied it onto poster board and had each child dip his hand in paint and make a handprint around the edge. Afterward, I displayed the poem in the classroom. We recite it at the end of each day. This has really helped my class remember to bring in their assignments!

Sue Potteiger, Bell Shoals Baptist Academy, Brandon, FL

I promise to do my homework
Every night that there is some!
I will write it down nice and neat,
Pack my books, and hit the street!
I promise to do my homework
Every night that there is some!
I will check it off when I am done
And have my parents sign it—how fun!
Then back to school it will come,
After every night that there was some!
I'll hand it in all nice and neat
And be so proud that it's complete!

Picture Border

I've started placing pictures of my students around the edges of my bulletin boards! I like to take photos of my students throughout the year as they're completing activities. Each time I develop a roll of film, I use the pictures as the border on a display. Students love looking at the photos and enjoy sharing them with classroom visitors.

Josette Bruno, Holy Trinity School, Pittsburgh, PA

Alternate Bulletin Boards

I create extra bulletin board space by purchasing a large sheet of polystyrene. I cut the foam into four pieces and decorate each one. Then I hang them on my wall wherever I need extra display space. These boards are great because they are portable and affordable!

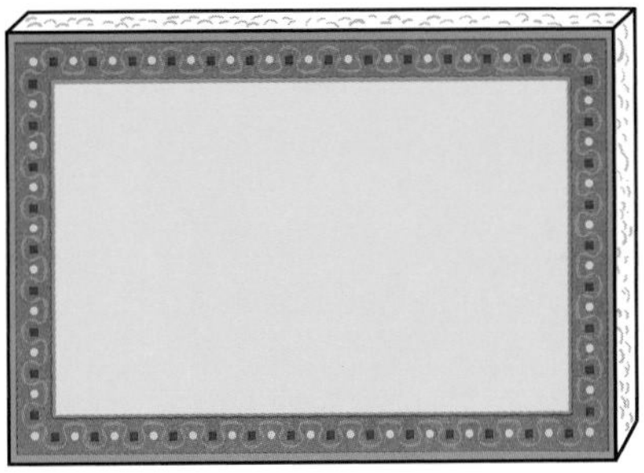

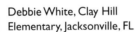

Debbie White, Clay Hill Elementary, Jacksonville, FL

Ready-to-Use Letters

I keep letter sticks on hand for students to use during lessons or centers. First, I laminate a file folder for each child. Then I gather a supply of Popsicle sticks and label each one with a letter of the alphabet. (Write the uppercase letter on one end and the lowercase letter on the other end, as shown.) Next, I attach Velcro fasteners to the folder and to each stick's back. Now I don't have to distribute individual sticks; I just give each child a folder, and we're ready to begin!

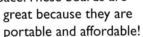

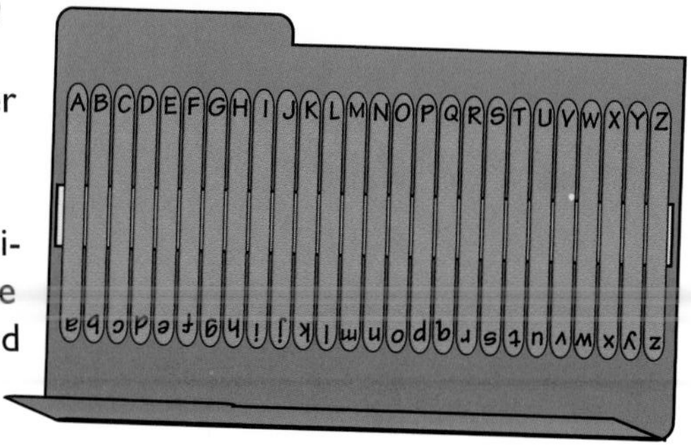
A B C D E F G H I J K L M N O P Q R S T U V W X Y Z

Kristi Langan, O'Neill Elementary, O'Neill, NE

Simple Storage

I keep all my overhead manipulatives in clear videotape cases that I bought at a discount store. I place each set of manipulatives in its own case. I label the spine on each one and store them near my overhead projector. Now my manipulatives are easy to find and keep organized!

Jennifer Warden, Rockwell Elementary, Rockwell, NC

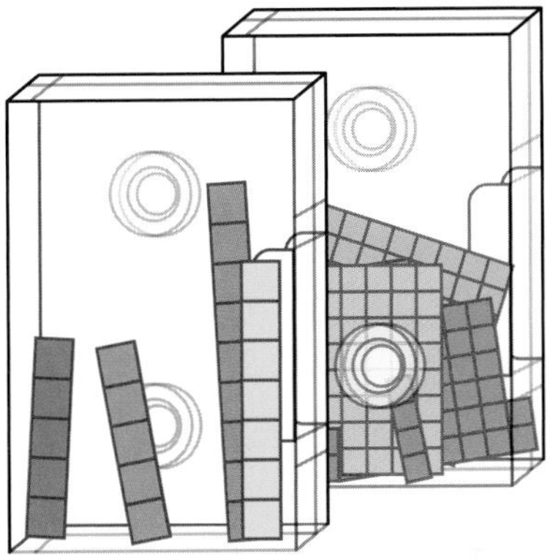

Dotted and Crossed

I use candy to help students remember to cross *t*'s and dot *i*'s! I place two jars on my desk: an empty one and another filled with Tootsie Rolls candy (to represent the crosses on a t) and individually-wrapped peppermint candies (to symbolize the dots on an i). Each time I find a missing dot or cross on a student's paper, I move a piece of the matching candy to the empty jar. At the end of the week, I divide the candies left in the original jar among my students. Now students double-check their work to ensure no crosses or dots are missing!

Laura Hess, Providence School, Waynesboro, PA

Our Readers Write

Tell Everybody

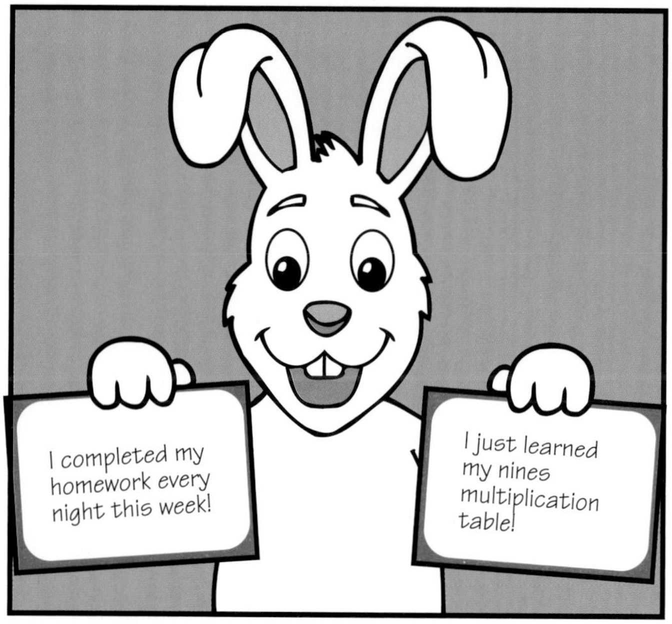

I completed my homework every night this week!
I just learned my nines multiplication table!

I use labels to recognize students' accomplishments! I purchase a supply of self-adhesive labels from an office supply store. Whenever one of my students reaches a goal or completes a difficult task, I write it on one of the tags. The child wears it throughout the day so everyone at school notices his accomplishment. Then he wears it home to share with his parents. These inexpensive labels make great mementos!

Joyce Lucas, Skyline Elementary, Ferndale, WA

Pick a Part of Speech!

This simple time filler is one my students love! I have each child write a noun, a verb, and an adjective each on a separate slip of paper. I place all the paper slips in a bag. Whenever we have extra time, I invite a student to select a strip from the bag. The child reveals the word to the class. Then all the students help her determine the word's part of speech. Afterward, we glue the words onto chart paper. As soon as we have a variety of words, students choose several of them to use in a silly sentence.

Karen Marzuk, Edith Slocum Elementary, Ronkonkoma, NY

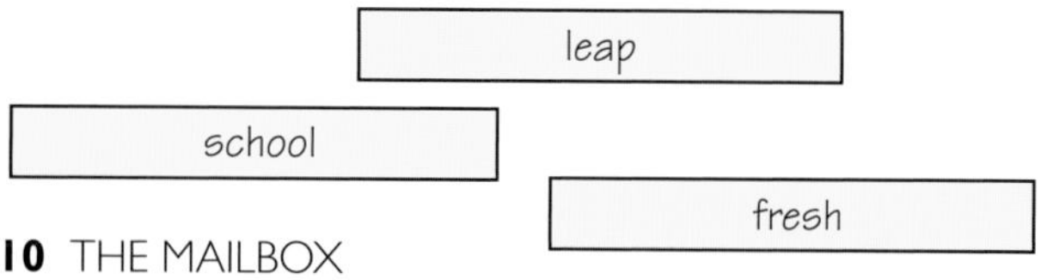

leap
school
fresh

Game Tip

I collect plastic bottle caps to make memory games! I program colorful dot stickers with synonym or antonym pairs (one word on each sticker) or basic facts and their answers. Then I place a programmed sticker inside each cap. I store the caps in a resealable plastic bag and place it at a center. Student pairs place the caps facedown and take turns trying to find the ones that match. These caps can even be used as game markers!

Laurie Tracey, Paul B. D. Temple Elementary, Kennedy, NY

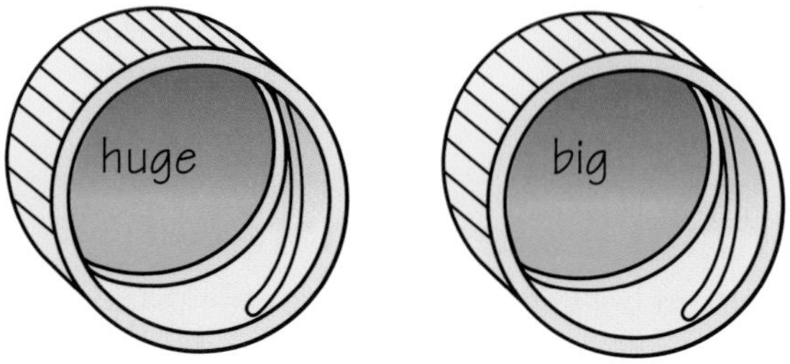

huge
big

Traveling Trivia

Small photo albums make great review books! To make one, I write on 4" x 6" index cards the skills that I want my class to review and then slide these into the photo sleeves. I take the book along when my students go to the cafeteria, restroom, or water fountain. While they wait in line, I quiz them on the concepts in the book. It's an easy way to make the most of our time during the day. I also create additional books and keep them at a center so student pairs can quiz each other!

Jessica Hines
Rivercrest Elementary
Bogata, TX

What plane figures have four sides and four corners?

T
H
A
N
K
Y
O
U

Multiplication Vest

I wear a vest to help my students memorize facts! I program index card halves with the multiplication facts I want my students to practice. Then I attach Velcro fasteners to an inexpensive vest and to each card's back. Throughout the day, I point to a fact and the class responds with the answer. I also use the vest to help students practice vocabulary words.

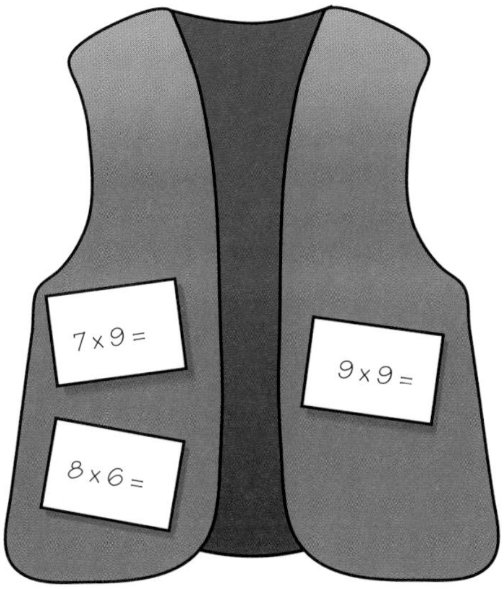
7 x 9 =
9 x 9 =
8 x 6 =

Chris Kirley
Lincoln School
Hartford, WI

Reference Book Song

Help students remember which reference books to use with this simple tune!

Colleen Hoover, Juniper Elementary, Hesperia, CA

Reference Book Song

(sung to the tune of "If You're Happy and You Know It")

An atlas is a book filled with maps.
An atlas is a book filled with maps.
If you really need to know
All the places you can go,
An atlas is just the book you need!

A thesaurus is a book of synonyms.
A thesaurus is a book of synonyms.
If you want to find a word
That means the same as *heard,*
A thesaurus is just the book you need!

A dictionary has words and what they mean.
A dictionary has words and what they mean.
If you need to know the meaning
Of a word that you are reading,
A dictionary is just the book you need!

Encyclopedias have all you need to know
About people, places, animals, and snow.
If you need information
About animals or nations,
An encyclopedia is just the book you need!

Thank-You Cards

Our classroom volunteers love receiving these sweet notes! To make one, I take a class photo, asking eight students to hold letter cards that spell "Thank You." I mount a copy of the photo on the front of a folded construction paper piece. Then I write a short thank-you message on the card's inside and have all my students sign it.

Sue Lake, Wright Elementary, Salem, OR

Lefty Writer Hint

This tip helps my left-handed students improve their handwriting! Whenever we practice handwriting, I usually write the letter to be practiced in a row across the top of each child's paper as a reference. But that doesn't work for my left-handed students because their hands cover the letters. Instead, I write their letter models in the right margin. Now they can easily see the letters and imitate them!

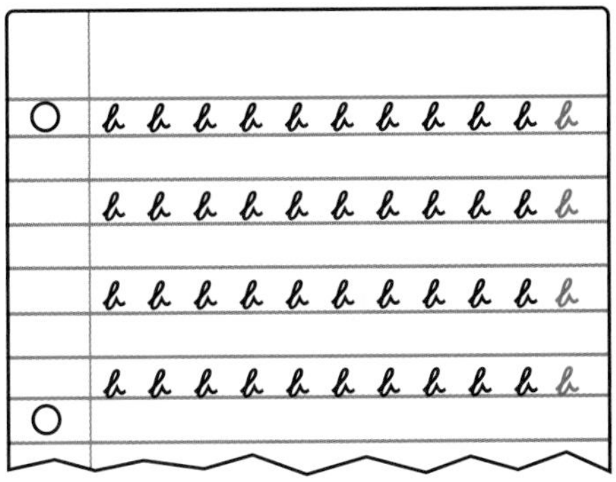

Santa Teresa
St. Gabriel School
Philadelphia, PA

Glitter Saver

I conserve glitter by storing it in resealable plastic bowls. My students use spoons to shake glitter on their projects. When they're done, they have plenty of room to pour off the excess, which falls neatly back into the bowl!

Pamela Grooms
Highland Lakes Elementary
Palm Harbor, FL

Our Readers Write

Manipulative Organization

UNIFIX CUBES

I use plastic baby food tubs for math manipulative storage and as paint containers! After washing each tub, I place manipulatives, such as plastic counters or dice, inside. Then I label the tub and place it in a cabinet so manipulatives are easy to find. When we paint, I simply pour a supply of paint in the tub. If the project lasts for a few days, I place the lid on the paint and it's ready to go for the next day. These tubs are lifesavers!

April Drake, Harvey Newlin Elementary, Burlington, NC

Candy Question

I use this simple idea to review important concepts with my students! Each day I ask a "Candy Question," a question that includes a fact or an idea from a lesson taught within the last week. I write the question on a slip of paper each morning. Then, sometime during the day, I pose it to students. The first student to raise his hand with the correct answer earns a piece of candy. After the question is answered, I place it in a jar on my desk. Then, every few weeks, I read an old question aloud and have students answer it as a review. My students love this activity! I like that it's simple and engages my class!

Elizabeth Compton, Western Union Elementary, Waxhaw, NC

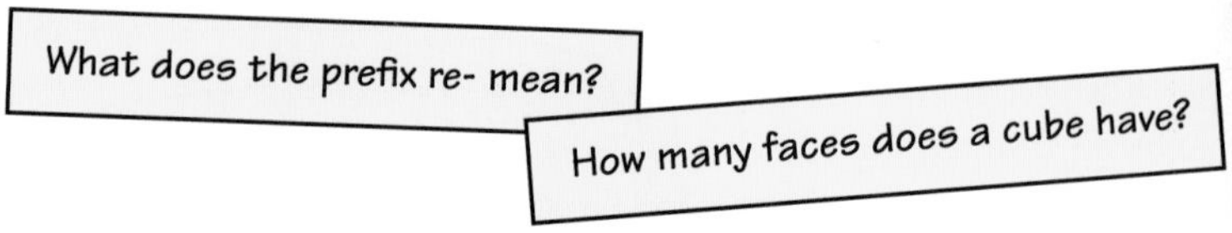
What does the prefix re- mean?
How many faces does a cube have?

Summer Correspondence

To keep students writing during summer vacation, I give each child a self-addressed stamped envelope. Then I invite her to write a letter, story, or poem during the summer and send it to me. I explain that I'll write back when I receive her note. My students have a great time writing messages and sending their stories, and I love corresponding with them!

Erin Matson
St. John the Baptist School
Cincinnati, OH

Ms. Erin Matson
100 Elm Street
Cincinnati, OH 00000

Ringed Reminders

To ensure that I can easily find ideas that worked well in the past, I make these nifty guides! First, I punch a hole in the top right corner of a supply of different-colored index cards. Next, I label each card with a different month or season and an activity appropriate for that time of year. I place the cards on a ring and keep them on my desk. Whenever I try a new activity that goes smoothly, I write it on a card and attach it to the ring. Now great activities are always at my fingertips!

Joyce Maher
Bellmawr Park School
Bellmawr, NJ

May
Time Filler
Write parts of speech on paper slips. A student draws one without looking at it. He shows it to classmates and they help him figure out the part of speech.

Write On!

Write On!

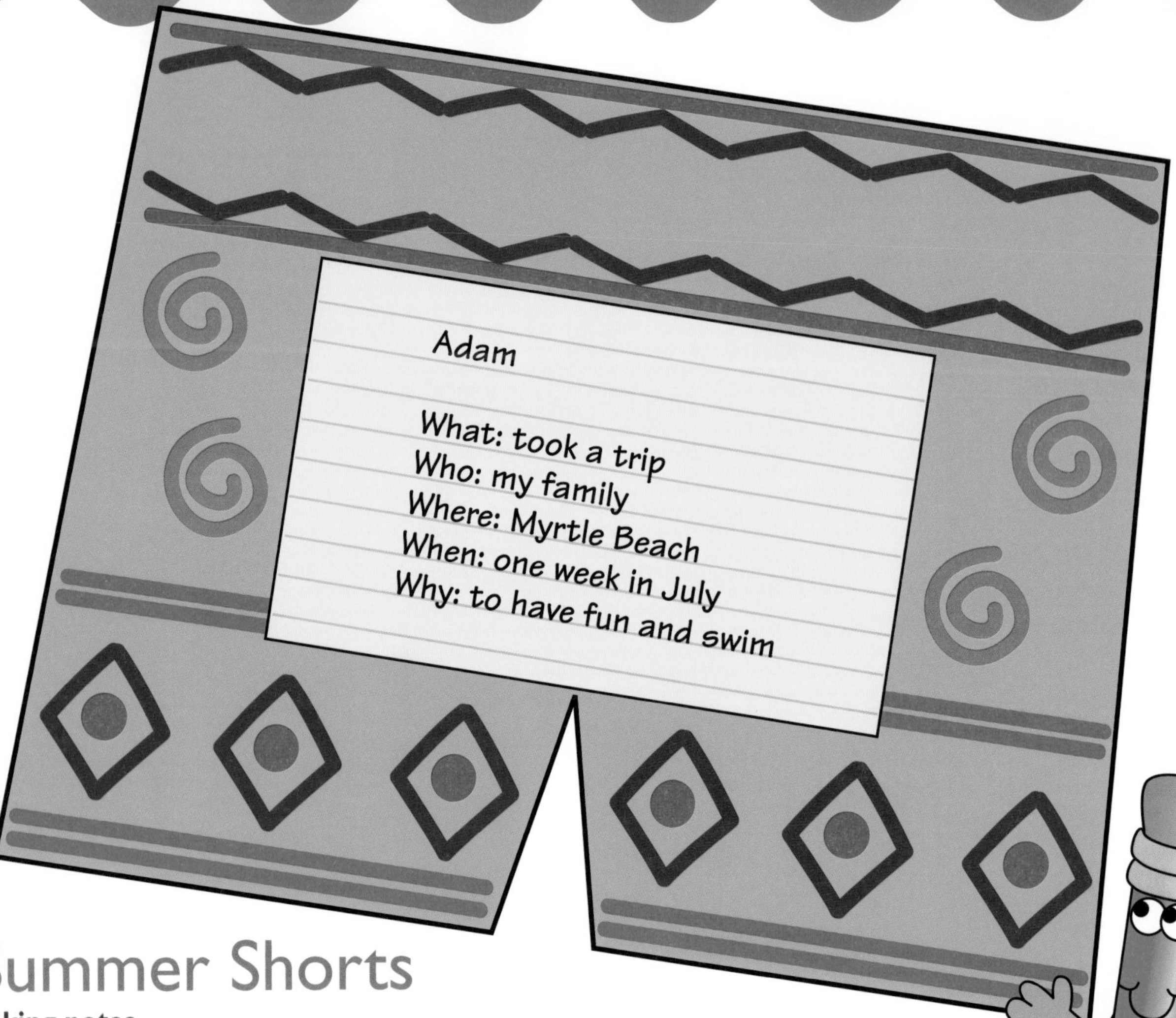
Adam
What: took a trip
Who: my family
Where: Myrtle Beach
When: one week in July
Why: to have fun and swim

Summer Shorts

Taking notes

This getting-to-know-you activity gives students practice with interviewing and note taking! First, pair students and have the students in each twosome use the following questions to interview each other.

- **What's one thing you did this summer?**
- **Who did you do this with?**
- **Where did you do the activity?**
- **When did you do the activity?**
- **Why did you do the activity?**

Each youngster writes his partner's answers on an index card, making sure to keep his notes brief. Next, he trims a sheet of light-colored construction paper to make a pair of shorts, personalizes them, and then glues his card in the center. Invite students to share their summer experiences with the class; then display the shorts and a list of interview questions on a bulletin board titled "Short Notes on Summer."

Dawn Maucieri, Signal Hill Elementary, Dix Hills, NY

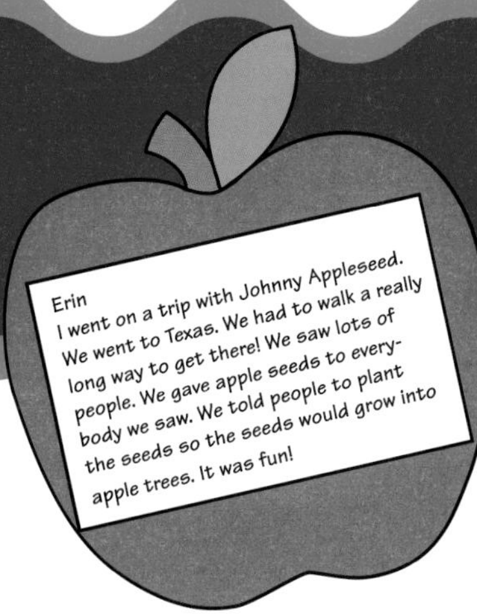
Erin
I went on a trip with Johnny Appleseed. We went to Texas. We had to walk a really long way to get there! We saw lots of people. We gave apple seeds to every-body we saw. We told people to plant the seeds so the seeds would grow into apple trees. It was fun!

Traveling With Johnny
Creative writing

Celebrate Johnny Appleseed's birthday with this sweet writing activity! Have each child imagine that she could travel with Johnny on one of his trips where he planted trees or gave seeds to people he met. Then have her write a story about the adventure, telling where they went and what happened there. Invite each child to share her story with the class. If desired, have the student mount her story on an apple cutout like the one shown, or combine students' stories into a class book titled "Traveling With Johnny."

Tisha Flowers, St. Paul Elementary, Highland, IL

Timely Prompts
Journal prompts

I brought my parrot, George, to school. He has really bright feathers. He's very friendly. He flew around the room and landed on people's shoulders. He even let some people pet him. Everyone thought he was really cool except my teacher. He kept repeating everything she said!

Celebrate students' return to school with these getting-acquainted prompts! Have each child respond to a favorite writing suggestion. Then provide time for students to share their responses.

- Imagine that you brought your pet (or any animal of your choice) to school. Write about what happened that day.
- Think about the best time you ever had with a family member. Who did you spend time with and what did you do?
- Pretend you are the principal of your school. Name one rule you would change. How would you make it different?

Picture-Perfect
Story elements

Setting a story scene has never been more fun! Give each child a clip art animal. Have him color the animal and then glue it to a sheet of light-colored construction paper. Next, instruct him to draw a background for his animal. Then have him write a story about the animal that describes the setting he drew and what the animal is doing. Invite students to share their writings and pictures with the class; then post each child's paper and illustration on a display titled "Setting the Scene."

Sonceria Zuckerman, Riley Elementary, Salt Lake City, UT

Once there was a bird. He lived in a park with pretty flowers and tall trees. The park also had a play-ground. People liked to go there and play. The bird wanted to play too. First, he flew to the slide. He slid down to the bottom. "This is fun!" he said. Next, he flew to the swings. But he couldn't swing because he was too little. Last, he tried the merry-go-round. It was like flying, but he didn't have to use his wings!

Write On!

Candy.
Yummy, orange.
Tasty, sweet, terrific.
I could eat a whole bag of it.
Sweet stuff.

Candy “Corn-quains”

Writing cinquains

Begin by giving each child a few pieces of candy corn. As a class, brainstorm words that describe the candy and list them on the board. Next, review with students the cinquain format. To complete the activity, each child writes a cinquain about candy corn on a pattern like the one shown. Then he cuts out the pattern and mounts it on a sheet of orange or yellow construction paper. Invite students to share their poems with the class. Post completed projects on a bulletin board titled “Candy ‘Corn-quains’.”

Pamela Earley, Bethel Manor Elementary, York County, VA

Scary Tales
Descriptive writing

Together with students, make a list of creepy Halloween characters, and write each one on a slip of paper. Repeat the process, this time naming spooky settings. Place the slips of paper in two containers, one labeled "Characters" and the other "Settings." To write a spooky tale, each child draws a slip from each container and uses her chosen character and setting to illustrate and write a descriptive paragraph on story paper.

Rita Skavinsky, Minersville Elementary Center, Minersville, PA

One night there was a bad storm. I heard something in the basement. I turned on the light, and my hand touched a cobweb. It felt sticky! Then I saw a giant, purple one-eyed monster! He was huge and slimy. The monster smelled like a trash can full of rotten bananas! I was so scared!

Believe It
Or Not

Believe It or Not
Personal and imaginative paragraphs

Start by having each child write a short narrative about an imagined event or an unusual event he has experienced. Then have the child make a sign like the one shown by folding a half sheet of construction paper in half. He labels one side "Believe It" and the other side "Or Not" and then glues the halves together, sandwiching a craft stick between them. Next, each child reads his story to the class. When he finishes, his classmates hold up their signs to show whether they think the story is real or imagined. Then have the student reveal whether his story was personal or imaginative.

Brooke Shaw, Columbia, SC

Timely Prompts
Journal writing

Have each child respond to a chosen prompt below. Then invite students to share their responses with the class.

- How would your life change if you had eight legs instead of two?
- Pretend you are a spider. Describe the best web you've ever spun. How big was it? How long did it take to finish?
- Spiders live anywhere they can find food. If you were a spider, where would you like to live? Why?

If I had eight legs instead of two, I'd be able to get to places more quickly! I'd never be late for anything, and I'd be able to run really fast during my soccer matches. But I would feel weird because I'd have to wear four different pairs of pants at the same time. And my mom would get really tired of doing my laundry!

Write On!

One morning I built a snowman. He was huge. I decorated him. Then the wind blew really hard. My snowman came to life! He talked to me. He told me his name was Flake. Then he threw snowballs at me! We had a snowball fight all morning long. When we went to have lunch we were soaked!

It's Alive!

Imaginative narrative

To begin the activity, each child draws and colors a picture of a snowman. He imagines that his snowman came to life and that they spent the day together. Then he writes a narrative explaining what he and the snowman did during the day. The first paragraph details the morning's events, the second tells about what they did in the afternoon, and the third paragraph tells about the evening. Encourage students to use vivid verbs and descriptive words throughout their stories. After each student finishes his writing, have him cut out his snowman and attach it to the top of his paper. Post students' papers on a display titled "It's Alive!"

Virginia Conrad
Bunker R-3 Elementary
Bunker, MO

Winter Senses
Poetry

During the first few days of winter, provide time for students to go outside and use all of their senses to observe the new season. After a few minutes, return indoors. Give each child a copy of page 120 and have her use her observations to finish the sentence starters. Then have her use the sentences to complete a five-line poem called "Winter Is," including one line about each sense. After the poems are written, invite students to share them with the class.

Laura Johnson, Blue River Valley Elementary, Mt. Summit, IN

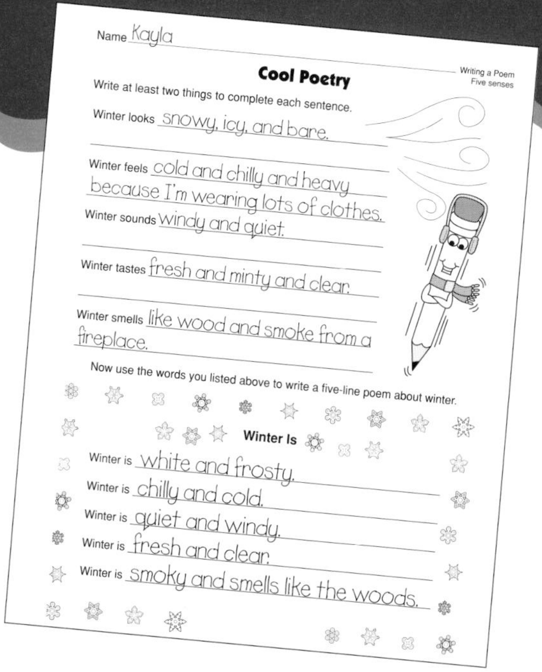
Name Kayla

Writing a Poem
Five senses

Cool Poetry

Write at least two things to complete each sentence.

Winter looks snowy, icy, and bare.

Winter feels cold and chilly and heavy because I'm wearing lots of clothes.

Winter sounds windy and quiet.

Winter tastes fresh and minty and clear.

Winter smells like wood and smoke from a fireplace.

Now use the words you listed above to write a five-line poem about winter.

Winter Is

Winter is white and frosty.
Winter is chilly and cold.
Winter is quiet and windy.
Winter is fresh and clear.
Winter is smoky and smells like the woods.

I'd Like a...
Descriptive writing

SALE!
Devonte
This year I'd like to get a really cool toy. It's red and it has four black round things on it. It makes a little bit of noise. It has another part that tells it what to do, like when to turn or to back up. Both parts need batteries.

In advance, gather several sales circulars from popular toy stores. Invite each child to browse through the circulars and select a toy that he would like to receive for the holidays. Then have him write a paragraph that describes the toy (including its size, color, and shape) without mentioning its name. Next, have him trade papers with a classmate. Each partner reads the paper he receives and uses the details to identify the toy. Giving the gift of descriptive writing has never been so easy!

Kim Bostick, Kernersville Elementary, Kernersville, NC

Timely Prompts
Journal writing

Invite each student to respond to a prompt below. Then have students share their responses with the class.

- Just as you are slipping on your mittens, they begin to talk to you. What do they say? How do you respond?
- One day when you're playing outside, you discover that the scarf you're wearing has the power to make things easier. Would you rather have it help you build a snowman or shovel the snow from the driveway? Explain.
- Which would you rather wear: summer clothes or winter clothes? Why?

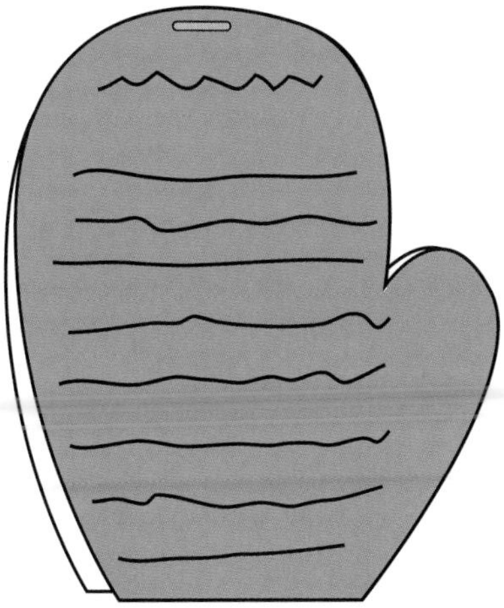

Name ____________________

Writing a Poem
Five senses

Cool Poetry

Write at least two things to complete each sentence.

Winter looks ____________________

____

Winter feels ____________________

____

Winter sounds ____________________

____

Winter tastes ____________________

____

Winter smells ____________________

____

Now use the words you listed above to write a five-line poem about winter.

Winter Is

Winter is ____________________

Winter is ____________________

Winter is ____________________

Winter is ____________________

Winter is ____________________

 Note to the teacher: Use with "Winter Senses" on page 119.

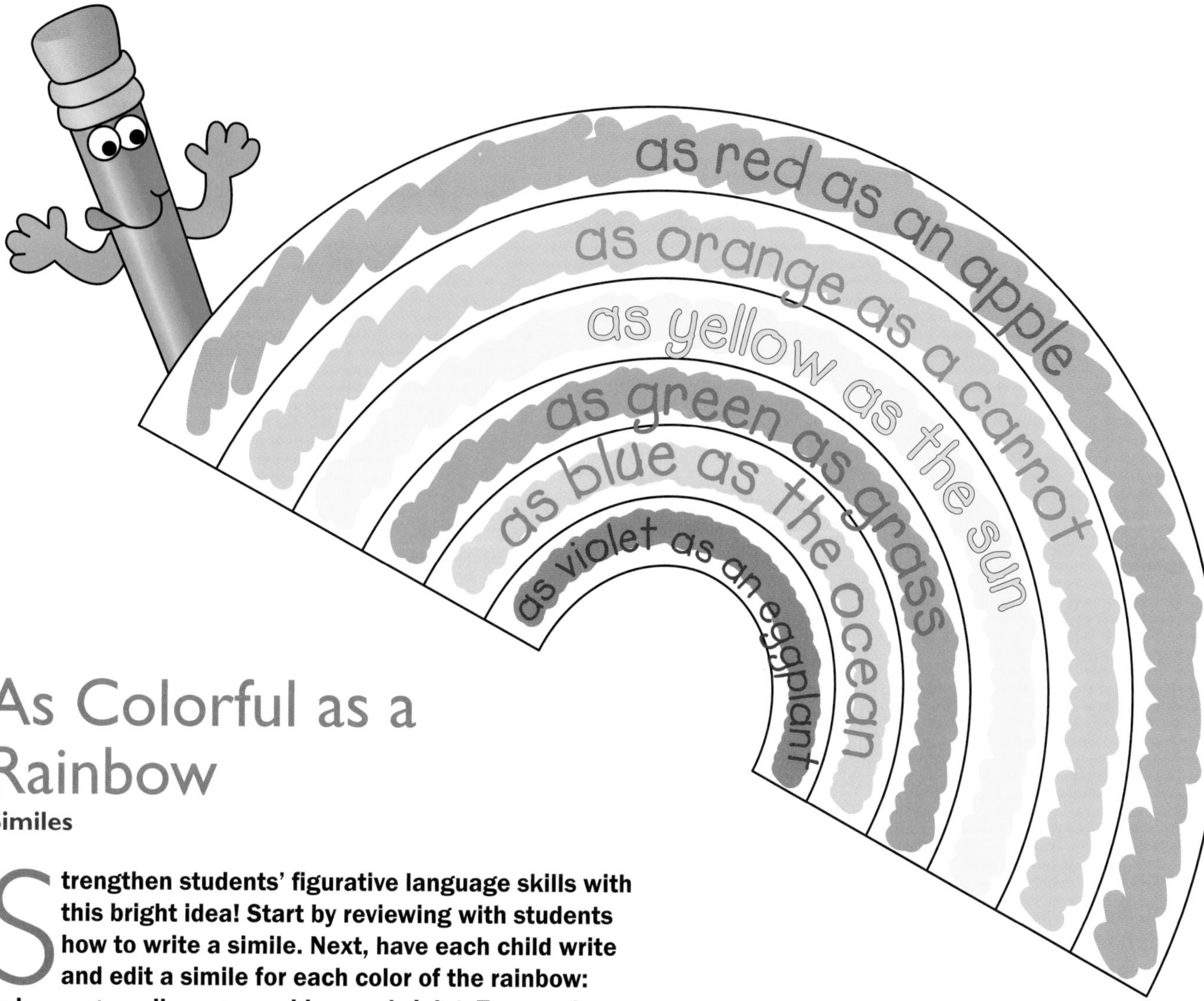
as red as an apple
as orange as a carrot
as yellow as the sun
as green as grass
as blue as the ocean
as violet as an eggplant

As Colorful as a Rainbow

Similes

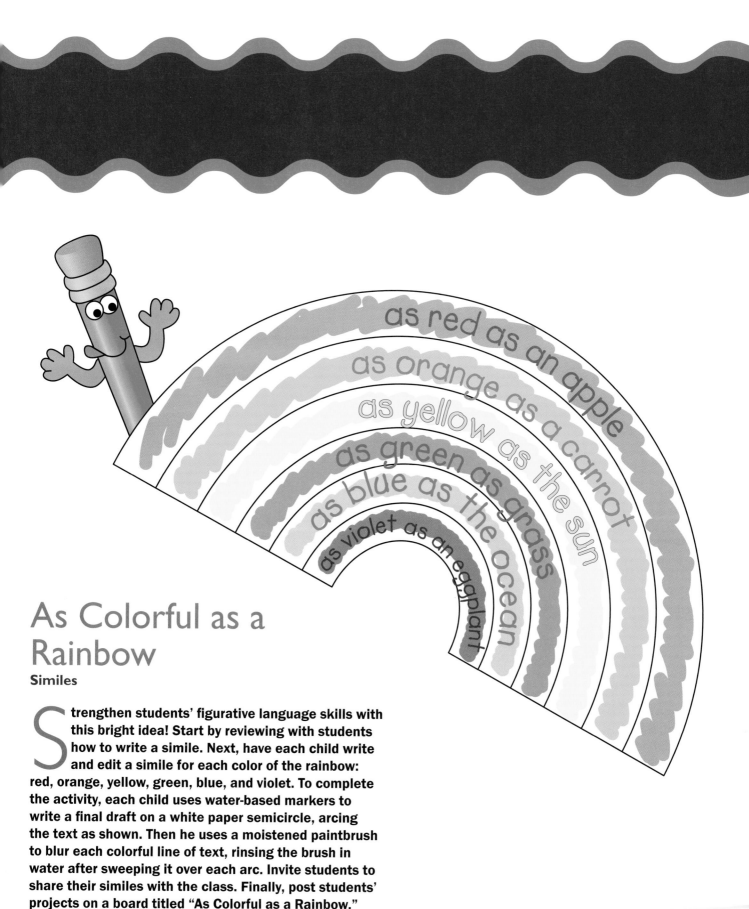

Strengthen students' figurative language skills with this bright idea! Start by reviewing with students how to write a simile. Next, have each child write and edit a simile for each color of the rainbow: red, orange, yellow, green, blue, and violet. To complete the activity, each child uses water-based markers to write a final draft on a white paper semicircle, arcing the text as shown. Then he uses a moistened paintbrush to blur each colorful line of text, rinsing the brush in water after sweeping it over each arc. Invite students to share their similes with the class. Finally, post students' projects on a board titled "As Colorful as a Rainbow."

Amy Barsanti, Pines Elementary, Plymouth, NC

Write On!

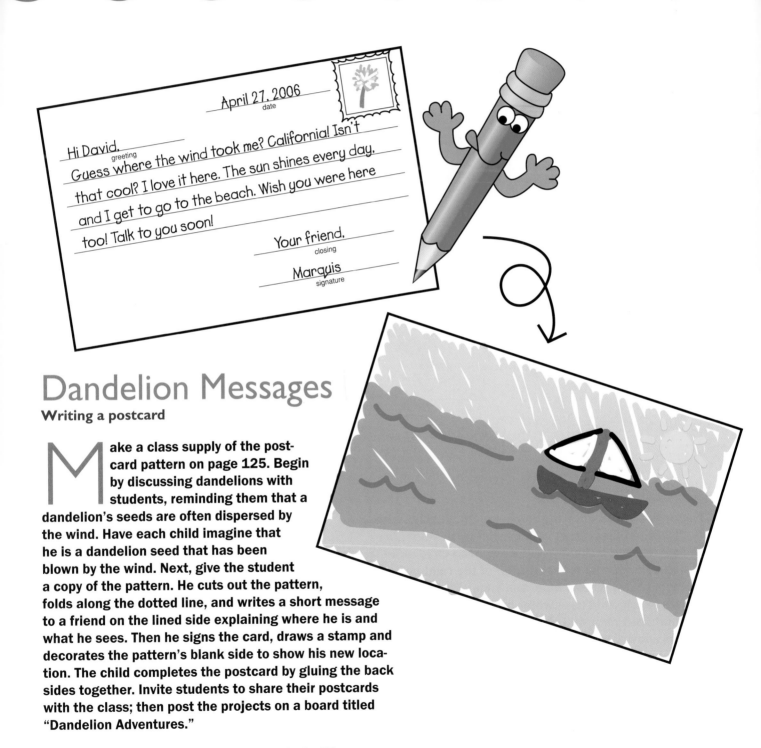

April 27, 2006
date
Hi David,
greeting
Guess where the wind took me? California! Isn't
that cool? I love it here. The sun shines every day,
and I get to go to the beach. Wish you were here
too! Talk to you soon!
Your friend,
closing
Marquis
signature

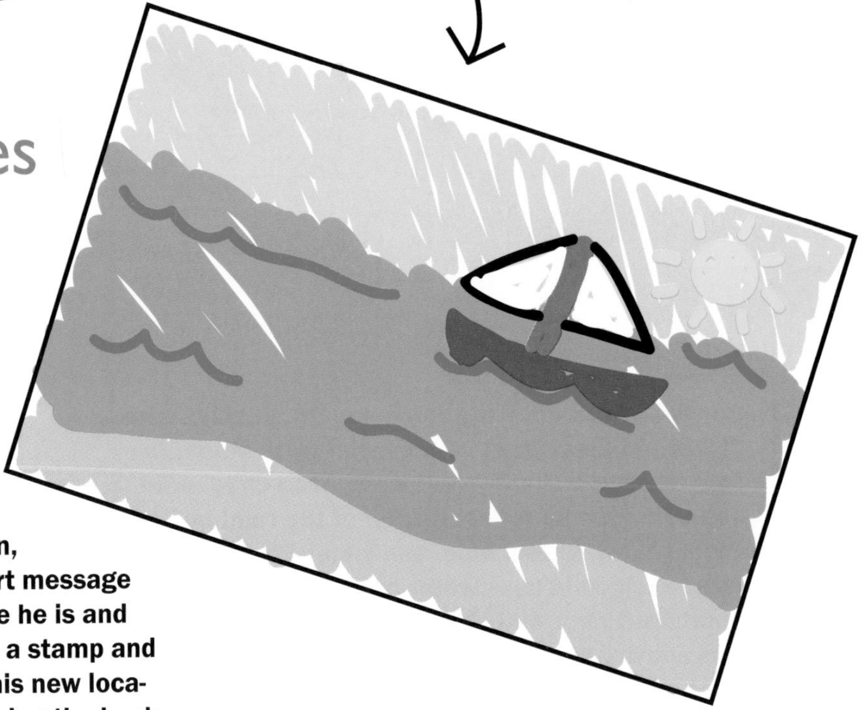

Dandelion Messages

Writing a postcard

Make a class supply of the postcard pattern on page 125. Begin by discussing dandelions with students, reminding them that a dandelion's seeds are often dispersed by the wind. Have each child imagine that he is a dandelion seed that has been blown by the wind. Next, give the student a copy of the pattern. He cuts out the pattern, folds along the dotted line, and writes a short message to a friend on the lined side explaining where he is and what he sees. Then he signs the card, draws a stamp and decorates the pattern's blank side to show his new location. The child completes the postcard by gluing the back sides together. Invite students to share their postcards with the class; then post the projects on a board titled "Dandelion Adventures."

adapted from an idea by Cindy Barber, Fredonia, WI

Mystery Writer
Writing a friendly letter, word choice

Begin by discussing with students the parts of a friendly letter. Next, have each child anonymously write a friendly letter to you. Instruct the student to write about herself, using descriptive words and phrases that provide clues to her identity. Collect the letters and place them in a box. Then, each day, read a letter aloud. Afterward, try to guess the writer's identity. Share with students the words and phrases you used to identify the author, showing them the importance of word choice in their writing.

Maria Blayter, Aguilar Elementary, Tempe, AZ

March 21, 2006

Dear Ms. Blayter,

I have brown hair and brown eyes. I love animals, especially dogs. I have a dog named Oscar. Math is my favorite thing to do at school. I also like to read. I like to go swimming in the summer.

Your student,
?

Wonderful Women
Interviewing, writing an expository paragraph

Celebrate National Women's History Month in March while building writing skills! Explain to the class that each child will interview a woman he knows. Next, as a class, create a list of questions that students might ask their chosen person. Each child selects five questions from the list and writes them on a sheet of paper. During the next few days, he interviews the person of his choice and records that individual's responses. Then the child uses his notes to write a descriptive paragraph about his subject. Post students' completed paragraphs on a bulletin board titled "Wonderful Women."

Dawn Maucieri, Signal Hill Elementary, Dix Hills, NY

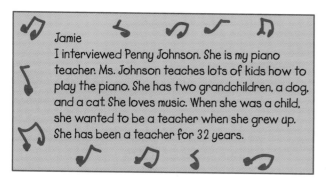

Jamie
I interviewed Penny Johnson. She is my piano teacher. Ms. Johnson teaches lots of kids how to play the piano. She has two grandchildren, a dog, and a cat. She loves music. When she was a child, she wanted to be a teacher when she grew up. She has been a teacher for 32 years.

Timely Prompts
Journal writing

Sail into March with these seasonal prompts! Have each child respond to a favorite prompt below. Then invite students to share their responses with the class.

- If you could design and build a kite, describe the kite you would create. What would it look like? What kinds of materials would you use to build it?
- Imagine that you found a lucky kite that could take you anywhere. Where would you go? What would you do when you got there?
- Pretend that you are a kite. Describe what it feels like when your owner sends you up into the air and when you are flying.

Let's go!

Dear Diary
Writing a diary entry

Start by reading aloud *Diary of a Worm* by Doreen Cronin. After finishing the story, discuss with students how a worm's life is similar to theirs and how it is different. Next, have each student select a different animal or insect and write and illustrate a diary entry from that creature's perspective. Instruct the child to use the book as a model for her entry. Finally, allow students to share their entries with the class; then post the completed projects on a bulletin board titled "Dear Diary."

Stacey Galasso, Center School, Stratford, CT

May 9
Today I helped build my first honeycomb. We had to use a lot of wax. We used bee glue to fix a crack.
It was going okay until I glued myself to the hive. Boy, was that hard to explain!

Class Photo Book
Writing captions

Provide expository-writing experience and create a class memento at the same time! Take photos of your students as they complete classroom activities. Give each twosome a few snapshots and have the pair affix each photo to a sheet of light-colored construction paper. Then the partners work together to write a few sentences below the picture to describe it. Afterward, combine the pages into a book. If desired, create additional books by having students use photos to write how-to paragraphs or summaries instead of captions.

Julie Lewis, J. O. Davis Elementary, Irving, TX

Jay and Lucia are using plastic grass, shredded paper, and ribbons to make a bird's nest. We made nests in April.

Timely Prompts
Journal writing

Invite each student to respond to a prompt below. Then have students share their responses with the class.

- What foods make a picnic perfect? Name five foods and explain why you chose each one.
- Write three things an ant might say to get you to share your picnic with him.
- Pretend that you're going on a picnic with your family. You find the perfect spot and spread out your blanket. Then you open the basket and discover that it's empty. What happens next?

Postcard Pattern

Use with "Dandelion Messages" on page 123.

date

greeting

closing

signature

TEC43024

Write On!

It was so hot...
Jaquan
...I drank 30 gallons of lemonade!
...that I swam in a sea of ice cream!

Summertime Treat

Using hyperbole

To create this cool project, copy the ice pop pattern on page 128 onto colored construction paper to make a class supply. Also gather a class supply of large craft sticks. Start by reviewing hyperbole with the class. Next, write "It was so hot..." on the board and have each child write two endings to the sentence on scrap paper, describing how he cools off during hot summer days. Instruct the student to use hyperbole in each ending. To complete the project, the child cuts out an ice pop pattern, folds it in half, and personalizes the front. On the inside he lists and illustrates both endings as shown. Then he glues a craft stick to the back of the project. Invite students to share their writing with the class. Afterward, post the ice pops on a display titled "Cooling Off."

adapted from an idea by Cindy Barber, Fredonia, WI

Guess Who?
Writing similes

Shannon
My eyes are as blue as the ocean.
My freckles look like crumbs on a white tablecloth.

These simple puzzles are easy to create and fun to solve! Each child draws a self-portrait on the blank side of an index card and writes her name below it. On the lined side, she writes two similes that describe her personality or physical appearance. Collect students' cards. Each day post a card in the classroom, making sure that only the similes are visible. Invite students to read the similes during the day and use them to guess the student's identity. At the end of the day, read the similes aloud. Allow students to share their guesses with the class. Then reveal the mystery student's identity. Repeat the process until each child's similes have been displayed and identified.

Stacie Stone Davis, Lima, NY

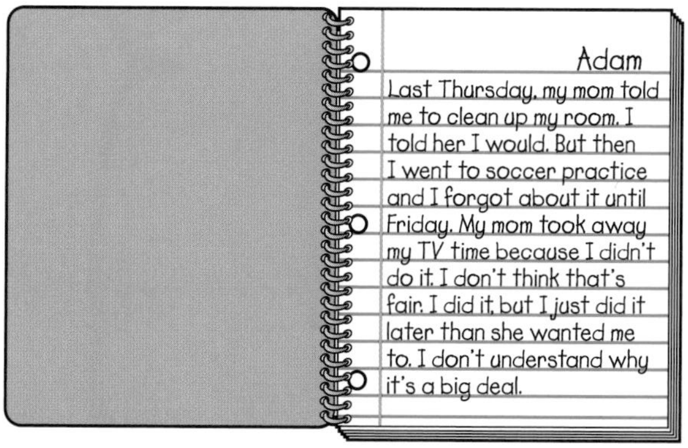
Adam
Last Thursday, my mom told me to clean up my room. I told her I would. But then I went to soccer practice and I forgot about it until Friday. My mom took away my TV time because I didn't do it. I don't think that's fair. I did it, but I just did it later than she wanted me to. I don't understand why it's a big deal.

Family Stories
Understanding point of view

Easily show students how perspectives can be different! Begin by dividing students into pairs. Have each child tell his partner a family story. After both partners have shared their stories, each child records his story in his journal. Then send the journal home with the student along with a note asking the child's parent to write his own version of the story and send it back to school. On the following day, have students re-read both versions of the story. Discuss as a class how the versions are similar and different.

Karen Pavlosky, Woodbrook Elementary, Charlottesville, VA

Timely Prompts
Journal writing

Have each child respond to a favorite prompt below. Then allow students to share their responses with the class.

- Imagine that you are a bee. Use descriptive words to tell about your favorite flower.
- If you were a bee, where would you build your hive? Give three reasons why you chose that place.
- Imagine that a bear and a bee are at a honeycomb at the same time. Write about the conversation that takes place between the two of them. Be sure to use correct punctuation, including quotation marks.

Ice Pop Pattern

Use with "Summertime Treat" on page 126.

It was so hot...
TEC43025

Language Arts Units

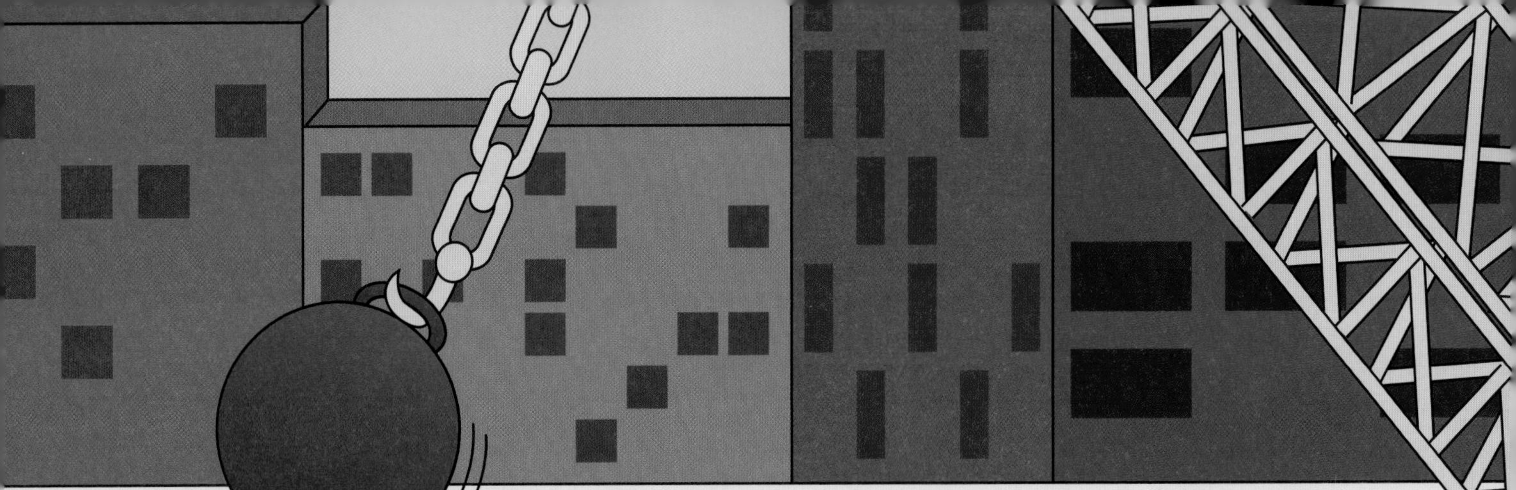

Hard Hat Area

Building Word Family Skills

Full House
b
r
l
p
s
w
_l_ump
_l_ock
_p_ack
ink
est
ack
_r_est
_r_ink
ock
ump
est
ack
ock
ock
ump

FULL HOUSE
Short-vowel rimes

Finishing last is the object of this center activity! Make a supply of the gameboard on page 132. Also copy the circular spinner on page 133 onto construction paper. Laminate the spinner for durability and then cut it out. Place the gameboards, the spinner, two different-colored crayons, a pencil, and a paper clip at a center. Confirm that students know how to use a paper clip and pencil to make a spinner. To play the game, a child spins the spinner. He then chooses a crayon and fills in one or two different boxes with the letter he spun, making a word or words. The student then reads aloud the word(s) he formed. Play continues in this manner until one student wins by filling in the last box and making a full house.

Miranda Babin, Southdown Elementary, Houma, LA

Construct a solid reading foundation while strengthening students' knowledge of word families!

with ideas by Jennifer L. Kohnke, Nature Ridge Elementary, Bartlett, IL

WORD WHEELS
Onsets and rimes

Put a spin on word families with this center activity! Divide a tagboard circle into four sections and program each section with one of the rimes shown. Laminate the circle for durability and cut it out. Also label a supply of wooden clothespins with the onsets shown. Place the circles and clothespins at a center. To use the center, a child selects a rime to practice. Then she tries each onset with that rime. She clips on the wheel the onsets that make words and then reads aloud each word from the resulting word family. Finally, she removes the clothespins and repeats the process using a different rime.

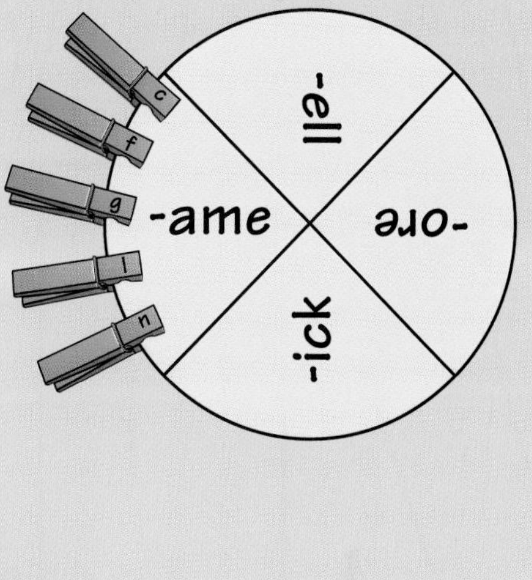

c
f
g
l
n
-ell
-ame
-ore
-ick

nice
BRICK BY BRICK
Start
-ail
-eat
-ay
-oke
-ice
m
n
h
p
s

BRICK BY BRICK
Long-vowel rimes

Use this ready-to-go game to build students' word family skills! First, copy page 134 and mount it on construction paper. Also copy the hexagonal spinner from page 133 onto construction paper. Color the gameboard. Store the spinner, two game markers, a paper clip, and a pencil in a resealable plastic bag. Place the gameboard and the bag at a center. Review with students how to use a paper clip and pencil to spin the spinner. Then have students visit the center in pairs and follow the directions on the gameboard to play the game.

APPLE ORCHARD
Forming word families

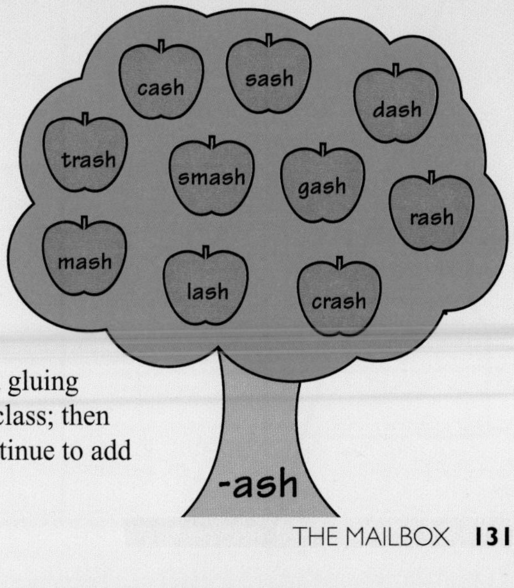

cash
sash
dash
trash
smash
gash
rash
mash
lash
crash
-ash

Branch out with a small-group activity that's a bushel of fun! Write on the board a list of onsets, including several blends and digraphs. Give each group of three or four students a supply of apple cutouts and a large tree cutout with a rime written on the trunk. Have the group form words by adding different onsets to its designated rime. Instruct team members to take turns writing the newly formed words on apple cutouts and gluing the cutouts to their tree. Invite each group to share its word family with the class; then post the groups' trees around the room, creating a word family orchard. Continue to add to the orchard as students learn new word families.

Full House

____ump	____ack	____est	____ock
____ock	____est	____ack	____ump
____ack	____ink	____ock	____est
____ink	____ock	____ump	____ink
____est	____ump	____ink	____ack

Note to the teacher: Use with "Full House" on page 130.

Circular Spinner

Use with "Full House" on page 130.

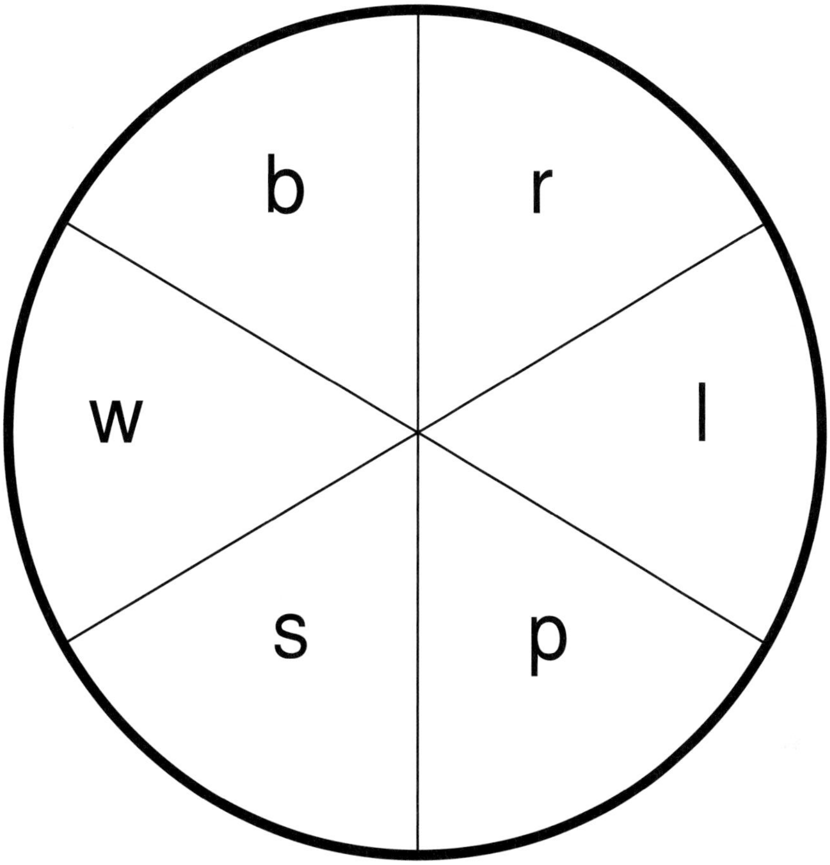
b
r
w
l
s
p

Hexagonal Spinner

Use with "Brick by Brick" on page 131.

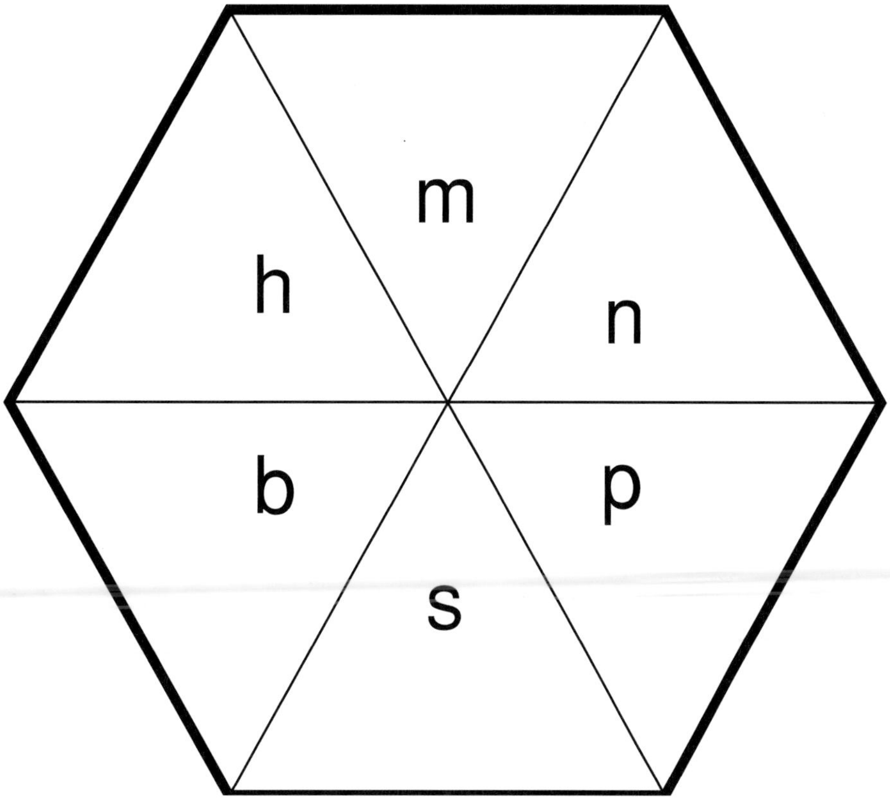
m
h
n
b
p
s

BRICK BY BRICK

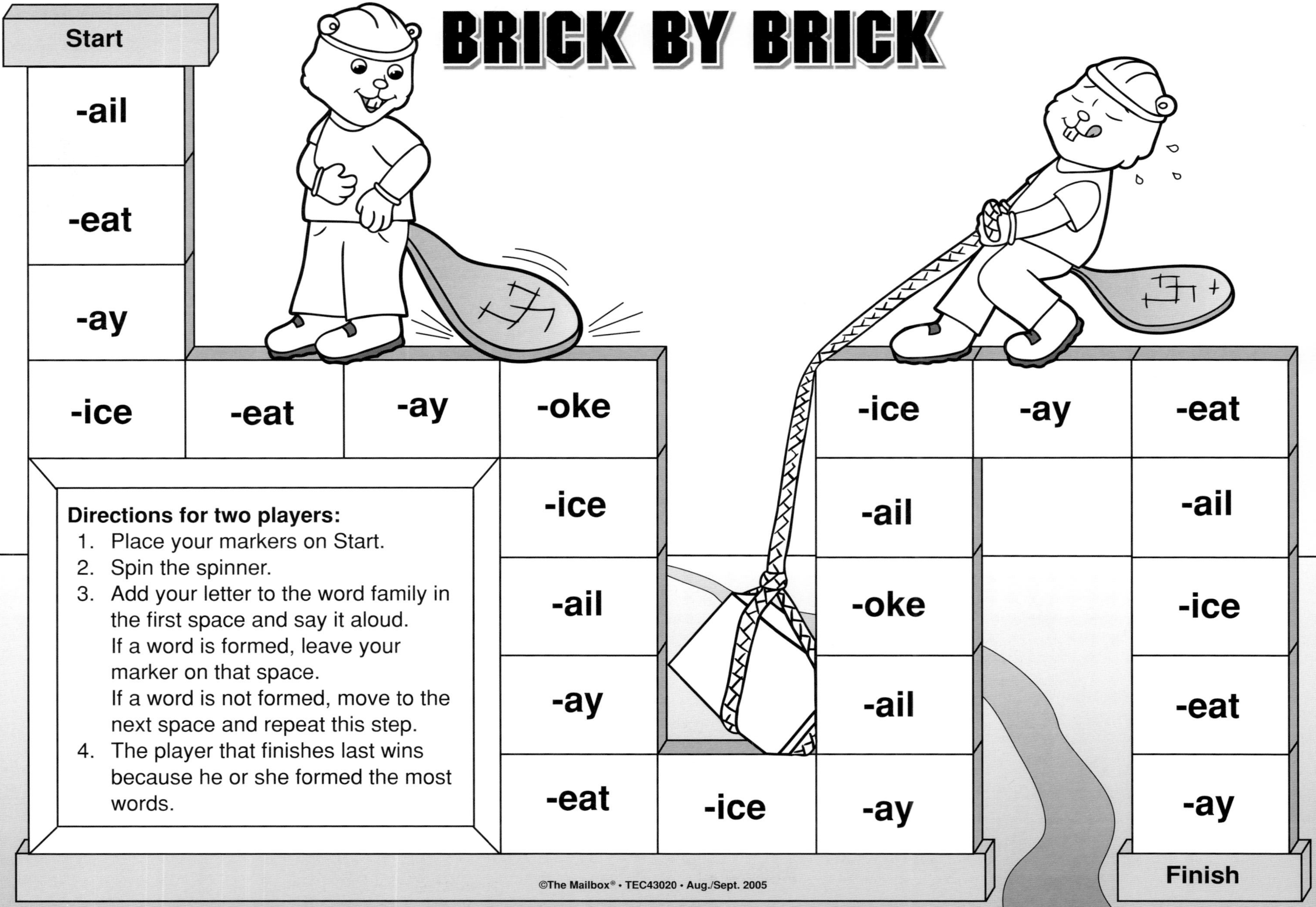
Start
-ail
-eat
-ay
-ice
-eat
-ay
-oke
-ice
-ail
-ay
-eat
-ice
-ay
-ail
-oke
-ail
-ice
-ay
-eat
-ail
-ice
-eat
-ay
Finish

Directions for two players:

1. Place your markers on Start.
2. Spin the spinner.
3. Add your letter to the word family in the first space and say it aloud.
   If a word is formed, leave your marker on that space.
   If a word is not formed, move to the next space and repeat this step.
4. The player that finishes last wins because he or she formed the most words.

Note to the teacher: Use with "Brick by Brick" on page 131.

Order Up!

A Serving of Sentence Skills

He
an
is
ie

SALAD SORT
Word order

Students improve their sentence skills at this center! In advance, write several sentences, each on a different-colored sentence strip. (If desired, use colors found in a salad, such as green, red, or orange.) Cut each strip, leaving one word on each piece. Toss the pieces into a plastic bowl and place it at a center along with paper and pencils. First, a student sorts the pieces by color. Next, he chooses a set of color cards and arranges them to form a complete sentence. He repeats the process for each remaining set of cards. Then he writes the sentences he formed on a sheet of paper and returns the cards to the bowl.

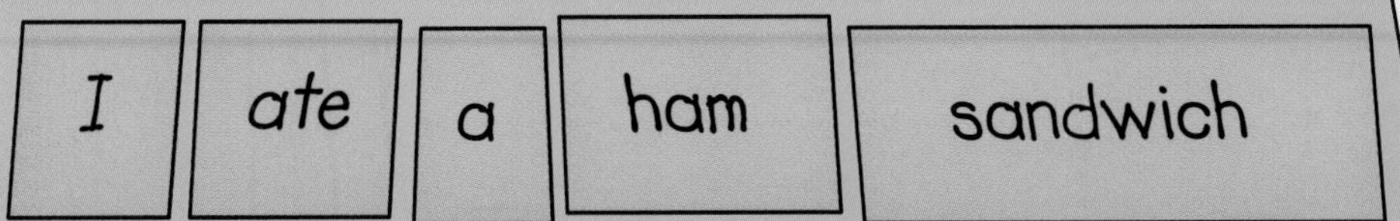
I
ate
a
ham
sandwich

This menu offers a variety of sentence skill activities that will please any palate!

with ideas by David Green, North Shore Country Day School, Winnetka, IL

WHAT'S COOKIN'?
Identifying types of sentences

Recognizing questions, statements, commands, and exclamations is the object of this whole-class game! Write on the board each sentence type and its ending punctuation. Also list movements to correspond with the ending punctuation (see the examples shown) and introduce each movement to the class. Then read a sentence aloud. Have students decide the sentence type and make the appropriate motion. Repeat the process, varying the sentence type each time.

statement—stirring the soup
command—putting the lid on a pot
question—icing the cake
exclamation—reaching for something on the top shelf

SENTENCE SENSE
Creating sentences with meaning

Cook up some fun with this small-group game! Before the activity, create a word bank for each of the following parts of speech: noun, verb, and adjective. Write each word bank on a separate sheet of chart paper and in a different color. Post the lists in the classroom. Begin the activity by dividing students into groups of three or four. Instruct each group to choose two nouns, one verb, and one adjective from the list. Then have the group write a sentence using the chosen words and othr words needed to form a complete sentence. Remind groups that their sentences may be silly, but they must have meaning. Continue having students serve up sentences in this manner for as long as desired.

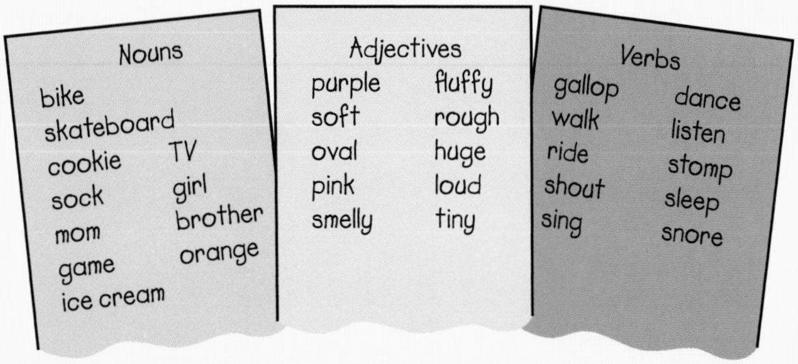
Nouns
bike
skateboard
cookie
TV
sock
girl
mom
brother
game
orange
ice cream
Adjectives
purple
fluffy
soft
rough
oval
huge
pink
loud
smelly
tiny
Verbs
gallop
dance
walk
listen
ride
stomp
shout
sleep
sing
snore

ONE OF EACH
Writing the four types of sentences

All that students need to practice writing questions, statements, commands, and exclamations is a sheet of paper and a few simple hand movements! Have each child fold a sheet of paper in half twice, creating four sections. Next, instruct the student to write one of the four types of sentences in each section. Then invite students to share their projects with the class. After a child finishes reading a sentence, have the remaining students use the hand gestures from "What's Cookin'?" to identify the sentence type.

Clean up your room.
Did you go to the park yesterday?
We won the game!
I like chocolate ice cream.

Name____

As Easy As Pie

Read each group of words.
Circle each sentence.

1. I am going to make a pie.
2. First, I will mix in the
3. Next, I will crack the eggs in a bowl.
4. some flour.
5. Now I will stir the filling.
6. on the oven.
7. I need to let the pie
8. Now I must cut the pie into slices.

Look at each group of words that is not circled. Add an end mark (if needed) and words to make a sentence. Write your new sentences on the lines below.

A. ____

B. ____

C. ____

D. ____

Name ______________________

Lunchtime!

Circle each run-on sentence.

1. We went to the diner for lunch.
2. Ollie was our waitress she took our order.
3. I ordered chili it looked good.
4. Steve wanted a hot dog.
5. He asked for mustard and relish.
6. We both ordered fries.
7. Steve wanted soda I asked for water.
8. Ollie brought our food to the table it was hot.
9. Our orders looked yummy.
10. I ate quickly Steve ate fast too.
11. Then we had apple pie.
12. That was the best meal I ever had!

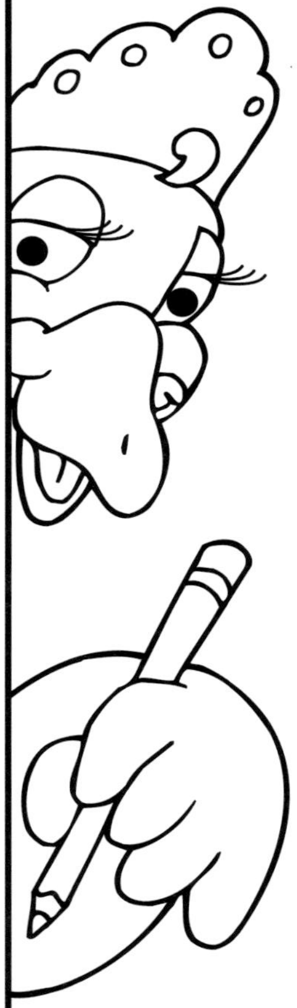

Add an end mark and a capital letter (if needed) to each run-on sentence to make two sentences.

A. ______________________

____

B. ______________________

____

C. ______________________

____

D. ______________________

____

E. ______________________

____

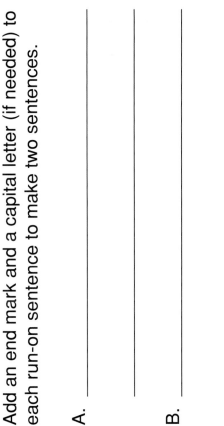

Name ____________________

Sentence Scramble

Write each group of words in an order that makes sense.
Use capital letters and end marks.

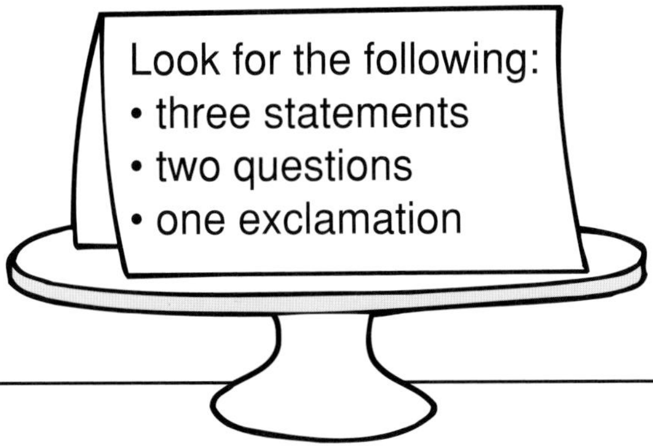
Look for the following:
• three statements
• two questions
• one exclamation

1. get did sandwich a you

   ____

2. burgers I three ate

   ____

3. the good here are fries

   ____

4. she dessert did order what for

   ____

5. like the I cake better

   ____

6. great meal was our

   ____

To the Rescue!

Activities to Use With Any Spelling List

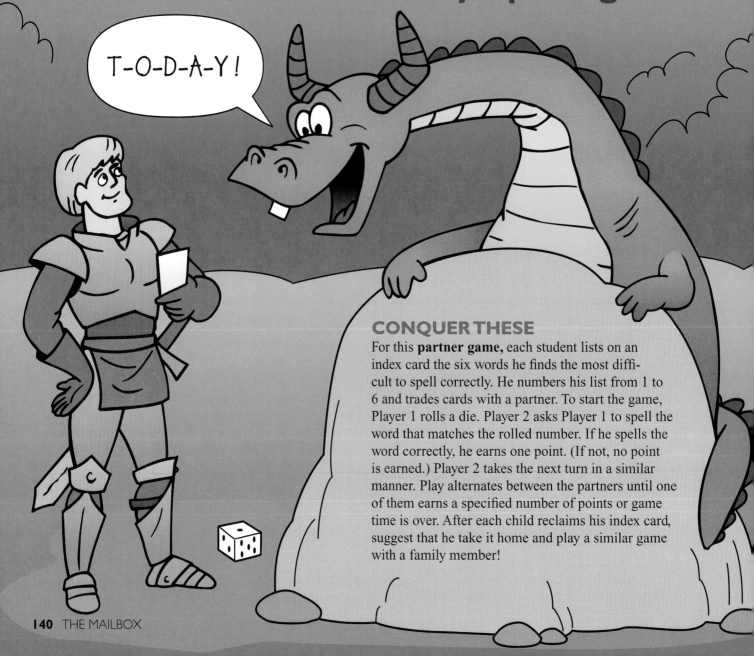

T-O-D-A-Y!

CONQUER THESE

For this **partner game,** each student lists on an index card the six words he finds the most difficult to spell correctly. He numbers his list from 1 to 6 and trades cards with a partner. To start the game, Player 1 rolls a die. Player 2 asks Player 1 to spell the word that matches the rolled number. If he spells the word correctly, he earns one point. (If not, no point is earned.) Player 2 takes the next turn in a similar manner. Play alternates between the partners until one of them earns a specified number of points or game time is over. After each child reclaims his index card, suggest that he take it home and play a similar game with a family member!

Welcome to Spell-a-lot, a place where shining examples of spelling reinforcement are waiting to save the day!

with ideas by Stacie Stone Davis, Lima, NY

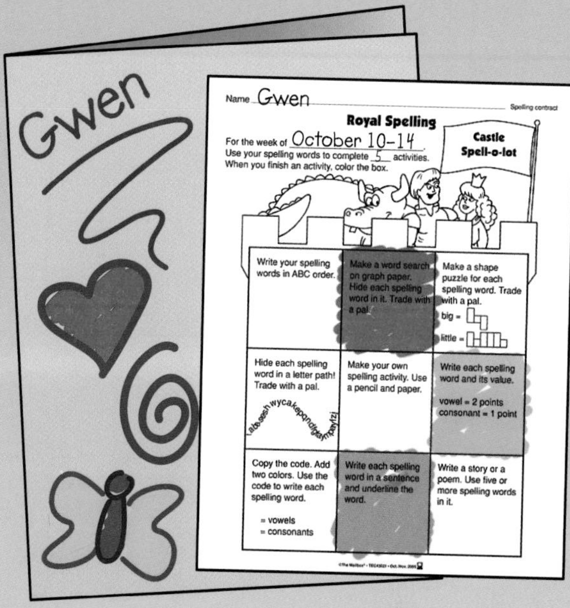

Gwen
Name Gwen
Spelling contract
Royal Spelling
For the week of October 10–14
Use your spelling words to complete 5 activities.
When you finish an activity, color the box.
Castle Spell-a-lot
Write your spelling words in ABC order.
Make a word search on graph paper. Hide each spelling word in it. Trade with a pal.
Make a shape puzzle for each spelling word. Trade with a pal.
Hide each spelling word in a letter path! Trade with a pal.
Make your own spelling activity. Use a pencil and paper.
Write each spelling word and its value.
vowel = 2 points
consonant = 1 point
Copy the code. Add two colors. Use the code to write each spelling word.
= vowels
= consonants
Write each spelling word in a sentence and underline the word.
Write a story or a poem. Use five or more spelling words in it.

ROYAL CHOICES

The pick-and-choose format of the **weekly spelling contract** on page 143 will make your spellers feel like royalty. To use, simply program a copy of the contract with the dates of the current week and the number of activities each child must complete. Then hand out student copies. If desired, have each child fold in half a large sheet of construction paper to serve as a spelling folder. Students can personalize the outside of the folders and store their weekly spelling contracts and completed spelling assignments inside.

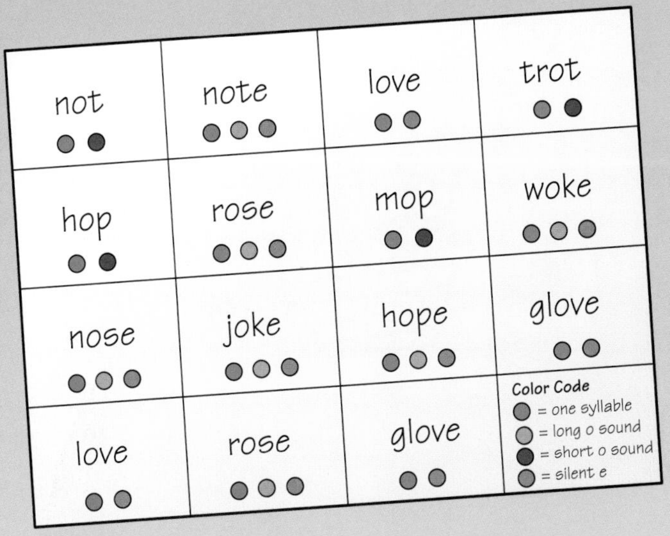

not
note
love
trot
hop
rose
mop
woke
nose
joke
hope
glove
love
rose
glove
Color Code
= one syllable
= long o sound
= short o sound
= silent e

DOT IT

Students can complete this **independent activity** numerous times with varying results. To make a 16-box grid like the one shown, have each child fold a sheet of blank paper in half four times, creasing each fold line. Next, have her unfold the paper and program one box with a desired dot code. (See the illustration for a sample code.) To complete the activity, a student writes a spelling word in each empty grid box, repeating spelling words as needed. Then she applies the code to each spelling word and colors in her results.

hot
h/click/t!

LETTER BY LETTER

Different auditory clues keep this **group activity** lively! Assign a sound such as a click, clap, or snap to replace all the vowels in oral spellings. For example, a child might click once; say, *"b;"* click twice; and say, *"t"* for *about* or click twice and say, *"c-h"* for *ouch.* Lead the class through several oral spellings while reinforcing similarities and differences in various spelling patterns. Change the auditory clues as often as desired. Encourage students to practice the technique when they study spelling words independently and with partners.

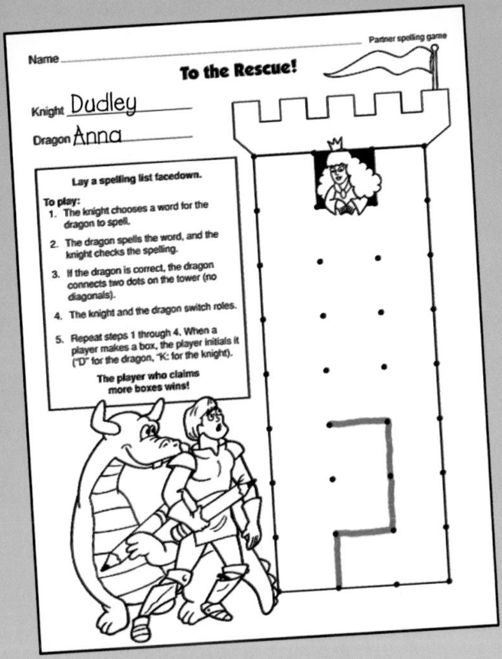

Name ______ Partner spelling game

To the Rescue!

Knight Dudley

Dragon Anna

Lay a spelling list facedown.

To play:

1. The knight chooses a word for the dragon to spell.
2. The dragon spells the word, and the knight checks the spelling.
3. If the dragon is correct, the dragon connects two dots on the tower (no diagonals).
4. The knight and the dragon switch roles.
5. Repeat steps 1 through 4. When a player makes a box, the player initials it ("D" for the dragon, "K: for the knight).

The player who claims more boxes wins!

SAVE THE DAY

Delivering this **game for two** does not require heroic measures! In fact, all you have to do is keep a supply of page 144 on hand. Your students will handle the rest!

hour
hour hour
hour hour hour
hour hour hour hour
hour hour hour
hour hour
hour
Kevin

SHAPING UP

This **independent activity** is great practice for words students are having trouble spelling correctly. Precut light-colored construction paper into a variety of geometric shapes. A student chooses a cutout and a tough-to-spell word. He repeatedly writes the spelling word on the cutout. When he finishes, he glues the labeled cutout onto white construction paper. Then he illustrates on the paper a scene or object that incorporates his programmed cutout. Invite students to repeat the activity as often as desired.

D!

DESKTOP SPELLERS

Begin this **large-group game** with every student sitting on her desk. Choose a student to begin and establish a sequence of play. Then say a spelling word. The first player says the first letter of the word, the second player says the second letter of the word, and so on until the word is spelled correctly. If a student gives an incorrect letter, she moves to her chair and the next player tries to give the correct one. A player who is seated continues to play and may return to her desktop once she supplies a correct letter.

Royal Spelling

For the week of ____________________.
Use your spelling words to complete ____ activities.
When you finish an activity, color the box.

Castle
Spell-a-lot

Write your spelling words in ABC order.	Make a word search on graph paper. Hide each spelling word in it. Trade with a pal.	Make a shape puzzle for each spelling word. Trade with a pal. big = little =
Hide each spelling word in a letter path! Trade with a pal. tabosesh wycakepqndtglaymmpayfzj	Make your own spelling activity. Use a pencil and paper.	Write each spelling word and its value. vowel = 2 points consonant = 1 point
Copy the code. Add two colors. Use the code to write each spelling word. = vowels = consonants	Write each spelling word in a sentence and underline the word.	Write a story or a poem. Use five or more spelling words in it.

Note to the teacher: Use with “Royal Choices” on page 141.

Name ____________________ Partner spelling game

To the Rescue!

Knight ____________________

Dragon ____________________

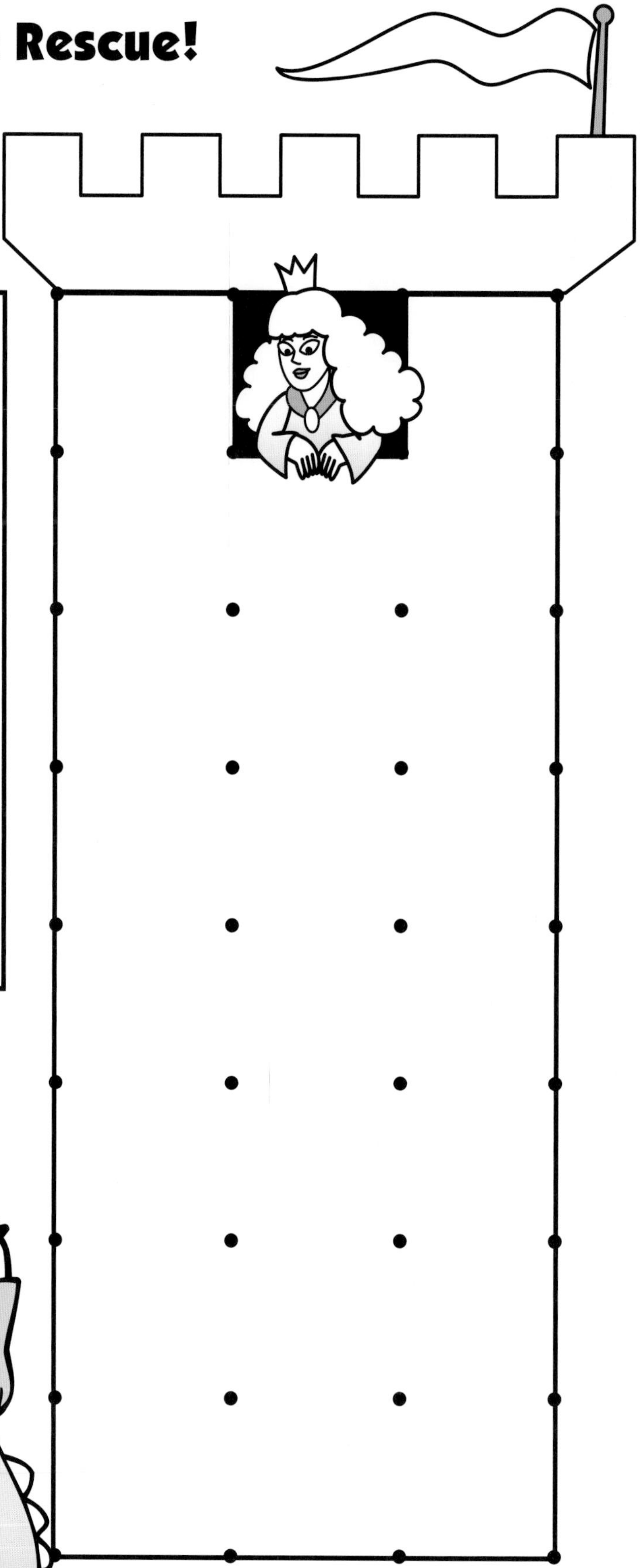

Lay a spelling list facedown.

To play:

1. The knight chooses a word for the dragon to spell.
2. The dragon spells the word, and the knight checks the spelling.
3. If the dragon is correct, the dragon connects two dots on the tower (no diagonals).
4. The knight and the dragon switch roles.
5. Repeat Steps 1 through 4. When a player makes a box, the player initials it ("D" for the dragon, "K" for the knight).

The player who claims more boxes wins!

 Note to the teacher: Use with "Save the Day" on page 142.

Aha!

Monitoring and Repairing Comprehension

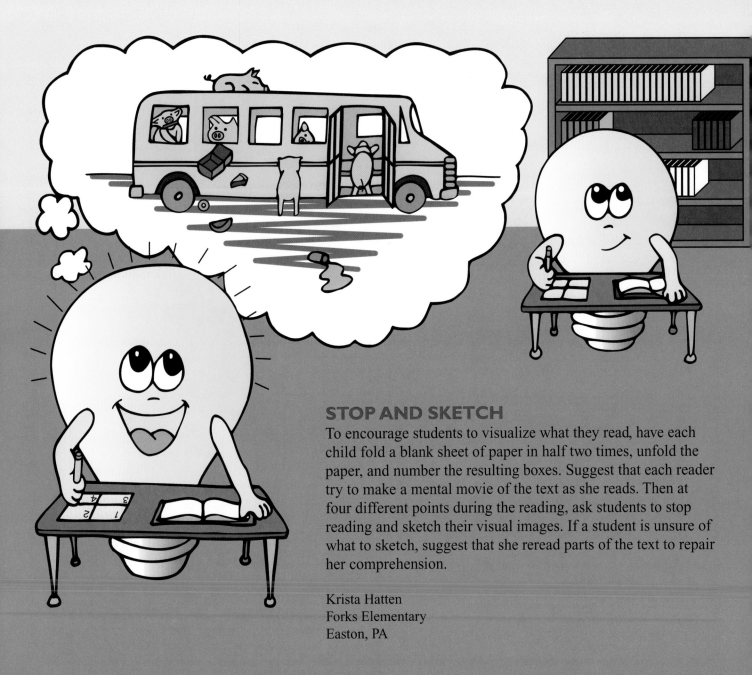

STOP AND SKETCH

To encourage students to visualize what they read, have each child fold a blank sheet of paper in half two times, unfold the paper, and number the resulting boxes. Suggest that each reader try to make a mental movie of the text as she reads. Then at four different points during the reading, ask students to stop reading and sketch their visual images. If a student is unsure of what to sketch, suggest that she reread parts of the text to repair her comprehension.

Krista Hatten
Forks Elementary
Easton, PA

Check out these bright ideas that help students bring meaning to their reading!

I think the cat knocked over the lamp!

TALK IT OUT

When students are engaged in guided reading or listening to a read-aloud, remember to stop and talk about the text. Ask volunteers to summarize what has happened, offer opinions about why something happened, or predict what could happen next. Encourage students to ask questions too.

Barclay Marcell
Theodore Roosevelt Elementary
Park Ridge, IL

STICK WITH IT

This coding technique works well with independent readers. Keep students supplied with small sticky notes. When a child becomes confused by his reading text, he labels a note with a question mark and places it at the point where he became confused. Next, he rereads or reads on for clarity. At the point where his confusion is cleared, he attaches a second sticky note labeled with an exclamation point. Ask students to leave the coding in place until their reading is complete, giving you another opportunity to assess comprehension.

?
!

STAY FOCUSED

To help students stay mentally engaged in their reading, promote the practice of "Read a page; check your gauge." For an additional reminder, give each child a copy of the bookmark below to color, cut out, and use.

Barclay Marcell

Read a Page;
✓ Your Gauge!
Read-o-meter
I can picture in my mind what has happened.
I understand what has happened.
I am wondering what will happen next!
©The Mailbox® • TEC43021 • Oct./Nov. 2005

Gliding Along

Ideas for Developing Fluid Readers

LET'S PERFORM!

Reading with appropriate pace and inflection

Put the spotlight on fluency with this readers' theater activity! Prepare by writing both versions of the poem below on separate sheets of chart paper; then post the poems in the classroom. First, read each version aloud to students on your own; then have the class read both poems chorally. Ask students whether the two poems are exactly the same and discuss their responses. Next, divide the class into four groups and give each group one of the poem cards on pages 150 and 151. Provide time for the group to practice reading its poem. Then have the group perform it for the class. Afterward, discuss with students how the poems sounded different even though they contained the same words. Guide students to see that the punctuation was different in each poem and that it affected how the poem was read.

The Monkey
My, oh my.
What do I see?
I see a huge monkey
Climbing up a tree!
Will he fall?
Oops, oops!
There he goes.
Get out of the way!
This monkey's not having a
very good day!
The Monkey
My, oh my!
What do I see?
I see a huge monkey
Climbing up a tree.
Will he fall?
Oops, oops.
There he goes!
Get out of the way.
This monkey's not having a
very good day.

Don't be afraid to step out on the ice! This unit provides plenty of support for readers!

with ideas by Jennifer Kohnke, Nature Ridge Elementary, Bartlett, IL,
and Stacie Wright, Millington School, Millington, NJ

READING SIGNALS

Using punctuation to guide fluency

Help students remember to pause for commas and stop for periods! Make a copy of the circles on page 152 for each child. Have the child color the "Stop" circle red and the "Pause" circle yellow. Next, he glues the circles together, sandwiching a craft stick between them. Then, as a class, chorally read a short passage. While reading, each student holds up his yellow circle when he reaches a comma and his red circle when he comes to a period. Continue to have students use their reading signals during reading to improve fluency.

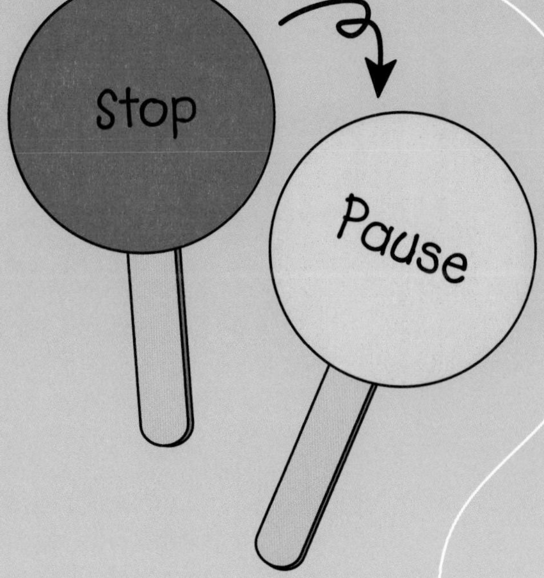
Stop
Pause

When did your soccer game start?

PUNCTUATION CARDS

Recognizing appropriate inflection

To prepare this partner game, label a supply of index cards with sentences, questions, and exclamations, writing each one on a separate card. Also label three additional cards with a period, a question mark, and an exclamation point. To play the game, give one child the sentence cards and the other partner the punctuation cards. Player 1 reads a sentence aloud with the correct inflection. Player 2 holds up the matching punctuation card, based on the inflection he heard. Play continues in this manner for as long as desired, with players periodically switching roles.

?

RHYME TIME
Using rhyme

This small-group activity uses familiar nursery rhymes to increase fluency. Begin by reading aloud a few familiar nursery rhymes. Then have each group select a short nursery rhyme or a section of a rhyme. Have the group rewrite the rhyme, using different words but keeping the same rhythm. After finishing, have the group copy its new rhyme onto a sheet of chart paper. Provide time to practice reading it together; then invite each group to read it to the class. Finally, hang the poems around the room so students can read them for extra practice.

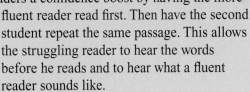

Old Johnny Brown
Had a big frown
Every single day.
Along came a clown,
Who tripped and fell down,
And made Johnny smile today.

READING FOCUS
Promoting fluency

Make partner reading more meaningful with this simple tip! After pairing students to read, have each twosome sit side by side and shoulder to shoulder, facing opposite directions. This helps keep students on task since the reader's mouth is always close to the listener's ear. Also, give struggling readers a confidence boost by having the more fluent reader read first. Then have the second student repeat the same passage. This allows the struggling reader to hear the words before he reads and to hear what a fluent reader sounds like.

Stacy Shumate, Eastside Elementary, Cabot, AR

Poem Cards

Use with "Let's Perform!" on page 147.

The Bear

Look over there,
In the green, fuzzy bush.
Is that a bear?
He has big claws and an awful stare.
Oh no, he's coming this way!
He doesn't look happy.
This isn't our day.

TEC43022

The Bear

Look over there,
In the green, fuzzy bush!
Is that a bear?
He has BIG claws and an awful stare!
Oh, no! He's coming this way.
He doesn't look happy.
This isn't our day!

TEC43022

The Fish

Splish, splash!
The fish swims all day.
Up and down the river,
Trying to find his way.
Where is his home?
Maybe he's lost,
Or maybe he likes swimming alone.

TEC43022

The Fish

Splish, splash,
The fish swims all day!
Up and down the river,
Trying to find his way.
Where is his home?
Maybe he's lost?
Or maybe he likes swimming alone!

Use with "Reading Signals" on page 148.

Be a Smooth Reader!

When you see...

.	Stop.
,	Wait a second.
?	Ask a question.
!	Show excitement.

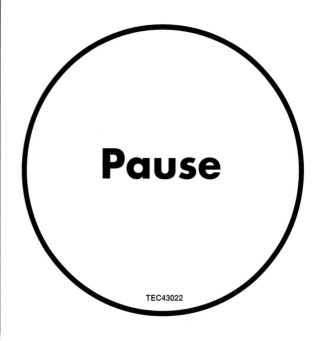

Stop

TEC43022

Pause

TEC43022

Note to the teacher: Make a class supply of the bookmark above and have each student decorate one. Encourage students to use it while reading to improve their fluency.

Aim and **Score!**

Game-Winning Verb Skills

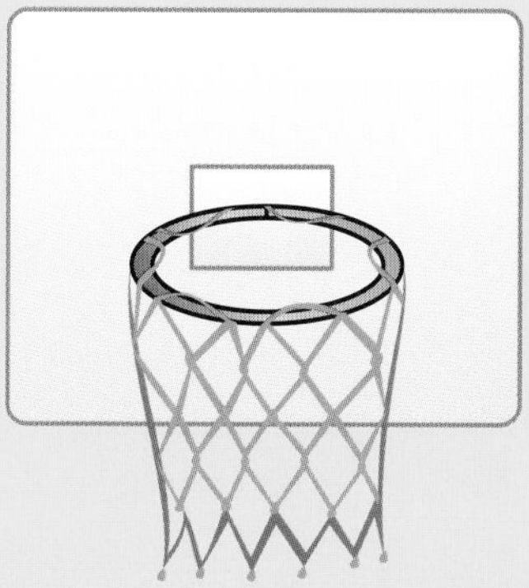

VERB LOTTO

Adding *-s* and *-es* to present-tense verbs, subject-verb agreement

This fast-paced whole-class game combines fun and practice! To prepare, write on a transparency the sentences shown. Have each child fold a sheet of paper in half four times, creasing each fold line. Next, he unfolds the paper and labels each space with "s" or "es" as desired. Begin the game by placing the transparency on the overhead, keeping the sentences covered. Designate a method to determine the winner (four in a row, four corners, etc.). Then reveal a sentence. Each student decides whether *-s* or *-es* should be added to the underlined word to make it correct, and then he writes the word in a corresponding space. Play continues in this manner until a student calls out, "Lotto!" If his answers are correct, give him a small treat. If not, play continues. Continue playing as long as desired.

s
es
fish
es
s
s
take
s
love
s
get
es
es
es
s
es
es
s
es
s

She love to eat cake.
He fish every day.
She get to play outside every day.
Every Monday Sam take me to the park.
He push me on the swing.
Megan play with her sister.
She rush to get to school on time.
He score a goal.
Kate catch the ball.
My mom brush her hair.

When it comes to verb tenses, these ideas are nothin' but net!

with ideas by Stacie Stone Davis, Lima, NY

TENSE SENSE

Past, present, and future tenses

In advance, stock a center with a supply of index cards and pencils. Each student visits the center and writes on separate cards three versions of the same sentence in the past, the present, and the future tense. Then collect the cards and teach students the hand motions shown. Read one card aloud and have students show the verb tense by making the corresponding hand motion. After repeating the activity several times, give each child a card, making sure that the other two matching sentences are distributed. Have the student find the two classmates with matching cards. Then have the threesome arrange themselves in past, present, and future tense.

Past:
Present:
Future:

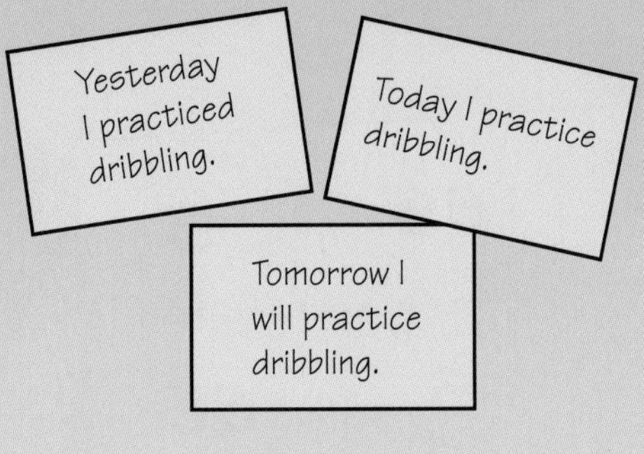
Yesterday I practiced dribbling.
Today I practice dribbling.
Tomorrow I will practice dribbling.

WHAT A WEEKEND!

Using past-tense verbs in writing

Dear Lucy,
I had a great weekend! On Saturday I went to the game. My mom bought me a t-shirt. My favorite player signed it. Then we got some pizza. On Sunday we went ice-skating. My dad fell twice! He looked really funny! Then we drove home. This weekend was great!

Your friend,
Meredith

Before the activity, write a short letter about a recent weekend on a sheet of chart paper, writing all verbs in the past tense. Post the letter and read it aloud. Ask student volunteers to identify and circle the verbs in the letter. Point out that the circled verbs show that the action took place in the past. Then have each child write a letter to a classmate about her weekend. Remind her to use verbs in the past tense. Finally, invite students to share their completed letters with the class.

Name ____

Verbs
Present tense, subject-verb agreement

Slam Dunk!

Find the verb that completes the sentence.
Circle its matching letter.

1. Henry ____ for the Hula Hippos basketball team.	L. play	Y. plays
2. The players ____ each day.	S. practice	M. practices
3. Henry _____ to dribble the ball.	R. like	F. likes
4. Two players ____ to catch a pass.	A. rush	W. rushes
5. Henry _____ it and shoots it.	E. catch	N. catches
6. The fans _____ for the team.	T. clap	O. claps
7. The players ______.	E. cheer	N. cheers
8. Henry's team _____ the game!	M. win	R. wins

How do the players stay cool during a game?
To solve the riddle, match each circled letter to a number below.

They ___ ___ ___ ___
(2) (6) (4) (1)

___ ___ ___ ___ the ___ ___ ___ ___!
(5) (7) (4) (8) (3) (4) (5) (2)

Name ____________________

At the Game

Circle the main verb or verb phrase in each sentence.
Check a box to show the verb tense.

	Past	Present	Future
1. I went to the Bears game.			
2. I bought a program when I got there.			
3. Then I found my seat.			
4. I see my favorite player over there!			
5. I will try to get his autograph.			
6. I run to talk to him.			
7. Then the game begins.			
8. I watch the players make their shots.			
9. Our team won the game!			
10. I will go to another game soon!			

4 Past Tense
4 Present Tense
2 Future Tense

Take Heart

Learning About Commas and Their Uses

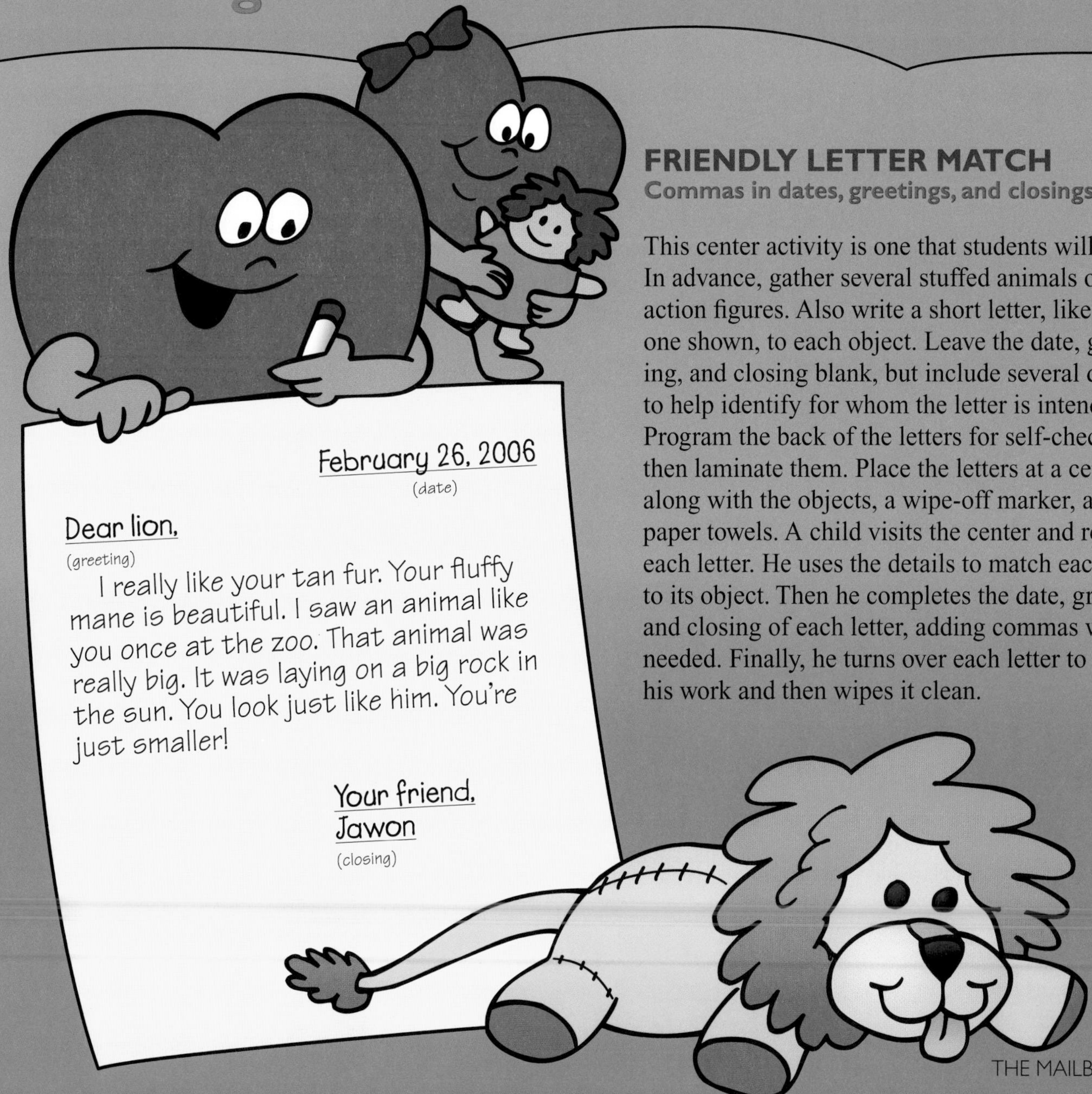
February 26, 2006
(date)
Dear lion,
(greeting)
I really like your tan fur. Your fluffy mane is beautiful. I saw an animal like you once at the zoo. That animal was really big. It was laying on a big rock in the sun. You look just like him. You're just smaller!
Your friend,
Jawon
(closing)

FRIENDLY LETTER MATCH

Commas in dates, greetings, and closings

This center activity is one that students will love! In advance, gather several stuffed animals or action figures. Also write a short letter, like the one shown, to each object. Leave the date, greeting, and closing blank, but include several details to help identify for whom the letter is intended. Program the back of the letters for self-checking; then laminate them. Place the letters at a center along with the objects, a wipe-off marker, and paper towels. A child visits the center and reads each letter. He uses the details to match each letter to its object. Then he completes the date, greeting, and closing of each letter, adding commas where needed. Finally, he turns over each letter to check his work and then wipes it clean.

From centers to team activities, these ideas are ones your students will love!

with ideas by Jean Erickson, Grace Christian Academy, West Allis, WI

IT'S IN THE BASKET
Commas in a series

To create this center, make a class supply of the reproducible at the top of page 159. Also gather three of each of the following items and store them in a basket: stuffed animals and red, round, soft, and flat objects. Place the basket and the reproducibles at a center. A child uses the items in the basket to fill in the blanks. Then she inserts commas where they are needed to complete the page.

Name Janie
Commas
Items in a series
A Basketful of Commas
Use items from the basket to complete each sentence.
Add commas where needed.
1. marble, ball, and orange are all round.
2. candy, apple, and pencil are all red.
3. and are all flat.
4. and are all animals.
5. and are all soft.

City comma
state—learning
this is really
great!
TEXAS
Dallas
El Paso
Austin
Houston
San
Antonio

MAP GAME
Using commas to separate a city and state

With the help of a rhyme and a map, learning this skill is a snap! Post a map of your state. Next, write on the board the rhyme shown and teach it to your class. Then divide students into two teams. To play, each team's Player 1 looks on the map and chooses a city. They each write the name of the city and the state, repeat the rhyme, and add a comma where it is needed. Then they consult with their teams to check their answers. When both players are finished, check their work. Award a point for each correct answer. Continue playing in this manner until time is up or one team earns a predetermined number of points.

MAGIC BEANS
Adding missing commas

Use this activity to wrap up your unit and practice a variety of comma skills! Write on several sentence strips a variety of sentences or phrases with missing commas like the ones shown. Place the strips at a center along with a handful of dried beans, paper, and pencils. A child selects a sentence strip, reads it, and uses the beans to add commas where needed. Then he copies the correctly punctuated sentence onto a sheet of paper. He repeats the process for as long as desired.

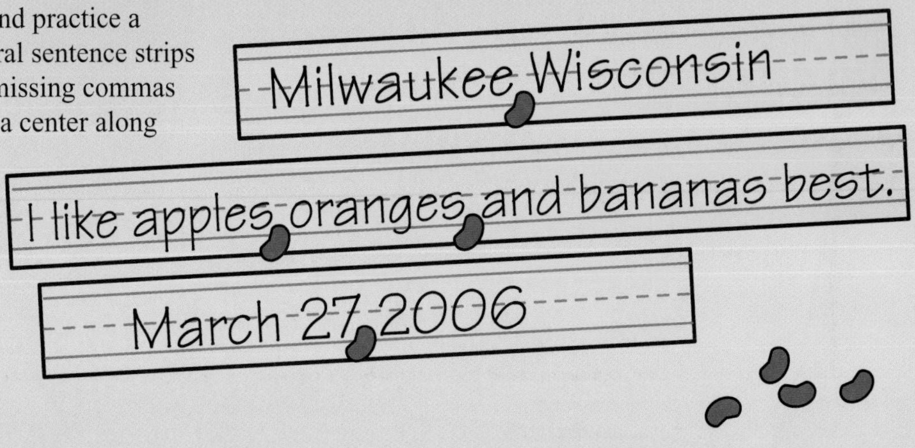
Milwaukee Wisconsin
I like apples oranges and bananas best.
March 27 2006

Name ____

A Basketful of Commas

Use items from the basket to complete each sentence.
Add commas where needed.

1. ____________ ____________ and ____________ are all round.

2. ____________ ____________ and ____________ are all red.

3. ____________ ____________ and ____________ are all flat.

4. ____________ ____________ and ____________ are all animals.

5. ____________ ____________ and ____________ are all soft.

Note to the teacher: Use with "It's in the Basket" on page 158.

Center Card

Add commas where needed.

March 23 2006

Dear Van

I'm having a great time here in Orlando Florida! I have been fishing shopping and eating lots of good food. I wish you were here! I'll see you soon!

Your friend
Vinnie

Note to the teacher: Copy and color this card. Cut out the card and laminate it. Place the card and a wipe-off marker at the center for extra practice.

Name ______________________________

Heartfelt Letters

Underline the city name with a blue crayon.
Underline the state name with a yellow crayon.
Add commas where needed.

1. I'm on my way to Orlando Florida.
2. My friend Val is going to Los Angeles California.
3. Vinnie is being sent to Honolulu Hawaii.
4. Vera is being mailed to New York New York.
5. Vickie is going to Myrtle Beach South Carolina.
6. Van will arrive in Chicago Illinois.
7. Vern is being mailed to Dallas Texas.
8. Vanna is flying to Nome Alaska.
9. Vic is going to Tucson Arizona.
10. Vita is taking a train to Denver Colorado.

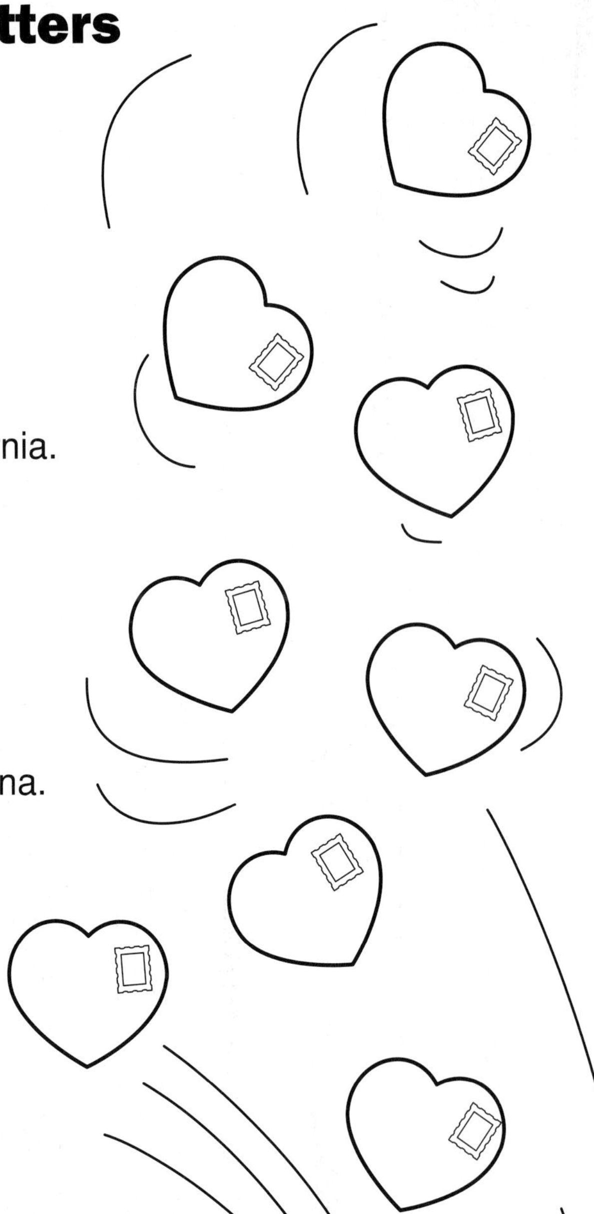

On the Trail
Investigating Expository Writing

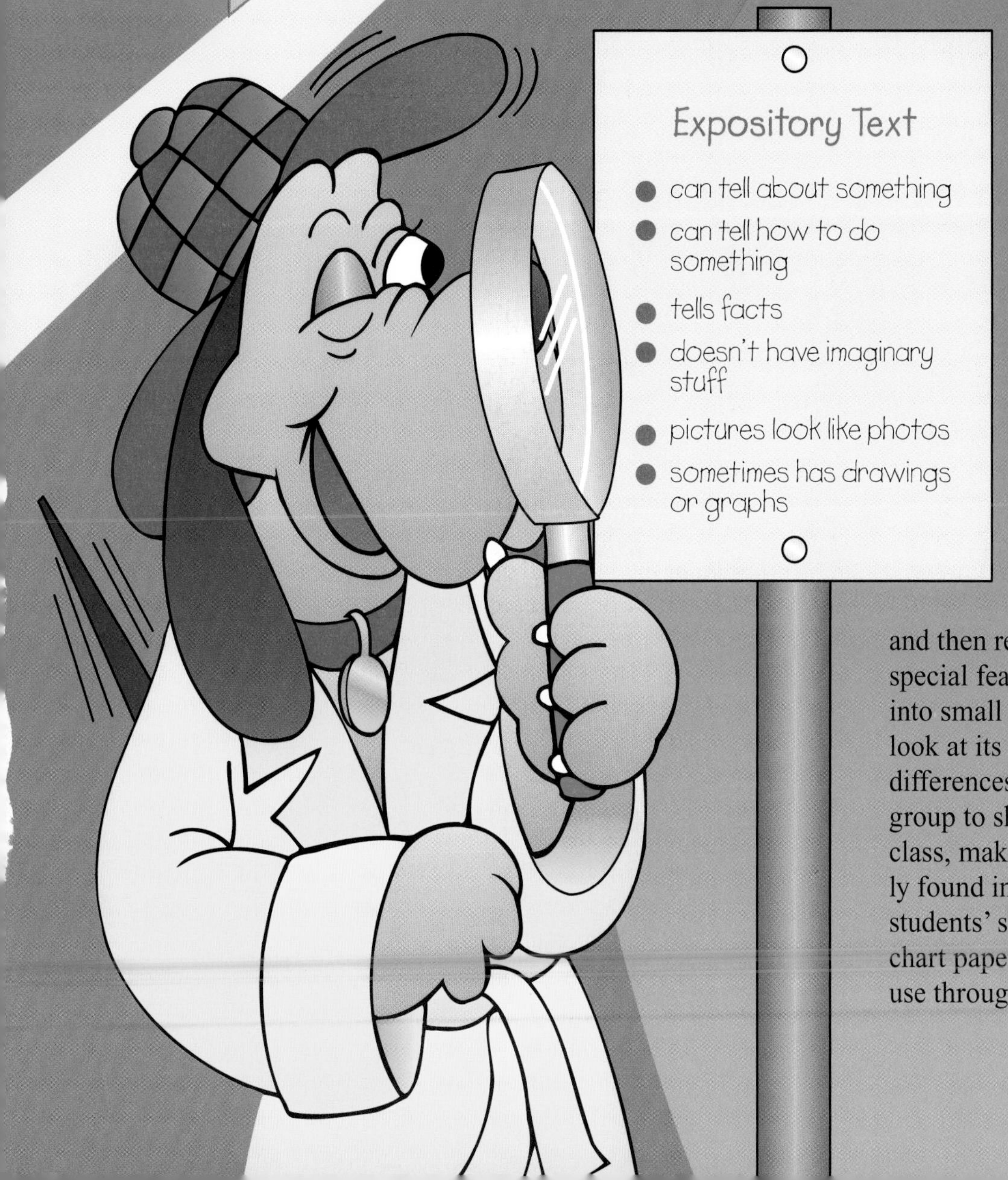
Expository Text
can tell about something
can tell how to do something
tells facts
doesn't have imaginary stuff
pictures look like photos
sometimes has drawings or graphs

STUDYING SAMPLES
Identifying features of expository writing

Shed some light on expository writing with this whole-class idea! In advance, gather from magazines, textbooks, and newspapers a supply of expository text samples that are on your students' reading levels. Begin by giving each child a sample. Instruct the student to look over and then read the sample, noting its special features. Then divide students into small groups. Have each group look at its samples for similarities and differences. Afterward, invite each group to share its findings. Then, as a class, make a list of features commonly found in expository text, recording students' suggestions on a sheet of chart paper. Post the list for students to use throughout the writing unit.

Searching for super expository-writing ideas? We've got just what you're looking for! Case closed!

with ideas by Jennifer L. Kohnke, Nature Ridge Elementary, Bartlett, IL

PARTNER PARAGRAPHS

Interviewing, writing an expository paragraph

In advance, make a class supply of page 163. Begin by reviewing with students the parts of an expository paragraph: the topic or main idea sentence and the supporting details. Next, pair students and give each child a copy of the reproducible. To complete the activity, one child interviews his partner, using the questions on the sheet as a guide. After recording the responses, the students switch roles. Then each student uses his completed page to write an expository paragraph about his partner. Afterward, invite students to share their paragraphs with the class.

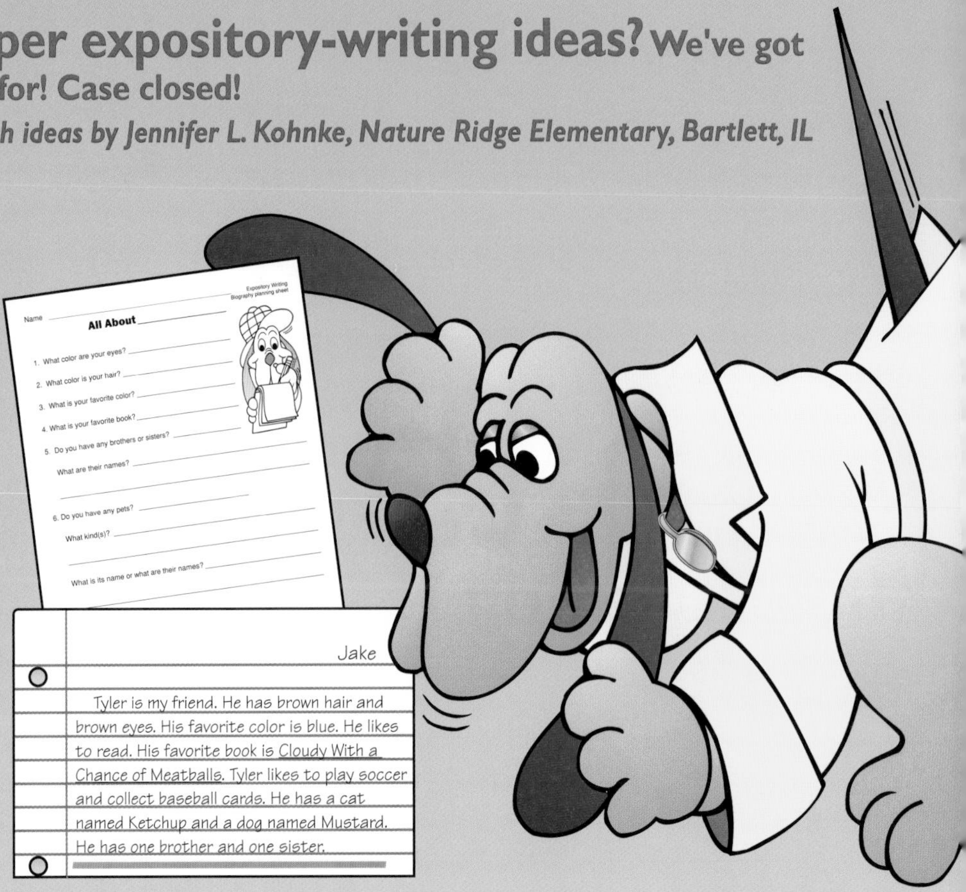
Expository Writing
Biography planning sheet
Name
All About
1. What color are your eyes?
2. What color is your hair?
3. What is your favorite color?
4. What is your favorite book?
5. Do you have any brothers or sisters?
What are their names?
6. Do you have any pets?
What kind(s)?
What is its name or what are their names?
Jake
Tyler is my friend. He has brown hair and brown eyes. His favorite color is blue. He likes to read. His favorite book is Cloudy With a Chance of Meatballs. Tyler likes to play soccer and collect baseball cards. He has a cat named Ketchup and a dog named Mustard. He has one brother and one sister.

FACT FILE

Taking notes

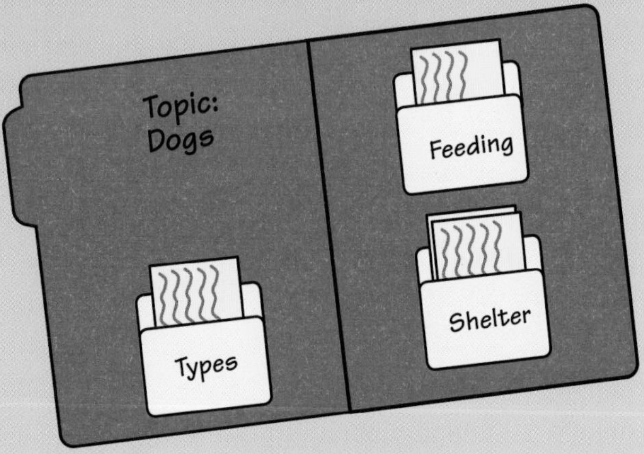
Topic: Dogs
Feeding
Types
Shelter

This unique approach to note taking helps students stay organized! After assigning a report topic, make a class supply of manila folders with several library pockets attached inside. Label each pocket with a subtopic. Give each child a folder along with a supply of index cards. Then, each time the student finds an important fact about his topic, have him rewrite it in his own words on an index card and file it in the corresponding pocket. After he has gathered the desired amount of information, he simply removes the cards from each pocket to write the paragraphs of his paper.

Laine Watts, Lincoln Elementary, St. Joseph, MI

WHAT'S GOING ON?

Descriptive writing

This simple activity helps students tune in to their senses. Begin by having each child create a chart like the one shown. Next, take the class to an area in the school, such as the playground or the library, where there are a variety of activities occurring. Have each student observe the area and record his thoughts in the corresponding sections of the chart. After a desired amount of time, return to the classroom and have each child use his observations to write a descriptive paragraph. Then post students' paragraphs and observation charts on a bulletin board titled "Our Observations."

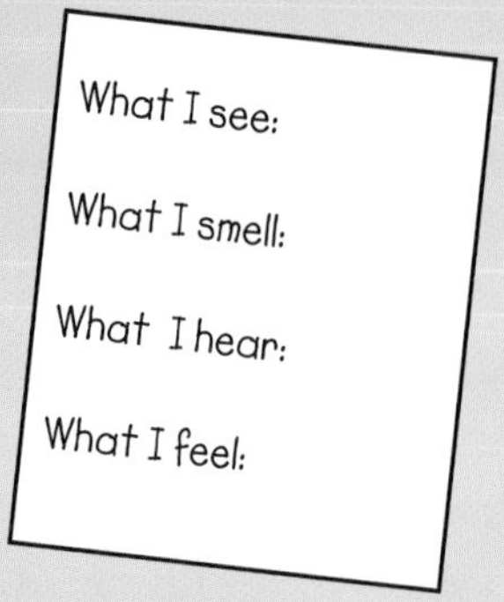
What I see:
What I smell:
What I hear:
What I feel:

Name ____________________

All About ____________

1. What color are your eyes? ____________

2. What color is your hair? ____________

3. What is your favorite color? ____________

4. What is your favorite book? ____________

5. Do you have any brothers or sisters? ____________

   What are their names? ____________

6. Do you have any pets? ____________

   What kind(s)? ____________

   What is its name or what are their names? ____________

7. What are your hobbies? ____________

Note to the teacher: Use with "Partner Paragraphs" on page 162.

Name ____________________ Expository Writing
Time-order words

Searching for Snacks

Cut.
Match each time-order word to a sentence.
Glue.

1. [ ] I looked in the closet because I thought I put them there.

2. [ ] I looked under the bed.

3. [ ] looking any longer, I asked my sister.

4. [ ] I asked my mom.

5. [ ] I asked my mom, I looked outside.

6. [ ] I found them in the yard!

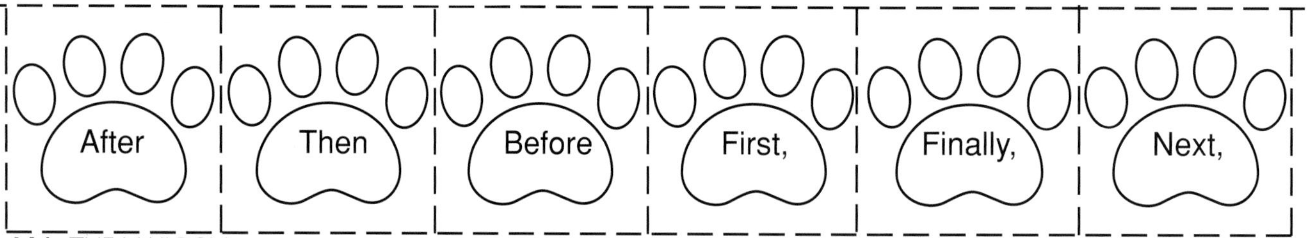
After
Then
Before
First,
Finally,
Next,

Taking Off!

High-Flying Literature Response Activities

My Father's Dragon
by Ruth Stiles Gannett
Zoo Exhibits
Tigers
Lion
Dragon
If this story took place at a zoo instead of on Wild Island, Elmer could get past the animals more easily. Also, he would have a place to throw away his tangerine peels.

A NEW VIEW
Creating a new setting

Get students to take a look at how time and place influence a story. Ask each child to change the setting of a favorite book and illustrate his idea on a 9" x 12" sheet of paper. Then have him glue the picture near the top of a 12" x 16" construction paper rectangle. In the space below the picture, have him write two or more ways the story would change because of its new setting. To complete the project, have each child cut from colorful construction paper two matching curtain shapes and a 1" x 12" rectangular curtain rod. After he decorates the cutouts as desired, help him staple them to the top of his project as shown. Before drawing this project to a close, invite students to share their work with the class. Then post the projects with the title "New Views on Books."

Merna Ahlemeyer
Crowders Creek Elementary, Clover, SC

Watch your brood soar **into understanding fiction with this pick-and-choose assortment of activities!**

with ideas by Jennifer Kohnke, Nature Ridge Elementary, Bartlett, IL

GETTING PERSONAL

Analyzing characters

Start this post-reading activity by challenging small groups of students to choose a recently read story and then describe the personality and actions of its main character. Have one member from each group list her group's ideas on chart paper. Post the lists and ask group members to share their work. Guide students to agree that good stories must have interesting characters. Next, have each child use construction paper scraps and the patterns on page 168 to make a character-related gumball machine. First, have her write the story title and character's name on a copy of the gumball machine and then color it. Then have her cut out both patterns and trace the gumball onto colorful paper several times. Ask her to cut out each gumball and label it with an interesting fact about the character, using the posted lists as a reference. Finally, have her glue the gumballs inside the machine.

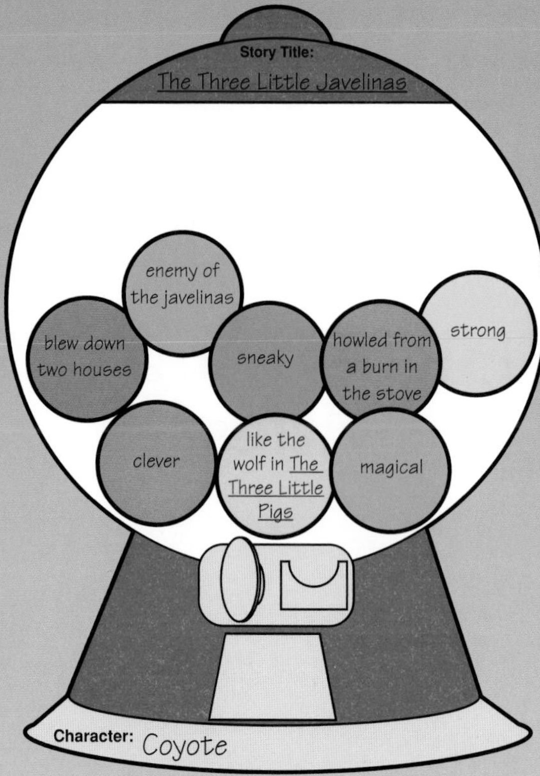
Story Title:
The Three Little Javelinas
enemy of the javelinas
blew down two houses
sneaky
howled from a burn in the stove
strong
clever
like the wolf in The Three Little Pigs
magical
Character: Coyote

Jack and Annie are on the plains in Africa and they see an animal coming from the trees. I predict the animal is an elephant. It wants to eat the peanut butter in Jack's backpack.

FICTION FORECASTERS

Making predictions

When students broadcast their thinking skills, everyone learns! During a read-aloud, stop at the end of selected chapters. Ask each child to use details from the text to predict what will happen next. While students record their predictions in literary response journals, take note of what they are writing. Then ask students with varying predictions to forecast upcoming story events. When you continue the read-aloud, revisit the predictions as appropriate. Be sure to alternate forecasters so that every child has a chance to share his ideas.

Stellaluna
Problem:
Stellaluna is hungry.
Solution:
She gets into a bird's nest and Mama Bird feeds her a grasshopper.
by Janell Cannon

BREEZY EXPLANATIONS
Problem and solution

For this kite-making project, each child needs four 4" x 4" squares in two different colors and an 8" x 8" paper square. Also give the student an 18-inch yarn length and five 12-inch yarn lengths. Begin by giving the class examples of problems and solutions from well-known books. Have each child choose a familiar book and identify in it one problem and its solution. The student positions one pair of cutouts to resemble diamond shapes. She writes the problem on one cutout and its solution on the other. Then she repeats the process, writing the book's title and author on the other pair of cutouts.

To make her kite, the student glues her programmed cutouts on the larger paper in the order shown, making sure that the colors alternate. She tapes the longer yarn length to the kite's back. Finally, she uses the remaining yarn lengths to tie bows along the kite string.

THIS STORY COMPUTES
Making connections

This partner activity is as simple as a click of a mouse. Give each student a copy of page 169. First, have her write the title of the story she and her partner have read. Then have her finish the sentence starter by describing an event or a character from the story. To complete the first related link, she fills in her name and writes how the story detail connects to her life, to another text, or to something she has learned. Next, partners exchange papers. Each student reads her partner's detail and first link. Then she completes the second link on the page, making sure it varies from what her partner wrote. When the partners return the papers, ask them to discuss the connections they made.

Name Danielle

Literature Response
Making connections

www. Flat Stanley .books
book title

In this book, Arthur is jealous because Stanley is getting so much attention.

Related Links:

1. www. Danielle .reader
student's name

I am jealous when my brother gets his name in the paper for soccer.

2. www. DeShawn .reader
partner's name

My friend gets jealous of me when I get a new video game.

Get Connected!

Gumball Machine and Gumball Patterns

Use with "Getting Personal" on page 166.

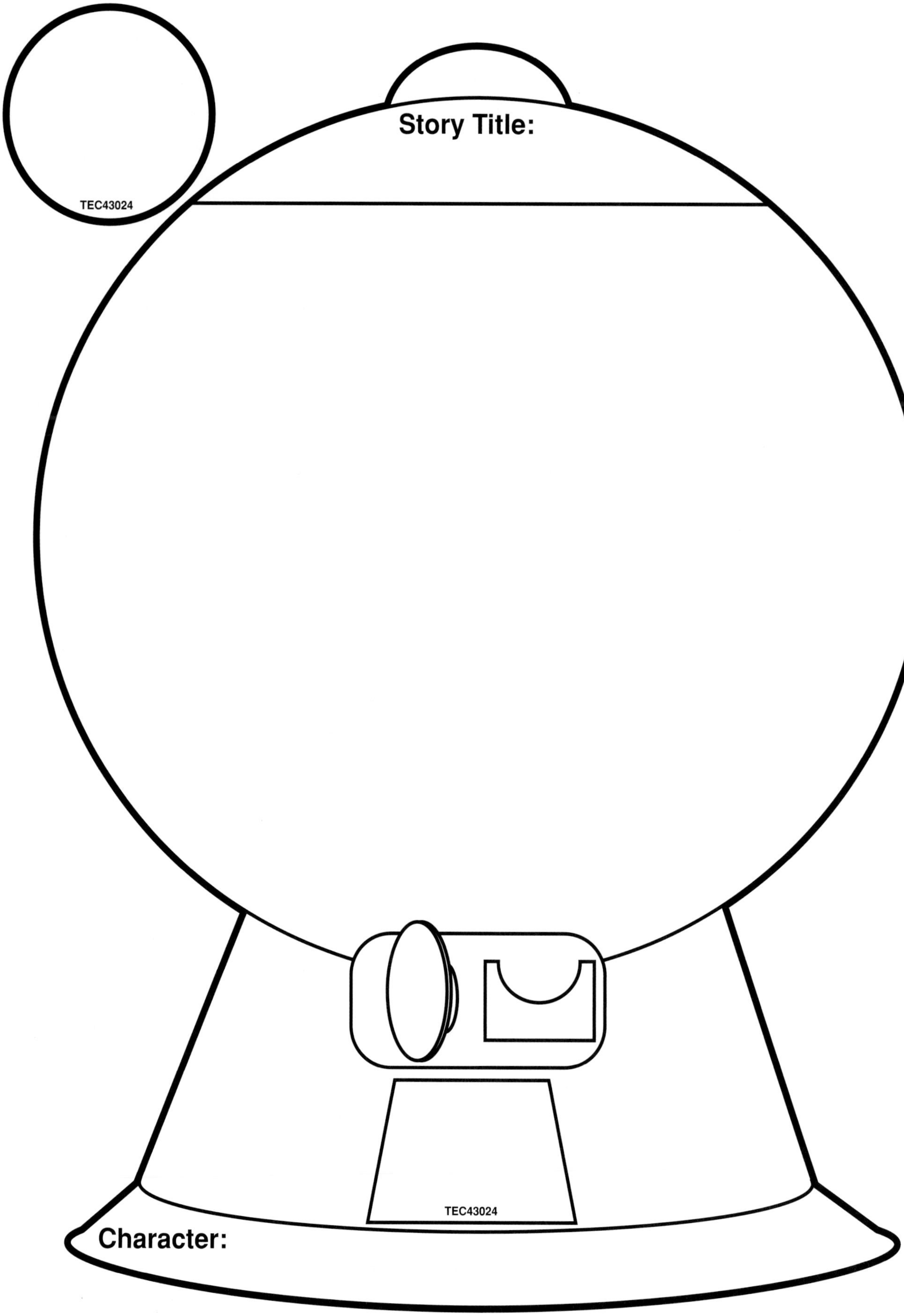
TEC43024
Story Title:
TEC43024
Character:

Name ______________________________

www.______________________________.books
book title

In this book, ______________________________

____

____

Related Links:

1. www.______________________________.reader
student's name

____

____

2. www.______________________________.reader
partner's name

____

____

Get Connected!

Note to the teacher: Use with "This Story Computes" on page 167.

Let's Shine!

Star-Studded Proofreading Activities

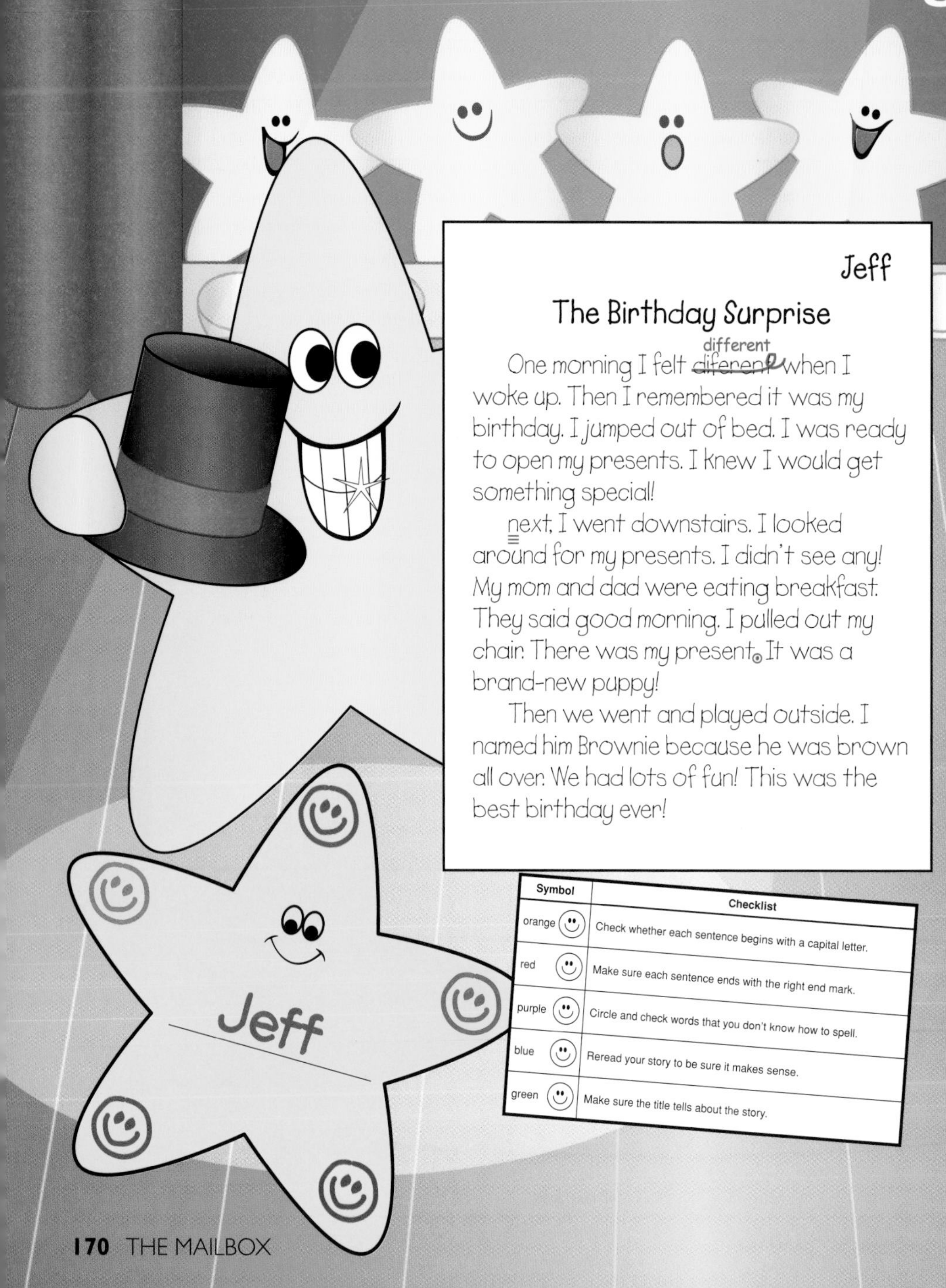
Jeff
The Birthday Surprise
One morning I felt diferent different when I woke up. Then I remembered it was my birthday. I jumped out of bed. I was ready to open my presents. I knew I would get something special!
next, I went downstairs. I looked around for my presents. I didn't see any! My mom and dad were eating breakfast. They said good morning. I pulled out my chair. There was my present. It was a brand-new puppy!
Then we went and played outside. I named him Brownie because he was brown all over. We had lots of fun! This was the best birthday ever!
Jeff
Symbol
Checklist
orange
Check whether each sentence begins with a capital letter.
red
Make sure each sentence ends with the right end mark.
purple
Circle and check words that you don't know how to spell.
blue
Reread your story to be sure it makes sense.
green
Make sure the title tells about the story.

SUPERSTAR EDITORS

Editing for grammar, spelling, and punctuation

In advance, make a class supply of page 172 on yellow construction paper. Store the copies in a folder and place it at a center. When a child is ready to proofread his paper, he cuts out the pattern and the chart and writes his name on the pattern. Next, he consults the chart for an editing task. After completing the task and correcting his errors, he draws the matching color-coded smiley face on one of the star's points. He continues in this manner until he has completed each task listed. Then he clips his star to his paper to show that he is ready for a teacher conference.

Who's the star of the proofreading show? Your students are, with the help of these bright ideas!

with ideas by Stacie Stone Davis, Lima, NY

NIFTY NINE

Evaluating handwriting

Team up with students to work on penmanship! Prior to the activity, make a class supply of the rubric on page 173. Store the copies in a place that is accessible to students. When each child completes a final draft, have her use the guidelines to evaluate her handwriting. After she finishes, she folds the paper on the dotted line to conceal her scores. Then she clips the rubric to her paper and turns it in. After you use the rubric to assess the child's penmanship, open the flap to reveal how the student scored herself. Meet with the child to discuss any differences between the two scores.

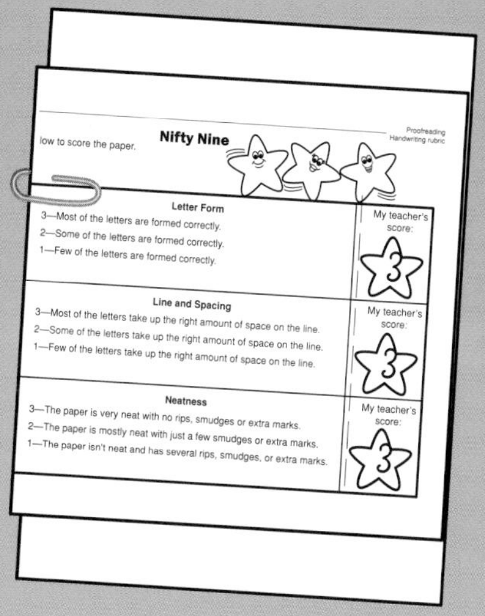
low to score the paper.
Nifty Nine
Proofreading
Handwriting rubric
Letter Form
3—Most of the letters are formed correctly.
2—Some of the letters are formed correctly.
1—Few of the letters are formed correctly.
My teacher's score:
3
Line and Spacing
3—Most of the letters take up the right amount of space on the line.
2—Some of the letters take up the right amount of space on the line.
1—Few of the letters take up the right amount of space on the line.
My teacher's score:
3
Neatness
3—The paper is very neat with no rips, smudges or extra marks.
2—The paper is mostly neat with just a few smudges or extra marks.
1—The paper isn't neat and has several rips, smudges, or extra marks.
My teacher's score:
3

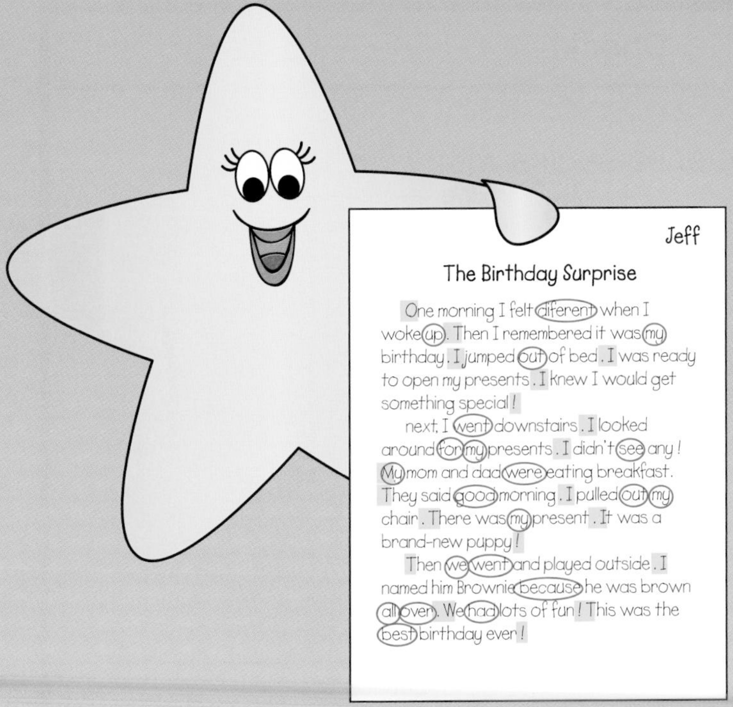
Jeff
The Birthday Surprise
One morning I felt different when I woke up. Then I remembered it was my birthday. I jumped out of bed. I was ready to open my presents. I knew I would get something special!
next, I went downstairs. I looked around for my presents. I didn't see any! My mom and dad were eating breakfast. They said good morning. I pulled out my chair. There was my present. It was a brand-new puppy!
Then we went and played outside. I named him Brownie because he was brown all over. We had lots of fun! This was the best birthday ever!

HIGHLIGHTER HELP

Self- and peer-editing

Have students use highlighters to reinforce correct grammar, spelling, and capitalization! After completing a piece of writing, have each child check it and correct any errors. Next, have him use a yellow highlighter to mark all the correctly capitalized words and correct end marks. If he finds an error, he circles it with a pencil. Then have the child exchange papers with a partner. His partner uses a different-colored highlighter to check word wall words, highlighting words that are spelled correctly and circling incorrect words with a pencil. This way, both students are internalizing correct spelling, grammar, and punctuation each time they look at a piece of writing.

Karen Slattery, Marie of the Incarnation School, Bradford, Ontario, CA

Star Pattern and Editing Chart

Use with "Superstar Editors" on page 170.

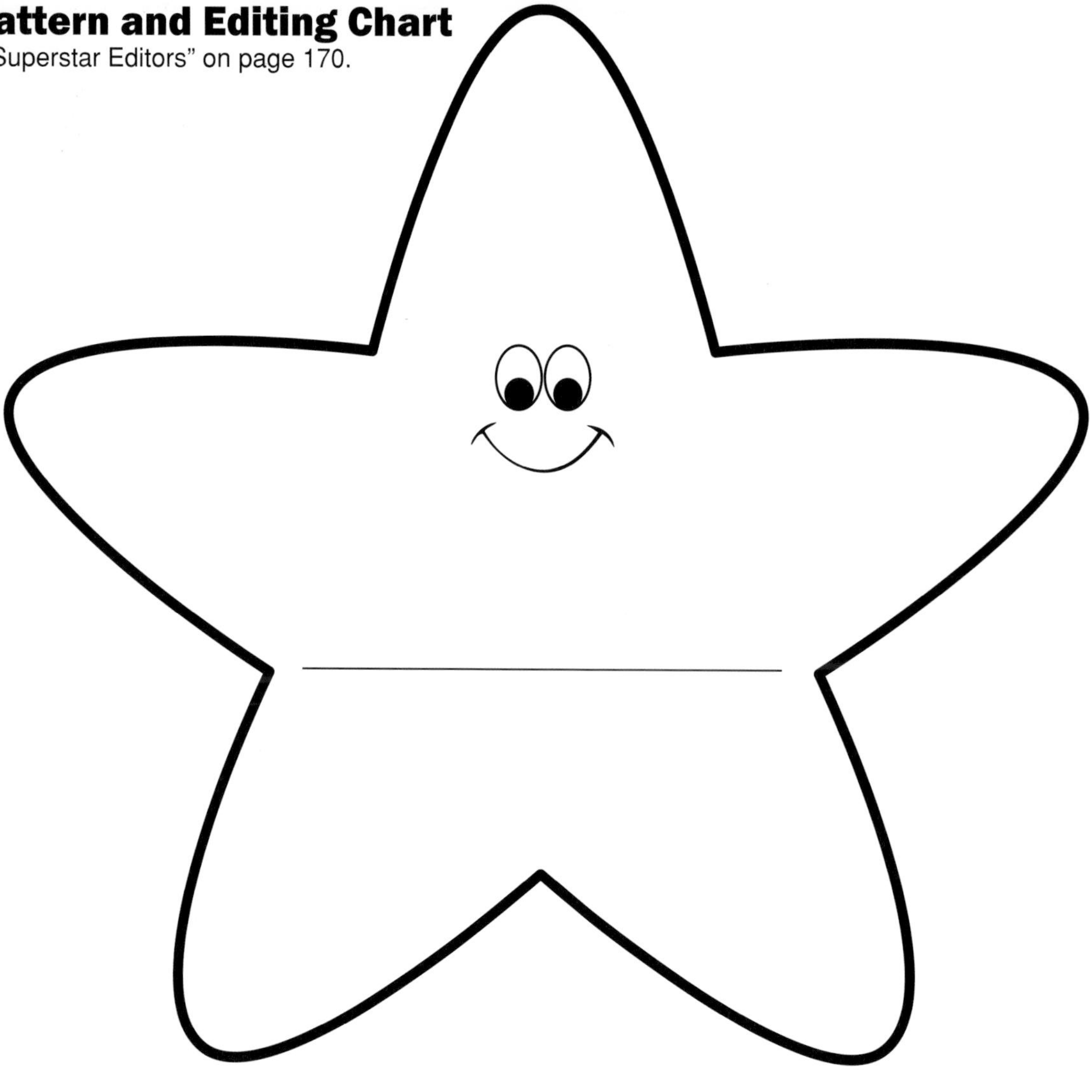

Symbol	Checklist
orange	Check whether each sentence begins with a capital letter.
red	Make sure each sentence ends with the right end mark.
purple	Circle and check words that you don't know how to spell.
blue	Reread your story to be sure it makes sense.
green	Make sure the title tells about the story.

Name ______________________________

Nifty Nine

Use the sentences below to score the paper.

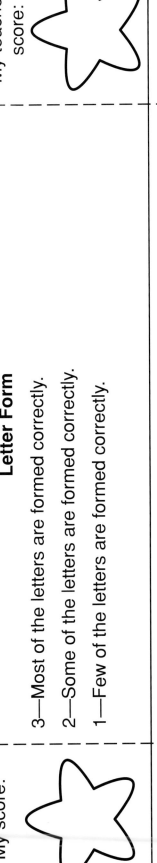

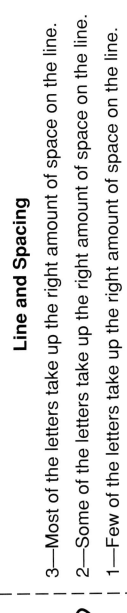

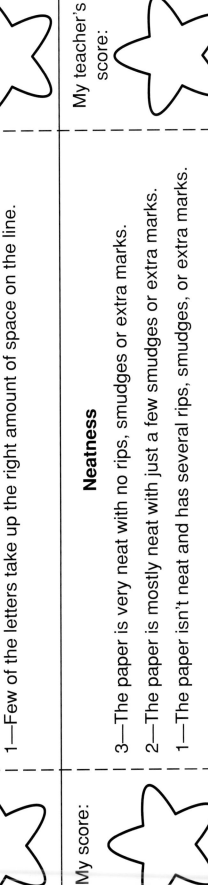

My score:	Letter Form	My teacher's score:
☆	3—Most of the letters are formed correctly. 2—Some of the letters are formed correctly. 1—Few of the letters are formed correctly.	☆

My score:	Line and Spacing	My teacher's score:
☆	3—Most of the letters take up the right amount of space on the line. 2—Some of the letters take up the right amount of space on the line. 1—Few of the letters take up the right amount of space on the line.	☆

My score:	Neatness	My teacher's score:
☆	3—The paper is very neat with no rips, smudges or extra marks. 2—The paper is mostly neat with just a few smudges or extra marks. 1—The paper isn't neat and has several rips, smudges, or extra marks.	☆

Note to the teacher: Use with "Nifty Nine" on page 171.

Having a **Ball**

Activities Using Multiple-Meaning Words

He swung
the bat and
hit the ball.
UNITED STATES 39¢

HOMOGRAPH BINGO

Matching words to their definitions

To prepare this whole-class game, cut apart a copy of the sentence cards on page 176 and place them in a paper bag. Next, give each child a set of the game cards on page 177, a blank sheet of paper, and a supply of bingo markers. The student cuts apart the game cards and then folds his paper in half four times, creasing each fold line. To create a bingo card, he unfolds the paper and glues a game card in each section. To play the game, draw a card from the bag and read aloud the corresponding sentence. If a child has the matching picture on his gameboard, he covers it with a bingo marker. Play continues in this manner until one child calls out, "Bingo!" signaling that he has covered four words in a row. Check his board; if he is correct, give him a small treat. If not, play continues. After finishing the game, collect students' papers. Keep them on hand and redistribute them to review multiple-meaning words throughout the year.

Juggling multiple word meanings is simple with these ideas and activities!

with ideas by Jennifer Kohnke, Nature Ridge Elementary, Bartlett, IL and Stacie Wright, Millington School, Millington, NJ

MISTAKEN MEANINGS
Identifying multiple-meaning words

All this simple activity requires is a popular book and good listening skills! In advance, locate any book from the Amelia Bedelia series by Peggy Parish. First, explain that as you read the book aloud, the class should listen carefully to what Amelia Bedelia does. Tell students that if Amelia confuses words or does something she's not supposed to, they should snap their fingers. Then read the book aloud, pausing each time students snap to write on the board the words that Amelia mixes up. After finishing the book, review the listed words with students. As a class, identify and record the multiple meanings of each word listed. Then circle the meaning that was used in the story.

change
dust
draw

The bat flew by the tree.

SILLY SCENES
Identifying multiple meanings of words

Together with students brainstorm a list of multiple-meaning words. Record the list on a sheet of chart paper. Next, have each child use one of the listed words in a sentence. The student writes the sentence at the bottom of a sheet of light-colored construction paper. Then she illustrates her sentence by using the word's other meaning to create a silly picture like the one shown. After each child's picture is complete, invite students to share their sentences and drawings with the class. Compile students' work in a class book titled "Silly Scenes."

MULTIPLE-MEANING MATCH
Using context clues to identify word meanings

Before starting the activity, copy pages 176 and 177. Next, mount the cards on construction paper and color the picture cards. Cut out the cards and program the back of each for self-checking. Place both sets of cards at a center. A child reads a sentence card and then finds the picture card that matches the meaning of the bold-faced word. After matching each sentence to a picture, he turns the cards over to check his work.

He gave her a **ring** on the phone.
She had a new

Sentence Cards

Use with "Homograph Bingo" on page 174 and "Multiple-Meaning Match" on page 175.

She had a new diamond **ring.** TEC43025	She stored her clothes in a **trunk.** TEC43025
He gave her a **ring** on the phone. TEC43025	Bark covered the **trunk** of the tree. TEC43025
The **mouse** ran across the floor. TEC43025	He heard the dog **bark.** TEC43025
She clicked the **mouse** to go to the next page. TEC43025	The tree was losing its **bark.** TEC43025
The **bat** flew through the air. TEC43025	She put her money in the **bank.** TEC43025
He hit the ball with the **bat.** TEC43025	He walked along the **bank** of the river. TEC43025
My **foot** is sore. TEC43025	She saw the bird **fly** away. TEC43025
The length of the box was a **foot.** TEC43025	That **fly** keeps buzzing in his ear. TEC43025
The plate had a **chip.** TEC43025	He put a **stamp** on the letter. TEC43025
This **chip** is tasty. TEC43025	She used a **stamp** to mark the book. TEC43025

Game Cards

Use with “Homograph Bingo” on page 174 and “Multiple-Meaning Match” on page 175.

TEC43025
TEC43025
TEC43025
TEC43025
TEC43025
TEC43025
TEC43025
TEC43025
TEC43025
TEC43025
TEC43025
TEC43025
TEC43025
TEC43025
TEC43025
TEC43025
TEC43025
TEC43025
UNITED STATES 39¢
TEC43025
TEC43025

Campout!

Writing Letters and Notes Home

Dear Mom and Dad,
I met a skunk here at camp. I named him Steve. I think he'd make a great pet. Can I bring him home? He's really friendly and he likes to play with me. He won't be any trouble at all. I promise I'll take care of him. Plus, other animals will stay out of our yard when they see our pet skunk! I think this is a great idea. Write back to me and tell me what you think.
Love,
Jeron

NEW PET

Writing a persuasive letter

Every student will enjoy trying to convince his parents that he should bring a camp critter home! Begin by having students imagine that they are at summer camp. Tell them to think about the different kinds of animals they would encounter there. Next, each child imagines that he has befriended one of the animals and wants to take it home as his new pet. He writes a letter to his parents, persuading them to let him bring the animal home. In his letter, he states his opinion and gives several reasons why he should be allowed to keep the pet. After each child has finished his letter, invite him to share it with the class.

Address letter-writing skills with this collection of activities!

with ideas by David Green, North Shore Country Day School, Winnetka, IL

CAMP RIDDLES

Writing a friendly letter

Strengthen students' writing skills with this activity! Have each child imagine she is an animal at summer camp. Instruct her to think about the things that animal might do at camp. She lists her ideas on a scrap sheet of paper, then uses them to write a friendly letter. She includes clues about the animal without revealing its identity. After checking to ensure that she included the five parts of a friendly letter, she turns the paper over and writes the animal's name in the bottom right corner. Collect the letters and post them on a bulletin board. Invite students to read each one and guess the animal's identity, turning the paper over to see if they are correct.

> June 28, 2006
>
> Dear Grandma,
>
> I'm having a great time here at camp! Yesterday we had a fly-eating contest and I won! Afterward, my friends and I hung out on a lily pad for the rest of the afternoon. Tomorrow, we're leaping into town for a field trip!
>
> I love you,
> ?

Dear Aunt Beth,
Thanks for the treats you sent! I shared them with my friends. The games you sent were cool too. We play them when it rains and we can't go outside.
Love,
Ben

CARE PACKAGE

Writing a thank-you note

Start by having the class imagine that they have just received a care package at camp. Instruct them to think about what the perfect care package would contain. List students' responses on the board. Then have each child write a thank-you note to his parents or another family member. Remind students that thank-you letters contain a salutation, body, signature, and closing and the writer usually explains why he appreciates the gift or the help he received. After students' letters are complete, compile them in a class book.

FRIENDLY LETTER POEM

Parts of a letter

Use this catchy poem as a letter-writing reminder!

Caryn Young, Mount Eagle Elementary School, Alexandria, VA

If you want to write a note
Or tell someone about your day,
Try writing a friendly letter.
It's a quick and easy way!

Start with the heading,
Including the month, day, and year.
Then add the salutation,
Which usually begins with *Dear.*

The body is next,
A really important part.
Share a story, ask a question,
Or say what's in your heart.

The closing uses words
Like *Sincerely* or *Your friend.*
And with your signature,
Your letter has come to an end.

Don't forget to proofread it
So your work will look even better.
Now you're done, my friend.
You've written a friendly letter!

Name____ Letter Writing
Revising

A Better Letter

Read the letter.
Write details in the blanks to make the letter more interesting.

June 27, 2006

Dear Grandpa,

I like camp. I have the neatest cabin. The food is good. Playing tag was fun. I got a small bump. I miss home.

Love,
Bobby

I like camp because ____

____.

I have the neatest cabin because ____

____.

The food is good, especially the ____.

Playing tag with ____ was fun.

I got a small bump when ____

____.

I miss home because ____

____.

Bonus Box: On the back of this page, rewrite the letter. Include the details to make it more interesting.

Math Units

Ready, Set, Go!

A Practice Lap of Basic Facts

Name
Basic Facts
Addition to 18
Taking a Spin
8 +7 15
2 +7 9
5 +7 12
1 +7 8
3 +7 10
6 +7 13
4 +7 11
+ 7

TAKING A SPIN

Addition to 18

Keep your students' knowledge of basic facts on course! For this partner center, remove the tens and face cards from a deck of playing cards and make a copy of page 184 for programming. To program the copy, write inside the box an addend from 0 through 9. Copy the programmed page to make a class supply and then place the copies at a center with the card deck, crayons, and pencils. To begin play, each partner draws one card from the deck. On his paper he writes a basic fact using the programmed addend and the card's face value and then he solves it. When his answer is verified by his partner, he colors the matching number of spaces on his racetrack. When both partners are ready, a new round begins. The student who is first around his track wins!

For a variation of this center activity, simply program another copy of page 184 with a different addend, make copies of the page, and restock the center. It's time to warm up those engines again!

Speedy recall of addition and subtraction facts is sure to follow up these crowd-pleasing maneuvers. Vroom!

with ideas by Beth Romie, New Albany Elementary, New Albany, OH

SPEED TRIALS
Fact memorization

Spark renewed interest in partner flash card drills! Keep several mats on hand like the one shown. To make a mat, write "see" and "say" on individual 4" x $4\frac{1}{2}$" cards. Glue the cards on a 4" x 9" construction paper strip and then laminate the strip for durability.

For a flash card drill, Partner 1 displays math facts from a customized or randomly selected deck of ten flash cards. Partner 2 taps "see" when she first sees a problem and "say" when she says the fact answer. The taps are concrete examples of a child's response rate and provide super motivation to reach speedy recall. If her answer is correct, Partner 1 (who can see the correct answer on the back of the card) sets the card aside and shows the next one in the deck. If her answer is incorrect, Partner 1 keeps displaying the card as she reads aloud the problem and its correct answer. Then she moves the card to the back of the deck. When Partner 2 has correctly answered every card in the deck, the partners switch roles (and card decks, if desired) and start again. Tap, tap!

5
+ 6
8
+ 3

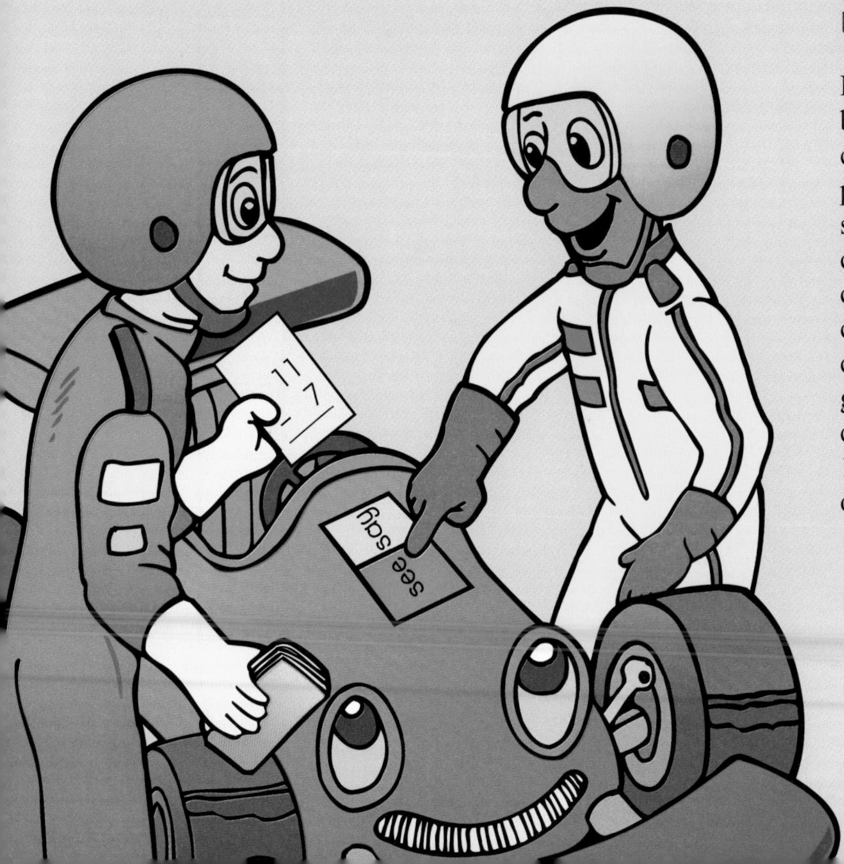
see
say

PIT STOP
Basic facts with equal solutions

Partners who pull into this math center refuel with basic facts! To make an addition game, make a construction paper copy of page 185. Laminate the paper for durability, cut out the cards, and attach a sticker to the back of each one. Store the cards at the center in a zippered bag. To play, Player 1 shuffles the cards and lays them facedown. Player 2 turns over a card and states the sum. Then he turns over a second card and states the sum. If the two sums match, he gathers the two cards and takes another turn. If the cards do not match, he turns the cards over and Player 1 takes a turn. The player with more cards at the end of the game wins!

Name____

Basic Facts
Addition to 18

Taking a Spin

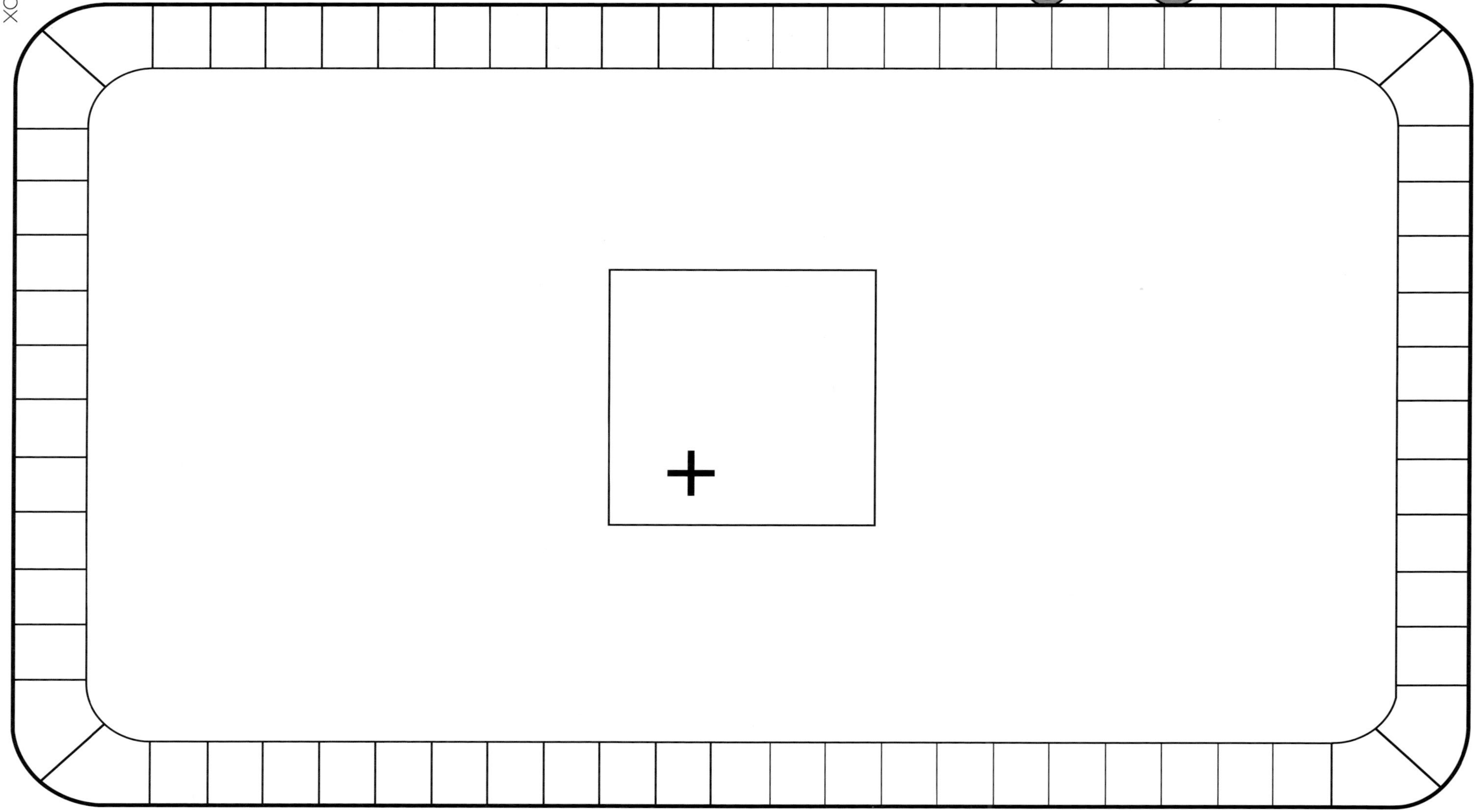
+

Note to the teacher: Use with "Taking a Spin" on page 182.

Use with “Pit Stop” on page 183.

7 + 5	6 + 6	4 + 6	3 + 7
9 + 5	7 + 7	5 + 6	8 + 3
7 + 8	9 + 6	4 + 5	6 + 3
2 + 5	6 + 1	2 + 4	1 + 5
6 + 2	5 + 3	7 + 6	8 + 5

Name ____________________

And the Winner Is...

Subtract.
Fill in the grid.
The first row is done for you.

★	– 0	– 4	– 6	– 2	– 5	– 3	– 7	– 1
5	5	1	★	3	0	2	★	4
7								
11	★							★
6							★	
4			★		★		★	
9								
10	★							★
12	★			★				★
8								

It's a Treasure!

Ordering and Comparing Numbers

5 2 9
<
less than
5 1 9
Terrell
350 > 192
256 < 874
529 < 716

NUMBER JEWELS

Using < and >

Comparing numbers is a cinch with this center activity! First, copy the jewel patterns on page 189 onto colored construction paper. Next, program each jewel with a different digit from 0 to 9; laminate the jewels for durability. Cut out the jewels and store them in a container that resembles a treasure chest. Also program a greater than and a less than symbol on index card halves. Place the chest, symbols, paper, and pencils at a center. A child removes the jewels from the chest and uses them to create two three-digit numbers. He arranges his numbers beside each other, as shown, and chooses the correct symbol to place between them to make the number sentence true. Then he copies the number sentence onto a sheet of paper. He repeats the process until he has created ten different number sentences and written them on his paper.

This treasure trove of number sense activities is beyond compare!

with ideas by Stacie Stone Davis, Lima, NY

BETWIXT AND BETWEEN
Before and after

Students gain practice with comparing numbers as they complete number sequences! Copy the coins on page 189 onto colored construction paper so that you have one coin per child. Program each coin with a different three-digit number. Laminate the coins for durability and cut them out. Begin by handing out the coins and instructing each child to write her number and the numbers that come before and after it on a blank sheet of paper. On your signal, the student trades coins with the classmate on her right and repeats the process. Have students continue in this manner for as long as desired. After the class completes the activity, collect the coins for future use.

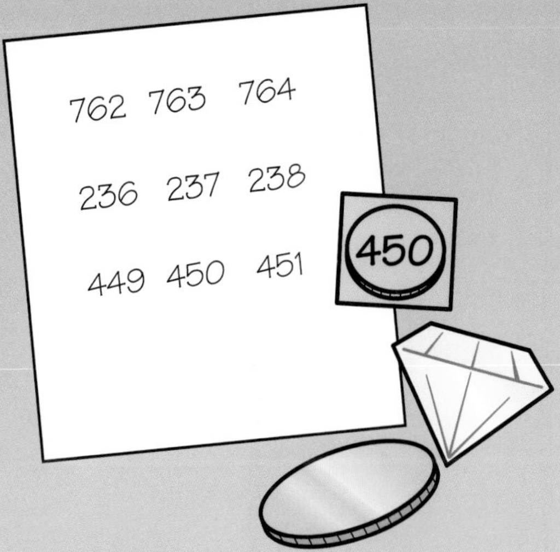

762 763 764
236 237 238
449 450 451
450

5 2 4
524
524
254
542
245
452
425
245
254
425
452
524
542

SMALLEST TO LARGEST
Generating and ordering numbers

Students continue to polish their sequencing skills with this group activity! Start by giving each child one of the programmed coins from "Betwixt and Between." Instruct the student to write each of the digits on the coin at the top of a sheet of paper and draw a circle around each one. Next, have him divide his paper in half. On the left side of the paper, have him generate a list of all the three-digit numbers that can be made using the digits on the coin. Then direct him to write the numbers in order from smallest to largest on the right side. After students finish, collect the coins. Then simply pass them out on the following day and repeat the process for additional practice with ordering numbers.

WHICH ONE?
Using < and >

This activity helps students decide which inequality sign to use! Create a symmetrical shark cutout like the one shown. Laminate the shark, cut it out, and attach a piece of magnetic tape to its back. Place the cutout at a center along with a set of magnetic numbers, a cookie sheet, paper, and pencils. A child creates two different two- or three-digit numbers on the cookie sheet, leaving a space between them. Next, she places the shark so that its mouth is opening toward the greater number. Then she copies the number sentence onto her paper using the correct inequality sign. Have the student repeat the process until she has created at least two number sentences using each sign.

Anne E. South, East Oro Public School, Orillia, Ontario, Canada

65
56

Coin Patterns

Use with "Betwixt and Between" and "Smallest to Largest" on page 188.

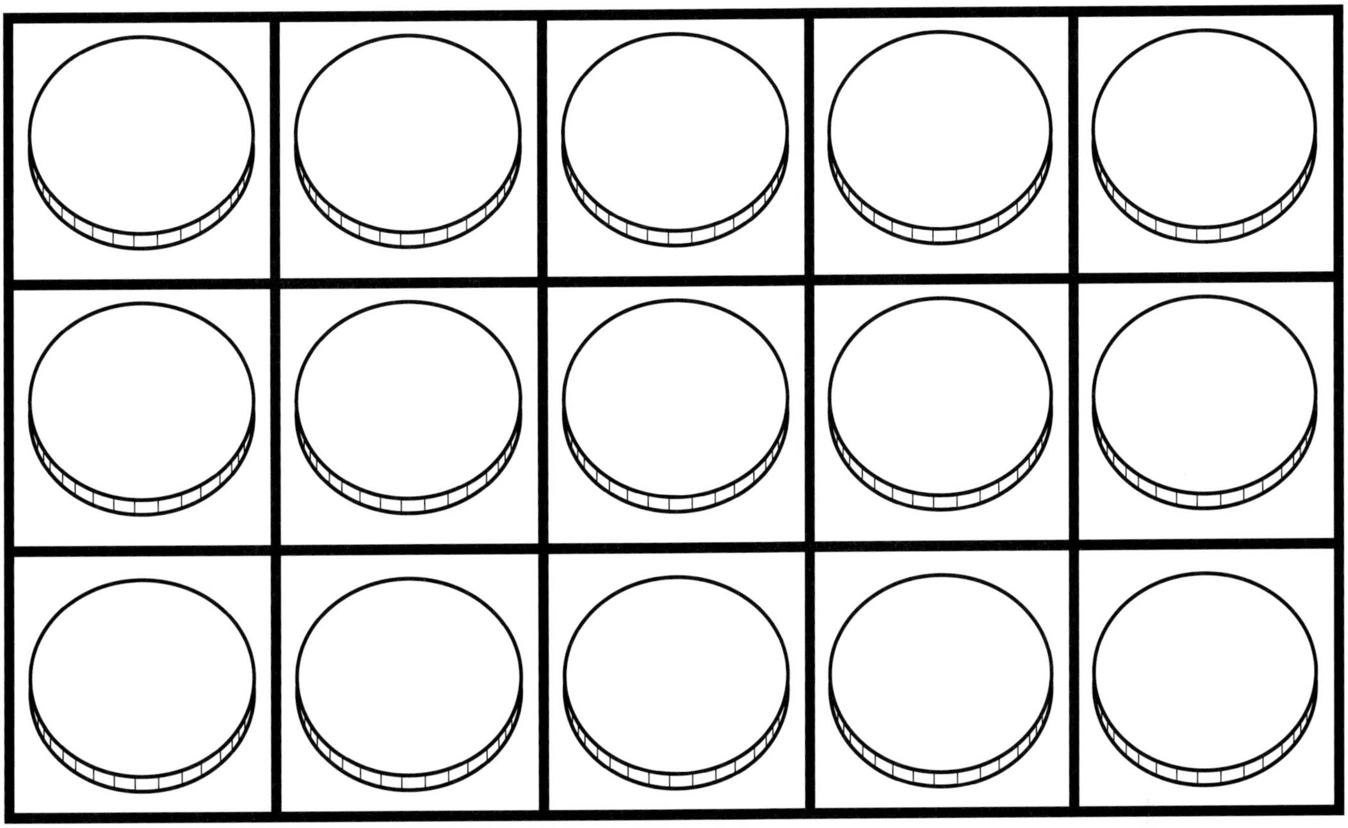

Jewel Patterns

Use with "Number Jewels" on page 187.

Name____

Number Sense
Comparing two-digit numbers

Pieces of Gold

Color the coin in each pair that has the greater number.
Write < or > to make a true number sentence.

C.	S.	B.	I.	E.	G.
31	28	18	81	36	32
M.	D.	F.	O.	U.	Y.
19	29	61	78	21	91
J.	R.	H.	Z.	P.	Q.
15	17	41	33	57	43
T.	V.	K.	A.	N.	W.
63	59	80	89	24	12

?

Where can you always find gold?

To solve the riddle, match the letters for the colored coins above to the numbered lines below.

81 24   63 41 36

29 81 31 63 81 78 24 89 17 91 !

Name ____

Number Sense
Ordering three-digit numbers

Which Key?

Order the numbers from least to greatest.
Use the clue to find the number that opens each chest.
Circle that number.

A. 428 561 487 294 322 506

______, ______, ______, ______, ______, ______

The number is between 250 and 310.

B. 987 854 971 755 898 926

______, ______, ______, ______, ______, ______

The number is between 860 and 900.

C. 695 548 632 616 583 624

______, ______, ______, ______, ______, ______

The number is less than 570.

D. 255 315 289 365 234 347

______, ______, ______, ______, ______, ______

The number is greater than 350.

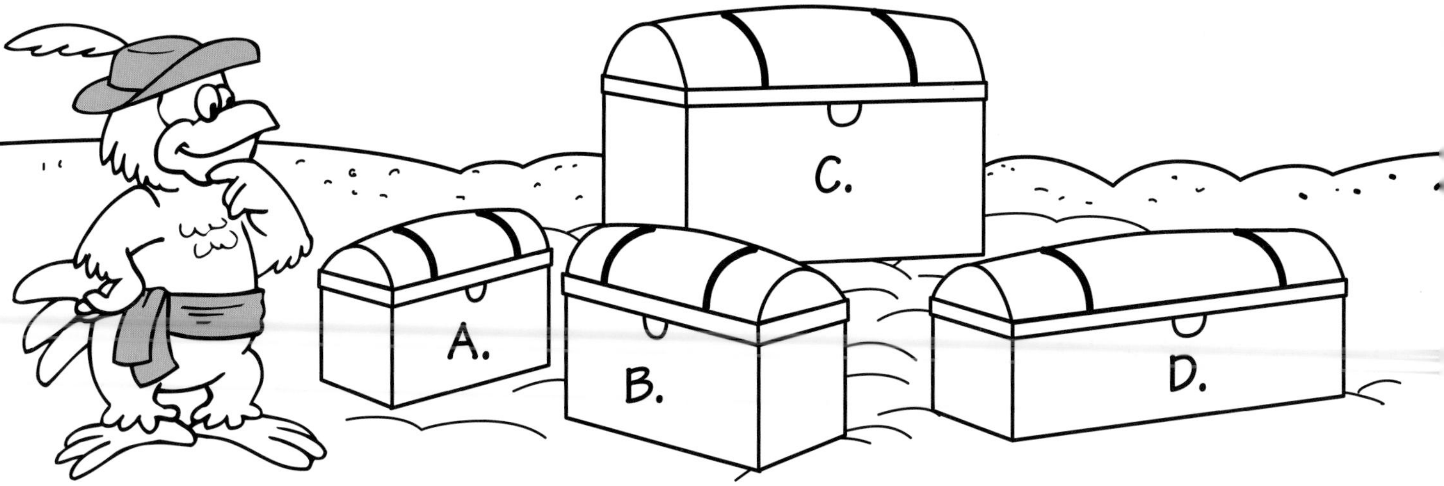
C.
A.
B.
D.

Saddle **Up!**

Tips for Roping Regrouping Skills

YES OR NO?

Identifying when to regroup is a snap with this center activity! First, copy pages 193 and 194. Mount both pages on construction paper. Color the mat and then cut out the cards. Use a permanent marker to program the back of each card for easy self-checking and place the activity at a center. A student sorts each card according to whether regrouping was used to find the answer. Then he flips the cards over to check his work.

SUBTRACTION SONG

This simple tune **reinforces when to borrow!**

Bobbi Roberts, Matilda Harris Elementary, Kingsland, GA

(sung to the tune of "If You're Happy and You Know It")
If it's smaller on the top, take a ten.
If it's smaller on the top, take a ten.
If it's smaller on the top, take a ten and start again.
If it's smaller on the top, take a ten.

Individual Scores					
WE	THEY	WE	THEY	WE	THEY
1					
6	4				
+2	9				
9	3				

A BRIDGE TO REGROUPING

Keeping numbers lined up in columns when adding and subtracting has never been easier! Purchase several notepads used to keep score in bridge, or create your own sheet with columns like the one shown. The columns help students keep numbers in their places and make regrouping easy. Have each child record and complete his problems on the sheets until he is comfortable with regrouping.

Kristen Murray
Hamilton County Math and Science Academy
Cincinnati, OH

Cal's Corral

Do you need
to regroup?
Yes
No

Sorting Cards

Use with "Yes or No?" on page 192 and the sorting mat on page 193.

27 + 34 61 TEC43021	326 + 13 339 TEC43021	78 + 11 89 TEC43021	226 + 105 331 TEC43021
63 + 25 88 TEC43021	31 + 49 80 TEC43021	514 + 78 592 TEC43021	85 + 14 99 TEC43021
176 + 217 393 TEC43021	408 + 114 522 TEC43021	73 − 19 54 TEC43021	192 − 131 61 TEC43021
58 − 47 11 TEC43021	96 − 17 79 TEC43021	421 − 160 261 TEC43021	87 − 54 33 TEC43021
529 − 416 113 TEC43021	26 − 12 14 TEC43021	66 − 25 41 TEC43021	76 − 48 28 TEC43021

Name ____________________

Regrouping Addition

Cowboy Capers

Add.

I. 27 + 63	U. 35 + 48	X. 261 + 355	K. 412 + 569
M. 304 + 617	N. 57 + 28	R. 556 + 124	P. 28 + 29
L. 76 + 17	O. 825 + 168	G. 463 + 195	A. 68 + 13
	N. 313 + 596	U. 38 + 48	D. 224 + 382

Why aren't cowboys good at math?
To solve the riddle, match a letter to each numbered line below.

They're always

____ ____ ____ ____ ____ ____ ____ ____ ____ ____ !

680 993 86 909 606 90 85 658   83 57

Seconds to Go

A Playbook of Telling-Time Activities

12:30
2:00
10:15
10:15
12:30
2:00

WHAT'S THE LINEUP?

Ordering times

Set up this small group activity by programming a class set of the clocks on page 199 each with a different time. Then make two additional class sets, each set in a different color, so that there are three different-colored clocks showing the same time.

Begin the activity by giving each child a clock of the same color. Each group of five orders its times from earliest to latest and glues the clocks in order on a sentence strip. Next, give each child a matching clock in one of the two remaining colors. Explain that one color clock represents A.M. and the other represents P.M. Have the group order its times again based on this information and glue the clocks in order on a second sentence strip. Then have each group look at both strips and discuss how they changed.

The goal is terrific time-telling skills, and these ideas easily score a touchdown!

with ideas by David Green, North Shore Country Day School, Winnetka, IL

PLAY BY PLAY
Reading a schedule

Begin by inviting students to suggest things they might do on a Saturday and the time needed to complete each activity. Create a schedule by listing their suggestions on a piece of chart paper. Post the schedule in the classroom; then write on the board a few story problems like the ones shown for students to solve. On each of several following days, post a problem for students to solve using the schedule. Or place the schedule at a center along with story problems for further practice.

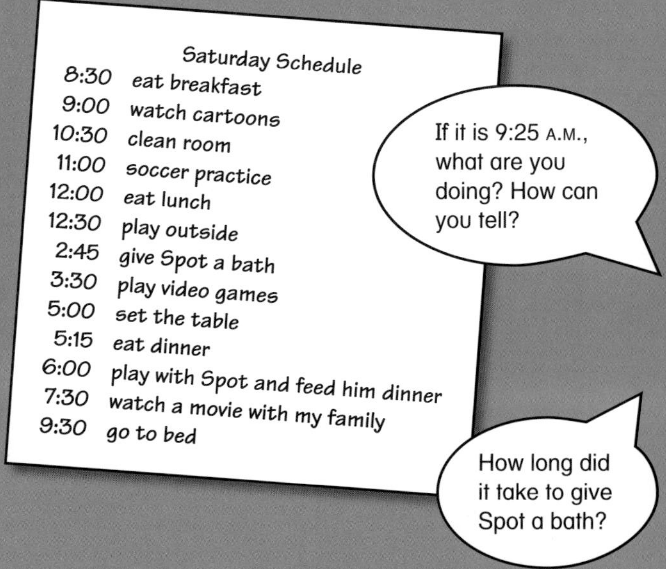
Saturday Schedule
8:30 eat breakfast
9:00 watch cartoons
10:30 clean room
11:00 soccer practice
12:00 eat lunch
12:30 play outside
2:45 give Spot a bath
3:30 play video games
5:00 set the table
5:15 eat dinner
6:00 play with Spot and feed him dinner
7:30 watch a movie with my family
9:30 go to bed
If it is 9:25 A.M., what are you doing? How can you tell?
How long did it take to give Spot a bath?

The show starts at 2:30.

EARLY OR LATE?
Vocabulary

Write a statement on the board like the one shown. Also display a class demo clock with a specific time. Then ask students a question such as "If you arrive at the time shown, will you be early or late?" Have students answer by giving a thumbs-up for early or a thumbs-down for late. Then ask how many minutes early or late they would be. Continue the activity for as long as desired to practice using time vocabulary.

WHEN TO WHEN?
Elapsed time

To start, ask each child to write on an index card an activity he recently enjoyed doing. Then have him estimate how long he spent doing it. Collect students' cards; then randomly select one and read it aloud. Give students a specific time the activity started and then have them use the start time and the information on the card to find the end time. Repeat the process several times, or place the cards at a center along with a class demo clock set to a certain time, paper, and pencils. Students visiting the center select a card and find the end time for the activity using the time shown on the demo clock.

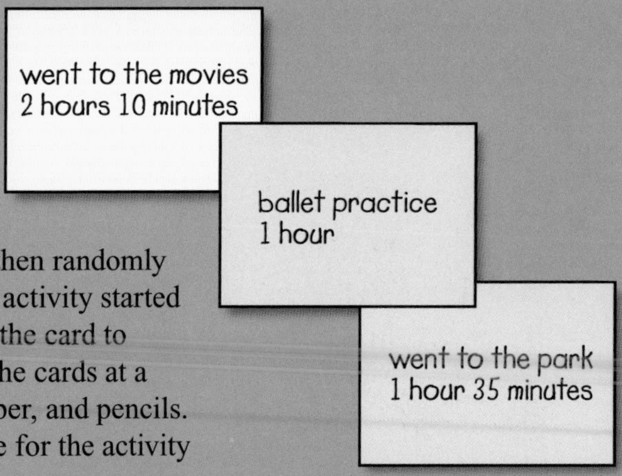
went to the movies
2 hours 10 minutes
ballet practice
1 hour
went to the park
1 hour 35 minutes

Name________________________________

What Time?

Draw a line from each clock to its matching time.
Circle the time in each column that you didn't use.

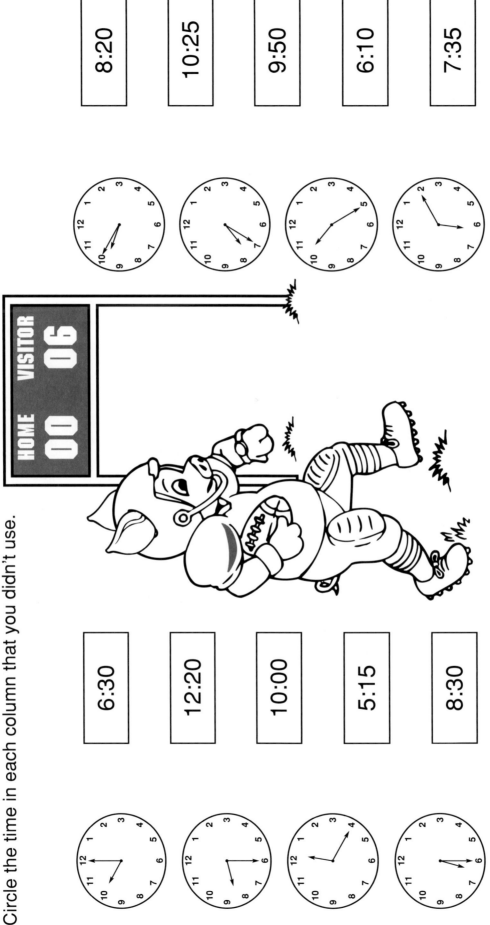

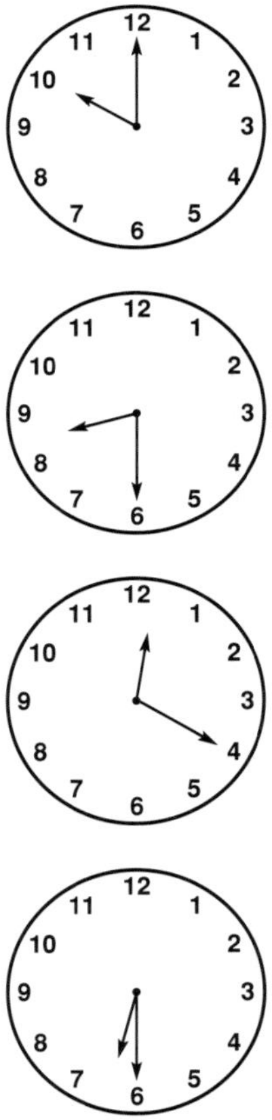

6:30	8:20
12:20	10:25
10:00	9:50
5:15	6:10
8:30	7:35

HOME
VISITOR
00
06

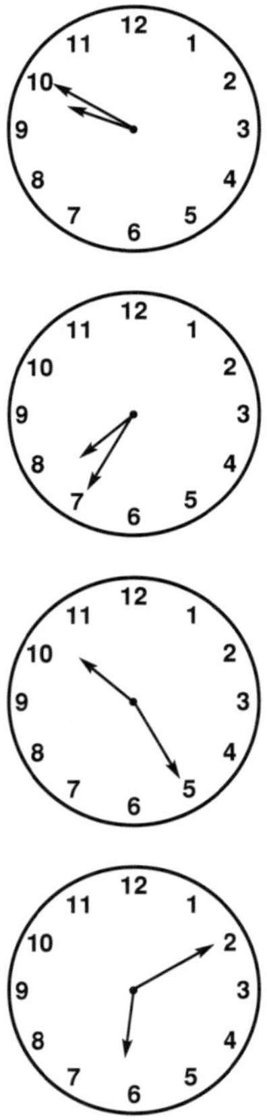

Bonus Box: If the circled times show when the game began and ended, how long did the game last?

Clock Patterns

Use with "What's the Lineup?" on page 196.

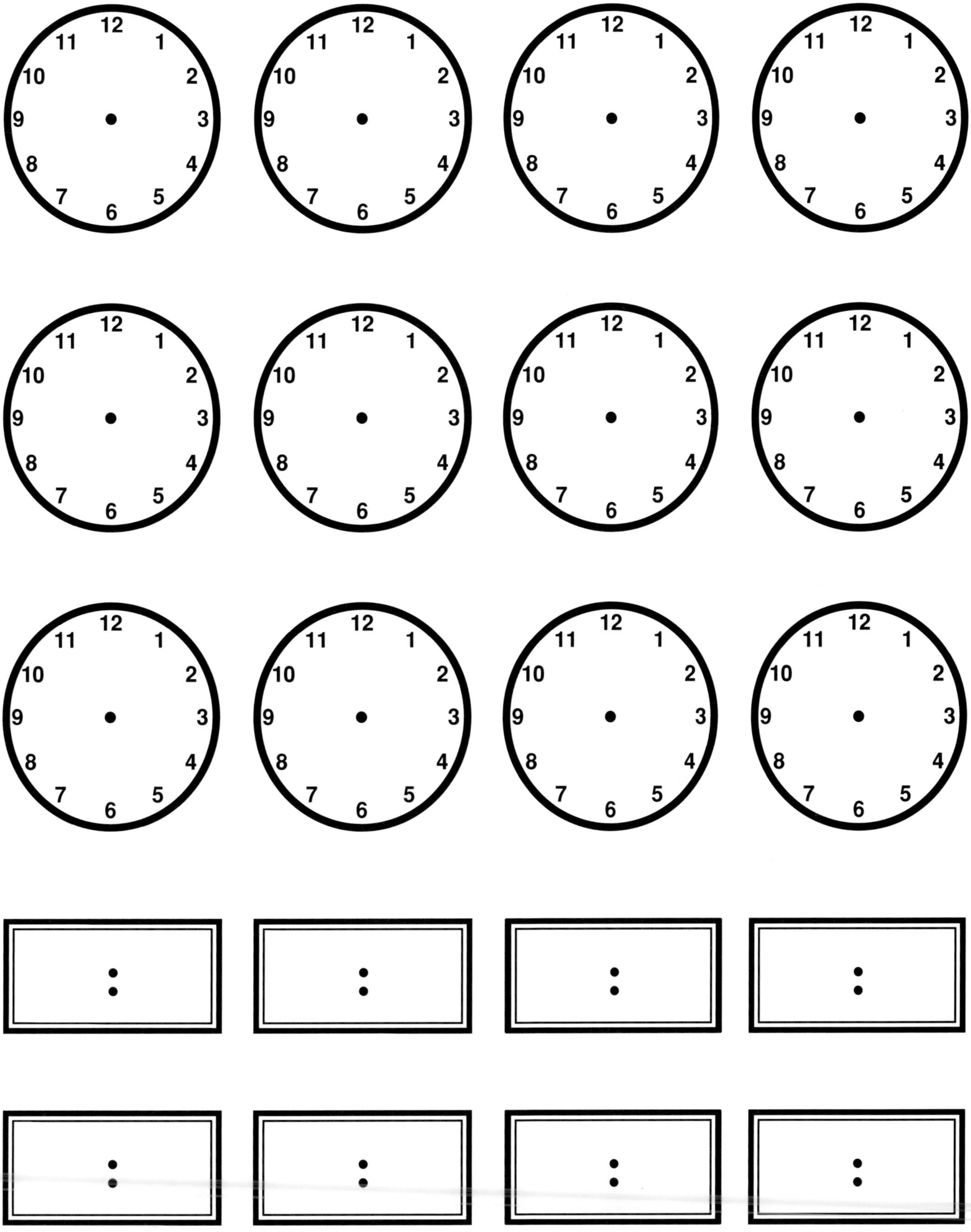

Cooling Off

Diving Into Multiplication

MEET IN THE MIDDLE

This **game for two** provides fact practice and is easy to prepare and play! In advance, make two copies of the tracks on the left side of page 202 for each student pair. Give the twosome the tracks, a set of double six dominoes, a multiplication table, paper, and pencils. To play, students turn the dominoes facedown and place their tracks end to end, leaving a space in the middle where the two sets meet. Then Player 1 draws a domino. He uses its pips to create a multiplication problem and solves it, using his paper if needed. His partner checks the multiplication table to verify his answer. If correct, the player places his domino on the track. If incorrect, the domino is discarded. Then Player 2 takes a turn in the same manner. Play continues until one student fills his tracks with dominoes and reaches the middle, winning the game.

3 x 3 =9
5 x 3 =15!

Sit back and watch your students' knowledge multiply

with these activities and games!

with ideas by Jean Erickson, Grace Christian Academy, West Allis, WI

12
4
2
20
10
8
0

SCOOPING OUT PRODUCTS

This simple **center** is a bowl full of fun! To prepare, gather ten plastic or paper bowls and a supply of wooden craft spoons. Label each bowl with a different digit from 0 to 9. Program each number's multiples on different wooden spoons as shown. Store the spoons in a large resealable plastic bag; then place the bag, the bowls, and a multiplication chart at a center. A student chooses a bowl and finds the number's multiples, placing the matching spoons inside the bowl. Then she uses the multiplication table to check her answers.

Check out the cool programmable reproducible on page 203! Just write the number that you want your students to multiply by.
Penguin Products

FOUR IN A ROW

Winning this **partner game** requires luck and knowledge of multiplication facts! Give each pair a copy of the gameboards on page 202, two different-colored crayons, and a pair of dice. To play, players take turns rolling the dice. Both partners find the product of the two numbers rolled. If the number is on a player's grid, he colors its square. Play continues in this manner until one player has four colored squares in a row and wins the game.

3	18	16	20
30	1	15	8
4	12	24	6
9	10	36	5

2	10	24	18
15	12	30	3
6	25	4	16
36	8	1	24

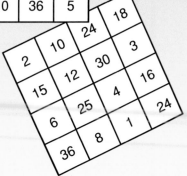

Domino Track Patterns

Use with "Meet in the Middle" on page 200.

TEC43022

TEC43022

Gameboards

Use with "Four in a Row" on page 201.

2	10	24	18
15	12	30	3
6	25	4	16
36	8	1	24

TEC43022

3	18	16	20
30	1	15	8
4	12	24	6
9	10	36	5

TEC43022

Name ____________________ Multiplication

Penguin Products

In each □ copy the number on Patti's mitten.
Multiply.

□ x 8 =

□ x 4 =

□ x 3 =

□ x 6 =

□ x 2 =

□ x 7 =

□ x 0 =

□ x 9 =

□ x 1 =

□ x 5 =

□ x 4 =

□ x 4 =

□ x 6 =

□ x 7 =

□ x 0 =

□ x 9 =

□ x 5 =

□ x 8 =

□ x 3 =

□ x 1 =

□ x 2 =

By Degrees

Turning Up the Heat With Temperature

F
110
90
80
50
10
0
10
20

110
100
90
80
94 °F

WHAT'S THE TEMP?

Reading a thermometer, relating temperatures to everyday situations

These easy-to-make booklets are a great reference for students! Make a class supply of page 206. Begin by asking the class what kinds of outdoor activities they would do in cool and then warm temperatures. After discussing students' responses, give each child a copy of page 206. To complete the activity, the student reads the thermometer on each page and writes its temperature on the line below. Then he draws a picture of himself doing an outdoor activity appropriate for the temperature shown. After completing the pages, he cuts them apart and arranges them from lowest to highest temperature. He places the cover on top and staples the pages together. Finally, invite students to share their booklets with the class.

These temperature-related activities won't leave you out in the cold!

with ideas by David Green, North Shore Country Day School, Winnetka, IL

The Warmest Place in School
100°
90°
80°
70°
60°
50°
40°
30°
20°
10°
0°
principal's office
our classroom
cafeteria
media center
art room
The cafeteria was the warmest. I think it's warm because they cook all our food in there. And it has a lot of windows, and it's a really sunny day.

SHOW ME THE TEMP
Using and reading a thermometer

To warm up students' temperature-reading skills, give each child a construction paper copy of the Fahrenheit or Celsius thermometer on page 208 and a 1" x 17" white construction paper strip. Have her follow the directions below to make a thermometer. Next, instruct each child to practice showing different temperatures on her thermometer by sliding the red and white strip. Then call out a specific temperature and have each student display it on her thermometer. As a class, discuss whether the stated temperature is cool or warm and how students would feel if that were the outdoor temperature. Repeat the process for as long as desired. Have students keep their thermometers handy to be used as a visual reminder throughout the unit.

Directions:

1. Color half of the strip red.
2. Cut a slit in the gray areas on the thermometer.
3. Slide the strip's red end through the bottom slit and its white end through the top slit.
4. Turn the thermometer over and tape the two ends together.

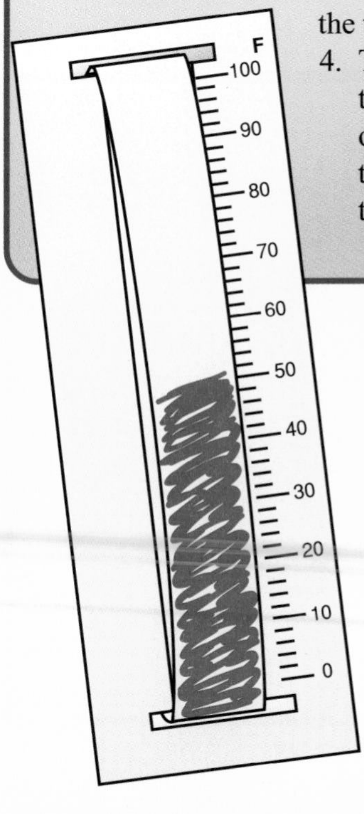

F
100
90
80
70
60
50
40
30
20
10
0

WHAT'S THE WARMEST?
Reading thermometers, making predictions

This experiment allows students to apply their knowledge of temperatures to a real-world setting! Tell students that you are growing a special kind of plant and need to find the warmest place in school. As a class, choose five locations to test, and have each student write on a slip of paper his prediction for the warmest place. Early the next morning, place a thermometer in each designated location. Then take small groups of students to check and record each location's temperature. Afterward, have each student construct a bar graph showing the experiment's results. At the bottom of the graph, have the child write the location of the highest temperature and list a few reasons why he thinks it is the warmest place in the school.

Michele Daughenbaugh
Park Forest Elementary
State College, PA

Booklet Cover and Pages

Use with "What's the Temp?" on page 204.

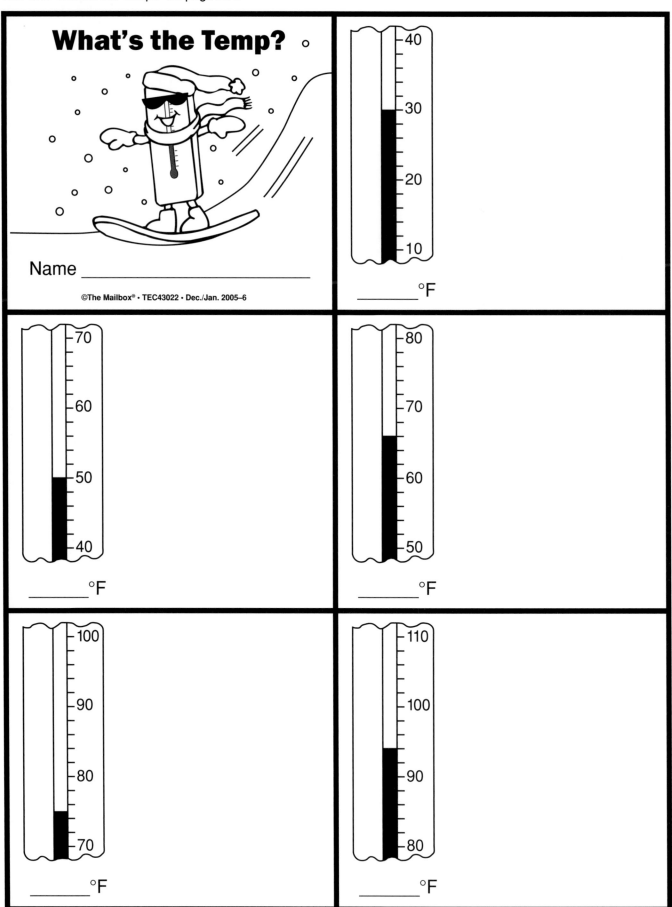

What's the Temp?

Name ______________________________

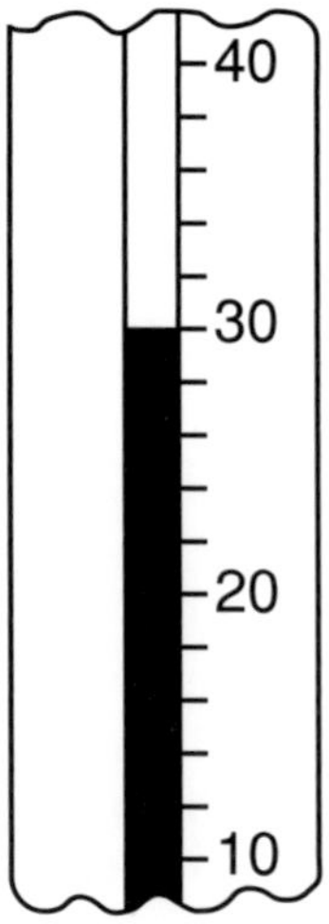

40
30
20
10

_______°F

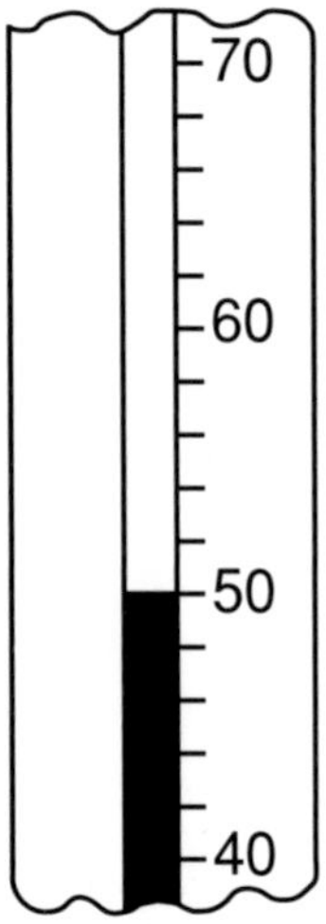

70
60
50
40

_______°F

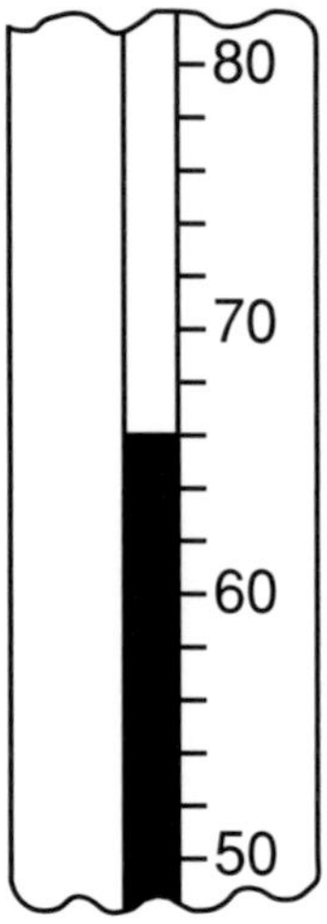

80
70
60
50

_______°F

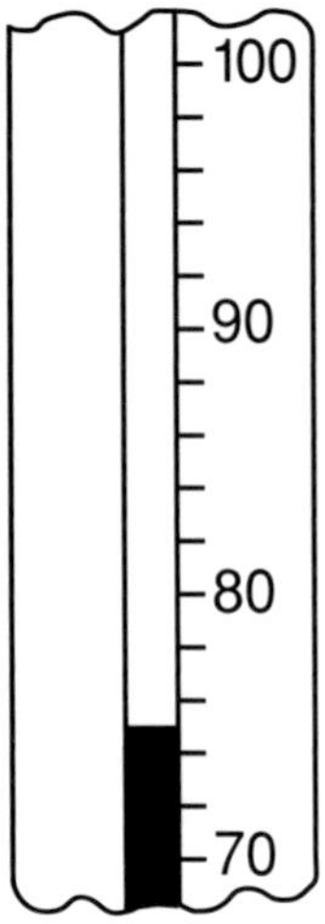

100
90
80
70

_______°F

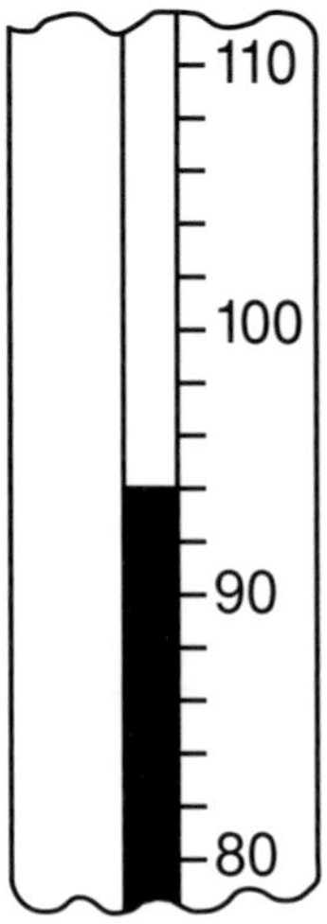

110
100
90
80

_______°F

Name ______________________________ Temperature Celsius

What to Wear?

Look at each temperature.
Circle the best clothing item for the pair.

0°C

25°C

10°C

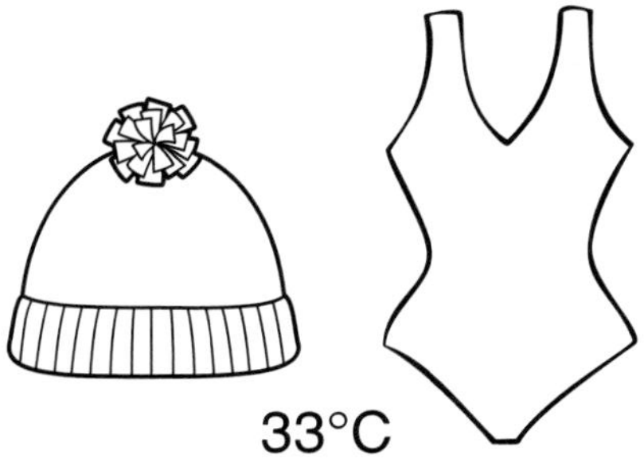

33°C

17°C

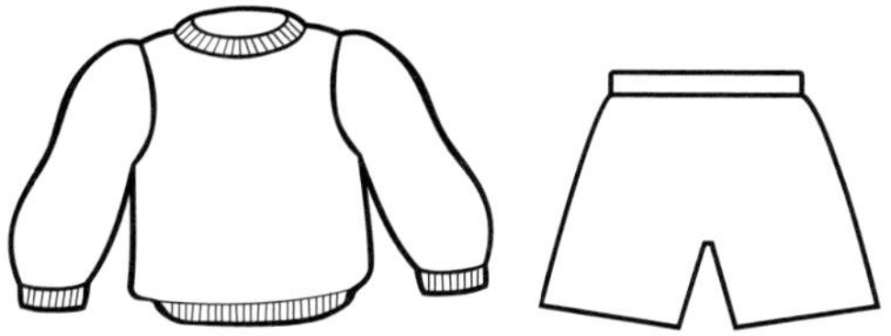

30°C

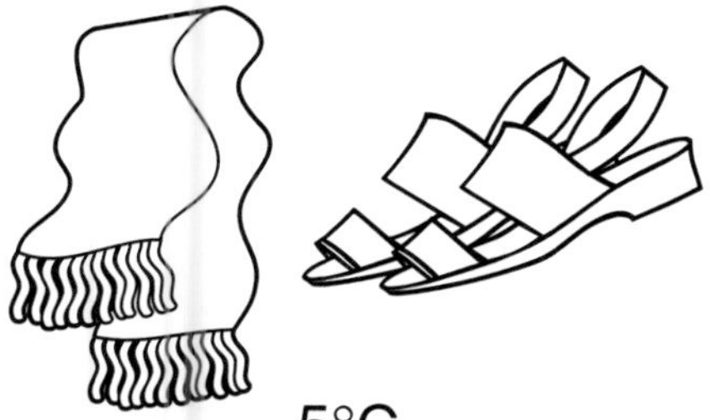

5°C

20°C

13°C

3°C

Thermometer Patterns

Use with "Show Me the Temp" on page 205.

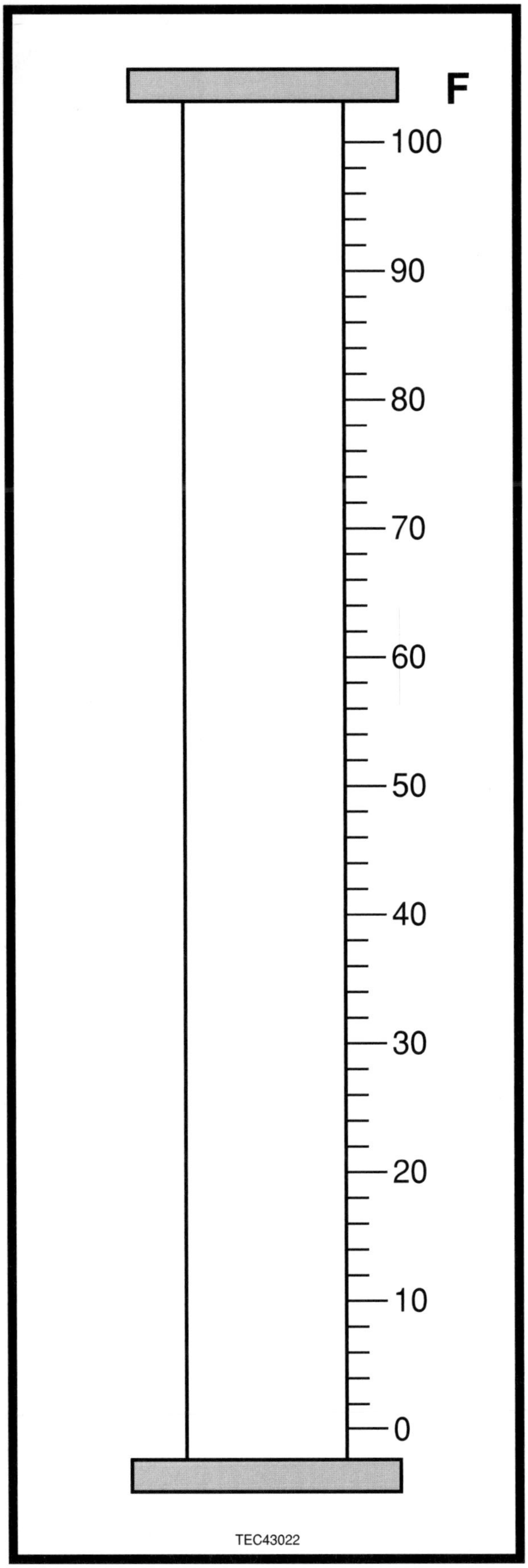
F
100
90
80
70
60
50
40
30
20
10
0
TEC43022

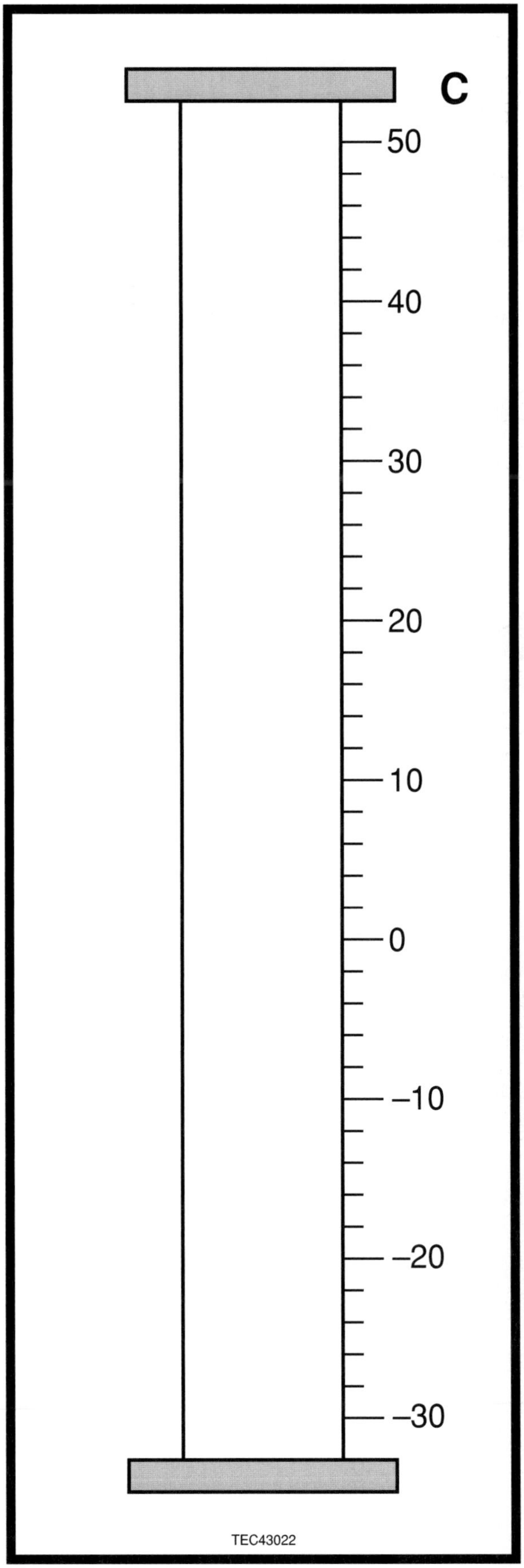
C
50
40
30
20
10
0
–10
–20
–30
TEC43022

Shaping Up

A Solid-Shape Workout

What am I?
I have 0 faces.
I have 0 corners.
I have 0 edges.
What am I?
I have 0 faces.
I have 0 corners.
I have 0 edges.
I can cannot roll.
I can cannot be stacked.

WHAT AM I?

Solid shapes' faces, edges, and corners

Use these minibooklets to help students identify three-dimensional figures! In advance, make a class supply of page 211. Have each child complete the blanks in each section to describe the picture of the corresponding shape. Next, the student cuts out the blank squares along the bottom of the page. He glues each one over a shape, creating a flap that hides the figure. Then he cuts out each page, arranges them in any order he chooses, and staples them between two construction paper covers. After he finishes his booklet, he finds a partner and reads aloud one page's clues. His partner uses the clues to identify the solid figure described. The child checks his partner's guess by lifting the flap and revealing the shape. The twosome takes turns describing and identifying solid shapes for as long as desired. Encourage students to take their booklets home to further practice identifying solid shapes.

Use these ideas and activities to strengthen students' understanding of solid shapes!

with ideas by Stacie Stone Davis, Lima, NY

3-D MATCHUP
Identifying solid shapes

Matching shapes to their names is easy with this game for two! Copy page 212, color the cards, and then cut them out. Mount them on construction paper. Color-code the back of the cards for self-checking; then place them at a center. To play, partners take turns turning over two cards at a time. If a child reveals a pair of cards whose name and shape match, he keeps them and takes another turn. If he turns over two cards that don't match, he replaces them and his partner takes a turn. Play continues in this manner until all cards are matched. The player with the most pairs wins.

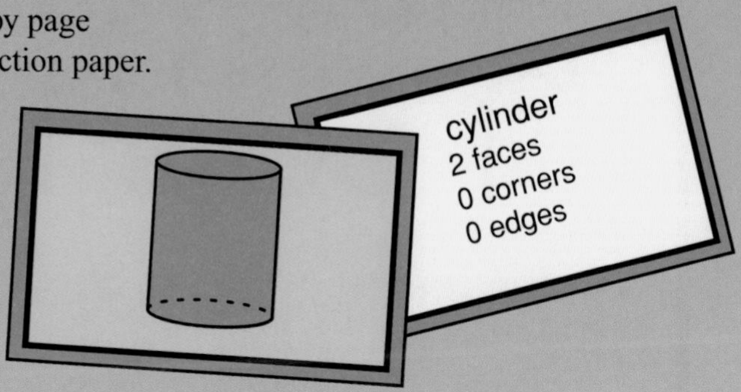
cylinder
2 faces
0 corners
0 edges

This object has a square face. All of its faces are the same shape. It has 8 corners.
cube
6 faces
8 corners
12 edges

GETTING A FEEL FOR SHAPES
Describing solid shapes

Solid shape examples and a blindfold are all you need for this partner activity! In advance, gather a supply of three-dimensional objects and place each one in a paper bag. Program the bag's outside with the shape's name and its number of faces, edges, and corners. Place the bags, the blindfold, paper, and pencils at a center. A student pair sits back-to-back. Partner 1 dons the blindfold and then selects an object from a bag. He uses his hands to feel the shape and describes it aloud to his partner using terms such as *faces, corners,* and *edges.* Partner 2 uses the description to write the shape's name on a sheet of paper. Then Partner 1 removes his blindfold, and the twosome uses the bag to check Partner 2's answer. Play continues with partners switching roles until all of the shapes have been described and identified.

SORTING SOLIDS
Classifying 3-D figures

Put students' reasoning skills to the test with this whole-class activity! Gather a supply of real-world solid shapes, such as canned food, cereal boxes, sugar cubes, and marbles, making sure that there are several examples of each solid shape. Then have students observe as you separate the objects aloud into two groups (for example, sorting objects by the number of faces, corners, or edges, or by the shapes of their faces). Invite students to guess how the objects are grouped. When a child identifies the sorting method, start a new round of the game, this time using a different method to sort the shapes.

How did I sort these?
WHOLE
Green
Beans

Use with "What Am I?" on page 209.

What am I?

I have ______ faces.

I have ______ corners.

I have ______ edges.

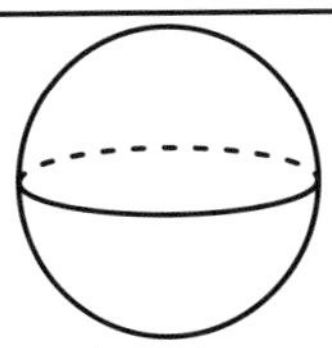

I am a sphere.

I can cannot roll.

I can cannot be stacked.

TEC43023

What am I?

I have ______ faces.

I have ______ corners.

I have ______ edges.

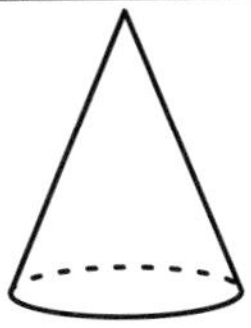

I am a cone.

I can cannot roll.

I can cannot be stacked.

TEC43023

What am I?

I have ______ faces.

I have ______ corners.

I have ______ edges.

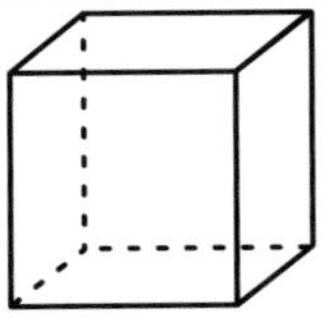

I am a cube.

All my faces are are not the same shape.

I can cannot roll.

I can cannot be stacked.

TEC43023

What am I?

I have ______ faces.

I have ______ corners.

I have ______ edges.

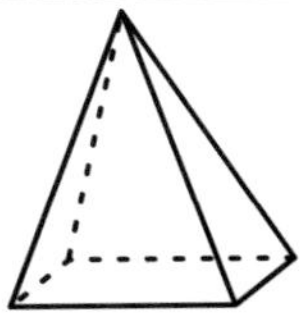

I am a square pyramid.

All my faces are are not the same shape.

I can cannot roll.

I can cannot be stacked.

TEC43023

What am I?

I have ______ faces.

I have ______ corners.

I have ______ edges.

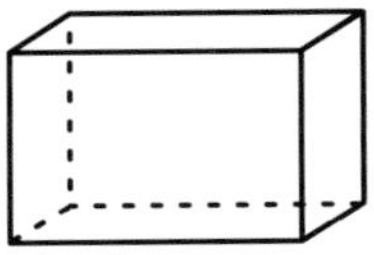

I am a rectangular prism.

All my faces are are not the same shape.

I can cannot roll.

I can cannot be stacked.

TEC43023

What am I?

I have ______ faces.

I have ______ corners.

I have ______ edges.

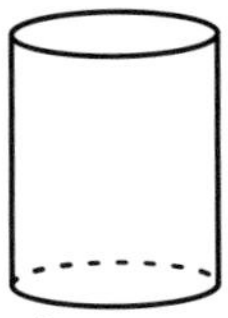

I am a cylinder.

All my faces are are not the same shape.

I can cannot roll.

I can cannot be stacked.

TEC43023

Center Cards

Use with "3-D Matchup" on page 210.

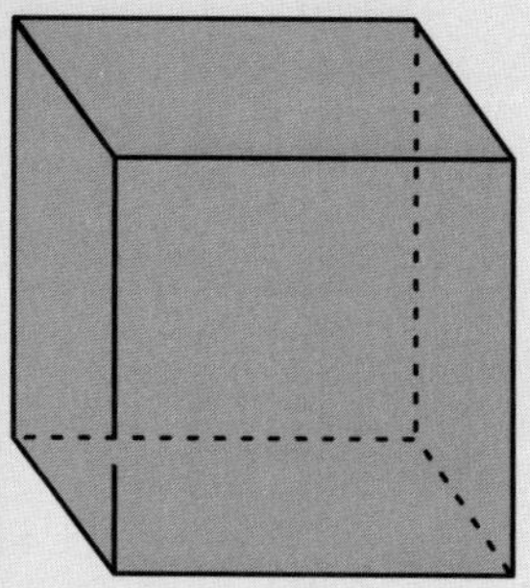

TEC43023

cube
6 faces
8 corners
12 edges

TEC43023

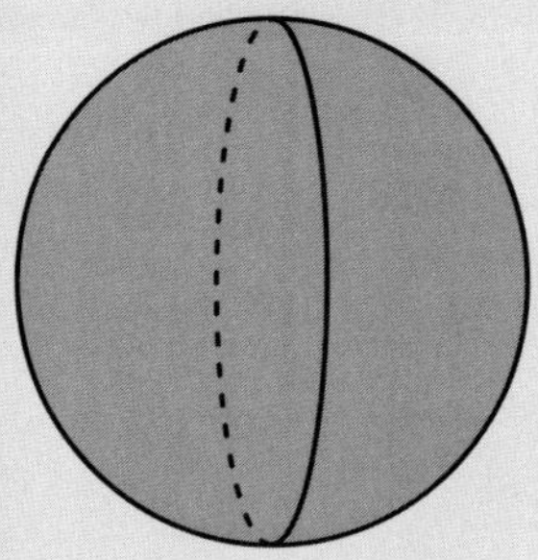

TEC43023

sphere
0 faces
0 corners
0 edges

TEC43023

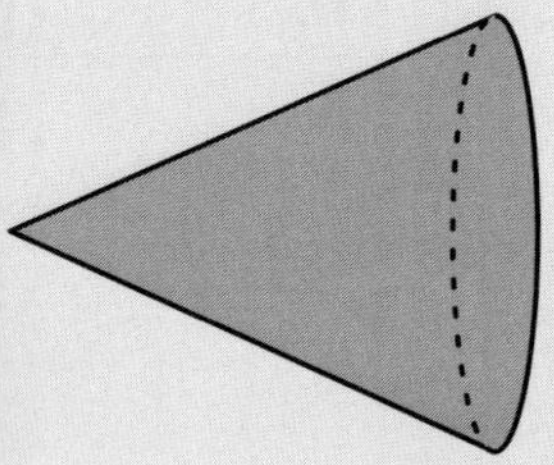

TEC43023

cone
1 face
0 corners
0 edges

TEC43023

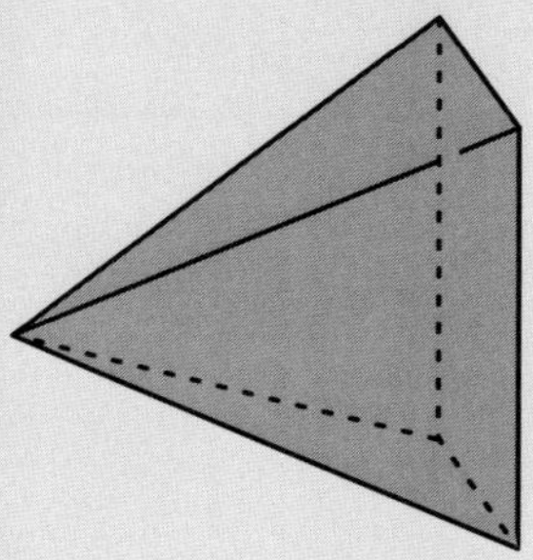

TEC43023

square pyramid
5 faces
5 corners
8 edges

TEC43023

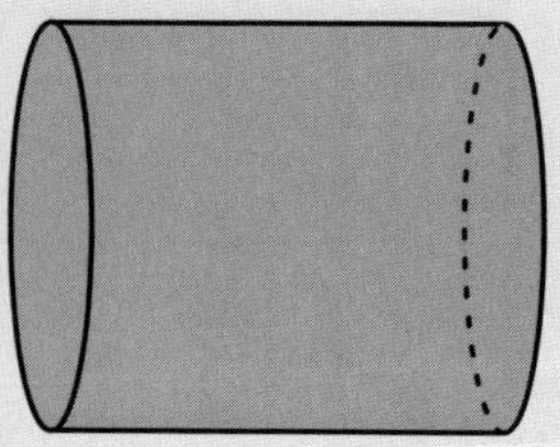

TEC43023

cylinder
2 faces
0 corners
0 edges

TEC43023

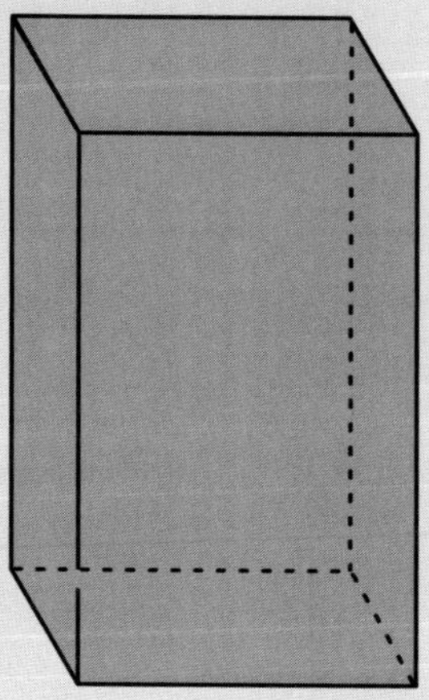

TEC43023

rectangular prism
6 faces
8 corners
12 edges

TEC43023

Name________________________________

When Did They Work Out?

Each solid shape went to the gym.
Find out when each shape worked out.

Read each clue and record what you know on the chart.
If a shape did not exercise at that time, color the box.
If a shape did exercise at that time, draw a star in the box.

	8:00	9:00	10:00	11:00	12:00	1:00
Sally Sphere						
Seth Square Pyramid						
Cole Cube						
Rita Rectangular Prism						
Cindy Cylinder						
Connor Cone						

Clues:

1. The shape with six faces that are all the same went last.
2. The shape with no faces, corners, or edges went before 10:00 but after 8:00.
3. The shape with one round face went at 8:00.
4. The shape with two round faces did not go at 11:00 or 12:00.
5. The shape with one square face and four triangular faces went at 11:00.

Tune-Up

Strengthening Math Skills

Gus's Number Racer
2 7 8 4

NUMBER RACER

Place value

These nifty booklets help students cruise to a better understanding of numbers! Give each child a 6" x 9" piece of construction paper, ten quarter sheets of white paper, construction paper scraps, and markers. To make a number racer, each child makes three cuts about an inch apart, in each quarter sheet of paper as shown. He labels each of the four flaps on the first sheet with the numeral 0, and each of the flaps on the second sheet with the numeral 1. He repeats the process with each remaining sheet, using a different digit from 2–9. Then he folds the construction paper in half and staples the quarter sheets inside. He uses construction paper scraps and markers to create a cover that resembles a car. After the booklets are complete, have students use them to practice several skills, such as creating numbers, reading and writing numbers, and finding a digit's value. Or place at a center the activity cards on page 217. Have students visit the center and use their booklets to complete the tasks on each card.

These games, centers, and whole-class activities are sure to have students' math engines running smoothly!

with ideas by Laura Wagner, Raleigh, NC

SPEED ZONE
Addition of two- and three-digit numbers

In this fast-paced game, students work in teams to hone their addition skills! Give each group of four a sheet of paper and a pencil. Also, write on the board four different numbers. Begin the game by having each group's Student 1 write the first number on her paper. Then announce a number for her to add to it. She solves the problem and then passes the paper to Student 2. This child checks Student 1's work and then adds the second number on the board to the solution. Students 3 and 4 repeat the process, using different numbers from the board. After all teams finish, check the problems as a class. Award a point to each team that correctly solved all four problems. Then post four new numbers on the board and begin another round of Speed Zone.

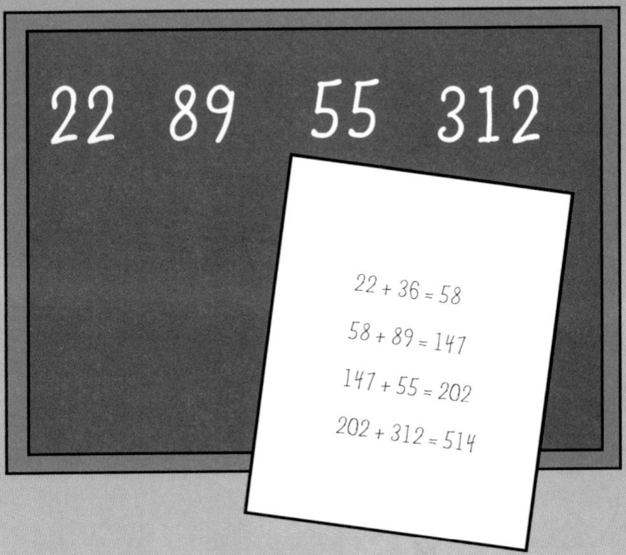
22 89 55 312
22 + 36 = 58
58 + 89 = 147
147 + 55 = 202
202 + 312 = 514

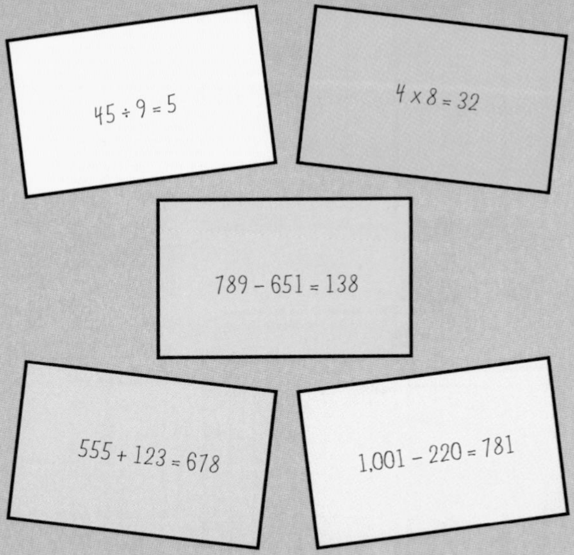
45 ÷ 9 = 5
4 x 8 = 32
789 – 651 = 138
555 + 123 = 678
1,001 – 220 = 781

COMPUTE AND COMPARE
Computation, ordering numbers

Cover two skills with one activity! Write different addition, subtraction, multiplication, or division problems on index cards. Make enough cards so that each student can have several. Give each child a card and then divide students into groups of five. When you say "Go!" each child solves the problem on his card. After he and his teammates have completed their problems, the students use their solutions to order themselves from least to greatest. Repeat the process with a new set of cards, this time having students order themselves from greatest to least. For further practice, place the cards at a center. Have a student draw five cards, solve the problems, and then order the cards according to their solutions.

BRAKE CHECK
Memorizing multiples

This quick time filler is a fun way to reinforce multiplication tables! To start, announce a number from two to twelve, such as six. Then have the class count aloud. When a multiple of the number is reached, have students make a braking sound instead of saying that number. Continue counting and braking until the class has counted the last basic-fact multiple for that number.

1, 2, 3, 4, 5, screech, 7, 8, 9, 10, 11, screech...

Name________________________

Fill 'er Up!

Write a fraction to show how full each tank is.

A.

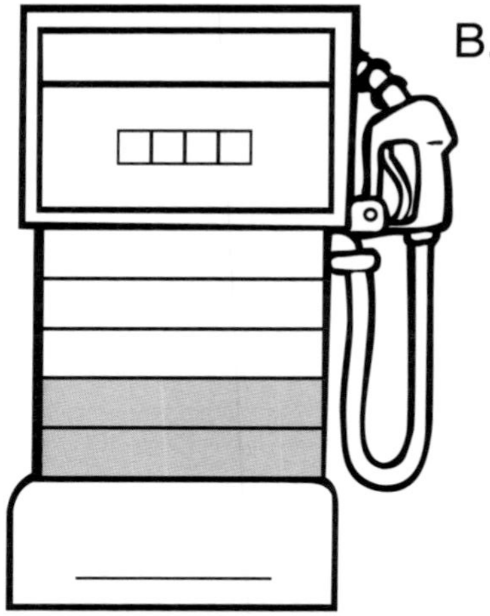

B.

C.

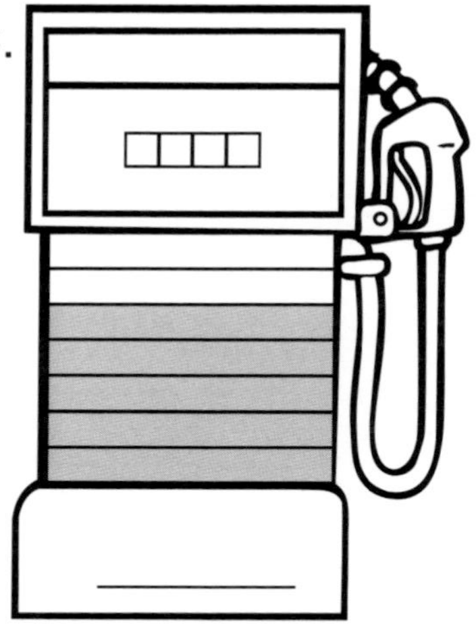

D.

E.

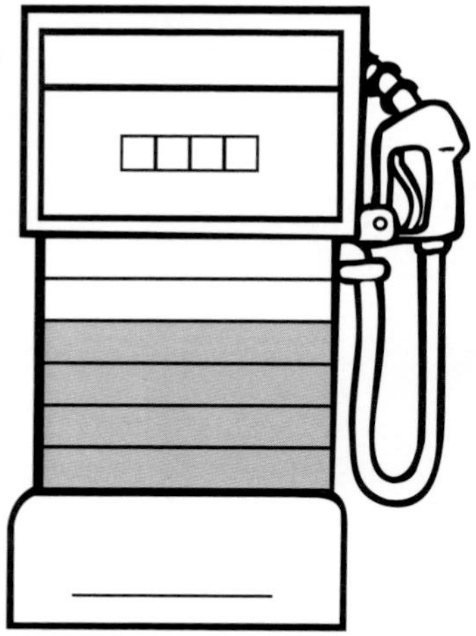

F.

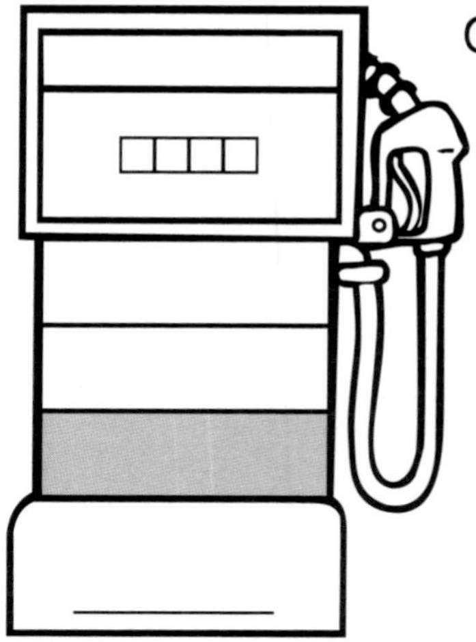

G.

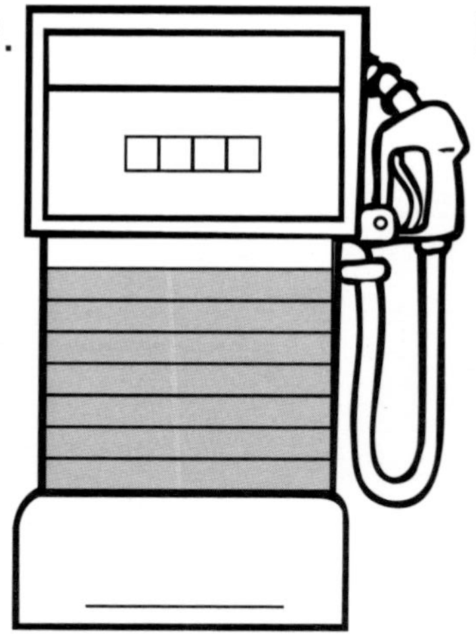

H.

I.

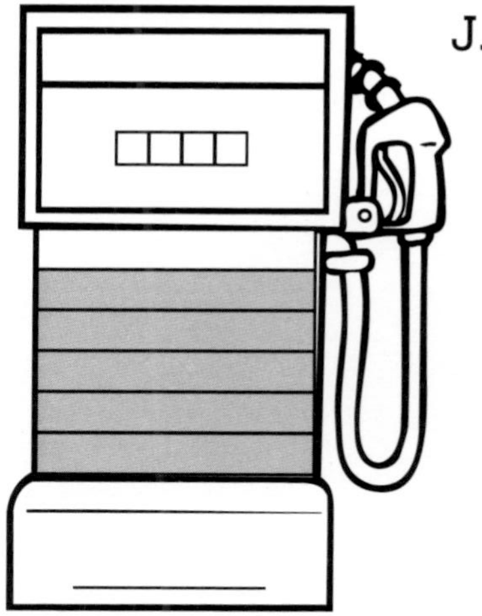

J.

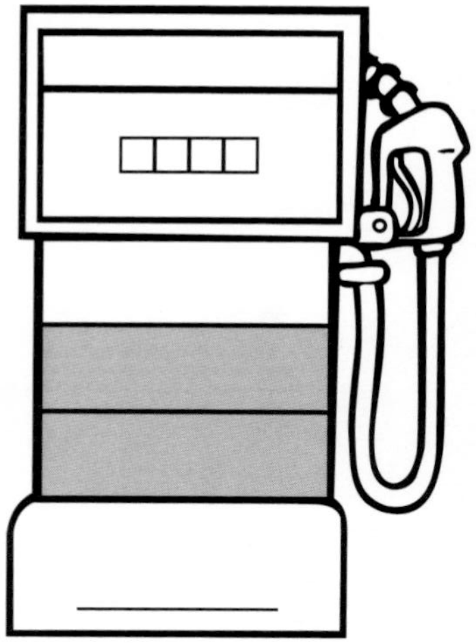

Directions

1. Copy this page and mount it on construction paper.
2. Color the cards and cut them out.
3. Place the cards at a center along with paper and pencils.
4. Have students use their number racers to complete each card and record their answers on paper.

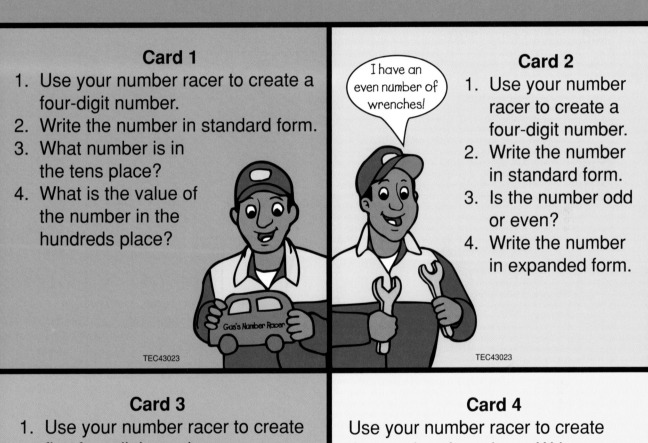

Card 1

1. Use your number racer to create a four-digit number.
2. Write the number in standard form.
3. What number is in the tens place?
4. What is the value of the number in the hundreds place?

Gus's Number Racer

TEC43023

Card 2

I have an even number of wrenches!

1. Use your number racer to create a four-digit number.
2. Write the number in standard form.
3. Is the number odd or even?
4. Write the number in expanded form.

TEC43023

Card 3

1. Use your number racer to create five four-digit numbers.
2. Write the numbers on a sheet of paper.
3. Order the numbers from greatest to least.

TEC43023

Card 4

Use your number racer to create three pairs of numbers. Write a number sentence for each pair using < or >.

1,000 spark plugs
2,500 spark plugs

TEC43023

Name__________________________________

Subtraction Lift

Subtract.
Cross out each answer
on the pole.

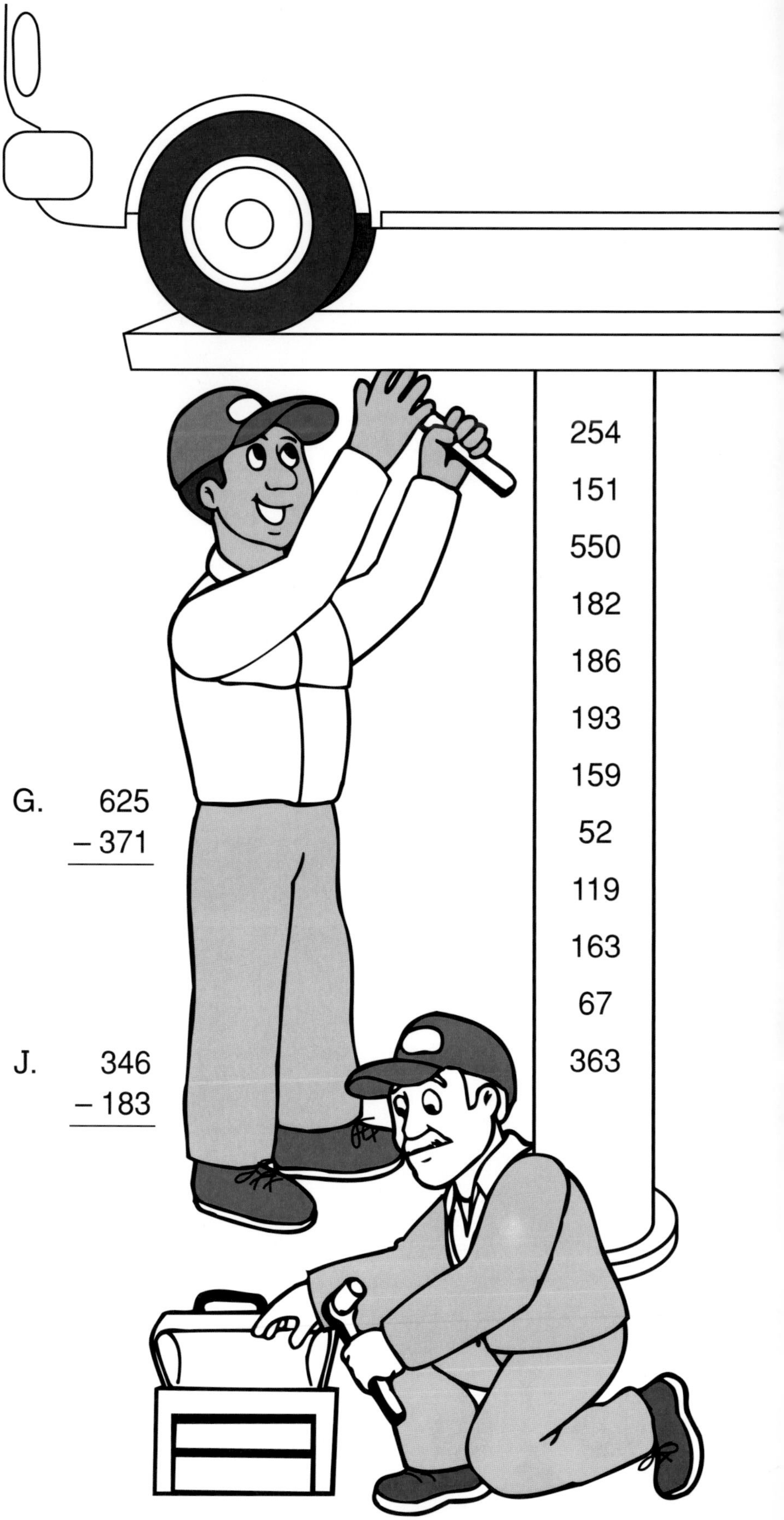
254
151
550
182
186
193
159
52
119
163
67
363

A. 257 − 138

B. 341 − 190

C. 554 − 361

D. 296 − 229

E. 923 − 764

F. 841 − 291

G. 625 − 371

H. 308 − 126

I. 222 − 170

J. 346 − 183

K. 749 − 386

L. 857 − 671

Goin' Buggy!

Practicing Number Patterns

Lulu's Pattern Puzzler
28, __, __, 37, __, 43, 46,
__, __, 55
28, 31, 34, 37, 40, 43, 46,
49, 52, 55
Add 3.
28, __, __, 37, __, 43, 46,
__, __, 55

PARTNER PUZZLERS

Identifying and completing number patterns

These puzzles are easy to create and fun to solve! Each child folds a sheet of paper to form a flap as shown. Next, he writes a number pattern and its rule under the flap. On the bottom of the paper he copies his pattern a second time, replacing several numbers with blanks. Then pair students. A student shows his pattern to his partner, making sure that the completed pattern and rule are concealed. His partner tries to guess a number to extend the pattern. If correct, his partner writes the number in the corresponding blank. The student then tries to identify the rule and complete the pattern. If he is unable to do this, his partner takes a turn in the same manner. Partners repeat the process until both students have correctly completed their partner's pattern and identified its rule. To vary this activity, place the puzzlers at a center instead. Invite each student to select a pattern and complete it on a sheet of paper. Finally, have him lift the flap to check his answer.

Spotting number patterns and their rules is simple with these activities!

with ideas by David Green, North Shore Country Day School, Winnetka, IL

NUMBERS IN A ROW
Identifying number patterns and their rules

To prepare this whole-class activity, write each number in the patterns shown on separate index card halves. Keep the cards in two separate groups, according to their pattern. Begin by randomly distributing one card set. Have those students come to the front of the room and display their cards so that their seated classmates can see each number. Invite the remaining students to guess the pattern rule. If a child identifies the rule, write it on the board. If no one is able to identify the rule, guide students to see it. Then have the seated students work together to order their classmates so that the pattern is complete. To play Round 2, have students change places. Distribute the second card set and repeat the process.

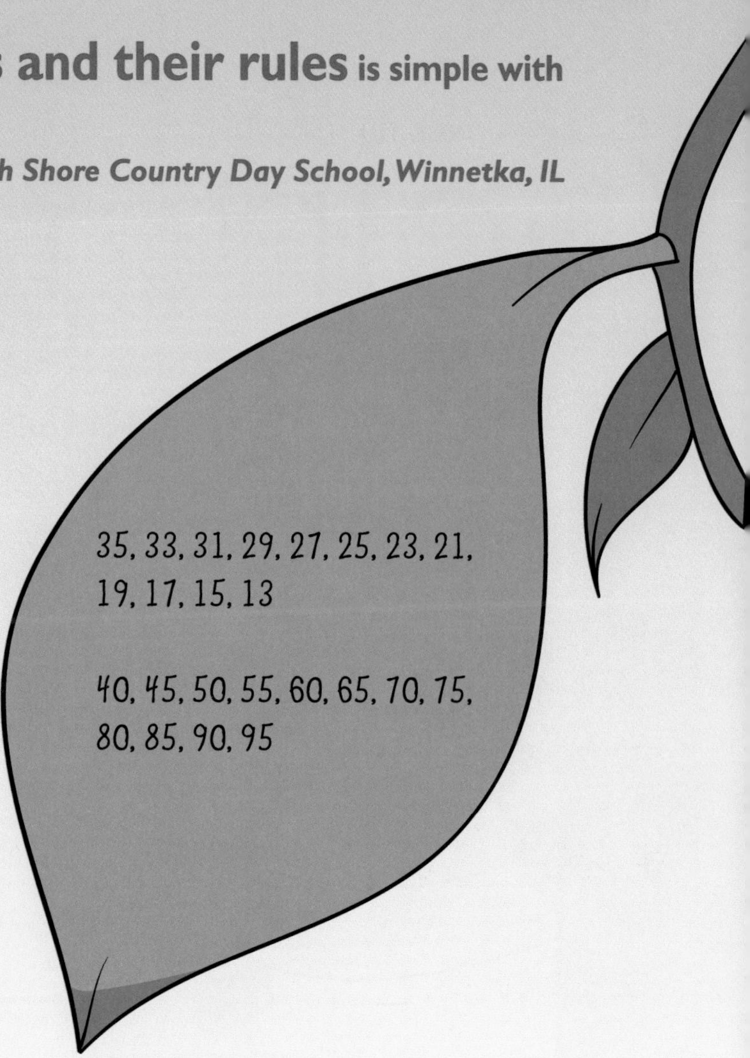
35, 33, 31, 29, 27, 25, 23, 21, 19, 17, 15, 13
40, 45, 50, 55, 60, 65, 70, 75, 80, 85, 90, 95

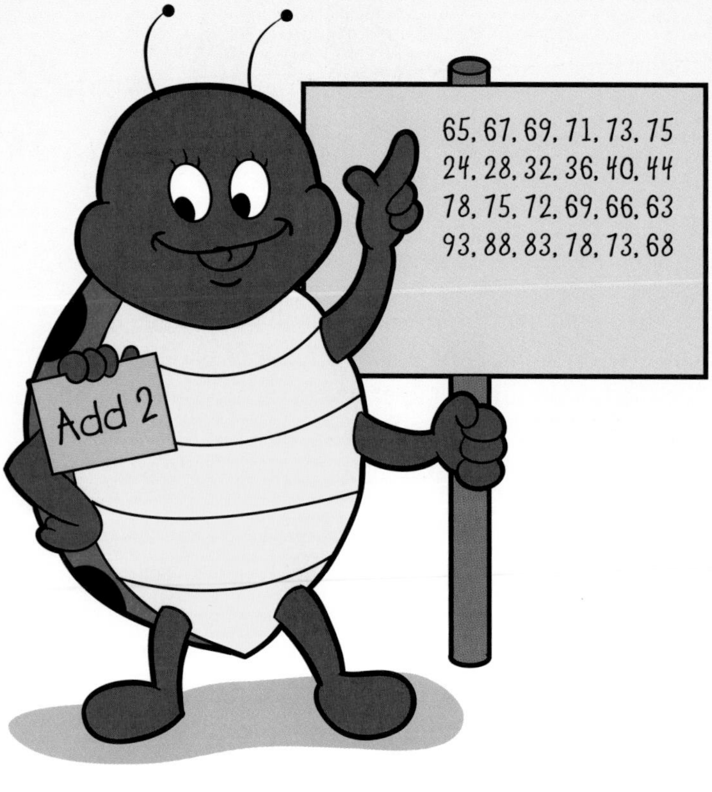
65, 67, 69, 71, 73, 75
24, 28, 32, 36, 40, 44
78, 75, 72, 69, 66, 63
93, 88, 83, 78, 73, 68
Add 2

PLAYING BY THE RULES
Identifying the pattern rule

Program a transparency with the number patterns shown. Also program four sets of index cards with the following pattern rules: add 2, add 4, subtract 3, and subtract 5. Then give each small group of students a set of cards and display the transparency on the overhead. Challenge each group to work quietly to identify each pattern's rule. After students are finished, read the first pattern aloud. Have groups hold up the card with the matching rule. Repeat the process for the remaining patterns.

Extend the lesson by having each group use the same rules to create four new patterns and write them on a transparency. Collect the group's patterns and card sets. For each of the next several days, begin the lesson by having students re-form their groups. Redistribute the cards and then post a different group's patterns on the overhead. Have students identify the pattern rule; then invite the pattern writers to repeat the process for checking.

Name____________________

Maid Service

Complete each number pattern.

A. 48, 50, ____ (E), 54, ____, 58, ____, 62, ____

B. 17, 20, 23, ____, ____ (S), ____, 35, 38, ____ (M)

C. 75, 65, ____, ____ (E), 35, ____, 15, ____ (T)

D. 30, 35, ____ (A), ____, 50, ____ (H), 60, ____

E. 88, 85, 82, ____, 76, ____ (T), ____, ____ (K), 64

F. 80, ____ (S), 60, ____, ____, 30, 20, ____

G. 55, 59, 63, ____, 71, ____, ____ (M), ____ (O), 87

H. 20, 18, 16, ____, ____, 10, ____ (L), 6, ____

I. 27, 32, ____ (E), 42, ____, ____, 57, ____ (P), 67

J. 13, 17, 21, ____ (S), 29, ____, 37, ____, ____

Why are ladybugs good at cleaning houses?
To solve the riddle, write the letters above on the matching numbered lines below.

They ____ ____ ____ ____   ____ ____ ____ ____
41 40 67 37   73 55 45 79

____ ____ ____ ____ ____ ____ ____ ____!
25 62 83 5 8 52 70 29

Sowing Seeds

Planting a Problem-Solving Garden

STEPPING STONES

Steps to problem solving

This activity helps students internalize the steps of problem solving! In advance, make one copy of the problem cards at the top of page 224. Also make five copies of the step cards at the bottom of page 224. Cut apart all the cards, and clip each set of step cards together. Begin the activity by dividing the class into five groups. Give each group two problem cards and a set of step cards. The group reads the first problem and uses the information on the step cards to solve it. One member records the group's answer on a sheet of paper. Then the group repeats the process with the second problem. After each group finishes, invite it to share one of its problems and the solution with the class. If desired, have students complete the reproducible on page 227 as a follow-up.

In all are clue words. They tell us to add to solve the problem!
1. Rex picked 27 carrots on Tuesday. He picked 39 carrots on Wednesday. Then he picked 43 carrots on Thursday. How many carrots did he pick in all?
3. What are the CLUE WORDS?

Plant these ideas in your classroom, and students will reap a better understanding of problem solving!

with ideas by Jean Erickson, Grace Christian Academy, West Allis, WI

DIGGING THE PROCESS
Matching key words to operations

In advance, copy pages 225 and 226 and mount them on construction paper. Cut out and program the back of each card with its corresponding operation sign for self-checking. Then place the cards and the sorting mat at a center. A child sorts each card by placing it on the matching shovel. Then she turns the cards over to check her work.

Subtraction
total
shared equally
left over
times

GET THE PICTURE?
Writing story problems

Problem solving is a snap with this simple partner idea! Throughout the week, take pictures of your students as they complete activities inside and outside the classroom. Write a number on the border or back of each photo. Next, give each pair a few pictures and index cards. Have the pair of students work together to write a story problem, like the ones shown, for each picture. Then have them label the card's front with the number found on the picture and write the answer to the problem on the card's back. Collect the cards and pictures and place them at a center. To use the center, a student selects a card (making sure not to choose one he's written with his partner) and finds the corresponding picture. Then he solves the problem and turns the card over to check his work.

1
2
1
Jamie is reading a book. If he reads 3 books each day, how many days will it take him to read 21 books?
Latoya and Donny are playing on the jungle gym. If they play on the jungle gym for 10 minutes every day, how long will they play in 4 days?

Problem Cards

Use with "Stepping Stones" on page 222.

1. Rex picked 27 carrots on Tuesday. He picked 39 carrots on Wednesday. Then he picked 43 carrots on Thursday. How many carrots did he pick in all?

TEC43024

2. Rex planted 9 rows of lettuce plants. Each row has an equal number of plants. If there are 81 plants in all, how many plants are in each row?

TEC43024

3. Rex picked 84 pounds of spinach. He also picked 67 pounds of cabbage. How many more pounds of spinach did he pick?

TEC43024

4. Rex made $29.00 selling vegetables on Monday. On Tuesday, he made $54.55. On Wednesday, he made $47.40. How much money did he make all together?

TEC43024

5. Rex packed 7 boxes of radishes. Each box has 10 radishes in it. How many radishes did Rex pack in all?

TEC43024

6. Rex worked for 3 hours and 15 minutes on Thursday. He worked 2 hours and 5 minutes on Friday. How long did he work in all?

TEC43024

7. Rex packed a crate that weighs 156 pounds. He packed a second crate that weighs 89 pounds. How much more does the first crate weigh?

TEC43024

8. Rex sells 4 pies each week at the farmer's market. How many pies will he sell in 9 weeks?

TEC43024

9. Rex plows 5 rows of corn each day. He plows the same number of rows each day. How many days will it take him to plow 35 rows?

TEC43024

10. Rex planted 6 rows of cabbage. Each row had 9 plants. How many total cabbage plants did he plant?

TEC43024

Step Cards

Use with "Stepping Stones" on page 222.

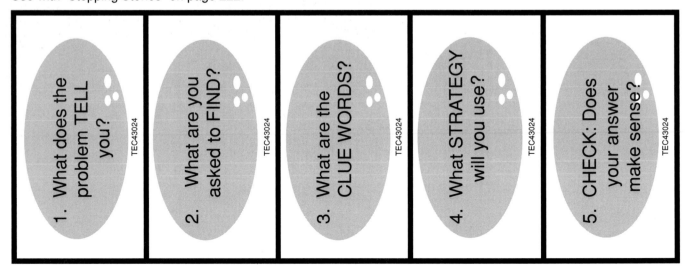

1. What does the problem TELL you?

TEC43024

2. What are you asked to FIND?

TEC43024

3. What are the CLUE WORDS?

TEC43024

4. What STRATEGY will you use?

TEC43024

5. CHECK: Does your answer make sense?

TEC43024

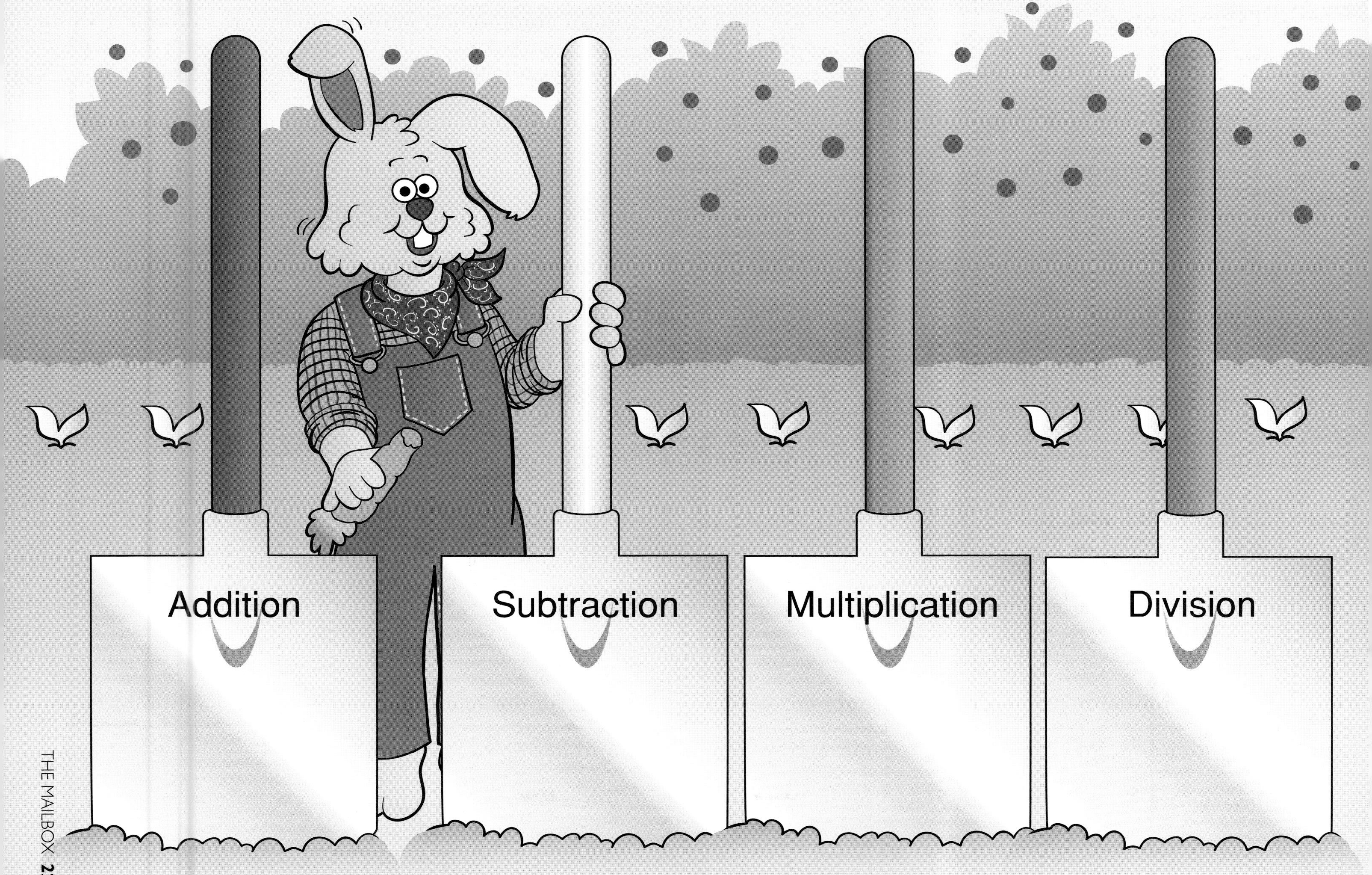
Addition
Subtraction
Multiplication
Division

Center Cards

Use with "Digging the Process" on page 223.

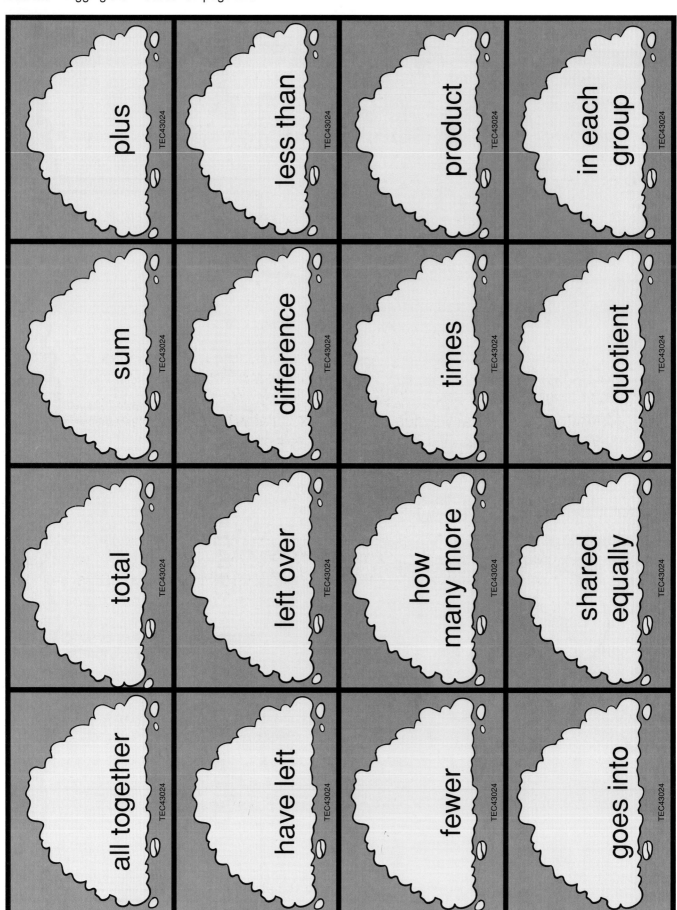

all together TEC43024	total TEC43024	sum TEC43024	plus TEC43024
have left TEC43024	left over TEC43024	difference TEC43024	less than TEC43024
fewer TEC43024	how many more TEC43024	times TEC43024	product TEC43024
goes into TEC43024	shared equally TEC43024	quotient TEC43024	in each group TEC43024

Name____

On the Farm

Solve.

1. Rex picked 74 carrots on Thursday. He picked 98 carrots on Friday and 92 carrots on Monday. How many carrots did Rex pick in all? ______________	2. Rex collected 239 gallons of milk during week 1. During week 2 he collected 328 gallons of milk. How many more gallons of milk did Rex collect during week 2? ______________
3. Rex's sister Rita takes care of the horses. She has 16 pounds of food to share equally among 8 horses. How much food will each horse get? ______________	4. Rita planted 6 rows of roses in her flower garden. Each row has 7 plants. How many roses did Rita plant in all? ______________
5. Rita also planted 8 rows of pansies. Each row has 5 pansies. How many pansies did she plant? ______________	6. Rex worked on the tractor for 15 minutes on Tuesday. He also worked on it for 35 minutes on Thursday and 20 minutes on Friday. How many total minutes did Rex work on the tractor? ______________
7. Both Rex and Rita helped harvest the lettuce. Rex picked 187 heads of lettuce. Rita picked 265 heads of lettuce. How many more heads of lettuce did Rita pick? ______________	8. Rex's mom baked 28 pies. She baked the same number of pies on each day. If she baked pies on 4 days, how many pies did she make each day? ______________

Celebrate!
A Star-Spangled Math Review

4 x 8 = 32
Jin
54 - 22 = 32
20 + 12 = 32
32
16 + 16 = 32
40 - 8 = 32

SHINE ON!
Computation

This simple activity is just the thing for practicing addition, subtraction, and multiplication skills! In advance, cut a class supply of star shapes from red and blue construction paper. Program each star's center with a different two-digit number, making sure that the number is a common multiple of at least two numbers. Next, give each child a star and have him create five different problems, each with a sum, difference, or product equal to the number on his star. He writes each problem on one of the star's points. Then he writes his name on the star and decorates it as desired. Post students' stars on a display titled "We're Math Superstars!"

Showcase your students' math skills
with this end-of-the-year review!

with ideas by Stacie Stone Davis, Lima, NY

MEASUREMENT MATCH
Finding perimeter

To create this center, first copy page 230 and mount it on construction paper. Color the cards and cut them out. Program the back of each card for self-checking; then place the cards at a center along with paper and pencils. A child selects a shape card and finds the perimeter by adding the measurements of the sides. She uses paper and pencil as needed. Then she finds the card with the matching perimeter. After she matches each shape to its perimeter, she turns the cards over to check her work.

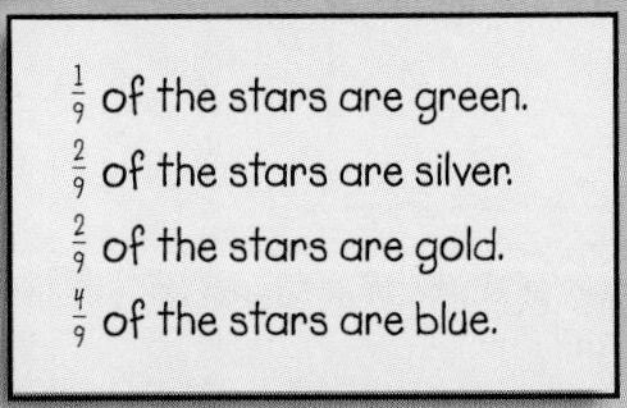
$\frac{1}{9}$ of the stars are green.
$\frac{2}{9}$ of the stars are silver.
$\frac{2}{9}$ of the stars are gold.
$\frac{4}{9}$ of the stars are blue.

5 cm
3 cm
4 cm
Perimeter = 12 cm

STARRY FLAGS
Finding the fractional part of a set

Before starting the activity, gather a supply of multicolored foil stars and cut out a class supply of 4½" x 6 " colored construction paper rectangles. Place the stars and rectangles at a center along with index cards and pencils. Each child visits the center, selects a rectangle, and uses any combination of stars desired to create a flag. After his flag is complete, he lists on an index card several fraction statements that describe the makeup of the stars. Then he writes his name on the back of the index card and the flag. After all students have created a flag and a clue card, invite them to visit the center again. This time, have each child read a clue card and find the corresponding flag. He flips the card and the flag over to see whether the names match. He continues matching clues and flags for as long as desired.

Center Cards

Use with "Measurement Match" on page 229.

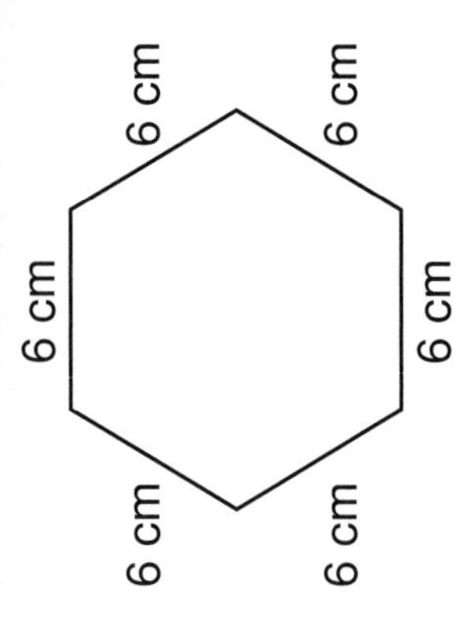
6 cm
6 cm
6 cm
6 cm
6 cm
6 cm

Perimeter = 36 cm

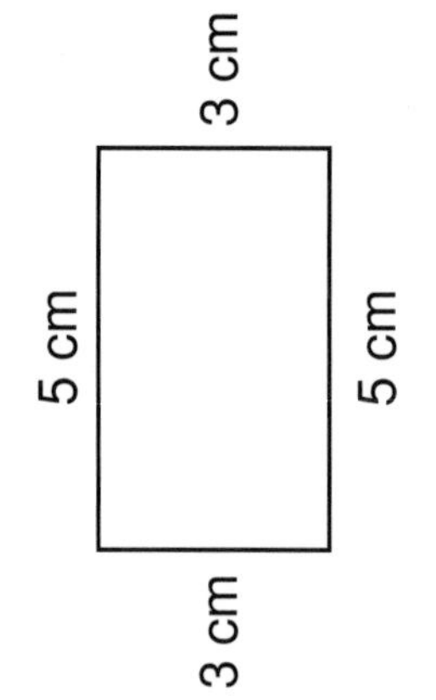
3 cm
5 cm
5 cm
3 cm

Perimeter = 16 cm

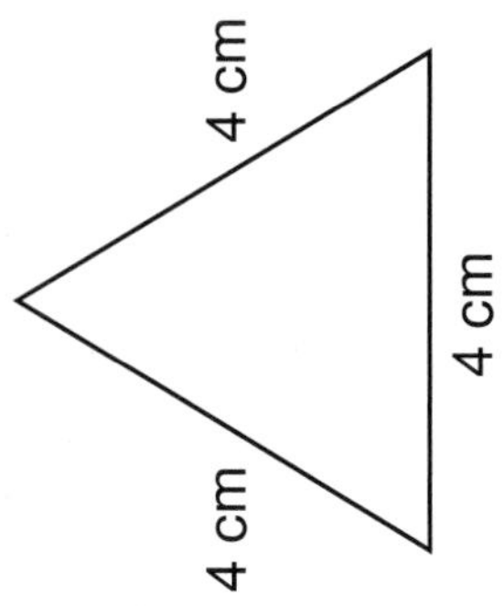
4 cm
4 cm
4 cm

Perimeter = 12 cm

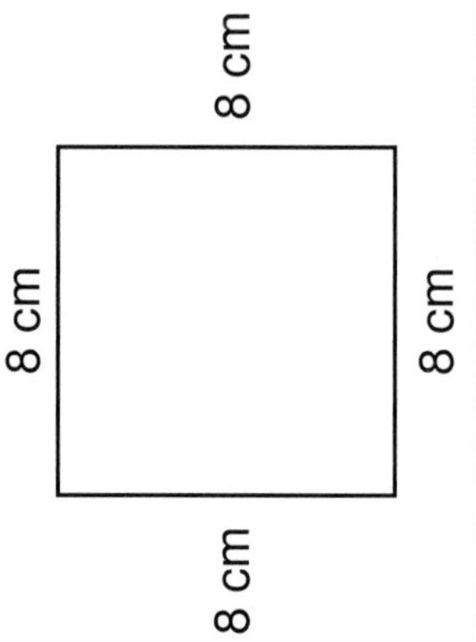
8 cm
8 cm
8 cm
8 cm

Perimeter = 32 cm

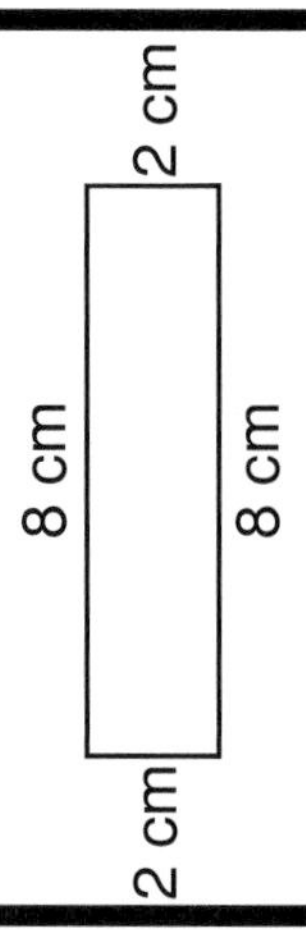
2 cm
8 cm
8 cm
2 cm

Perimeter = 20 cm

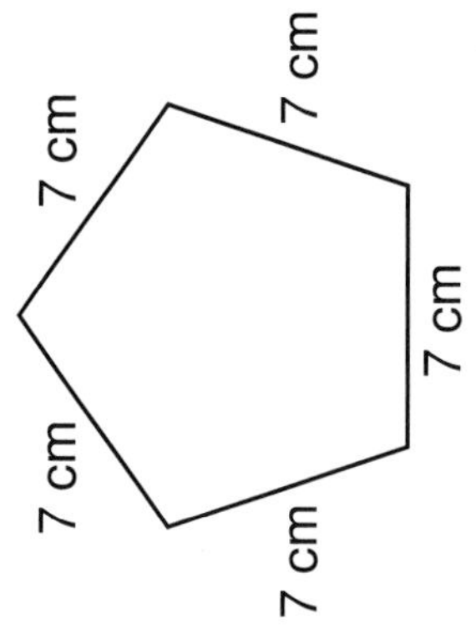
7 cm
7 cm
7 cm
7 cm
7 cm

Perimeter = 35 cm

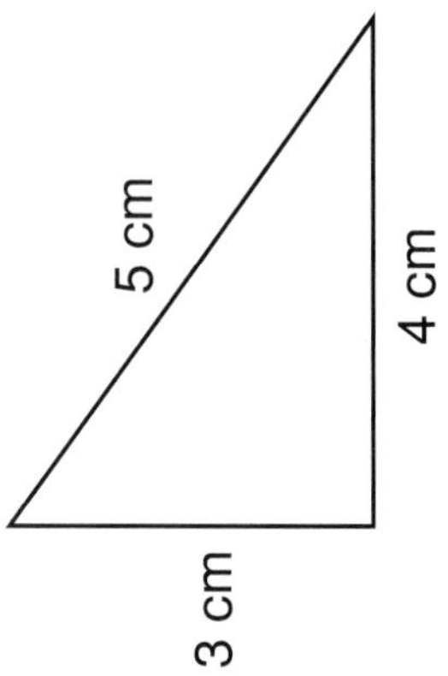
5 cm
4 cm
3 cm

Perimeter = 12 cm

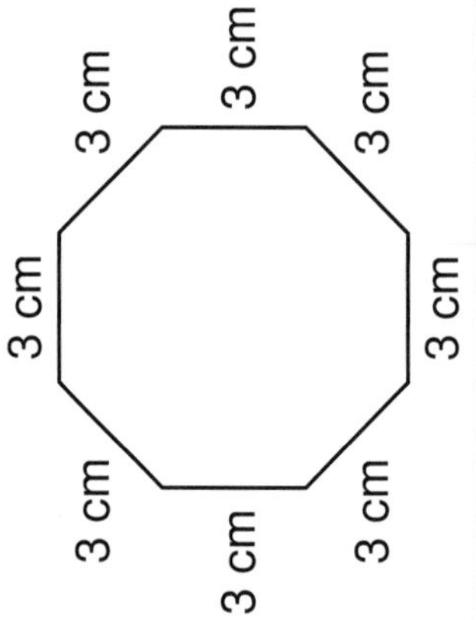
3 cm
3 cm
3 cm
3 cm
3 cm
3 cm
3 cm
3 cm

Perimeter = 24 cm

Name____

Flo's Flags

Use the graph to answer the questions.

Flags Sold

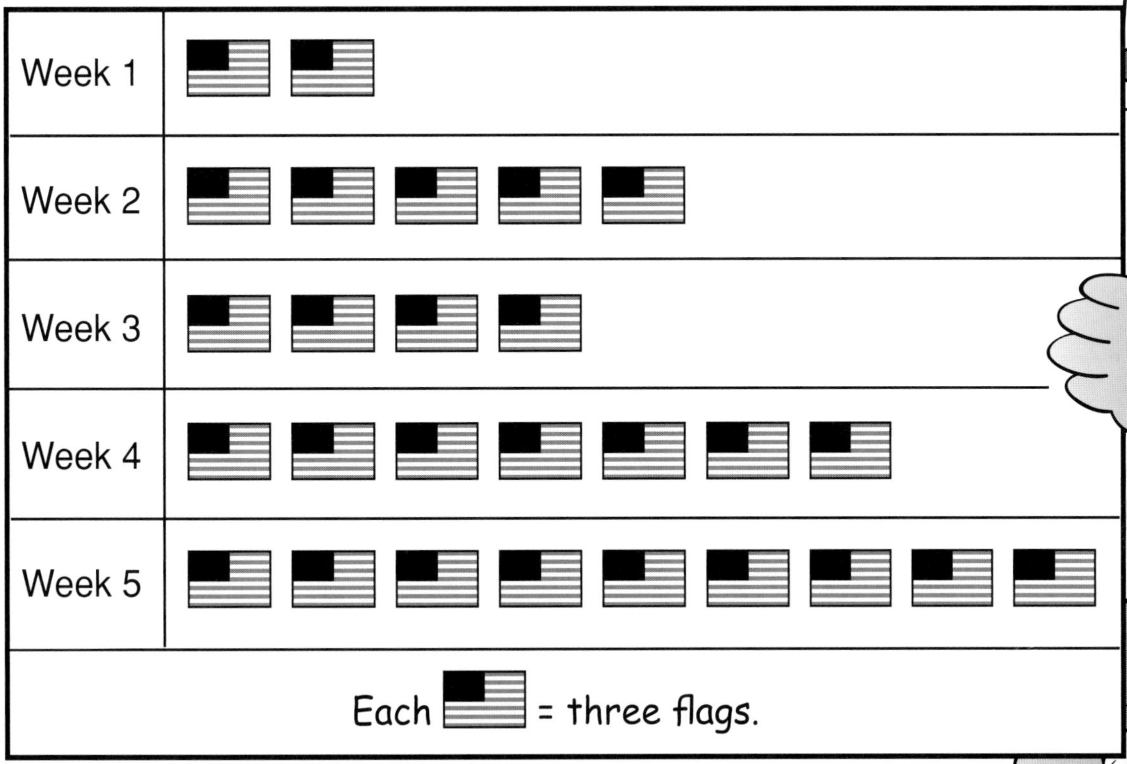
Week 1
Week 2
Week 3
Week 4
Week 5
Each = three flags.

1. In which week were the most flags sold? ________________
2. How many flags were sold then? ___________
3. How many flags were sold during Weeks 2 and 3? ___________
4. In which week were the least number of flags sold? ________________
5. How many flags were sold during that week? ___________
6. How many more flags were sold during Week 4 than Week 1? ___________
7. How many total flags were sold during Weeks 4 and 5? ___________
8. Flo's goal is to sell 15 flags each week. How many more flags did she need to sell during Week 1 to reach her goal? ___________

Name____

Math Review
Logical reasoning

Flag Facts

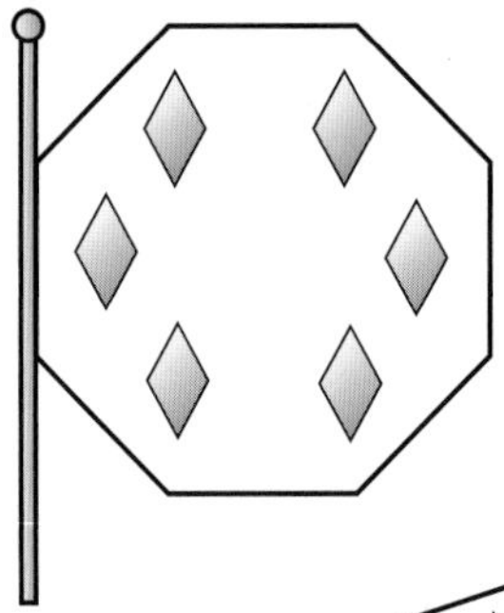

Each eagle has a different flag.
Find out which flag belongs to each eagle.

Read each clue and record what you know on the chart.
If the flag does not belong to the eagle, color the box.
If the flag does belong to the eagle, draw a star in the box.

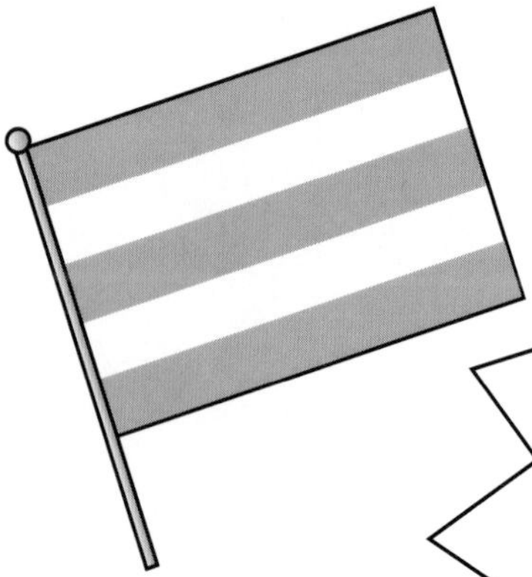

Clues

1. Ellie's flag is not shaped like a rectangle.
2. Evan's flag has circles on it.
3. Ernie's flag has eight sides.
4. Erin's flag does not have stripes.
5. Eva's flag does not have stars.

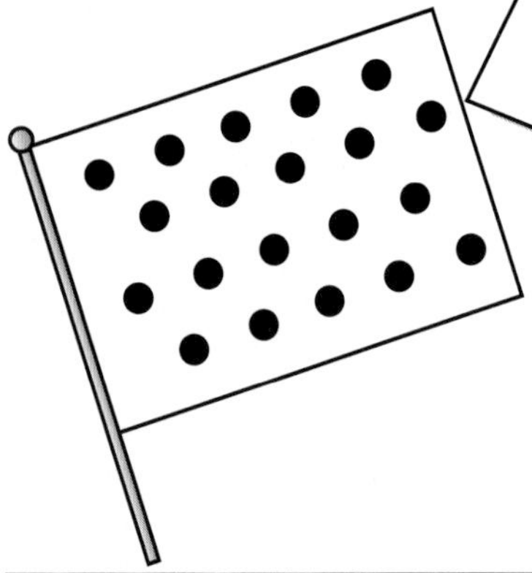

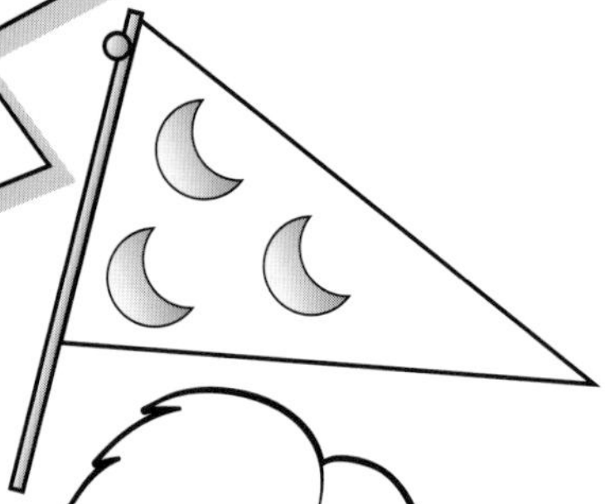

	Striped Flag	Polka-Dot Flag	Starry Flag	Triangular Flag	Octagonal Flag
Ernie					
Evan					
Erin					
Eva					
Ellie					

Take a **Chance!**

Probability Activities

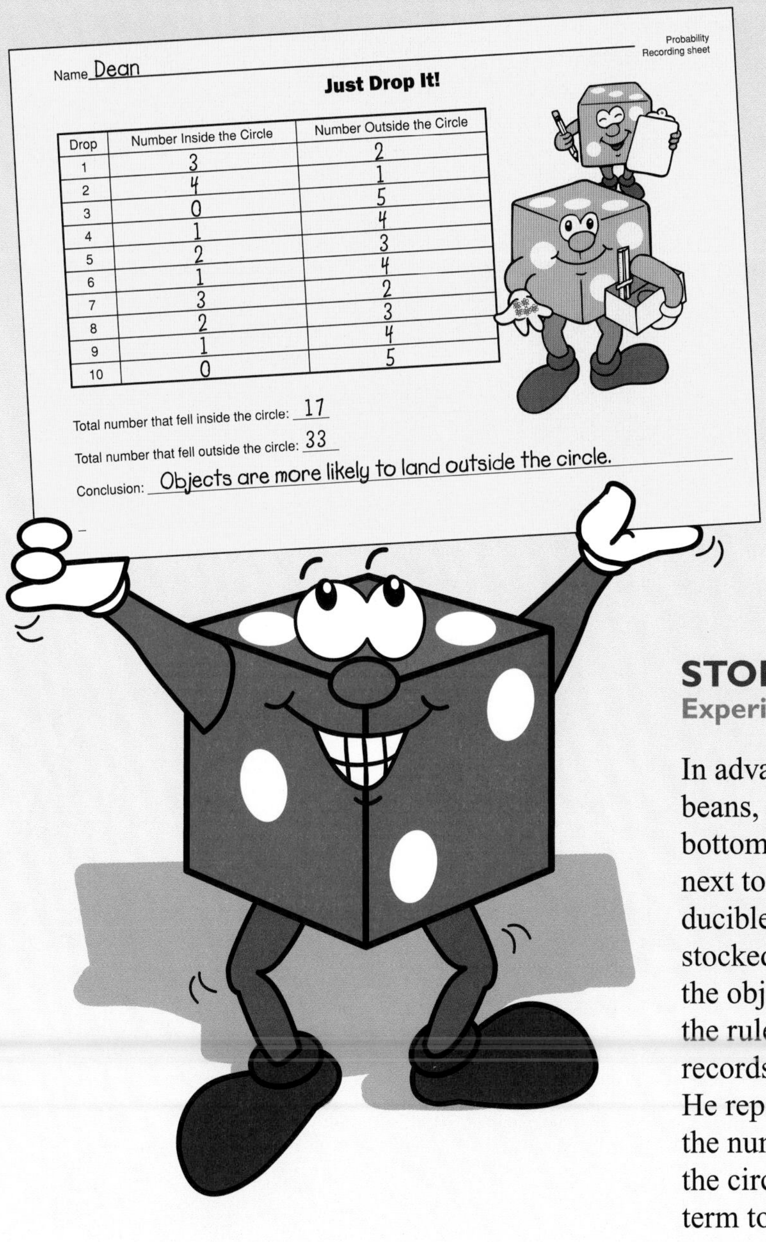

Name Dean

Probability
Recording sheet

Just Drop It!

Drop	Number Inside the Circle	Number Outside the Circle
1	3	2
2	4	1
3	0	5
4	1	4
5	2	3
6	1	4
7	3	2
8	2	3
9	1	4
10	0	5

Total number that fell inside the circle: 17

Total number that fell outside the circle: 33

Conclusion: Objects are more likely to land outside the circle.

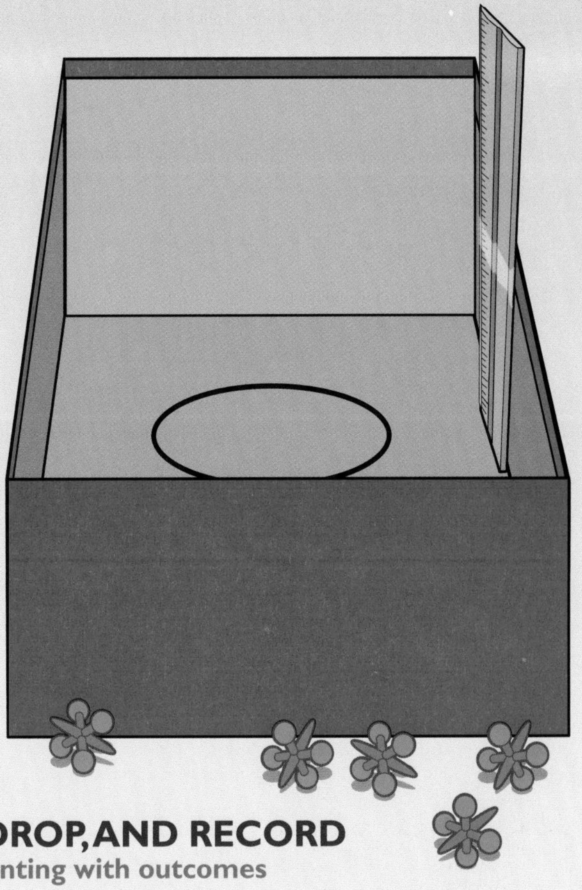

STOP, DROP, AND RECORD

Experimenting with outcomes

In advance, gather a shoebox, a ruler, and five dried beans, counters, or jacks. Draw a four-inch circle in the bottom of the box, and tape the ruler to the box's side, next to the circle. Also make a class supply of the reproducible on page 235. Then place the materials at a center stocked with pencils. A child visits the center and holds the objects in his hand, at the same height as the top of the ruler. He drops the objects at the same time and then records the number that fell inside and outside the circle. He repeats the process nine times. Afterward, he totals the number of times the objects landed inside or outside the circle. He uses this information and a probability term to write a conclusion for the experiment.

Use these activities to get students on a roll with probability!

with ideas by Jean Erickson, Grace Christian Academy, West Allis, WI

PREDICTING OUTCOMES

Using *certain, more likely, less likely,* and *impossible*

It will snow three inches.
I will see the sun.
I will wear long pants every day.
I will go to the beach.

This simple activity helps students become familiar with probability terms! In advance, write several summertime events and other seasonal events, like the ones shown, each on a different paper slip. Make sure to include events that are certain, are more likely, are less likely, and would be impossible to occur in the summer. Place the slips in a paper bag. Begin by sharing with students the hand motions shown. Then draw a paper slip and read it aloud. Each child listens to the statement; thinks about summer; decides whether the event is certain, more likely, less likely, or impossible; and shows the corresponding hand motion. Continue in this manner until each event has been read aloud and identified.

certain	=	two thumbs up
more likely	=	one thumb up
less likely	=	one thumb down
impossible	=	two thumbs down

CENTERED ON PROBABILITY

Conducting an experiment and recording the results

Toss your penny 20 times.
Use tally marks to record each toss.
Heads
Tails
On which side did the penny land the most?

To set up these centers, make a class supply of the reproducible on page 236. Also gather the items listed below and place them at four different centers.

- Center 1: penny
- Center 2: die
- Center 3: three sets of five items that are the same shape and size, but different colors (for example, five green blocks, five red blocks, and five blue blocks)
- Center 4: a spinner divided into four sections, with each section having one of the following shapes inside: triangle, square, rectangle, and circle

To start, give each child a copy of the reproducible. The student cuts apart the pages, stacks them, and staples them together between two construction paper covers. She visits each center and writes a prediction of the experiment's outcome on the back of the page. Then she uses the directions on the page to complete the experiment and record the results.

Name ______________________________

Just Drop It!

Drop	Number Inside the Circle	Number Outside the Circle
1		
2		
3		
4		
5		
6		
7		
8		
9		
10		

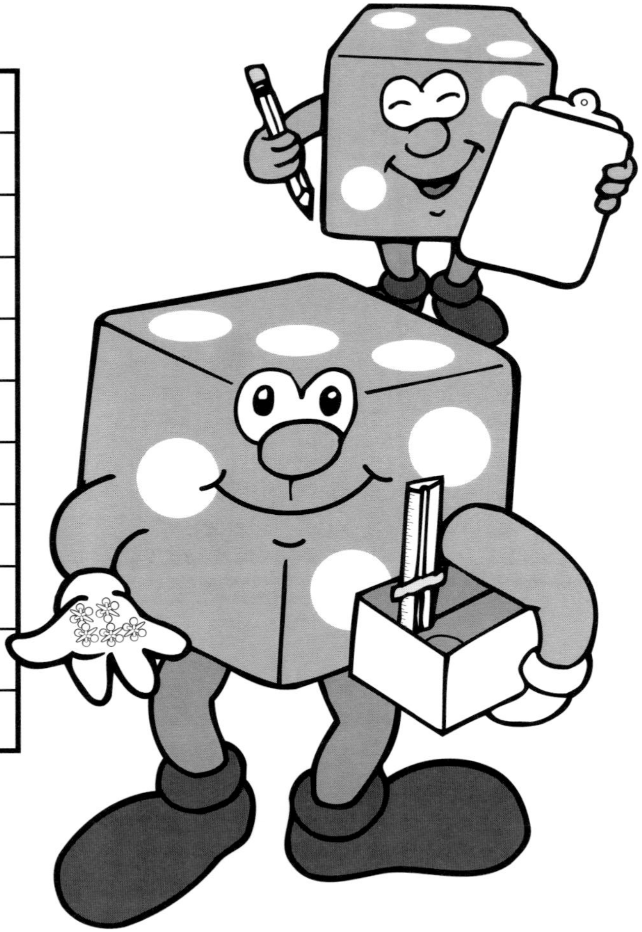

Total number that fell inside the circle: _____

Total number that fell outside the circle: _____

Conclusion: ______________________________

Note to the teacher: Use with “Stop, Drop, and Record” on page 233.

Recording Booklet

Use with "Centered on Probability" on page 234.

Toss your penny 20 times.
Use tally marks to record each toss.

Heads	Tails

On which side did the penny land the most? ______________________

TEC43025

Roll the die 20 times.
Draw an X in the matching box each time.

1	2	3	4	5	6

Which number was rolled the most?

______

TEC43025

Draw an item from the bag.
Color a circle in the matching row.
Return the item to the bag.
Repeat until you have colored 20 circles.

Red	○ ○ ○ ○ ○ ○ ○ ○ ○ ○ ○ ○
Blue	○ ○ ○ ○ ○ ○ ○ ○ ○ ○ ○ ○
Green	○ ○ ○ ○ ○ ○ ○ ○ ○ ○ ○ ○

Which color was drawn the most?

_

TEC43025

Spin the spinner 20 times.
Use a tally mark to record each spin.

 △	
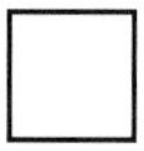 □	
 ▭	
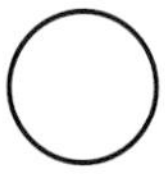 ○	

Which shape was spun the most?

_

TEC43025

Science and Social Studies

Give a Hoot!

Practicing Good Citizenship

A Better Me
At School
At Home
In My Neighborhood
treat my classmates as I want to be treated.
At School
At Home
In My Neighborhood
Good Citizens Give a Hoot!

A BETTER ME

Goal setting

The goal of this booklet project is to remind students that they can practice good citizenship in more than one place. Challenge each child to determine one or more ways she can be a better citizen in each of the following locations: school, home, neighborhood (or community). Prompt students' thinking by asking volunteers to share their ideas. When a child has determined her citizenship goals, have her make a flip booklet. To do this, she stacks two half sheets of blank paper and then she slides the top sheet upward about one inch. Next, she folds the papers forward to make four graduated layers. Staple her booklet near the fold. Next, instruct her to title the front cover "A Better Me" and draw and color her self-likeness there. Then have her label the lower edge of each booklet page as shown and program the pages with her goals for becoming a better citizen. Very impressive!

"Whooo" knows the traits of a good citizen? Use these activities, and your students will be all the wiser!

with ideas by David A. Green, North Shore Country Day School, Winnetka, IL

Scenario suggestions:
• A child drops his lunch tray. No one stops to help him.
• A student gives the wrong answer. Her classmates giggle.
• A student passes a note to a classmate when the teacher isn't looking.
• A student tells an untrue story about a classmate.
Good Citizens Give a Hoot

TAKING NOTICE
Evaluating behavior

Expand your students' understanding of good citizenship with fictitious scenarios like the ones provided. After students explain why the exhibited behaviors do not promote good citizenship, have them propose behaviors that do. For an individual assessment, ask each child to complete a copy of page 240.

STAR CITIZENS
Good citizen traits

Encourage good citizenship all year long! Title a star-themed bulletin board "Good Citizens Make Good Choices." Nearby, provide a supply of blank cards, star-shaped stickers, and a container for completed cards. Explain to students that the good choices they make can inspire others to make good choices too. Next, ask each child to contribute one or more completed cards per week. To complete a card, a child writes his name, the date, and a description of the good choice he made. Then he adds a star sticker and drops the card in the container. Post the cards on the bulletin board and update the display weekly. When it becomes necessary to remove cards, file them by student name. At the end of the school year, each child can compile his cards into an impressive booklet of good citizenship!

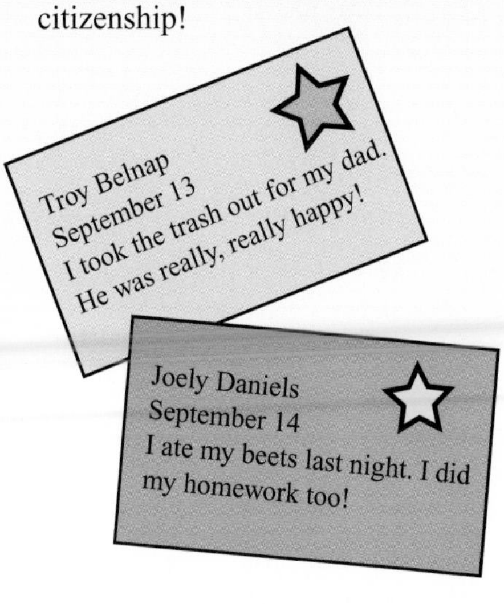

Troy Belnap
September 13
I took the trash out for my dad.
He was really, really happy!
Joely Daniels
September 14
I ate my beets last night. I did my homework too!

Get the word out:
Put the trash in!
TRASH

SPREAD THE WORD
Problem solving

Remind students that communities benefit from citizens who help solve problems. Then ask them to identify problems in their school community. As you list the students' suggestions on the board (for example, litter, excessive noise, unsafe behaviors), have them talk about the effects of each problem and offer solutions for it. Next, help the class select one problem to spotlight in a schoolwide poster campaign. Provide the materials and time needed to design and display posters that encourage citizens to make good choices. When students see the positive results of their campaign, they'll be eager to tackle another school-related issue!

Name ______________________________

Citizenship
Evaluating behavior

Be a Good Citizen

Write why each action is wrong.
Write what a good citizen would do.

My dog ate it.

Telling your teacher a lie

It is wrong because ______________________

____

A good citizen would ______________________

____

Ha! Ha! Ha!

Laughing when someone slips and falls

It is wrong because ______________________

____

A good citizen would ______________________

____

Did you see the moon last night?

Talking during a movie

It is wrong because ______________________

____

A good citizen would ______________________

____

 Note to the teacher: Use alone or as a follow-up to “Taking Notice” on page 239.

Picture This

Mapping Skills

North

WHERE, OH WHERE?

Cardinal directions

For this group activity, label each classroom wall with an appropriate direction (north, south, east, west). Also have each student color, cut out, and personalize a turkey pattern. When the turkeys are ready, ask each child to hide her bird in the classroom. Emphasize that she must remember its location. For a quick review of cardinal directions, sing "Where Did Turkey Go?" below. Ask students to look and point in a direction each time it is named. Then pair students and have each child, in turn, use cardinal directions to orally guide her partner to her hidden turkey. To repeat the activity, have each student move her bird to a different location; then pair the students with new partners.

Where Did Turkey Go?

(sung to the tune of "Mary Had a Little Lamb")

Turkey just ran out of sight,
Out of sight,
Out of sight.
Turkey just ran out of sight.
He's nowhere to be found.

Better look both north and south,
North and south,
North and south.
Better look both north and south.
To see if he's around.

Maybe he went east or west,
East or west,
East or west.
Maybe he went east or west.
Now where did turkey go?

"Wattle" it take to keep your students' geography skills on track? These curriculum-savvy birds have some fine-feathered suggestions!

with ideas by Jean Erickson, Grace Christian Academy, Milwaukee, WI

Northwest
North
Northeast
Center of Classroom
West
East
Southwest
South
Southeast

TIC-TAC-TURKEY
Intermediate directions

Before you begin, have each child ready a copy of page 243 by coloring the pictures and cutting out the grid, the labels, and the pictures. Then start by telling each child to glue the turkey in the center of his grid. Next, have him point to the box that is north of the turkey and glue the "North" label at the top of the box. Continue the process with each remaining cardinal and intermediate direction. Last, have students follow your directional clues to glue the remaining pictures on the grid.

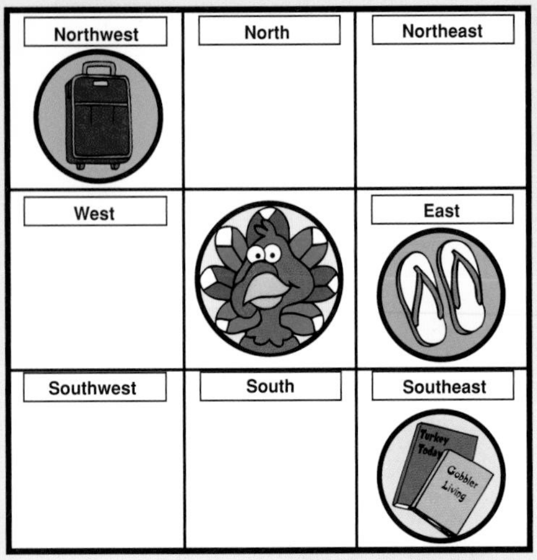

Northwest
North
Northeast
West
East
Southwest
South
Southeast
Turkey Today
Gobbler Living

IN PLAIN VIEW
Making a map

Show students how a grid labeled like the one shown above helps a mapmaker! Label a large sheet of white paper like the one shown. Ask a child to stand in the center of the classroom, face north, and name an object in plain view. Sketch the object in the "North" grid box. Repeat the process for each remaining direction, recruiting a different volunteer each time. Identify the completed project as a simple map of the classroom. Ask students to think of places around school and their homes that can be mapped in a similar way. Mapmakers can draw and label grids or use the grid and labels from copies of page 243. Then set a date on which each student will share her map with the class.

MAKING SENSE OF SYMBOLS
Map key

To set the stage for this activity, remind students that every day during math, they interpret symbols. Then list on the board in a vertical line several symbols that might appear on a map. Invite students to interpret each one, encouraging multiple ideas per symbol. Explain that a symbol on a map has a greater possibility of being misunderstood than a math symbol. Next, beside each symbol on the board, list one meaning. Title the resulting list "Map Key" and draw a box around it. Now ask students whether there is any confusion about what each symbol represents. Students' understanding of keys and symbols will be much clearer!

Map Key
Gobble Lake
Turkey Trail
Feather Lodge
Wattlesville

Grid, Label, and Picture Patterns

Use with "Tic-Tac-Turkey" and "In Plain View" on page 242.

South	West	Northwest	Southwest
North	East	Northeast	Southeast

Turkey Today
Gobbler Living

Name ______________________________

Turkey Trot

Write what the turkeys take on their hike.
Use the map grid.

	1	2	3	4	
A	shades	hat	CD	gum	A
B	camera	raisins	watch	basketball	B
C	whistle	bandage	map	water	C
D	seeds	compass	journal	flashlight	D
	1	2	3	4	

Tug	Tug and Taz	Taz
(3, A) ____________	(4, C) ____________	(3, C) ____________
(2, B) ____________	(1, D) ____________	(1, B) ____________
(1, C) ____________	(2, A) ____________	(4, A) ____________
(2, D) ____________	(3, B) ____________	(3, D) ____________
(4, D) ____________	(1, A) ____________	(2, C) ____________

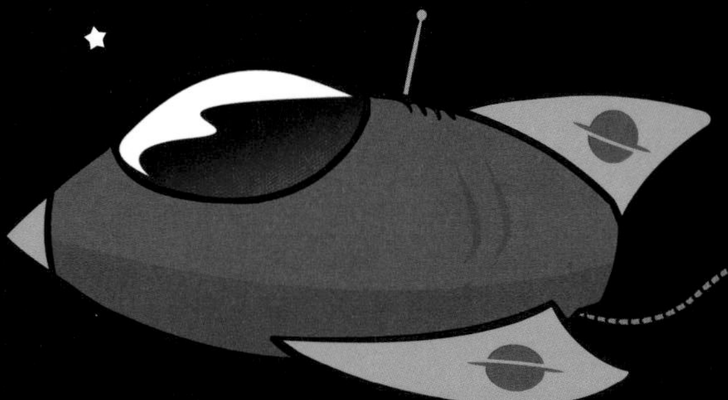

3, 2, 1 . . . Liftoff!

Exploring the Solar System

North Star
Fall

STAR BRIGHT

Patterns of stars

Make a copy of the pattern and cards on page 247 for each student and prepare a class supply of matching blank circles. Begin the activity by asking the class whether the patterns of the stars change. Invite students to share their responses. Next, give each child a copy of the pattern and cards, a blank circle, and a brad. To complete the project, the student cuts out the wheel and the cards and glues each card on the wheel in seasonal order. Then he draws and colors a picture of the night sky on one side of the blank circle. He places the circle atop the wheel and then inserts a brad through the center of both. The child carefully cuts a wedge in the top circle as shown. Have students study the groups of stars on their wheels. Guide them to see that even though each group of stars looks different, it is arranged the same way. The only difference is that it is being seen from four different angles.

Set a course for a better understanding of sky objects with these stellar activities!

with ideas by Julie Hamilton, Renaissance Academy, Colorado Springs, CO, and Stacie Wright, Millington School, Millington, NJ

PLACES, PLEASE!
Ordering the planets

Before starting the activity, gather a variety of books about the planets. Have each child use the books to discover the order of the planets. Then have the student use her knowledge of planet order to make a space booklet. First, she cuts through ten half-sheets of writing paper to form a rocket shape. She creates a cover by decorating the top sheet to resemble a rocket and labels each remaining page with a different planet's name. Next, she uses the books to find two facts about each planet. She writes them on the matching pages and then staples the pages in order. Afterward, pair students and have them create a story about an imaginary trip through the solar system. Challenge the twosome to use facts from their booklets in the story.

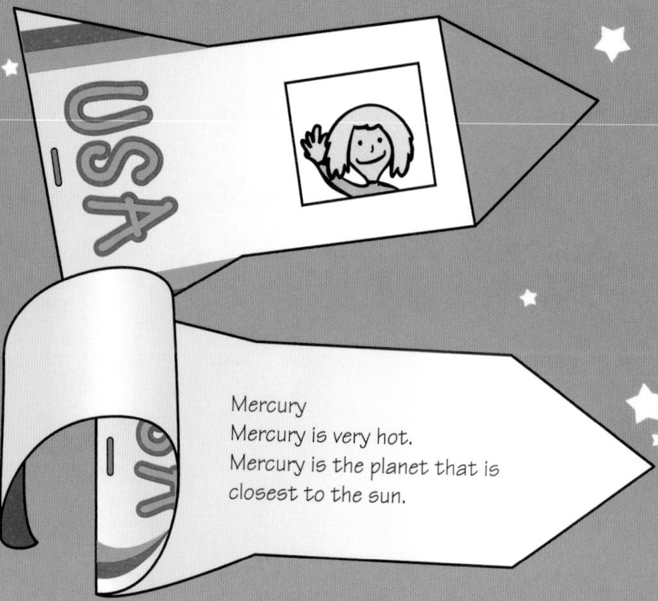
USA
Mercury
Mercury is very hot.
Mercury is the planet that is closest to the sun.

First quarter moon!

SWEET EATS
Phases of the moon

In advance, gather a supply of vanilla wafers and several dark-colored food coloring pens. Begin by giving each child four cookies. To make the phases of the moon, the student colors one whole cookie to represent the new moon, half a cookie for the first quarter, and half a cookie for the last quarter. He leaves one cookie uncolored to symbolize the full moon. After finishing, have each child arrange his cookies on a napkin in the order of the moon phases. Then wrap up the activity by having students eat each cookie when you announce its matching phase.

Kim Haab, Coal City Elementary, Coal City, IL

STARRY SCENES
Investigating constellations

Stock a center with a supply of black construction paper, white crayons, cotton swabs, glow-in-the-dark paint, and pictures of various constellations. Each child selects a favorite constellation and creates a picture of it by dipping a cotton swab into the paint and dotting her paper. She continues the process until she has created the desired constellation. Then she uses a white crayon to write the constellation's name at the bottom of the page. After the paint dries, turn off the lights to view students' starry creations.

Ursa Major-Great Bear

Wheel Pattern and Cards

Use with "Star Bright" on page 245.

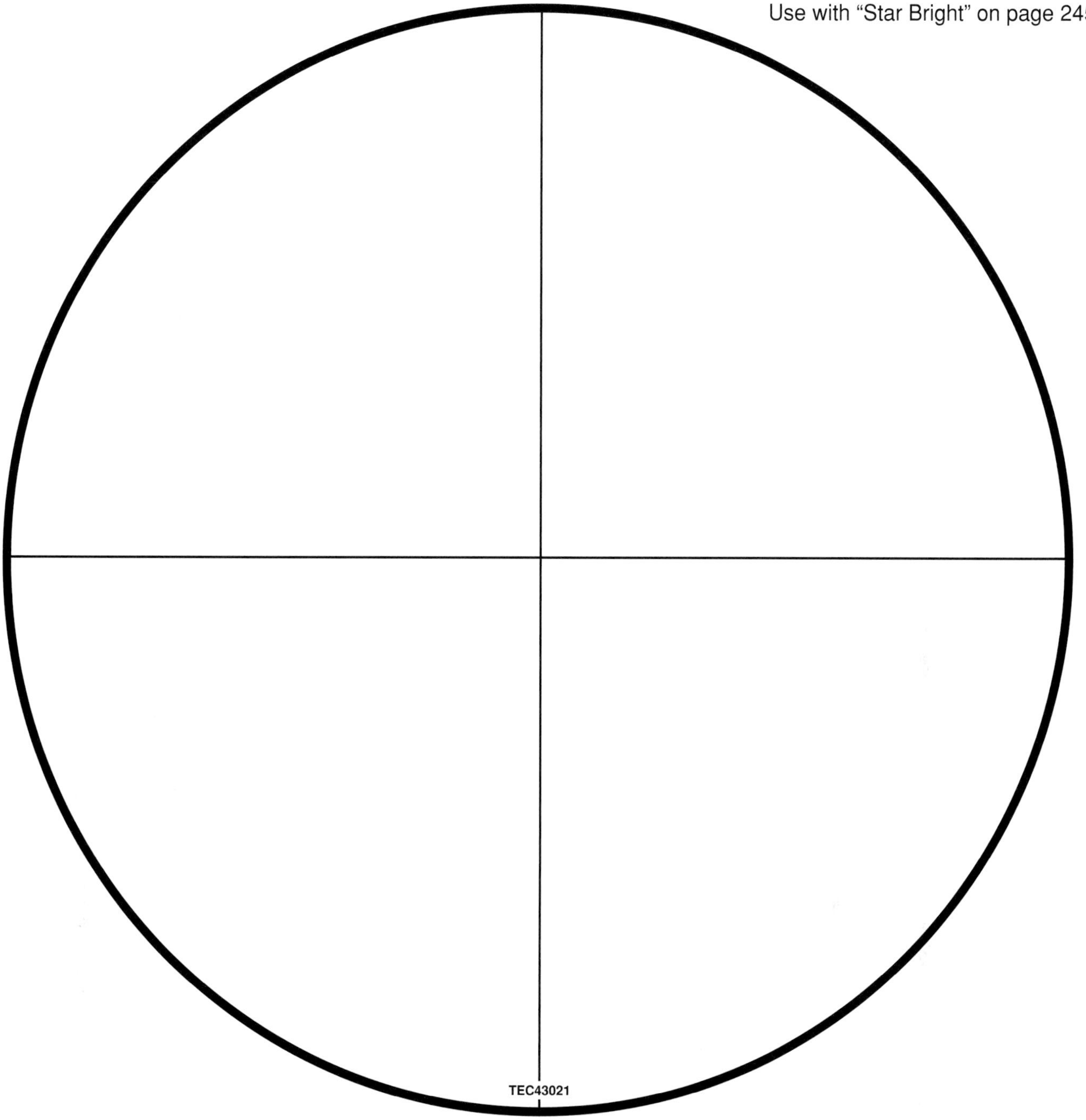
TEC43021

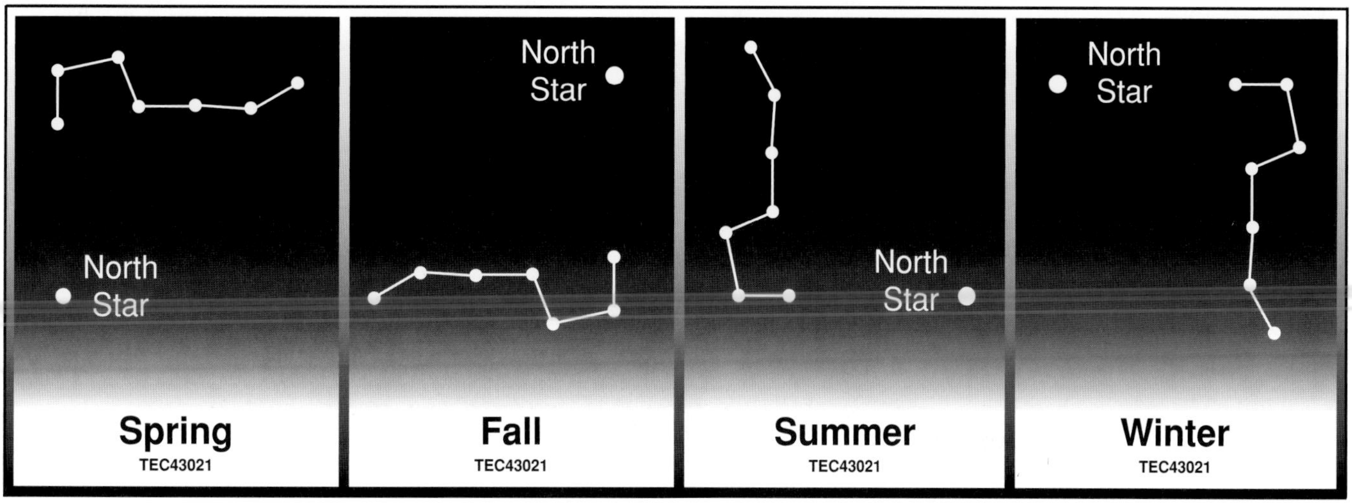
North Star
Spring
TEC43021
North Star
Fall
TEC43021
North Star
Summer
TEC43021
North Star
Winter
TEC43021

Here to **There**

Animal Migrations

Caribou
in
northern
Canada
Stay for the Winter?
Yes No
There is plenty of food.
It is not too cold.
There is safe shelter.
My young could live.
Stay
Go

WHY NOT STAY?

Basic needs

This booklet project reminds students that migration and survival go hand in hand. Give each child a copy of the animal cards from page 250 to color and cut out. Also have her cut out and stack six booklet pages (patterns on page 250). Staple her pages between colorful paper covers and then have her add her name, the title "Stay or Go?" and desired artwork to the cover. To complete each page, specify an animal card for students to glue in their booklets. Have different volunteers read aloud the statements on the page and as a class decide whether "Yes" or "No" should be checked for each one. Then, depending on whether the animal's needs can be met, each student circles "Stay" or "Go" at the bottom of the page. *(Only the needs of the grizzly bear and the beaver are met.)*

Address core science skills and leave the legwork to this select group of animals!

HOW DO THEY KNOW?
Inherited behaviors

To help students better understand migration, write "cry," "laugh," "sleep," and "read" on the board. Invite students to describe ways these human behaviors are and are not alike. Lead them to identify reading as the only learned behavior. Explain that migration is also a behavior. Then ask students whether or not they think it is learned. After plenty of discussion, tell students that wild animals do not need to learn this behavior because they instinctively know when and where to migrate.

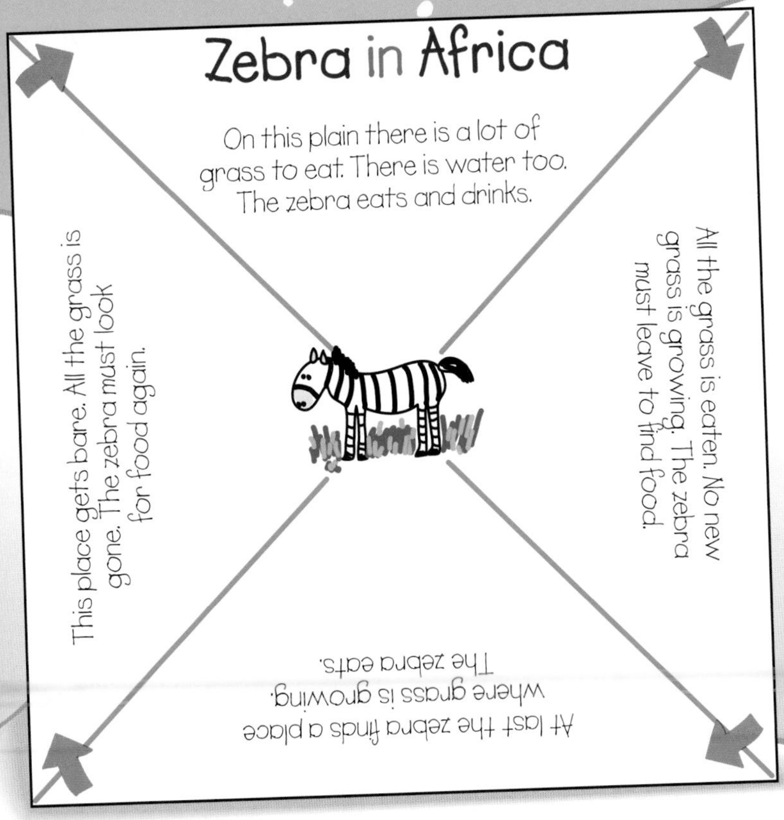
Zebra in Africa
On this plain there is a lot of grass to eat. There is water too. The zebra eats and drinks.
All the grass is eaten. No new grass is growing. The zebra must leave to find food.
At last the zebra finds a place where grass is growing. The zebra eats.
This place gets bare. All the grass is gone. The zebra must look for food again.

A MATTER OF SURVIVAL
Adaptation

These student-made webs spotlight migration as a repeated pattern of behavior that is necessary for survival. To make his web, a child illustrates a migrating animal in the center of a nine-inch square of drawing paper. Next, he draws four colorful lines and arrows, as shown, and writes the animal's name and habitat as the title. Then, using his knowledge of the animal's migratory habits, he programs the web so that a cycle of adaptation is described. Post the completed projects with the title "On the Move!" To make the display interactive, use one pushpin to showcase each project. Insert the pin directly above the illustration. Invite students to gently turn the projects clockwise as they read how the animals adapt to survive.

Booklet Pages and Animal Cards

Use with "Why Not Stay?" on page 248.

Stay for the Winter?

Yes	No	
☐	☐	There is plenty of food.
☐	☐	It is not too cold.
☐	☐	There is safe shelter.
☐	☐	My young could live.

Stay **Go**

Stay for the Winter?

Yes	No	
☐	☐	There is plenty of food.
☐	☐	It is not too cold.
☐	☐	There is safe shelter.
☐	☐	My young could live.

Stay **Go**

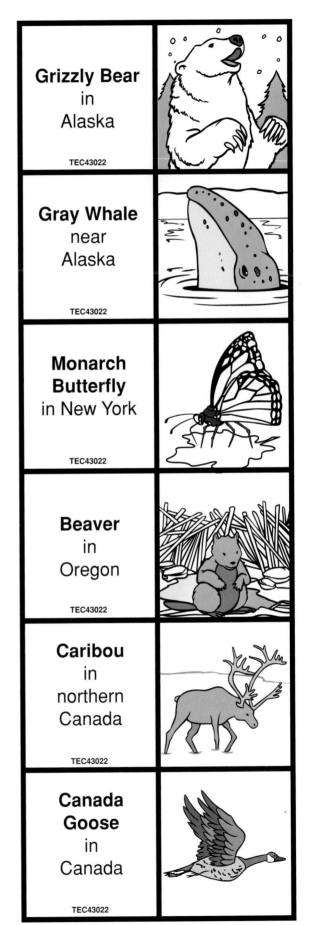

Grizzly Bear
in
Alaska

TEC43022

Gray Whale
near
Alaska

TEC43022

Monarch Butterfly
in New York

TEC43022

Beaver
in
Oregon

TEC43022

Caribou
in
northern
Canada

TEC43022

Canada Goose
in
Canada

TEC43022

In Motion

Using a Simple Experiment to Understand the Scientific Process

What we think will happen:
We think the M&M's candy will fly off the table.
Our group thinks all of the markers will move.

WHAT WILL HAPPEN?

Forming a hypothesis

In advance, gather five of each of the following objects: quarters, chocolate-coated candies, buttons, whiteboard markers, and cookies. Make sure that each set of objects is the same size. Start by dividing students into groups of five. Give each group a set of objects and an enlarged copy of the clipboard pattern at the bottom of page 252. Explain to students that they will be conducting an experiment and that first they must predict what will happen. Next, have the groups think about and discuss what will happen if they line up their objects, slide one piece back, and then sling that piece forward. Then each group works together to form a hypothesis and writes it on the clipboard. Allow each group to share its hypothesis with the class; then post the predictions on the board. Afterward, have each group conduct the experiment on page 252.

Shed some light on force, motion, and the scientific process with this quick and easy experiment!

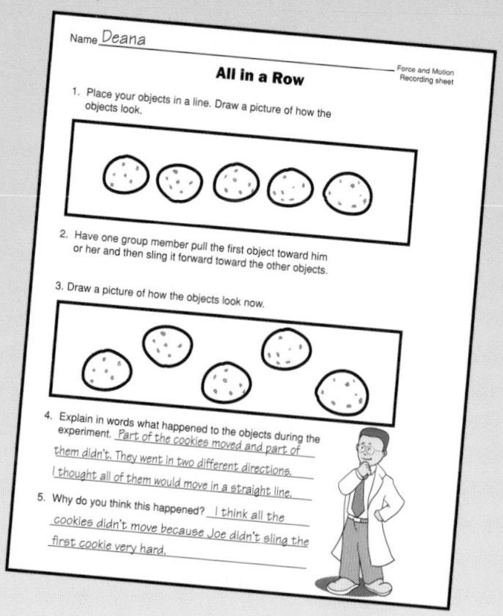
Name Deana

Force and Motion Recording sheet

All in a Row

1. Place your objects in a line. Draw a picture of how the objects look.
2. Have one group member pull the first object toward him or her and then sling it forward toward the other objects.
3. Draw a picture of how the objects look now.
4. Explain in words what happened to the objects during the experiment. Part of the cookies moved and part of them didn't. They went in two different directions. I thought all of them would move in a straight line.
5. Why do you think this happened? I think all the cookies didn't move because Joe didn't sling the first cookie very hard.

ALL IN A ROW
Conducting an experiment, recording observations

Before the activity, make a class supply of page 253. Begin by reviewing with students the words *force* and *motion* and what they mean. Then give each student a copy of the reproducible. To complete the experiment, each group places its objects in a row, on a hard surface such as a desk or a table. The student draws a picture on the reproducible showing where the objects are placed. Next, one group member slides back the object at the beginning of the line and slings it toward the end of the line. Then each child writes and illustrates on her recording sheet the experiment's results and completes the page.

Our class thinks that the size and weight of the objects affected their motion. We also think that the force, or how hard the objects were pushed, made a difference.

WRAPPING IT UP
Using observations to form a conclusion

After completing the experiment, revisit each group's hypothesis as a class. Then invite the groups to share their results. Allow students to share their ideas about what might have affected each group's results. Guide students to see that the size of each group of objects and the amount of force that was used to slide the object could affect the results. Then, as a class, write a conclusion for the experiment incorporating the words *force* and *motion.*

Clipboard Pattern
Use with "What Will Happen?" on page 251.

What we think will happen:

Name ____________________

All in a Row

1. Place your objects in a line. Draw a picture of how the objects look.

2. Have one group member pull the first object toward him or her and then sling it forward toward the other objects.

3. Draw a picture of how the objects look now.

4. Explain in words what happened to the objects during the experiment. ____________________

5. Why do you think this happened? ____________________

Note to the teacher: Use with "All in a Row" on page 252.

How Useful!

The Importance of Natural Resources

Natural Resource: river
How is this resource used?
The river provides food for us to eat. People also use the river to travel.

COMMUNITY BOOKLETS

Identifying natural resources

Help students recognize the resources all around them! In advance, make two copies of page 256 for each student. Begin by brainstorming as a class the natural resources that are present in your community. List students' responses on the board. Next, give each child two copies of the booklet patterns. To make a booklet, the student cuts out the patterns and staples them between two construction paper covers. He writes a title on the cover and personalizes it as desired. Then he selects a natural resource from the list. He completes a page by writing the name of the resource, drawing a picture of it, and explaining in a complete sentence how it is used. He repeats the process until each page is complete.

Guide students to see all that the earth gives us with these resourceful ideas!

with ideas by Stacie Wright, Millington School, Millington, NJ

SCAVENGER HUNT
Identifying natural resources used every day

Send your class on a mission to see how valuable resources can be! Have each child create a T chart like the one shown. Next, share with the class a few examples of items in the room that come from natural resources, such as a textbook. Then give students ten minutes to move around the classroom and find as many items as possible that come from natural resources. Each child writes down the examples he finds and the resources that they come from. When time is up, invite students to share their lists with the class. If desired, compile a class list. Challenge students to look for other examples around the school and at home, and add their responses to the list.

Item	Natural Resource Used to Make It
bookcase	tree
pencil	tree
counters	beans
brick	clay

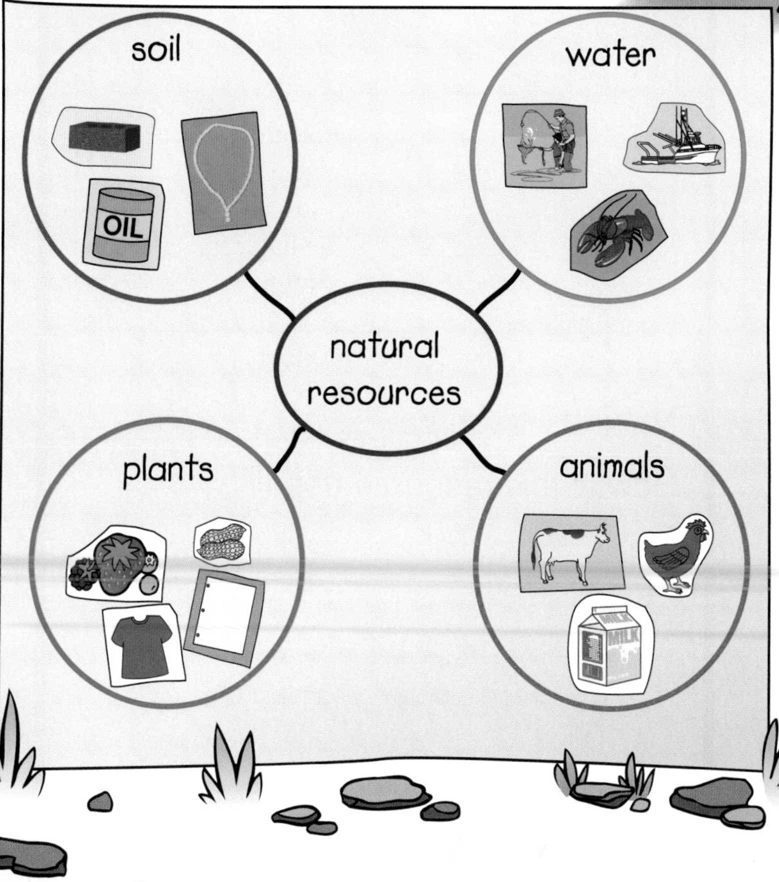
soil
OIL
water
natural resources
plants
animals
MILK

RESOURCE WEB
Types of natural resources

Show off students' knowledge with this group activity! Before starting, create a web like the one shown on a large piece of bulletin board paper and post it in your classroom. Also gather a supply of newspapers and magazines. Start by reviewing with students the definition of a natural resource. Next, divide students into groups of four and give each group a stack of magazines and newspapers. Have each child look through her group's stack and find and cut out pictures of the following: natural resources, items that natural resources were used to make, or people using natural resources. After a designated period of time, each group combines its pictures and sorts them according to the categories on the web. Then invite groups to post their pictures on the chart under the corresponding headings.

Booklet Pages

Use with "Community Booklets" on page 254.

Natural Resource: ________________

How is this resource used?

Natural Resource: ________________

How is this resource used?

Natural Resource: ________________

How is this resource used?

Natural Resource: ________________

How is this resource used?

Name ____________________

Our Resources

Write each answer in the puzzle.
Use the word bank.

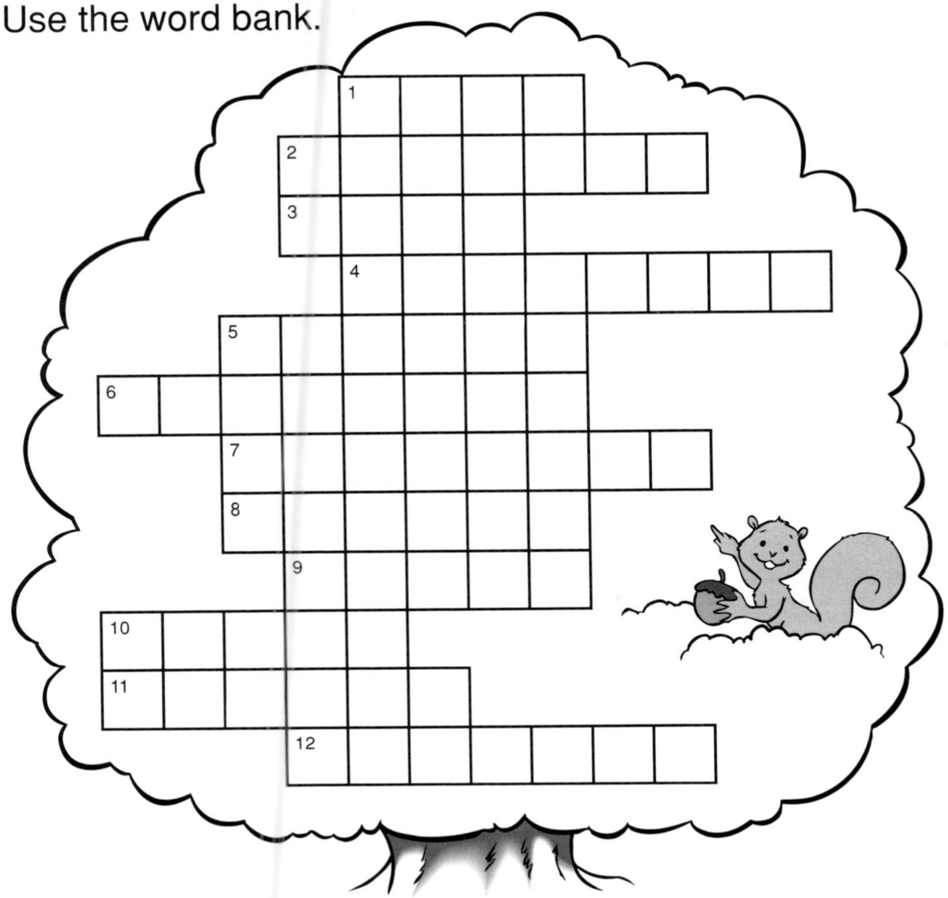
1
2
3
4
5
6
7
8
9
10
11
12

Study the puzzle from top to bottom. Find a three-word phrase. Use it to finish the sentence.

Natural resources are things that we use every day. They come ____________________!

Word Bank

clean air	cotton	fish	minerals	oceans	paper
plants	protect	shelter	soil	sunshine	water

1. ____________ live in water, and people can eat them.
2. We should ____________ our resources so they don't run out.
3. Plants need rich ____________ to grow in.
4. ____________ are found in all rocks. They are used to make many things, such as jewelry and cement for buildings.
5. The fibers from ____________ plants are used to make clothes.
6. ____________ provides warmth and energy.
7. People need to breathe in ____________ ____________.
8. Many people travel in ships on rivers and ____________.
9. Trees are often used to make ____________.
10. ____________ is a resource that we drink.
11. Corn and pumpkins are foods that we get from ____________.
12. Trees provide ____________ for many animals.

Plentiful Plant

The Saguaro Cactus Habitat

roots
saguaro has thick, waxy skin to help it
water. It has long roots that are not
very deep. This also helps it save water.
Animals live in the cactus both when it is alive and dead. They get food from its fruit. The cactus can even give the animals shade from the sun.
The cactus needs animals to help it grow. Birds, insects, and bats carry pollen to flowers when they get a drink of nectar. Animals also carry its seeds.
The Saguaro Cactus

COUNT ON ME

Interdependency between plants and animals

Picturing the saguaro household will be a snap with this classification project! Begin by sharing with students that a saguaro cactus is a desert plant that provides food and shelter for the animals in its habitat. Then, to make a picture slide, cut a 6" x 9" construction paper rectangle (frame) and a 4" x 24" paper strip. Each child measures one inch on both sides of the frame and scores a four-inch-long line as shown. Next, he labels the frame "The Saguaro Cactus." He feeds the paper through the scored lines so the left side is flush with the left edge of the frame. In the first section, he writes a sentence describing the characteristics of the cactus and draws a matching scene above it. Then he pulls the strip from the left until the right side of the illustration meets the frame's left edge. In this section, he writes and illustrates a sentence about how animals depend on the cactus. He pulls the strip one final time and writes about how the cactus depends on the animals and adds an illustration.

Journey into the Sonoran Desert and explore the world of the giant cactus with these succulent ideas!

SPONGY SIMILARITY
Plant adaptations

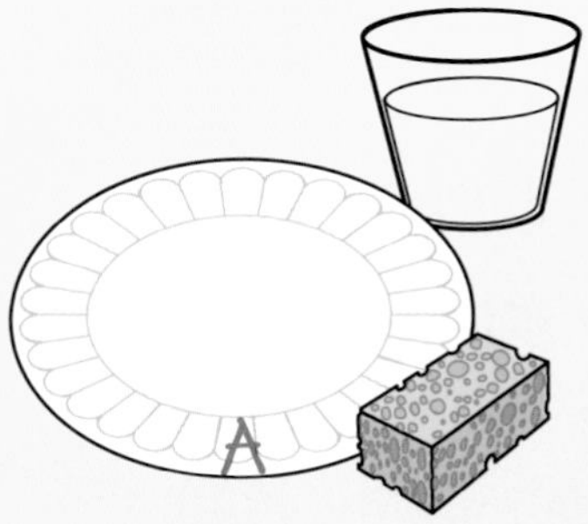
A

Help students soak up an understanding of how cacti rely on their waxy skin to store water. To prepare for the activity, make a class supply of page 260. Also cut a supply of kitchen sponges into fourths, making enough for each small group to have two. Use a permanent marker to label two foam plates for each group, one "A" and the other "B." Discuss with students how storing water helps the cactus survive, and that animals can get water by eating its pulp. Then give each small group the materials listed at the top of page 260 and have the group complete the page as directed.

Food, Shelter, or Both?
A bat drinks the saguaro flower's nectar.
Food
Place cards here.
Both
Place cards here.
Shelter

FOOD, SHELTER, OR BOTH?
Interdependence

First, copy pages 261 and 262. Mount the sorting mat and the cards on construction paper. Color the mat and the cards and cut them out. Program the back of each card with the letter *F* (food), *S* (shelter), or *B* (both) to make the center self-checking (see the answer key on page 313). Put the cards in a plastic bag and place them and the mat at a center. A student pair works together to sort the cards onto the correct cacti. Then the partners turn the cards over to check their work.

DESERT CHARADES
Interdependence

White-winged dove

This game will have students acting like desert animals! To prepare, place the cards from "Food, Shelter, or Both?" in a deck. Shuffle the cards and then write the names of the animals on the board as a reference. Next, divide your class into two teams and place a chair in the game area. A child chooses a card from the deck and reads it. Then she acts like the chosen animal, using the chair to represent the cactus. To show an animal that lives underground, she sits on the floor next to the chair. She sits in the chair to represent an animal that lives in the cactus. To show an animal that lives in the dead plant, she turns the chair on its side. Her teammates get three tries to name the animal; if they cannot, the turn goes to the opposing team. Play continues until all animals have been named or time is called.

Name ____

Saguaro Cactus
Recording sheet

Cactus Connection

Materials for each group:

2 sponges
water
5" x 5" piece of waxed paper
2 foam plates, labeled "A" and "B"
2 plastic cups
petroleum jelly
tape

Directions:

1. Fill both cups with equal amounts of water. Place each sponge in a cup of water. Hold them underwater to soak for about ten seconds. Gently wring them out.

2. Place one sponge on plate A. Apply a layer of petroleum jelly to the waxed paper and wrap it around the second sponge. Secure the ends with a piece of tape and place the sponge on plate B.

3. Set the plates in a sunny spot for 24 hours.

   Which sponge do you predict will dry out more? ______ Why? ______________

   ____

   ____

4. When time is up, observe the sponges.

   Which sponge dried out more? ______ Why? ______________

   ____

   ____

   How is sponge B like a saguaro cactus? ______________

   ____

   ____

 Note to the teacher: Use with "Spongy Similarity" on page 259.

Food, Shelter, or Both?

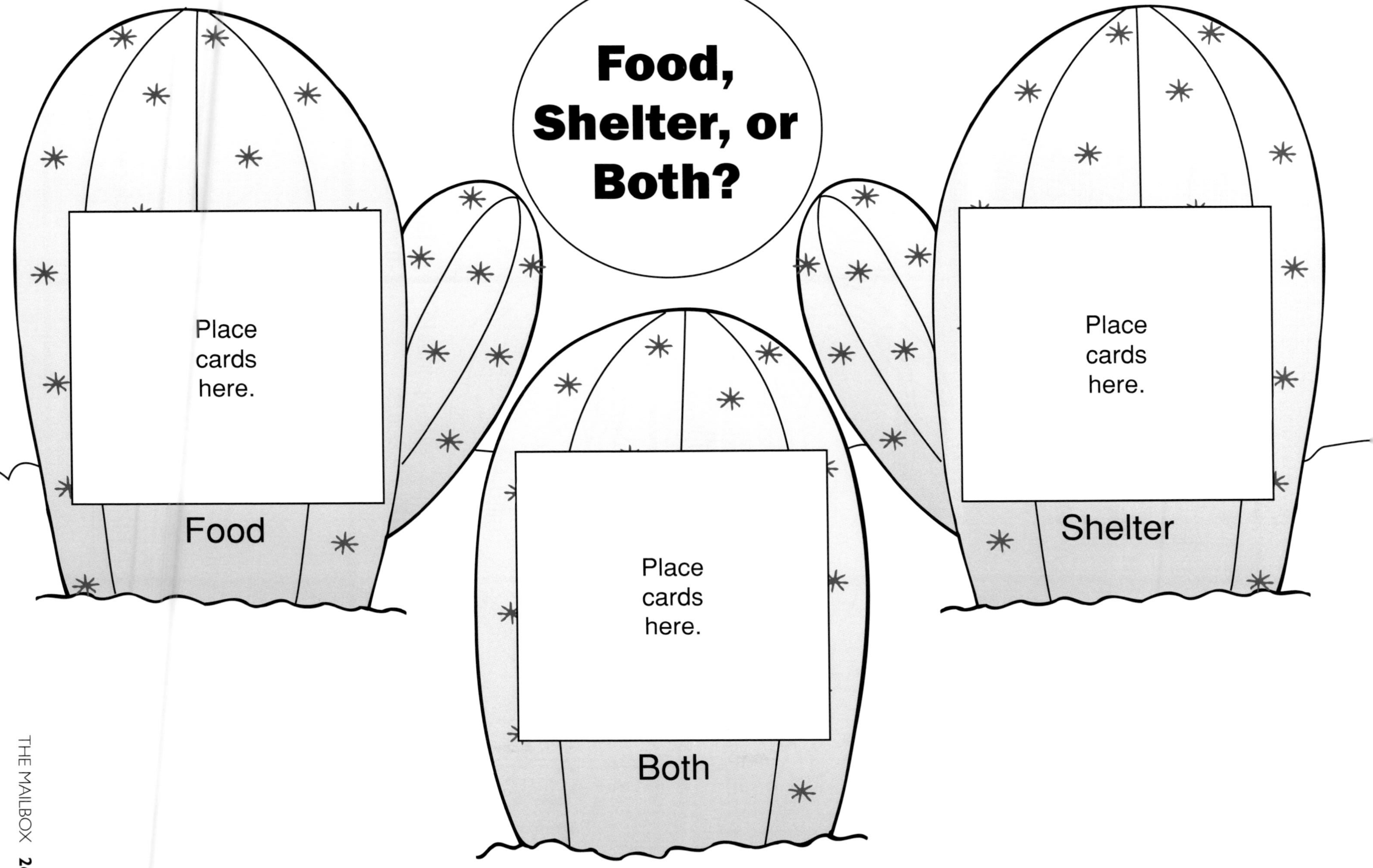
Place cards here.
Food
Place cards here.
Both
Place cards here.
Shelter

Animal Cards

Use with “Food, Shelter, or Both?” and “Desert Charades” on page 259.

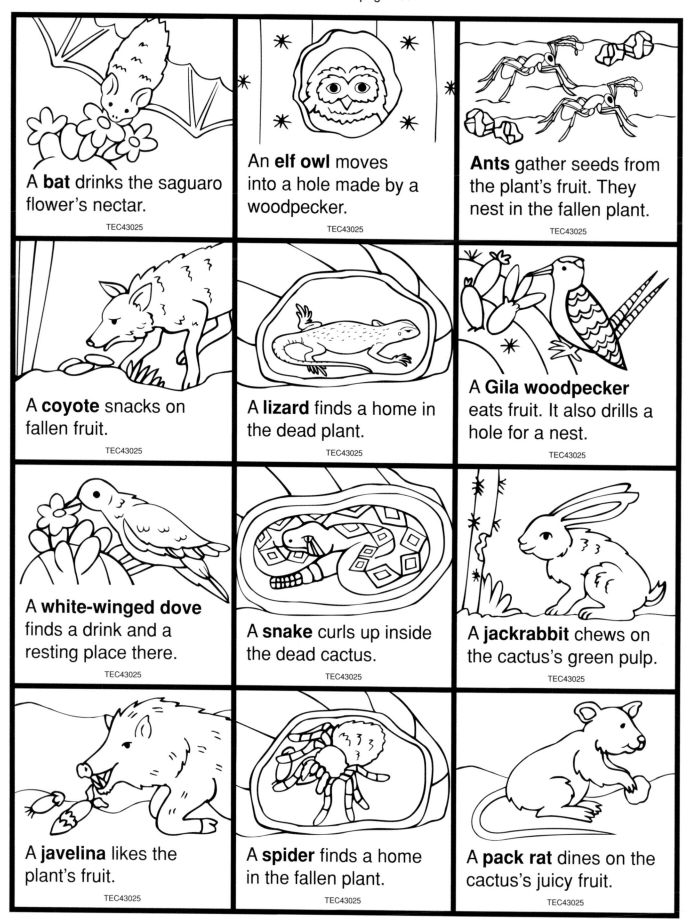

A **bat** drinks the saguaro flower’s nectar.

TEC43025

An **elf owl** moves into a hole made by a woodpecker.

TEC43025

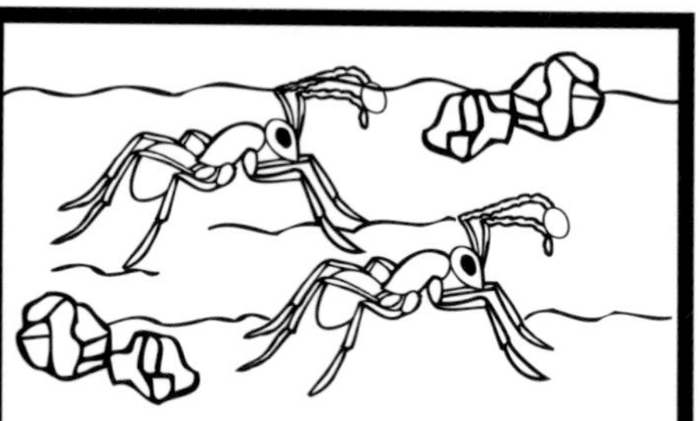

Ants gather seeds from the plant’s fruit. They nest in the fallen plant.

TEC43025

A **coyote** snacks on fallen fruit.

TEC43025

A **lizard** finds a home in the dead plant.

TEC43025

A **Gila woodpecker** eats fruit. It also drills a hole for a nest.

TEC43025

A **white-winged dove** finds a drink and a resting place there.

TEC43025

A **snake** curls up inside the dead cactus.

TEC43025

A **jackrabbit** chews on the cactus’s green pulp.

TEC43025

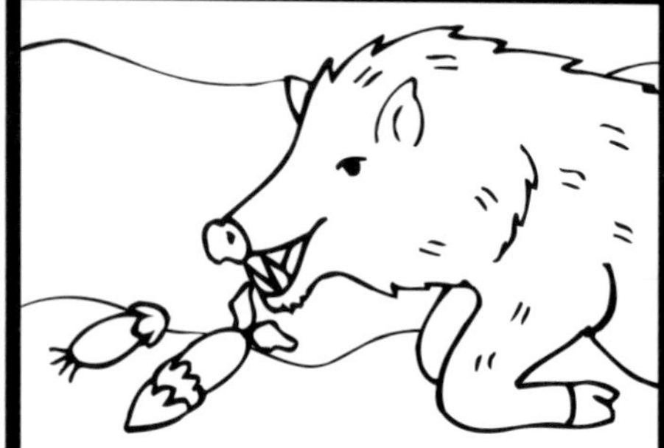

A **javelina** likes the plant’s fruit.

TEC43025

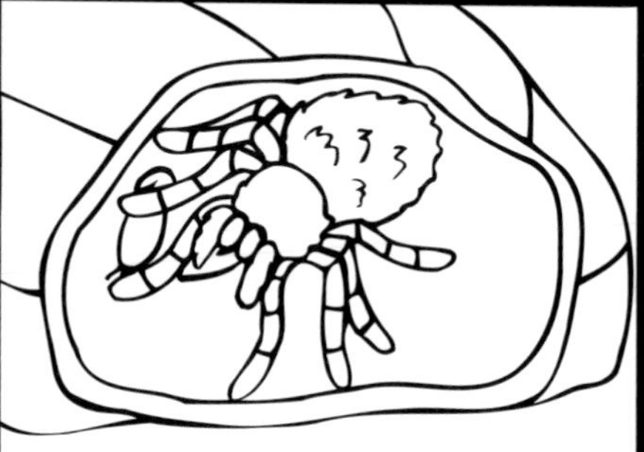

A **spider** finds a home in the fallen plant.

TEC43025

A **pack rat** dines on the cactus’s juicy fruit.

TEC43025

It's a "Shoe-In"!

Economics Activities That Fit Your Curriculum

STARTING UP

Identifying wants and needs

In advance, write on a transparency the bulleted information below. Begin by discussing with students products that they want and ones that they need. List students' responses on a T chart. Next, explain that companies make and sell goods and services to supply people's wants and needs. As a class, name some of the companies that make the products listed. Then divide students into small groups and explain that each group is a company that makes sneakers. The group will be responsible for creating a new sneaker, making several examples of it, and making an advertisement for it. To complete the activity, show students the questions on the transparency. Have group members work together to answer each question, recording their final decisions on a sheet of paper. After each group has finished, collect the papers for use in the next activity.

David, Lamar, and Annie
Our company name is Happy Feet Company.
We make sneakers for running.
People wear our shoes when they go running. Our shoes are light, so you can run fast. And they have extra padding so your feet won't get sore.
Our shoes will look like this:
We need craft foam, feathers, scissors, glue, yarn, and markers to make an example of our shoe.

- What is the name of your company?
- What type of sneaker do you make?
- What activities can people do while they wear your sneakers?
- What will your sneaker look like? Draw a picture of it.
- If you were making an example of your sneaker, what arts-and-crafts materials would you need?

Want to help students gain a better understanding of economics? Then these activities are just what you need!

with ideas by Felice McCreary, Dripping Springs Primary, Dripping Springs, TX

MAKING THE GOODS

Understanding an assembly line

Before starting the activity, make three copies of the sneaker patterns on page 265 for each group. Begin by reviewing the assembly line concept with students, explaining that companies often use it to produce products quickly. Next, hand out each group's plan from the previous lesson. Have the group use its illustration and materials list to plan the most efficient way to make three pairs of shoes. Instruct the group to create a different job for each group member to make the shoes; for instance, one child might cut materials, another might glue, and a third might decorate. Explain that groups may have different jobs based on their shoe designs. Then give each group three copies of the shoe patterns and its listed materials. Each person in the group does his assigned job to help make three pairs of shoes. When groups are done, invite them to share their plans and finished products with the class. Afterward, discuss as a class how the assembly line process helped them make their shoes.

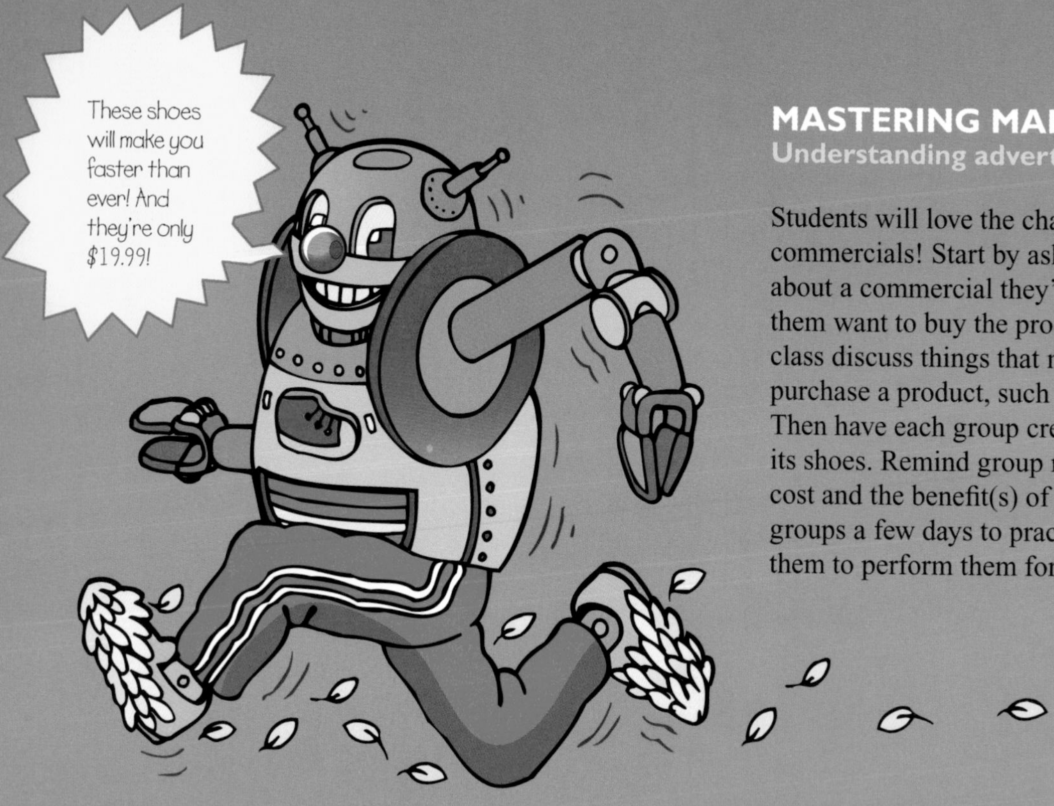
These shoes will make you faster than ever! And they're only $19.99!

MASTERING MARKETING

Understanding advertising

Students will love the chance to create their own commercials! Start by asking students to think about a commercial they've seen recently that made them want to buy the product advertised. Have the class discuss things that might influence a person to purchase a product, such as need, price, or benefit. Then have each group create a short skit to advertise its shoes. Remind group members to include the cost and the benefit(s) of buying the shoes. Give groups a few days to practice their skits; then invite them to perform them for the class.

Sneaker Patterns

Use with "Making the Goods" on page 264.

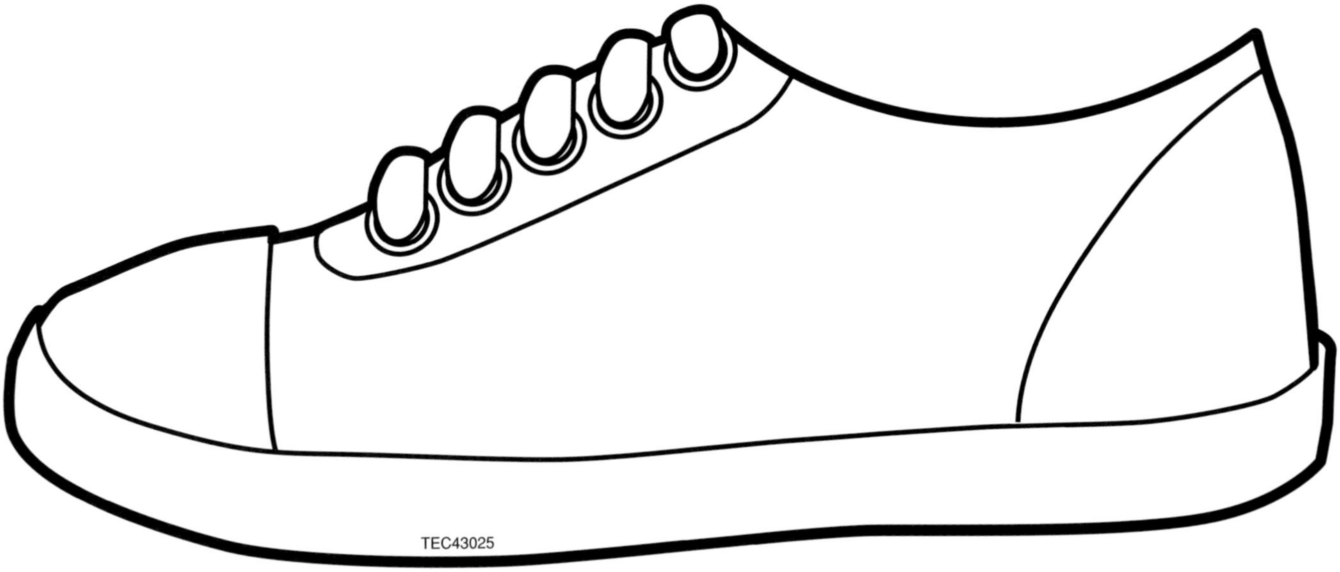
TEC43025

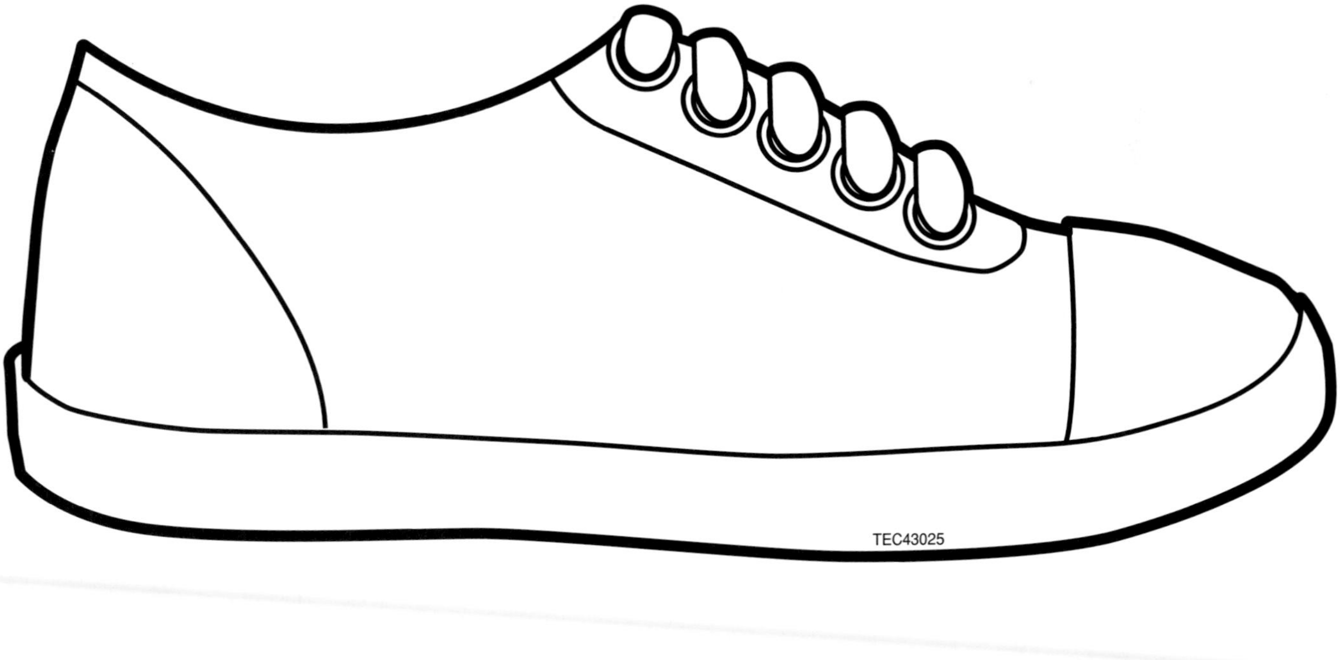
TEC43025

Name____

Money Matters

Write the matching word in the blank.
Use the word bank to help you.

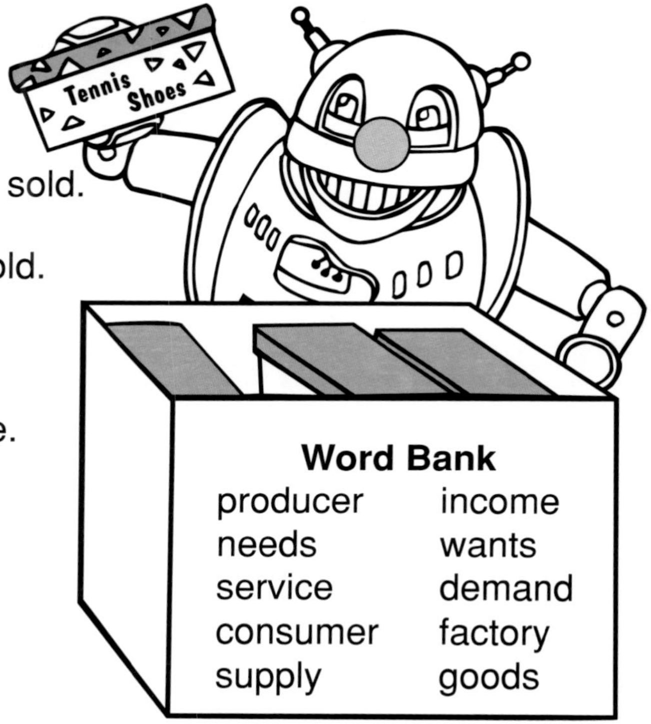
Tennis Shoes

Word Bank

producer	income
needs	wants
service	demand
consumer	factory
supply	goods

1. __ ◯ __ __ __ are things that are made or grown. They are often sold.
2. __ __ __ __ ◯ __ is how much of a product or service can be sold.
3. __ __ __ ◯ __ are things people must have.
4. __ __ __ ◯ __ __ is how much people need a product or service.
5. A __ __ __ __ __ __ __ __ makes or grows things.
6. A __ __ __ __ __ __ __ __ buys a service or product.
7. A ◯ __ __ __ __ __ __ is a place where goods are made.
8. A __ __ __ __ ◯ __ __ is something that a person does for another person.
9. __ __ __ ◯ __ are things that people would like to have.
10. __ ◯ __ __ __ __ is money that is made or earned.

How can you double your money?

To solve the riddle, write the circled letters from above on the matching numbered lines below.

__ __ __ __ (7 1 2 3) __ __ (8 9) __ __ (8 10) H __ __ __! (4 2 7)

Cross Curricular & Seasonal Units

Howdy Do!

Riveting Skill-Based Introductions

2+2+2+2+2=10

1. These people are in my family: ______________
2. My favorite color is ______________
3. I have a pet named ______________
   I don't have a pet, but if I did I would name it ____________
4. After school I like to ______________
5. My favorite thing about school is ______________
6. My favorite food is ______________

WHO'S WHO?
Writing

Foster new friendships through penmanship? You bet! Instruct each child to use proper word and letter spacing as he copies and completes six sentences about himself and his family. Next, give him a zippered bag and a construction paper copy of a puzzle template like the one shown. Ask him to illustrate his sentences on the template, cut out the puzzle pieces, and store the pieces in the bag. Collect the puzzle bags and post the penmanship papers with the title "Get to Know Us!"

Next, give each student a puzzle bag (other than his own) and a sheet of colorful construction paper. Have him assemble the puzzle and glue it on the colorful paper. Provide plenty of time (a day or two) for each child to read the posted writing samples, decide whose puzzle he has, and verify his hunch. Then set aside time for each student to introduce the classmate whose puzzle he assembled. Follow up by displaying each student's artwork with his writing sample.

adapted from an idea by Lynn L. Caruso, Littlebrook Elementary, Princeton, NJ

Make these high-performance ideas for getting acquainted the nuts and bolts of your back-to-school plans!

NOTABLE NUMBERS
Math

Numbers are the key to this get-acquainted booklet. Give each child several quarter sheets of blank paper. Ask her to label one sheet with a number that describes something about herself or her family. Then have her write a sentence that includes the number and explains its significance. Instruct her to repeat the process for each remaining blank page, using a different number each time. When she's finished, ask her to sequence her pages from the smallest to the largest number, staple the stack between two construction paper covers, and write "Numbers About [student's name]" on the front cover. Collect the booklets and display them in your classroom library for all to enjoy.

adapted from an idea by Stacie Stone Davis, Lima, NY

1
I have one sister.
6
My dad is six feet tall.
4
I got four stitches last summer.

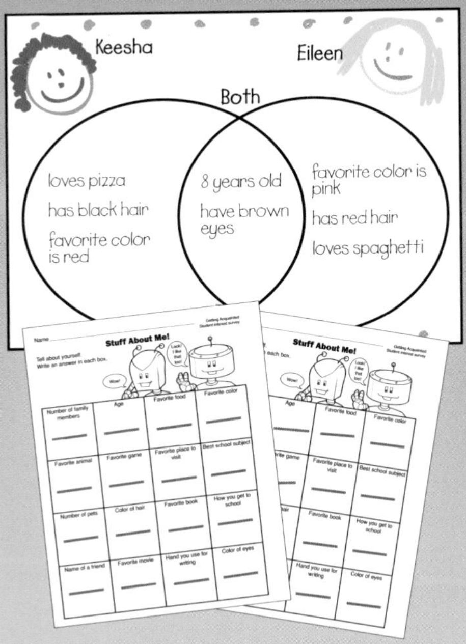

Keesha
Eileen
Both
loves pizza
has black hair
favorite color is red
8 years old
have brown eyes
favorite color is pink
has red hair
loves spaghetti
Stuff About Me!

YOU TOO?
Comprehension

Comparing and contrasting personal interests is a fun way for students to learn a lot about each other. For a quick and easy approach, have each child complete a copy of the survey on page 270. Next, pair students and have each twosome draw a large Venn diagram on a 12" x 18" sheet of light-colored construction paper. Instruct the partners to label the diagram and use their surveys to program it with their unique and shared interests. Encourage partners to decorate the resulting poster. Then post the projects around the classroom so other potential pals can take a peek!

Rhonda Chiles, South Park Elementary, Mission, KS

FAVORITE PLACES
Social Studies

Here's a mapping activity that's sure to please! Give each child a copy of page 271. Ask the child to list in the map key eight places where he likes to spend time. Then have him draw and color a symbol for each place. Next, have him use his symbols to make a map of a special location that has all of his favorite places! Remind students to name the streets, and encourage them to add other map details. When the maps are finished, provide time for each mapmaker to share his work with a partner, a small group, or the entire class. Collect the projects and display them for open house visitors. Or use the maps as story prompts at a writing center!

adapted from an idea by Amy Beck, Sleepy Hollow Elementary, Falls Church, VA

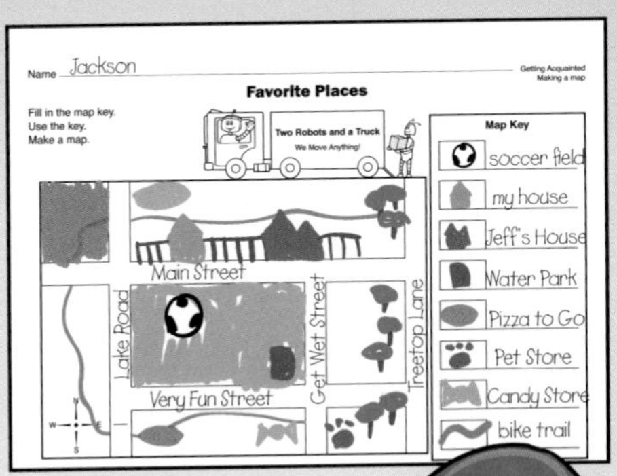

Name Jackson
Favorite Places
Fill in the map key.
Use the key.
Make a map.
Two Robots and a Truck
Map Key
soccer field
my house
Jeff's House
Water Park
Pizza to Go
Pet Store
Candy Store
bike trail
Main Street
Lake Road
Get Wet Street
Treetop Lane
Very Fun Street

Name____

Stuff About Me!

Tell about yourself.
Write an answer in each box.

Wow!
Look! I like that too!

Number of family members	Age	Favorite food	Favorite color
Favorite animal	Favorite game	Favorite place to visit	Best school subject
Number of pets	Color of hair	Favorite book	How you get to school
Name of a friend	Favorite movie	Hand you use for writing	Color of eyes

 Note to the teacher: Use alone or with "You Too?" on page 269.

Name ______________________

Favorite Places

Fill in the map key.
Use the key.
Make a map.

Two Robots and a Truck
We Move Anything!

N
W
E
S

Map Key

Note to the teacher: Use alone or with "Favorite Places" on page 269.

Take Your Pick

Skill-Based Seasonal Selections

STEP BY STEP
Writing steps in logical order

Begin by having each child imagine that he grew the world's largest pumpkin in his backyard, and have him think about how he would carve it. To complete a booklet, he writes each step of the carving process on a separate quarter sheet of blank paper, using time and order words as needed. Next, he illustrates a cover for his booklet using the pumpkin pattern on page 274. Then he places the pages in order, staples the cover atop them as shown, and cuts around the cover's edges. To display the projects, post the pumpkins on a bulletin board along with a vine. Title the board "The Pick of the Patch."

Next, I'd put a ladder next to the pumpkin so I could reach the top.

We've harvested a crop of core curriculum activities
students will fall for!

ideas by Jennifer Kohnke, Nature Ridge Elementary, Bartlett, IL

MAKING PREDICTIONS
Math

Place at a center a large pumpkin, a few pencils, and a class supply of the data sheet on page 274. Have each child visit the center and record her predictions for the pumpkin's circumference, its weight, and the number of seeds. Then, as a class, find the pumpkin's actual circumference and weight. Instruct each student to record these amounts on her data sheet and to find the difference between the predicted and actual weights and circumferences. Before class on the following day, cut the pumpkin open and remove the seeds. After allowing them to dry, give each group of five students a portion of the seeds to count. List each group's total on the board and then have students add the totals to find the number of seeds in the pumpkin. Finally, have the class complete the data sheet.

Name Susan
Actual
Difference
37 inches
15 pounds
97

Problem
Solution
The pumpkin was really big, and it started rolling down a hill. The more it rolled, the faster it got. When everyone saw it, they thought about how good it would taste if Grandma cooked it. But nothing could make it stop. It crashed into the pigsty and the chicken coop. Then it kept on going.
Poppa saw it coming. He made a pumpkin bed, and the pumpkin rolled to a stop.

WHAT'S THE PROBLEM?
Literature

Start by reading aloud *The Runaway Pumpkin* by Kevin Lewis to students. Review the terms *problem* and *solution* with the class. Next, have each child fold in half a sheet of white paper and label one side "Problem" and the other "Solution." To complete the activity, each child illustrates the book's problem, then writes a few sentences describing it. Then she repeats the process for the book's solution.

PUMPKIN PLURALS
Grammar

Before preparing this center activity, copy page 275. Glue the page onto construction paper; then color and cut out the mat and the cards. Use a permanent marker to program the back of each card for easy self-checking. Then place the activity at a center. A student sorts each word by whether an *s* or an *es* is needed to make it plural. Then he flips the cards over to check his work.

pumpkin
dish
Add s.
Add es.

Pumpkin Pattern

Use with "Step by Step" on page 272.

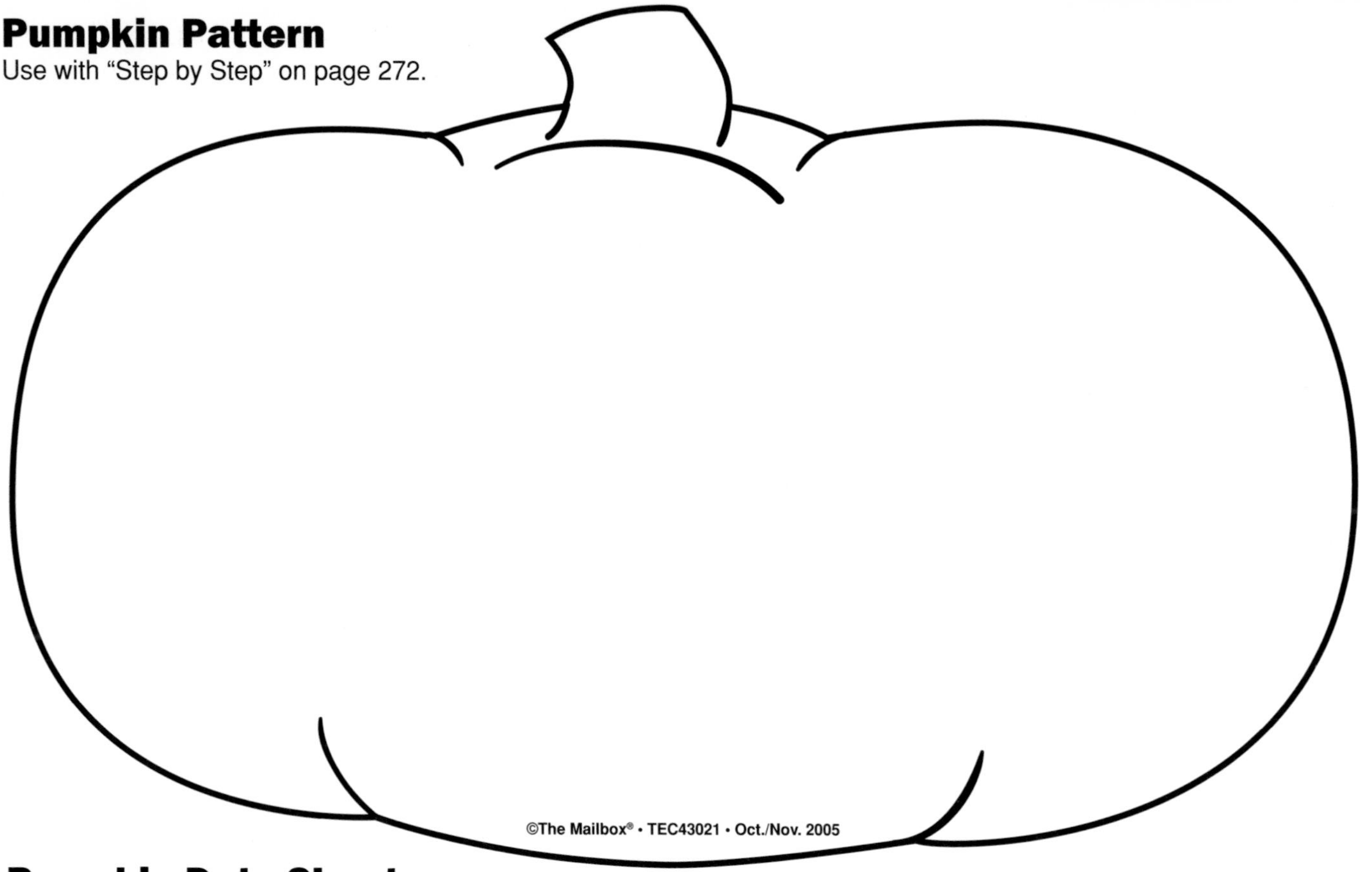

Pumpkin Data Sheet

Use with "Making Predictions" on page 273.

Name ______________________________

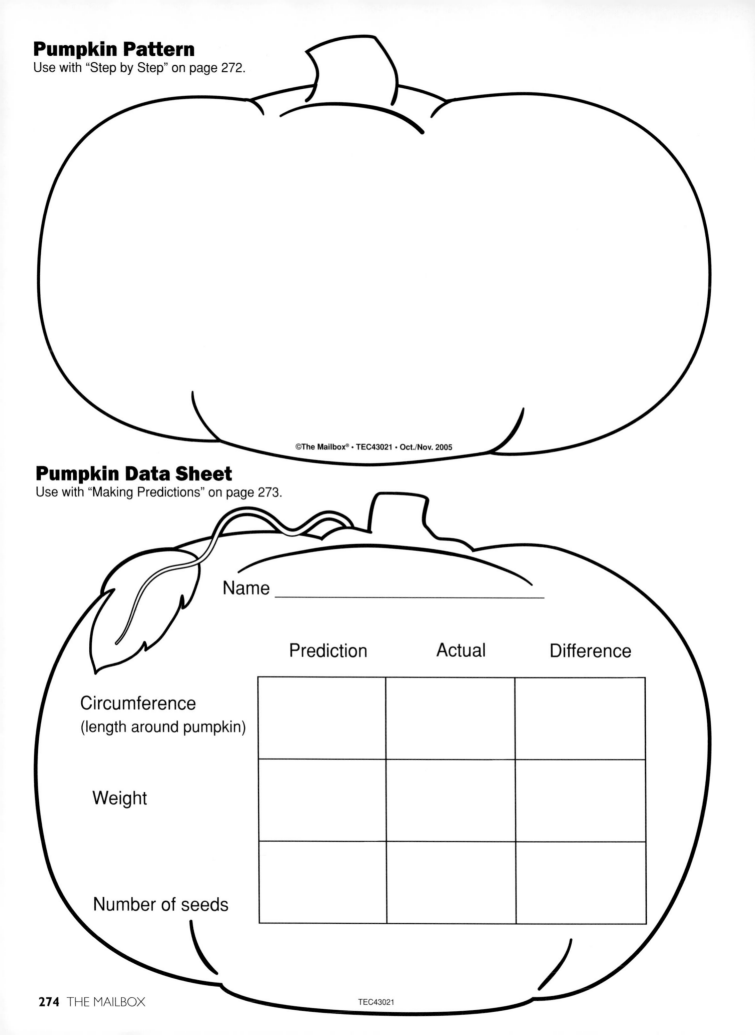

	Prediction	Actual	Difference
Circumference (length around pumpkin)			
Weight			
Number of seeds			

Sorting Mat and Word Cards

Use with "Pumpkin Plurals" on page 273.

Add *s*.
Add *es*.
©The Mailbox® • TEC43021 • Oct./Nov. 2005

pumpkin	seed	pie	dish
tree	branch	vine	apple
acorn	lunch	spider	web
bat	fox	peach	turkey
box	bush	brush	wish

Name________________________________

Pumpkin Patch

Write the value of each underlined digit.
Color the pumpkin with the matching number.
Two pumpkins will not be colored.

A. 966 ________

B. 222 ________

C. 615 ________

D. 874 ________

E. 337 ________

F. 492 ________

G. 617 ________

H. 734 ________

I. 209 ________

J. 544 ________

K. 921 ________

L. 362 ________

N. 778 ________

N. 868 ________

O. 690 ________

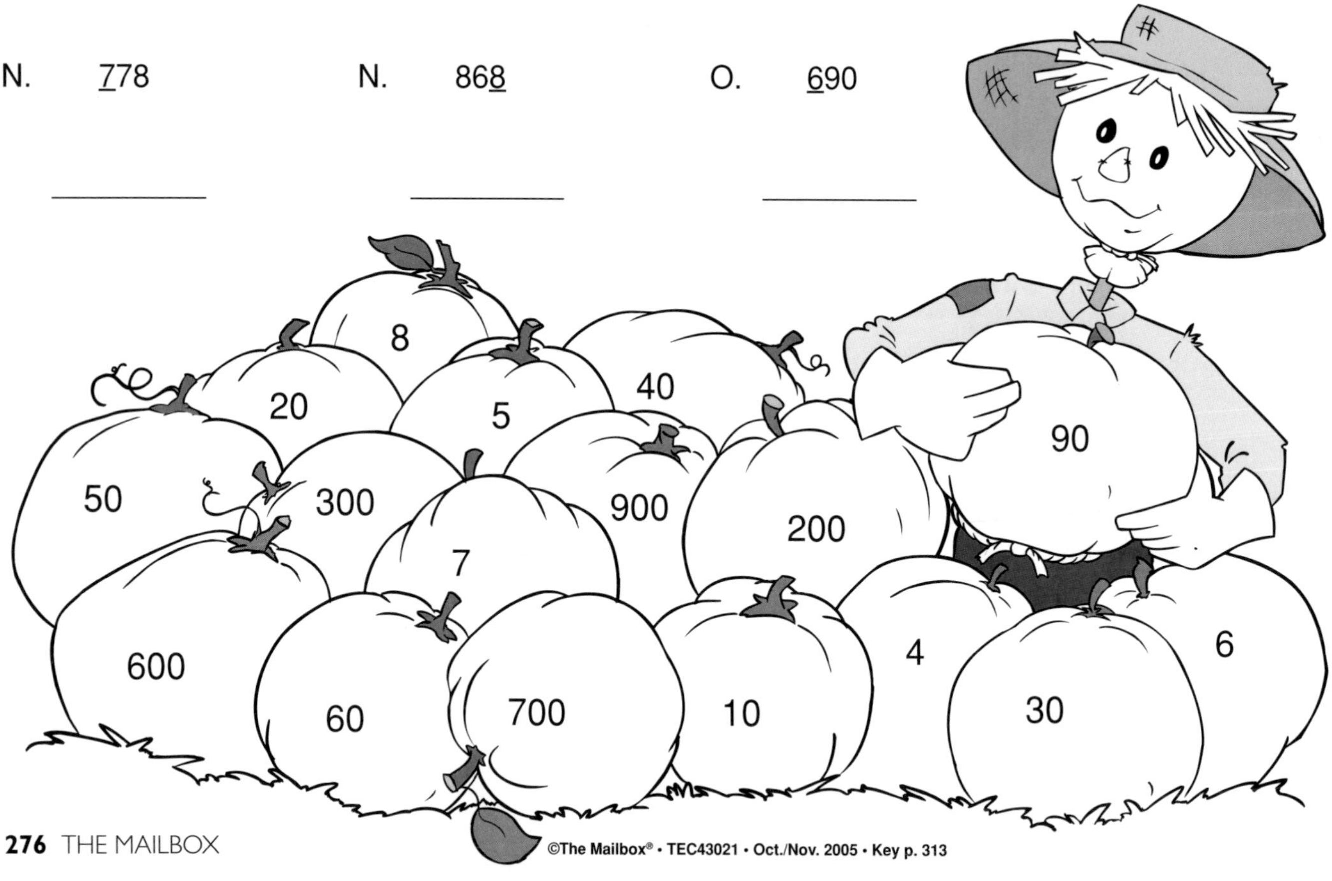
8
20
5
40
90
50
300
900
200
7
600
60
700
10
4
6
30

Warming **Up**

A Serving of Seasonal Skills

COUNTING ON COCOA
Math

Hot Chocolate
Math

Name Joseph

Counting Coins

Count the coins in each box.

Box	Total
A	73 ¢
B	29 ¢
C	¢
D	¢
E	¢
F	¢

Cook up a batch of money practice at this sweet center! In advance, fill six boxes each with a different amount of coins. Label each box with a letter, and make a key listing each box's total amount. Also make a class supply of the reproducible and the mug and marshmallow patterns on page 279. Place the reproducibles and the boxes at a center. Begin the activity by giving each child a mug pattern and have him personalize it. He visits the center and counts the money in each box, writing the amount on his recording sheet. For each correct amount, he receives a marshmallow to attach to the top of his mug. Post students' mugs around the classroom, and reward students with hot chocolate and marshmallows for a job well done!

C
Joseph
D
E

Deb Jenkins
Woodburn Elementary
Woodburn, IN

Like hot chocolate? Then you'll love these ideas, packed with an extra helping of curriculum-based activities!

MARSHMALLOW MELT
Science

Take a short trip through the scientific process with this sweet experiment! Each child needs a cup of hot chocolate, four marshmallows, and a copy of the reproducible on page 281. To complete the experiment, each child predicts how long it will take the marshmallows to melt in warm cocoa and records it at the top of the page. Then she places her marshmallows inside the cup of cocoa and writes her observations. At the one-, three-, and five-minute mark, ask her to record what she sees. After the marsh-mallows melt completely, have students complete the page. Then allow students to sip their cocoa as you discuss the results together.

Hot Chocolate Science
Name Shayla
Marshmallow Melt
Prediction: I think the marshmallows will melt in five minutes.
Observations
After I put the marshmallows in
After 1 minute in the cup
After 3 minutes in the cup
After 5 minutes in the cup
It took the marshmallows ______ to melt.
Conclusion (what I learned):

COMMON OR PROPER
Grammar

Whip up easy grammar practice at this center! Make a copy of page 280 and mount it on construction paper. Color the cups; then cut out the cups and the whipped toppings. Program each piece's back for easy self-checking, and place the pieces at a center. A child decides whether each noun is common or proper and places the corresponding topping on the cup. Then he flips the pieces over to check his work.

proper
Kwanzaa
common
gift

COCOA SHAPE POEM
Writing

In advance, prepare a small cup of hot chocolate for each child and make a class supply of the mug pattern on page 279. As each student sips her cocoa, ask her to write on a sheet of paper sentences and phrases that describe it. To complete the activity, she cuts out the mug and glues it to a half sheet of light-colored construction paper. Then the child writes the words from her list around the outside of the mug. She decorates the mug as desired and paints a small amount of chocolate syrup inside the mug as shown. Invite students to share their poems with the class. Post the poems on a bulletin board titled "Cups of Cocoa."

Warm, sweet, chocolatey. Good in my tummy. Makes me feel warm and cozy. Smells sweet. I like it with marshmallows.

Laura Johnson, Blue River Valley Elementary, Mt. Summit, IN

Mug and Marshmallow Patterns

Use with "Counting on Cocoa" on page 277 and "Cocoa Shape Poem" on page 278.

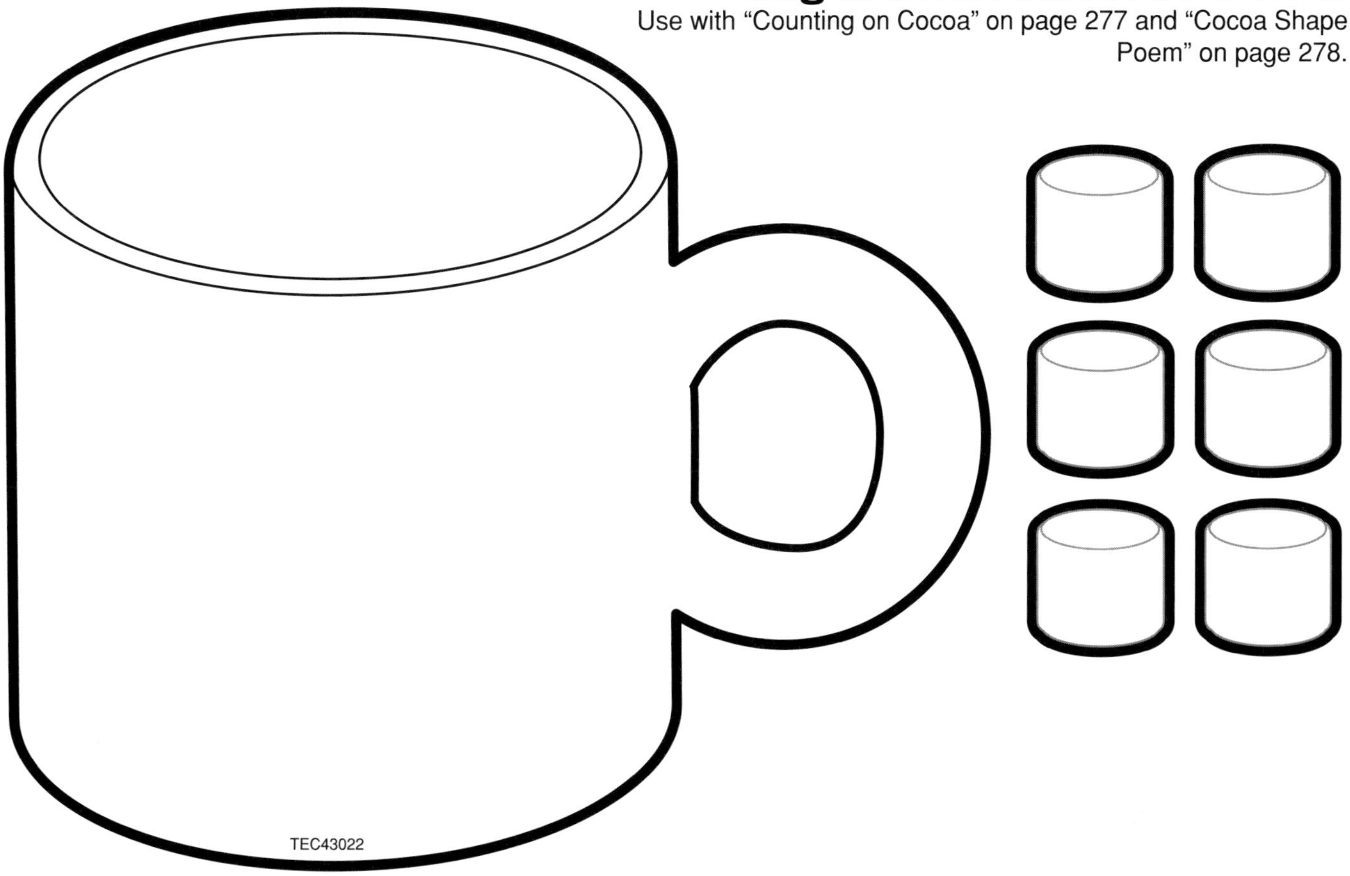
TEC43022

Name ______________________________ Hot Chocolate Math

Counting Coins

Count the coins in each box.

Box	Total
A	¢
B	¢
C	¢
D	¢
E	¢
F	¢

Note to the teacher: Use with "Counting on Cocoa" on page 277.

Sorting Cards

Use with "Common or Proper" on page 278.

Hanukkah
TEC43022
latke
TEC43022
menorah
TEC43022
Santa
TEC43022
holiday
TEC43022
Kwanzaa
TEC43022
friend
TEC43022
gift
TEC43022
candle
TEC43022
mat
TEC43022
December
TEC43022
Christmas
TEC43022

common
TEC43022
common
TEC43022
common
TEC43022
common
TEC43022
common
TEC43022
common
TEC43022
common
TEC43022
proper
TEC43022
proper
TEC43022
proper
TEC43022
proper
TEC43022
proper
TEC43022

Name ______________________________ Hot Chocolate Science

Marshmallow Melt

Prediction: ______________________________

Observations

After I put the marshmallows in	
After 1 minute in the cup	
After 3 minutes in the cup	
After 5 minutes in the cup	

It took the marshmallows ________________ to melt.

Conclusion (what I learned): ______________________________

____

Note to the teacher: Use with "Marshmallow Melt" on page 278.

Doing What's Right

The Life of Martin Luther King Jr.

ideas by Laura Wagner, Raleigh, NC

POEMS FOR MARTIN
Character traits, adjectives

This writing activity is the perfect way to remember Dr. King! As a class, discuss Dr. King's life and his accomplishments. Have students name different character traits they think Dr. King showed through his actions; list their suggestions on the board. To complete the activity, each student selects one word from the list that he thinks best describes Dr. King and writes it vertically on a sheet of white paper. Then he creates a poem about Dr. King, using each letter to begin a new line as shown. Encourage him to include as many descriptive words as he can. After he finishes his poem, he circles each adjective. Then he illustrates his work. Invite students to share their poems with the class; then post the poems on a bulletin board titled "Poems for Martin."

Martin Luther King Jr.
Born in an unfair time,
Raised to know right from wrong.
A strong leader,
Very kind—
Everyone was his friend.

Someone takes the seat you want at lunch.
A classmate takes your markers without asking.
Someone tries to stop your swing while you are on it.
Classmates laugh when you answer a question wrong.

If Someone Takes Your Stuff Without Asking...
It's okay to borrow the ball if you ask first. Please give it back when you finish.

PROMOTING PEACE
Problem solving

Help students find peaceful solutions to everyday problems! Remind students that Dr. King tried to solve the problems he encountered in a peaceful, nonviolent way. Challenge your class to walk in Dr. King's shoes. To do this, have each group of four make a list of school situations that could lead to conflict (see box). The group chooses one situation from the list and thinks of a peaceful way to solve it. Then the group illustrates the situation and its solution on a poster. Display the posters around your classroom or throughout the school as visual reminders of how to solve problems peacefully.

Name ____________________

Dr. King's Dream

Read the passage.
Answer the questions.

Years ago, black people and white people did not have the same rights. They had different schools and bathrooms. If a black person rode a bus, he had to give his seat to a white person. Martin Luther King Jr. felt that these things were wrong. He thought all people were equal. He wanted all people to be treated the same.

Dr. King tried to change things. He wrote speeches. He went to one town and helped people start a bus boycott. Black people stopped riding buses until they could sit in the same seats as white people. A few years later Dr. King led a peaceful march. He made a famous speech called "I have a dream."

Dr. King kept working to make sure that blacks and whites were treated fairly. He was killed in 1968. Each year on his birthday, we honor him because he solved problems in a peaceful way.

1. What was Dr. King's dream? ____________________

2. Name two ways black people and white people weren't treated the same. ____________________

3. Why do we celebrate Dr. King's birthday? ____________________

4. How do you think Dr. King solved problems peacefully? ____________________

5. Circle the letter of the best title for this passage.

   a. How to Treat People
   b. A Famous Person
   c. Dr. King and His Dream
   d. Being the Same

Name ______________________________ Martin Luther King Jr. Timeline

Dr. King's Life

Use the timeline to answer the questions.

1. Where was Dr. King born? ____________________
2. When did Dr. King become a minister? ____________________
3. Which event happened first? ________

   a. gave "I have a dream" speech   b. led bus boycott

4. In what year did Dr. King's birthday become a holiday? __________
5. What was Dr. King's wife's name? ____________________
6. When did Dr. King lead a march in Washington, DC? __________

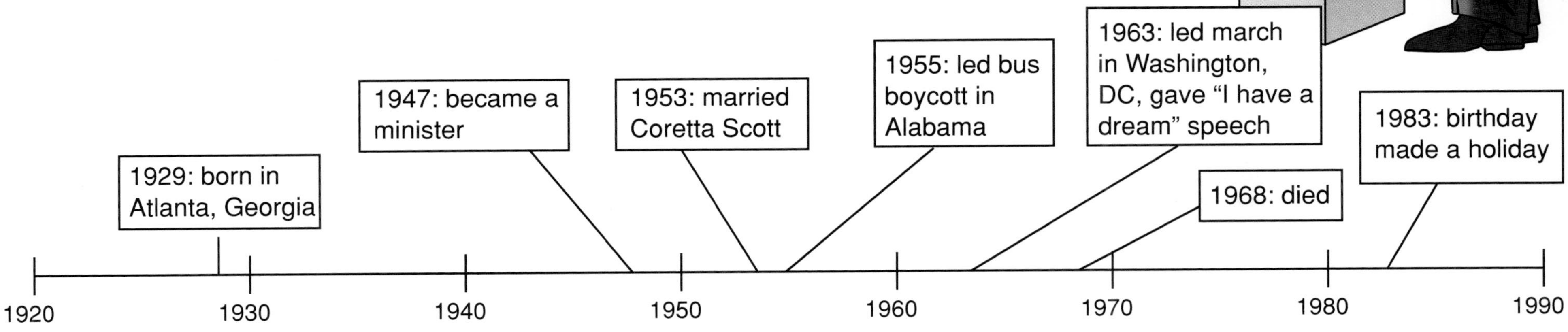
1929: born in Atlanta, Georgia
1947: became a minister
1953: married Coretta Scott
1955: led bus boycott in Alabama
1963: led march in Washington, DC, gave "I have a dream" speech
1968: died
1983: birthday made a holiday
1920
1930
1940
1950
1960
1970
1980
1990

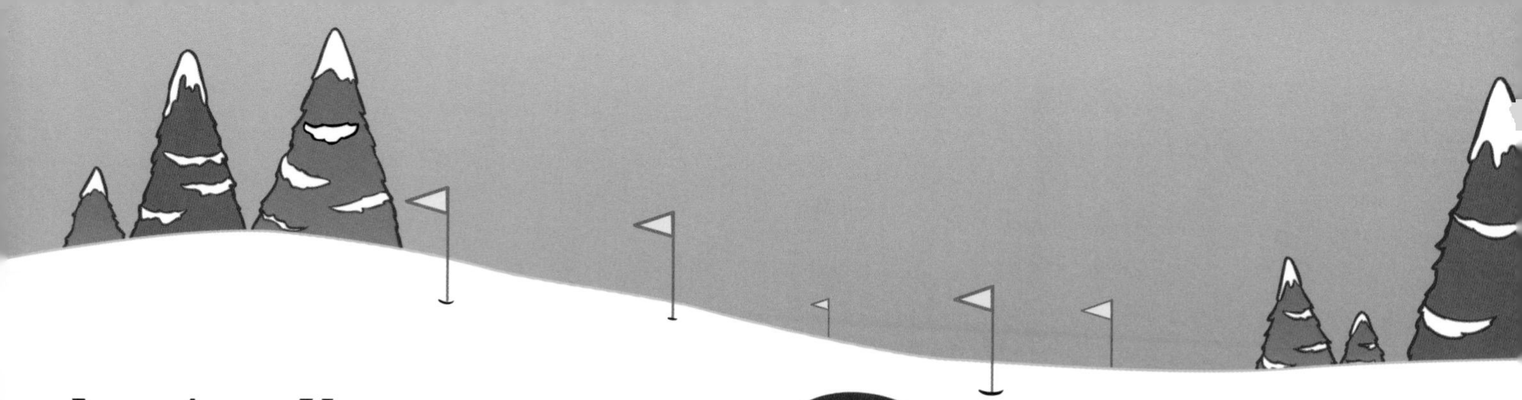

Winter Games

A Wonderland of Skill Practice

ICE RINK
Science

This simple experiment is the perfect small-group activity! In advance, create individual ice rinks by freezing a thin layer of water in several large baking pans. Also gather a paper clip, a pencil, a rock, a marble, and a small ball of yarn for each group. Begin by giving each group its own ice rink, the items listed above, and a copy of page 287 for each member. Have each child predict which item will slide over the ice the easiest. To complete the experiment, group members take turns sliding different objects and recording the results. After each group finishes the experiment, discuss which items would be best for scoring a goal. Then invite students to share why they think some objects slid on the ice easier than others.

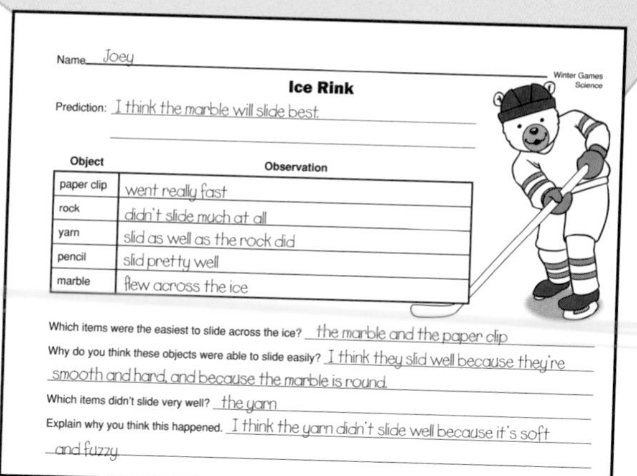

Name Joey

Winter Games
Science

Ice Rink

Prediction: I think the marble will slide best.

Object	Observation
paper clip	went really fast
rock	didn't slide much at all
yarn	slid as well as the rock did
pencil	slid pretty well
marble	flew across the ice

Which items were the easiest to slide across the ice? the marble and the paper clip

Why do you think these objects were able to slide easily? I think they slid well because they're smooth and hard, and because the marble is round.

Which items didn't slide very well? the yarn

Explain why you think this happened. I think the yarn didn't slide well because it's soft and fuzzy

Celebrate winter sports with these winning ideas and activities!

with ideas by Stacie Wright, Millington School, Millington, NJ

CURLING COINS
Math

This partner activity is easy to prepare! In advance, make a paper target like the one shown, and label each section with a different coin amount. Place the target and a rolled-up sock at a center along with a variety of play coins, paper, and a pencil. Each child starts the game with $1.00. Player 1 curls, or rolls, the sock onto the paper target. He subtracts the amount he lands on from his total, writing the math problem and using coins as needed. Then he writes his new amount on a sheet of paper. Player 2 takes a turn in the same manner. If a child lands on a space and does not have enough money to subtract to zero, he takes another turn. Play continues until one child has no money left and wins the game.

50¢
5¢
25¢
10¢

MAKING THE GOAL
Grammar

Making the Goal
Singular Possessive
Plural Possessive
girl's
players'

Score some practice with singular and plural possessive nouns at this center! Copy page 288, color the sorting mat, and then cut out the mat and cards. Mount the cards and mat on construction paper. Program each card's back for easy self-checking. Place the cards and the mat at a center. A child decides whether each noun is singular or plural and places the card on the corresponding box on the mat. Then he flips the cards over to check his work.

PERSONAL FLAGS
Social Studies

Help students understand symbolism by having them create their own flags! Tell students that each country has its own flag that is displayed during the Olympic Games. Explain that each country's flag has symbols or colors that represent something special about it. Then, as a class, discuss the American flag and the symbolism behind its 13 stripes and 50 stars. Afterward, give each child a sheet of blank paper and have him create his own personal flag. Encourage him to use pictures, symbols, and colors that represent something special about him. When students finish, invite each child to show his flag and explain its symbols.

My flag is green because that's my favorite color. I drew three circles because there are three people in my family. The things in the clouds are the things that are the most important to me.

Name ____________________

Ice Rink

Prediction: ____________________

____

Object	Observation
paper clip	
rock	
yarn	
pencil	
marble	

Which items were the easiest to slide across the ice? ____________________

Why do you think these objects were able to slide easily? ____________________

____

Which items didn't slide very well? ____________________

Explain why you think this happened. ____________________

____

Sorting Mat and Word Cards

Use with "Making the Goal" on page 286.

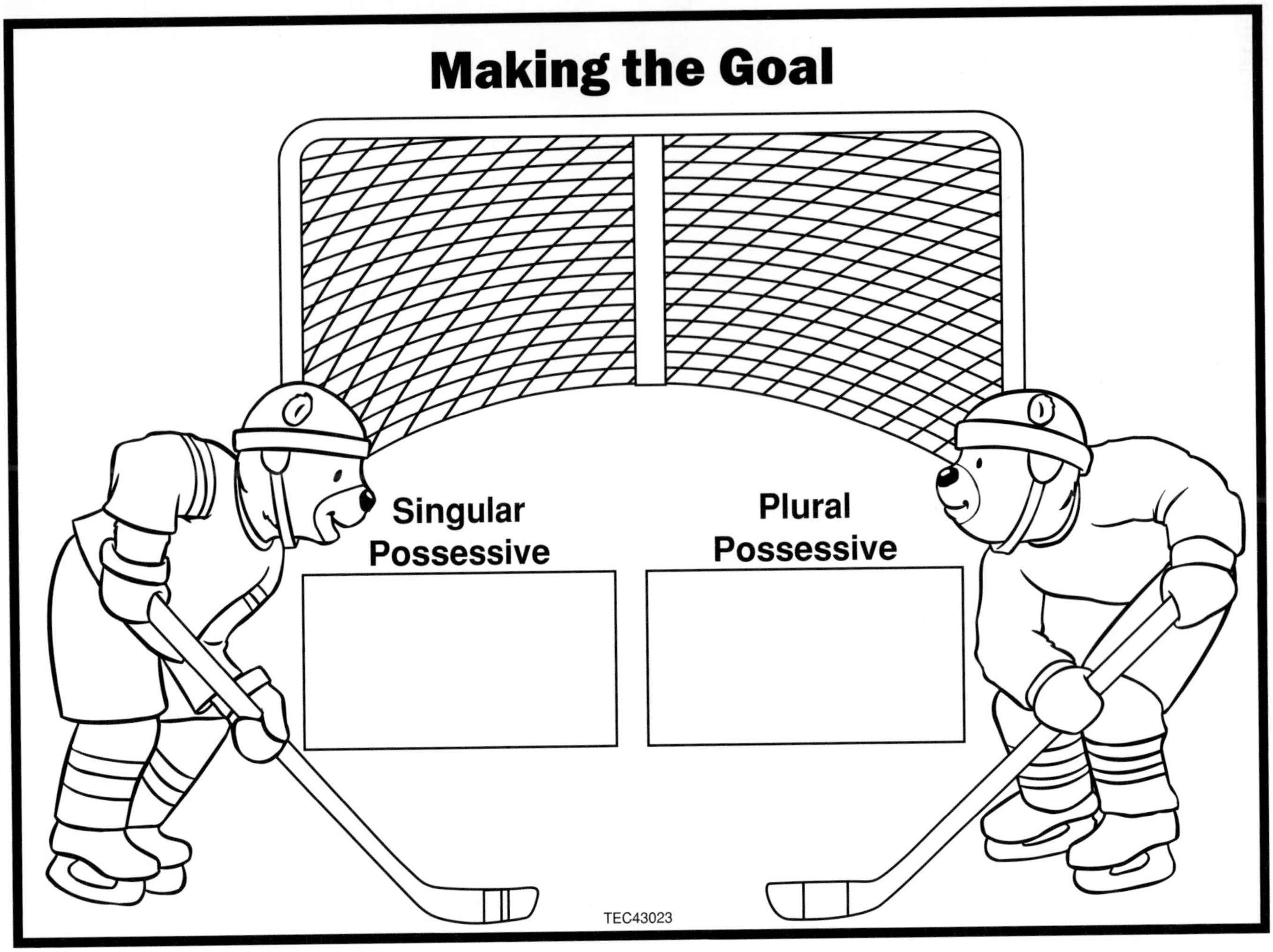
Making the Goal
Singular Possessive
Plural Possessive
TEC43023

friends' TEC43023	coach's TEC43023	team's TEC43023	fans' TEC43023
person's TEC43023	boy's TEC43023	judges' TEC43023	girl's TEC43023
sister's TEC43023	children's TEC43023	schools' TEC43023	game's TEC43023
players' TEC43023	teachers' TEC43023	doctor's TEC43023	brothers' TEC43023

Name____________________

Possible combinations, money
Winter Games

Ticket Types

Write the ten different combinations of tickets that are $10.00 or less.

Ticket Prices
Luge $3.75
Skiing $4.25
Snowboarding $4.50
Figure Skating $4.75
Ice Hockey $5.25

Ticket 1	Ticket 2	Total
$.	$.	$.
$.	$.	$.
$.	$.	$.
$.	$.	$.
$.	$.	$.
$.	$.	$.
$.	$.	$.
$.	$.	$.
$.	$.	$.
$.	$.	$.

Superstars

Celebrating Black History Month

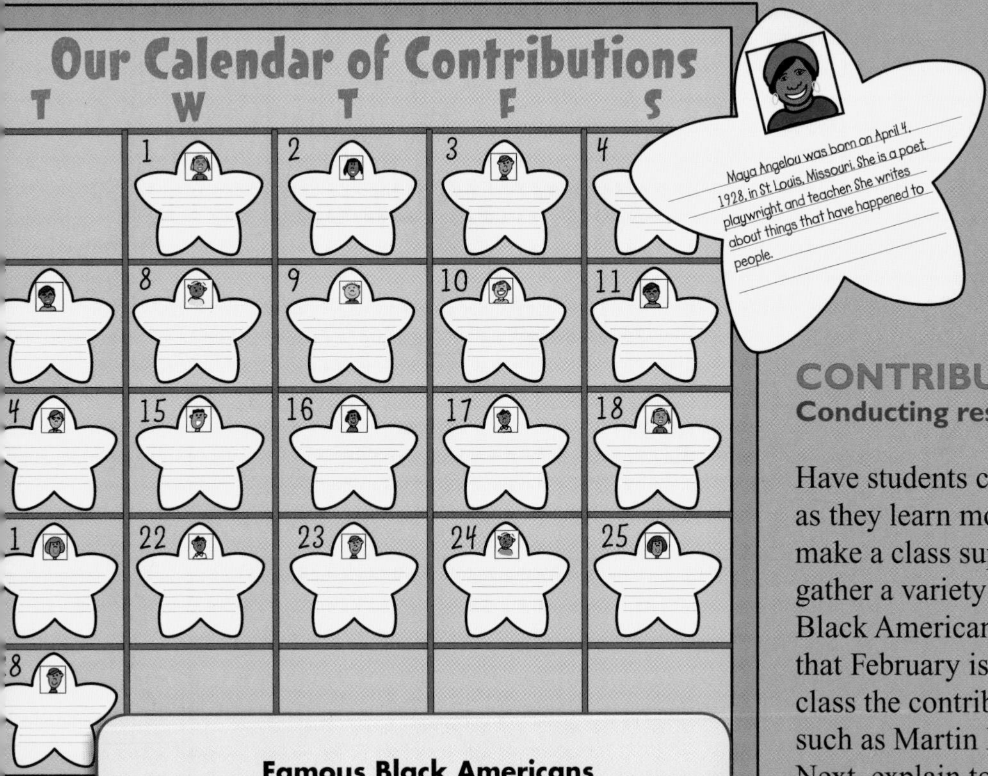
Our Calendar of Contributions
T W T F S
1 2 3 4
8 9 10 11
15 16 17 18
22 23 24 25
Maya Angelou was born on April 4, 1928, in St. Louis, Missouri. She is a poet, playwright, and teacher. She writes about things that have happened to people.

Famous Black Americans

Marian Anderson	Mae Jemison
Maya Angelou	Michael Jordan
Louis Armstrong	Jackie Joyner-Kersee
Mary McLeod Bethune	Martin Luther King Jr.
Carol Moseley Braun	Thurgood Marshall
Gwendolyn Brooks	Elijah McCoy
Ralph Johnson Bunche	Jesse Owens
George Washington Carver	Rosa Parks
Shirley Chisholm	Colin Powell
Bessie Coleman	Wilma Rudolph
Bill Cosby	Harriet Tubman
Charles Drew	Booker T. Washington
Matthew Henson	Oprah Winfrey
Langston Hughes	Tiger Woods

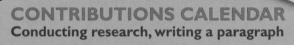

CONTRIBUTIONS CALENDAR

Conducting research, writing a paragraph

Have students create a unique informational display as they learn more about black history! In advance, make a class supply of pages 291 and 292. Also gather a variety of books and resources about famous Black Americans. Begin by sharing with students that February is Black History Month. Discuss as a class the contributions of famous Black Americans, such as Martin Luther King Jr. and Harriet Tubman. Next, explain to students that the class will create its own February calendar showing the contributions of 28 famous Black Americans—one for each day of the month. To complete the activity, each child chooses a person from the list shown. Then he uses research materials to gather information about his assigned person and records the facts on a copy of the organizer on page 291.

After the child has completed his organizer, he uses his notes to write a paragraph about his person. He carefully edits his paragraph, writes his final version on a copy of page 292, and draws a picture of the individual in the space given at the top of the pattern. Finally, invite students to share their paragraphs with the class. Post students' paragraphs on a display with a title like the one shown.

Name ______________________________

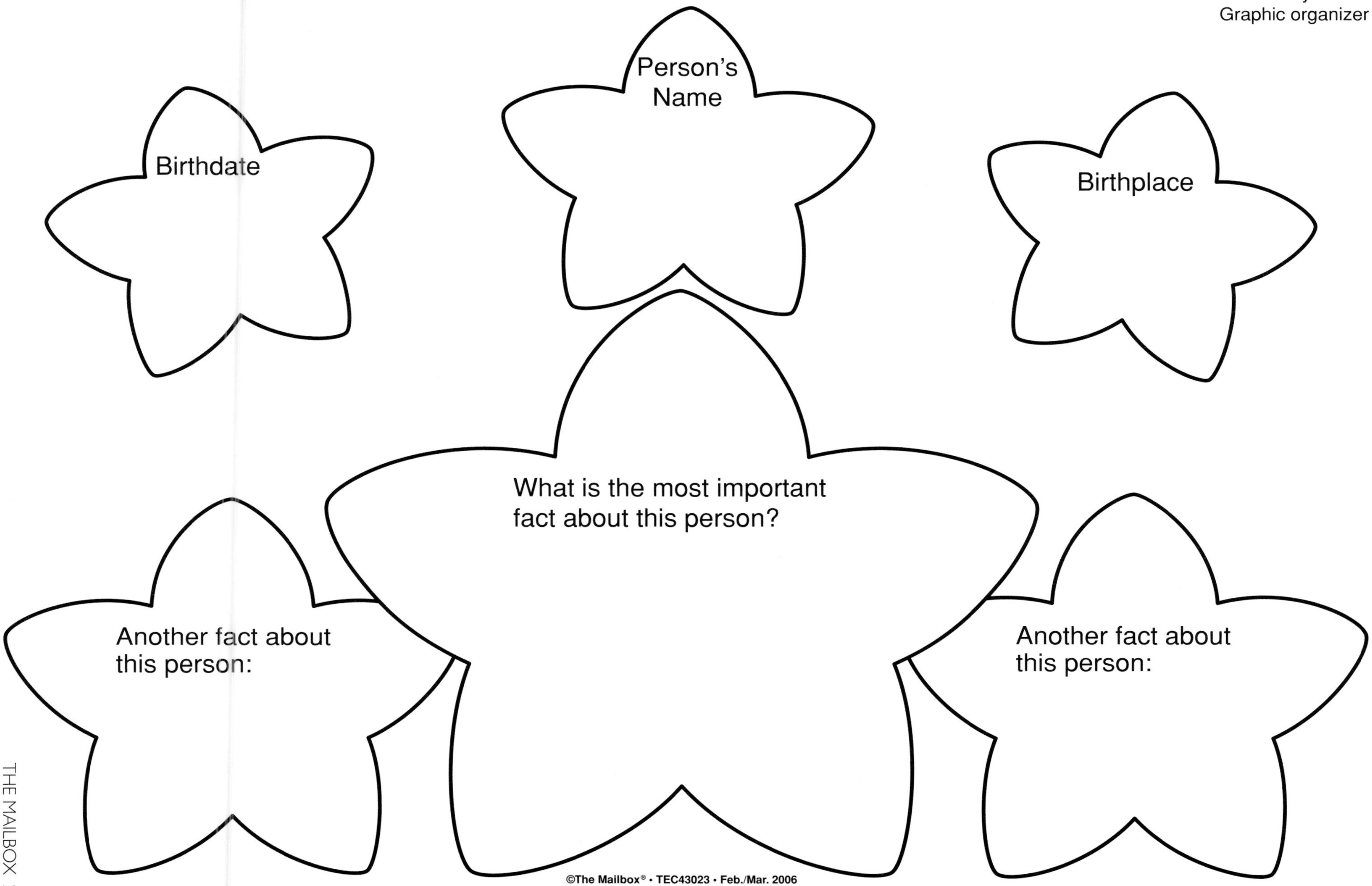
Person's
Name
Birthdate
Birthplace
What is the most important
fact about this person?
Another fact about
this person:
Another fact about
this person:

Note to the teacher: Use with "Contributions Calendar" on page 290.

Star Pattern

Use with "Contributions Calendar" on page 290.

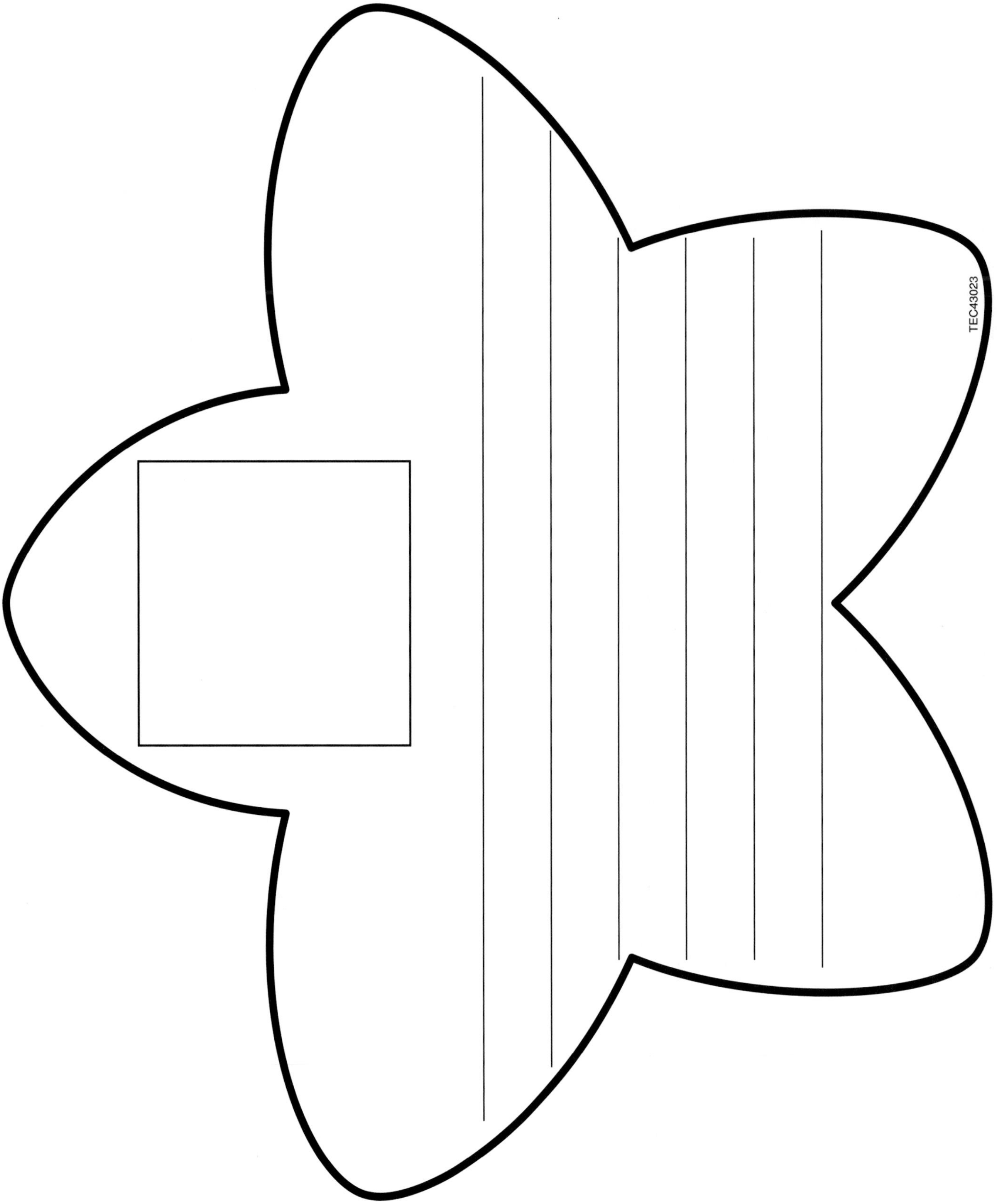
TEC43023

In Bloom!

Skill-Based Activities on Flowers

FLORIST
Sam's
SMELL-O-RAMA

CRAFTY PLANTS
Science

Have students make unique models that showcase the parts of a flowering plant! In advance, gather a supply of craft materials such as fabric scraps, feathers, pipe cleaners, beads, craft foam, and craft glue. Each child arranges any combination of craft materials desired to form a plant with the following parts: roots, stem, leaf, petal, stamen, and pistil. Next, the student uses craft glue to affix the model to a 9" x 12" sheet of colored construction paper. Then he attaches an index card listing each flower part and the materials used to create it. Invite students to share their creations with the class; then post the completed diagrams on a bulletin board.

Jason

Here's my flower. It has six parts.
1. roots–moss
2. stem–green pipe cleaner
3. leaves–green craft foam
4. stamen–yellow and brown pipe cleaners
5. pistil–yellow pipe cleaner and brown bean
6. petals–blue feathers

This collection of core curriculum activities will help students' knowledge blossom!

with ideas by Laura Wagner, Raleigh, NC

POLLINATION POSTERS
Writing

Cultivate students' persuasive-writing skills! Begin by discussing with the class why plants have flowers. Remind students that a flower's main job is to make seeds. Also explain that flowers are often brightly colored or have an odor to attract insects and animals so that pollination will occur. Next, pair students and have each twosome brainstorm words and phrases that might persuade an animal or insect to visit and pollinate a flower. To create a poster, each twosome draws a picture of a flower on a sheet of 9" x 12" light-colored construction paper. Then the pair writes a few of their brainstormed ideas on the poster. Display the completed posters on a board titled "Pollination Persuasion"!

Eat here! This pollen tastes best! Share it with your friends!
Come try our delicious pollen! It's made fresh every day!

Sam's SMELL-O-RAMA
Card 1
1. The yellow flower is last.
2. The red flower is third.
3. The purple flower is next to the yellow one.
4. The pink flower is between the red and purple flowers.
5. The orange flower is first.
6. Where does the blue card go?

FLOWER ARRANGEMENTS
Math

To create this logical-reasoning center, copy page 295. Color the cards, making certain there is a pink, yellow, red, orange, purple, and blue flower. Cut them apart. Laminate the cards and store them at a center. Also make a copy of the answer key on page 313 and place it at the center. A child visiting the center selects a problem-solving card and reads the clues. Then she uses all of the flower cards to find the correct order. When she thinks she has arranged the flowers correctly, she consults the answer key to check her work. Then she selects a different card and repeats the process as time allows.

Use with "Flower Arrangements" on page 294.

Card 1

1. The yellow flower is last.
2. The red flower is third.
3. The purple flower is next to the yellow one.
4. The pink flower is between the red and purple flowers.
5. The orange flower is first.
6. Where does the blue card go?

TEC43024

Card 2

1. The yellow and red flowers are beside each other.
2. The orange flower is last.
3. The pink flower is between the red and orange flowers.
4. The purple flower is beside the yellow flower.
5. The purple flower is to the right of the blue flower.

TEC43024

Card 3

1. The yellow flower is between the orange and purple flowers.
2. The purple flower and the blue flower are side by side.
3. The red flower is first.
4. The pink flower is between the red and orange flowers.
5. The blue flower is last.

TEC43024

Card 4

1. The pink flower is next to the last flower.
2. The purple flower is first.
3. The yellow flower is on the pink flower's left side.
4. The red flower is last.
5. The blue flower is between the orange and yellow flowers.

TEC43024

TEC43024

TEC43024

TEC43024

TEC43024

TEC43024

TEC43024

Name____

Flower Finale

Add the suffix in the flower's center to each word.
Write the new words on the lines.

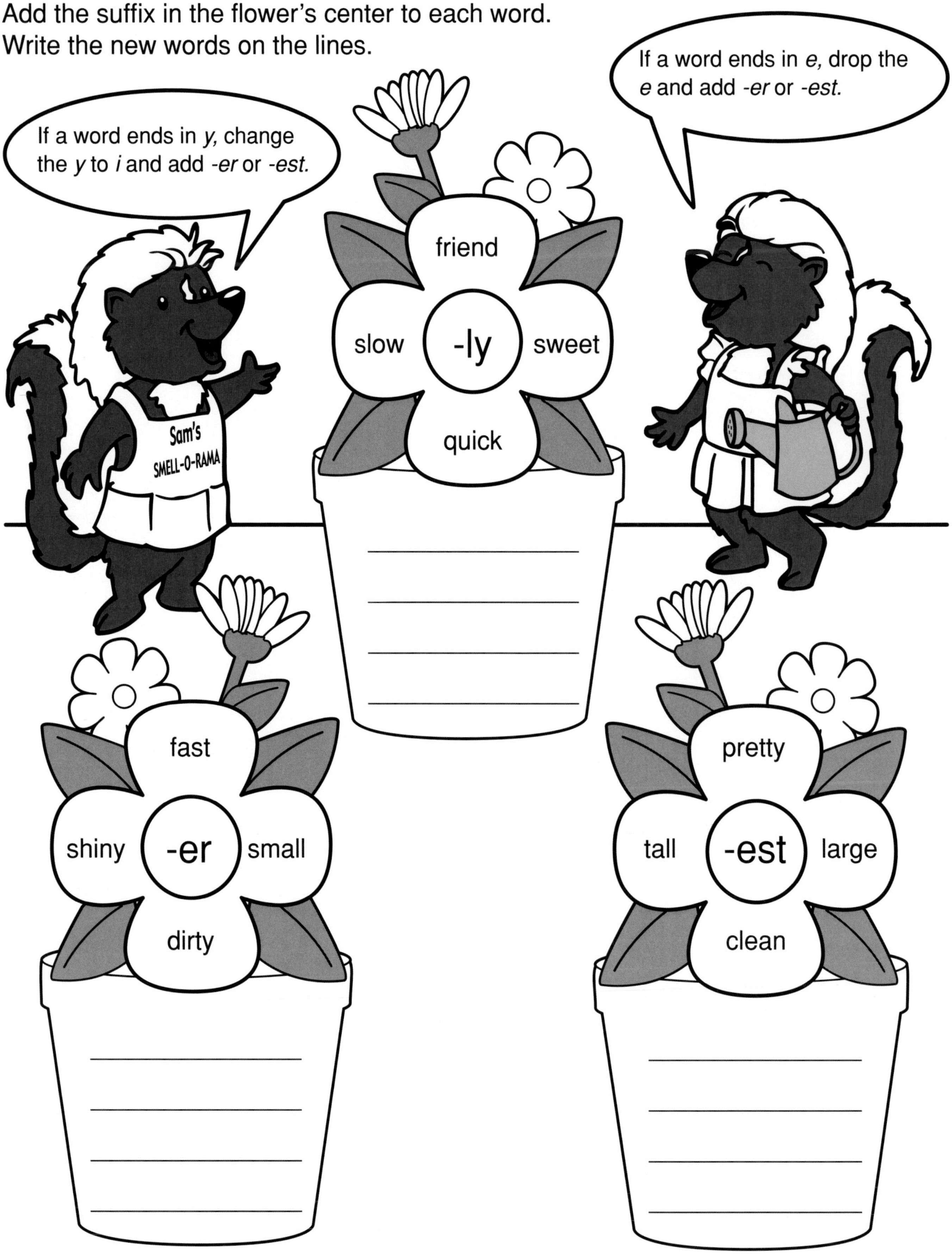
If a word ends in *e,* drop the *e* and add *-er* or *-est.*
If a word ends in *y,* change the *y* to *i* and add *-er* or *-est.*
Sam's
SMELL-O-RAMA
friend
slow
-ly
sweet
quick
fast
shiny
-er
small
dirty
pretty
tall
-est
large
clean

Get the **Scoop!**

A Serving of Ice-Cream Ideas

SODAS
MILK SHAKES

Jeff
5 x 8 = 40
8 x 5 = 40
40 ÷ 5 = 8
40 ÷ 8 = 5
10
7
4
3
6
5
8

JUST THE FACTS
Math

This multiplication partner center is a bowlful of fun! In advance, gather 20 Ping-Pong balls. Program each with a different digit from 0 to 9, resulting in two balls with the same number. Place the balls in a bowl; then store it at a center along with an ice-cream scoop, paper, and pencils. Partners take turns scooping up two balls. Each child uses the numbers on the balls to write a multiplication problem on his paper. He solves the problem; then below it, he writes the remaining multiplication and division problems in the fact family. Students continue scooping up numbers and creating multiplication problems as long as desired.

Celebrate summertime with these cool ideas!

with ideas by Laura Wagner, Raleigh, NC

Delia's
Super Sundae
First, you scoop
ice cream into
the bowl.

SUPER SUNDAES
Writing

Begin by brainstorming with the class the ingredients needed to make the perfect ice-cream sundae. Write students' responses on the board. Next, each child lists the steps to make a sundae, using time and order words as needed. Then she writes and illustrates each step on a separate quarter sheet of blank paper. She puts the completed pages in order and staples them between two construction paper covers. After cutting around the booklet's edges to create an ice-cream scoop shape, she decorates the cover as desired. To display the projects, post them on a bulletin board along with a large bowl and the title "Sundae Perfection."

Jennifer Kohnke
Nature Ridge Elementary
Bartlett, IL

EATING TREATS
Grammar

Showcase students' drama skills as they practice adverbs! Before the activity, create a paper ice-cream cone like the one shown below. Also write the following sentence on the board: "I eat my ice-cream cone _______." Begin by reviewing with students adverbs and three things that an adverb tells *(how, when, and where)*. Then give a child the paper cone and have him say the sentence aloud, including an adverb. He uses the paper cone to dramatize his sentence and then gives it to the next student, who repeats the process. Continue passing the cone around the room until each student has had a chance to complete the sentence and act it out.

I eat my ice-cream cone quickly.

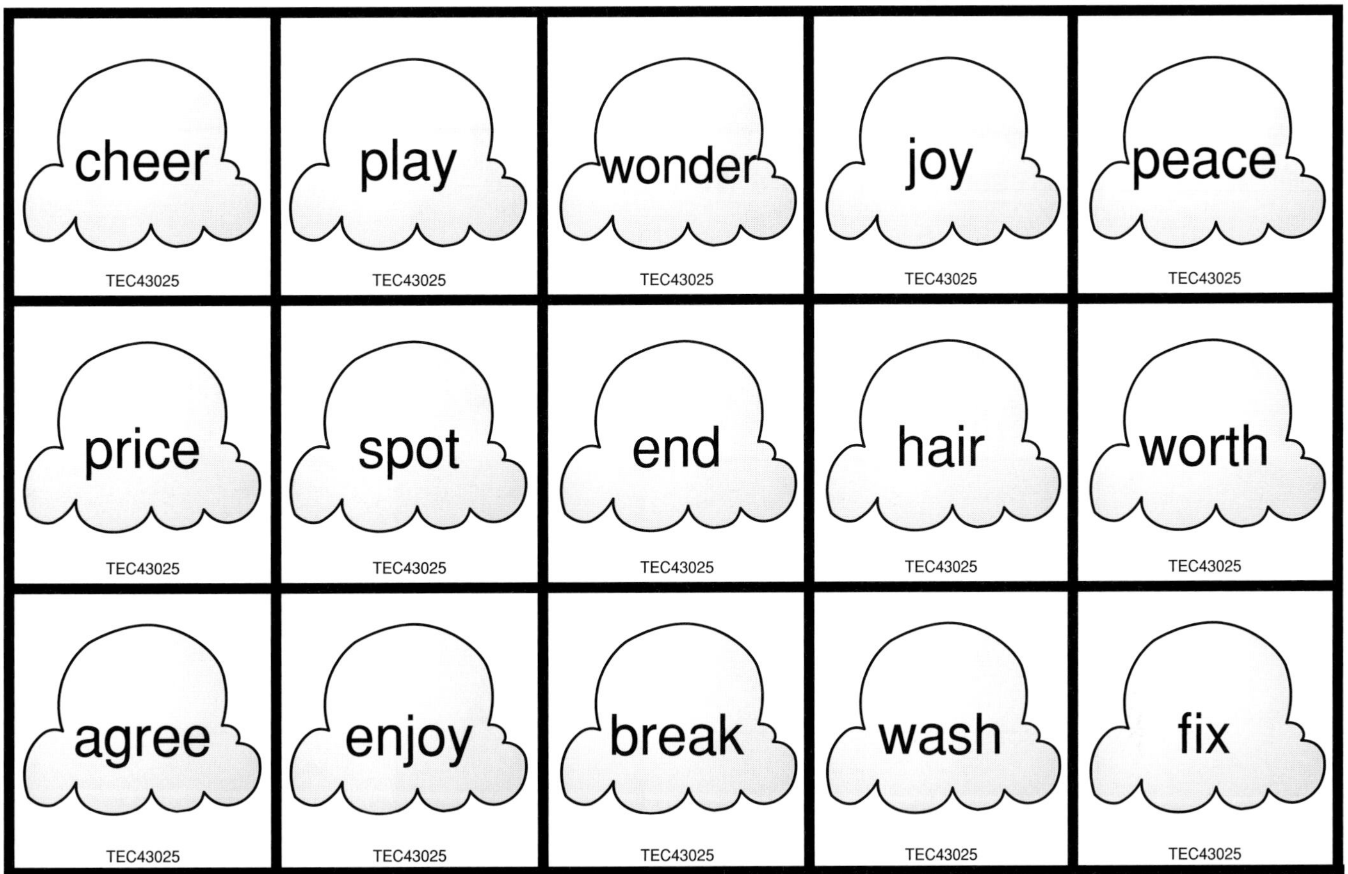
cheer
TEC43025
play
TEC43025
wonder
TEC43025
joy
TEC43025
peace
TEC43025
price
TEC43025
spot
TEC43025
end
TEC43025
hair
TEC43025
worth
TEC43025
agree
TEC43025
enjoy
TEC43025
break
TEC43025
wash
TEC43025
fix
TEC43025

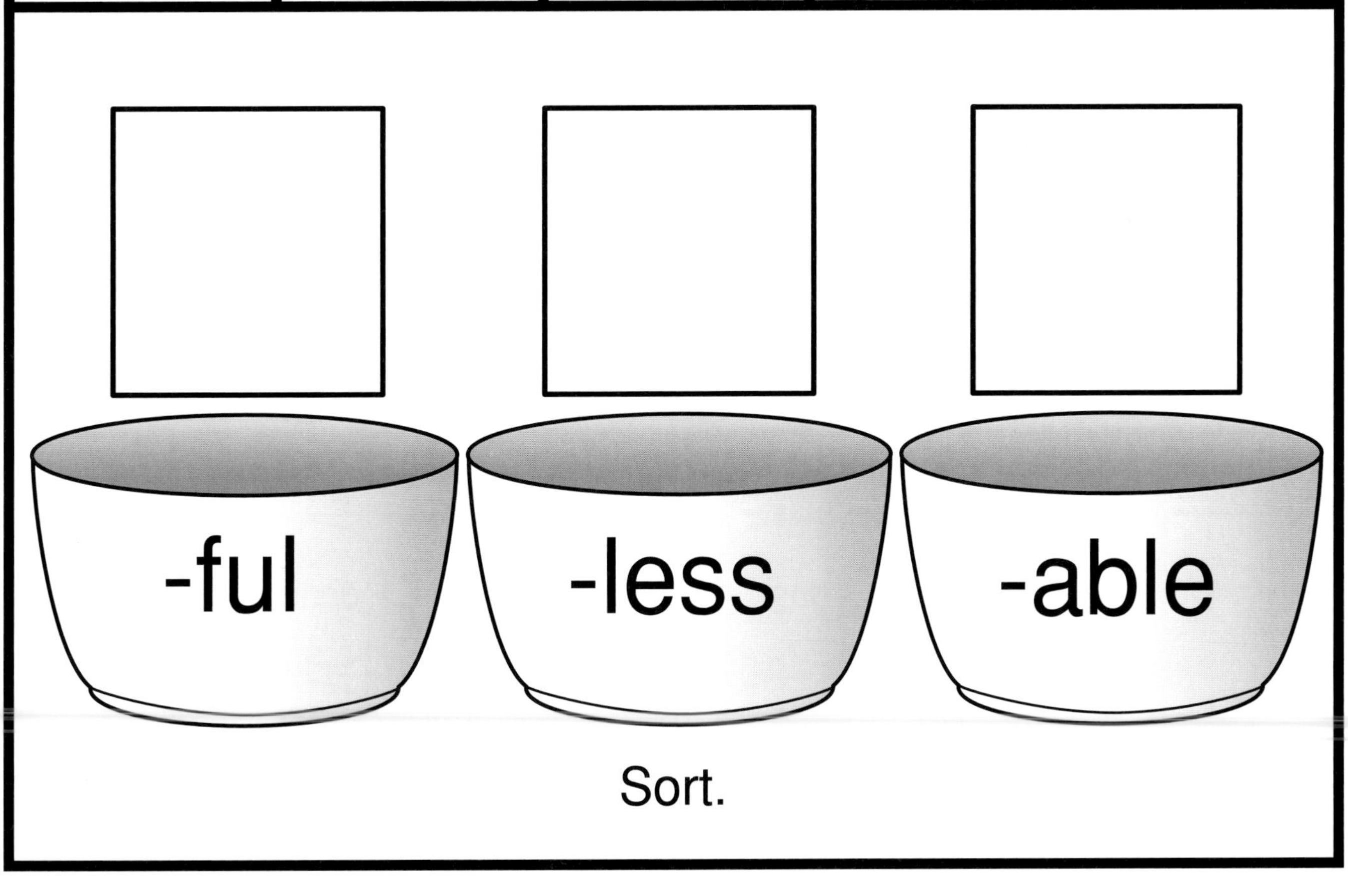
-ful
-less
-able
Sort.

Note to the Teacher: Copy this page; then mount the cards and mat on construction paper. Color the sorting mat and cards; then cut them out. Program each card's back for self-checking. Place the cards and mat at a center. A child sorts each card by placing it on the suffix that, when combined with the base word, forms a new word. After sorting the cards he turns them over to check his work.

Name____________________

Ice Cream
Singular and plural possessives

Scoop Sort

Cut the scoops apart.
Glue each scoop above the dish that shows the correct rule.
Then write the possessive form of the word on the line.

Add *'s.*

____
____
____
____
____
____

Add an ' after the *s.*

____
____
____
____
____
____

Add *'s.*

Add an ' after the *s.*

brothers	dog	girls	dancer
students	children	Carrie	Mom
cats	teachers	author	players

Teacher Resource Units

Field Trip Next Friday

Come On In!

Making the Most of Open House

Welcome!
Me
Favorite Food
hot dog
Favorite Subject
math
Favorite Place
water park
Favorite Hobby
soccer
Favorite Color
red
Guess Who?
Me
I am proud because...
you are my son and you treat others well.
Thank you for...
trying hard at school and keeping a neat desk!

GUESS WHO?

Encourage **open house attendance** with student-made riddles! Make a class supply of page 304 and then cut the forms apart. Have each child complete a "Welcome!" form by illustrating himself in the center of the paper and describing and illustrating the five favorites listed. Next, have him paper-clip his clues atop his desktag so his name is hidden from view. Explain to students that parents who come to open house will use the papers to locate their child's desk!

For a return surprise, ask parents to complete "Guess Who?" forms during open house and clip the clues to their children's desktags. Be sure to fill out a few forms yourself, and clip your clues to the desktags of students whose families were unable to attend. You can anticipate plenty of smiles the following day!

Lisa Funk
Herbert Hoover Elementary
Buffalo, NY

Make a BIG impression on parents with this fine catch of open house suggestions!

Thank you so much!
Signature Phone/Email
Supplies
1. Otis Octopus 555-0100
2. Larry Lobster 2claws@sealink.com
3.
4.
Chaperones
1. Sally Shark ibite@sealink.com
2.
3.
4.
Guest Readers
1. Jada Jellyfish 555-0176
2.
3.
4.

ALL IN A DAY

Parents are often curious about how a **typical school day** unfolds. To show them, design a brief presentation on your computer that explains the daily routine. Use a digital camera to photograph students engaged in the activities you've outlined, making sure every child is photographed. Then insert the images into your presentation. Next year, simply update the photos (and text pages as necessary) and your presentation is ready!

Jen Ratka
Hillview Elementary School
Lancaster, NY

Our School Day
Centers 9:30 – 10:15

THE FISH POND

Reel in **family support** at this clever open house display. Label a class supply of fish-shaped sticky notes with an opportunity for parent involvement, such as donating supplies, chaperoning field trips, and being guest readers. Also make a corresponding contact sheet like the one shown. Showcase the programmed notes on a large paper pond titled "Our FISH Pond—**F**amily **I**nvolvement **S**tarts **H**ere!" Place the contact sheet and pencils nearby. Invite parents to take fish from the pond and sign the contact sheet beside the corresponding category. Family support is the catch of the evening!

Liana Mahoney
Beaver River Central School
Beaver Falls, NY

TAKE A NUMBER, PLEASE!

You'll earn rave reviews with this **organizational tip!** Number a class set of cards and arrange the cards numerically in a pocket chart. Then make a sign that invites each family to take a numbered card and explains that you look forward to spending quality time with your guests in the order of their arrival. Display the sign and pocket chart just inside your classroom door. Families who are visiting more than one teacher can choose their cards accordingly. Your visitors are sure to appreciate this thoughtful approach!

Allie Arksey
Northridge Public School
London, Ontario, Canada

3
6

Open House Forms

Use with "Guess Who?" on page 302.

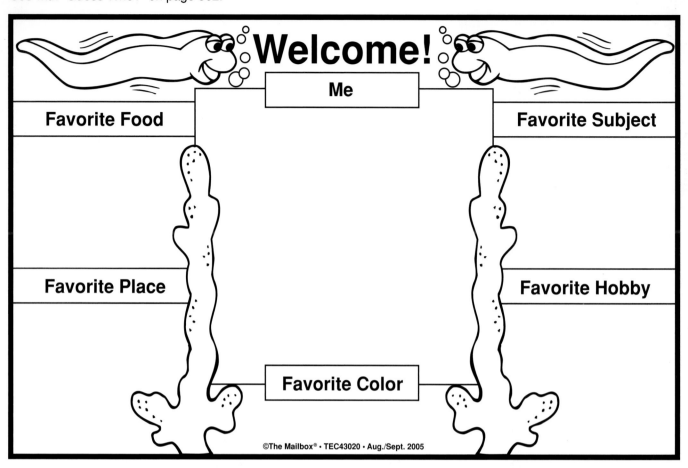

Welcome!

Me

Favorite Food

Favorite Subject

Favorite Place

Favorite Hobby

Favorite Color

Guess Who?

Me

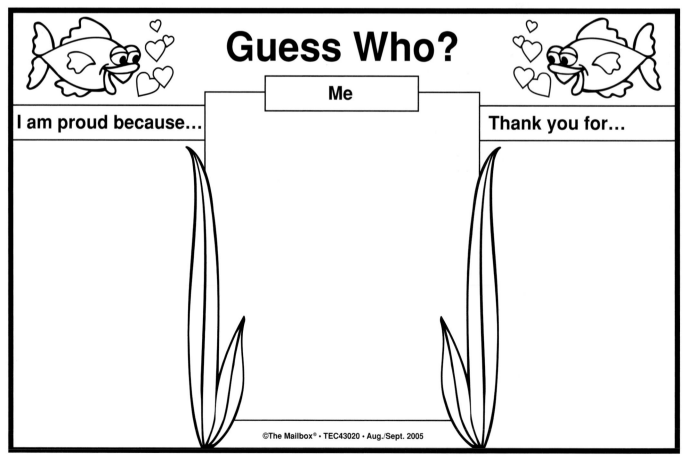

I am proud because...

Thank you for...

In the Field

Pointers for Parent-Teacher Conferences

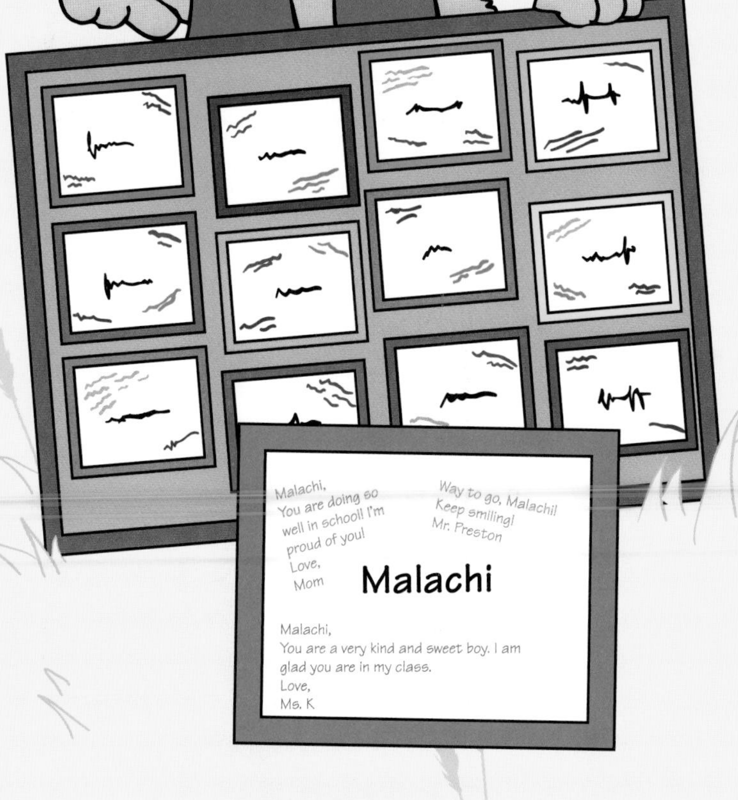
Malachi,
You are doing so well in school! I'm proud of you!
Love,
Mom
Way to go, Malachi!
Keep smiling!
Mr. Preston
Malachi
Malachi,
You are a very kind and sweet boy. I am glad you are in my class.
Love,
Ms. K

MESSAGE BOARD

Before conferences begin, lay the groundwork for a one-of-a-kind hallway display. Write each child's name on a sheet of blank paper. Then post the papers in the hallway with an uplifting title or quote. Store a container of colorful markers nearby. Each time you wrap up a conference, step over to the display and ask the parent to write a personalized note of encouragement to her child. (If you think parents need advance notice of the display, explain it in your preconference correspondence.) Add your own personalized messages to the display and invite your school principal and colleagues to do the same. Make sure every student has two or more positive messages by the time fall conferences come to a close.

Erica Kremitzki
Riddle Elementary
Mattoon, IL

Who "nose" where to sniff out suggestions for successful parent-teacher conferences? We do!

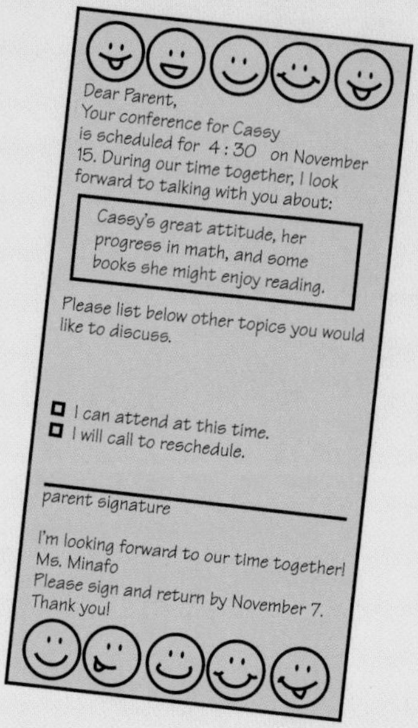
Dear Parent,
Your conference for Cassey is scheduled for 4:30 on November 15. During our time together, I look forward to talking with you about:

Cassey's great attitude, her progress in math, and some books she might enjoy reading.

Please list below other topics you would like to discuss.

- [ ] I can attend at this time.
- [ ] I will call to reschedule.

parent signature

I'm looking forward to our time together!
Ms. Minafo
Please sign and return by November 7.
Thank you!

PLAN AHEAD

Make every minute count! For each child, prepare a personalized conference form like the one shown that invites a parent to add to your agenda. Then ask that the form be signed and returned to school before the conference. Parents will appreciate your thoroughness and thoughtfulness, and you'll feel more relaxed and prepared for each meeting.

Kim Minafo
Dillard Drive Elementary School
Raleigh, NC

PICTURE THIS

Put each visitor at ease by spending a few minutes at the start of a conference looking at snapshots of students in action. Make sure every child appears in one or more photographs. This personal touch begins each conference on a positive note. If you've used a digital camera, consider sending each family home with a paper version of a favorite photo!

Anna Parrish
Joseph Keels Elementary
Columbia, SC

THE SANDWICH STRATEGY

Structure each conference for success! When planning your comments, think of a sandwich or cream-filled cookie. Start with positive comments that clearly recognize and appreciate a student's qualities and strengths. Next, sandwich areas of weakness for the student and invite his parent to help you develop strategies for improvement. Then end the conference on a positive note, just as you began it!

Joyce Ornam
Carden Traditional School
Surprise, AZ

Blast Off!

Boosting Testing Confidence

HOORAY, HOORAY!

Before students take a **standardized test,** read aloud *Hooray for Diffendoofer Day!* by Dr. Seuss, Jack Prelutsky, and Lane Smith. After sharing the book, discuss how the students at Diffendoofer feel about taking their test and how they handle their worries. Then point out that your class has a lot in common with the Diffendoofer students; they have been taught everything they need to know in order to do well, so there's no reason to be afraid. Capitalize on this feeling by having student pairs make motivational posters for an upcoming test. Display the posters in your classroom and around the school to boost everyone's spirit!

Linda Biondi, Robbinsville, NJ

Don't stress—it's just a test!
Take your time and you'll do just fine!

HEADS DOWN, HEADS UP

This simple tip works wonders before giving students a **test or quiz!** Two minutes before handing out the test, have students put their heads on their desks and think about what they know and remember about the test topic. This helps students relax and moves them into test-taking mode. At the end of the two minutes, say, "Heads up." Now students are focused and ready to take the test!

Krista Hatten, Forks Elementary School, Easton, PA

MEALTIME WRITING

Make taking a **writing test** stress free for your students! In the weeks before the test, tell students that writing a story is like eating a meal: there's an appetizer, a main course, and a dessert. The appetizer gets things started and grabs the reader's attention. The main course is the main part of the story, and the dessert wraps everything up. Encourage students to use this idea to plan their papers. On the day of the test, as soon as they see the prompt they'll be ready to go!

Lisa Massey, Ezard Elementary, Conway, MO

Taking the Grade

High-Scoring Assessment Tips

MAGIC NUMBERS

Assign each student a number and use it instead of her name when recording assessment information. This saves time and provides anonymity for your records.

PRESET FORMS

Use your computer to **create your own assessment templates.** To make one, type the subject at the top of a page. Create a table with your students' names in the rows in the first column and the related skills you are observing in the following columns. Be sure to include space to record the score as well as comments. To make this template suitable for any subject, keep the table and change the headings.

To organize student data for standards-based report cards, start with a template like the one described above. Add a content strand to the top of each page and then list the related objectives below it. Make similar pages for other subjects and print the pages for each subject on like-colored paper. Organize the pages by color and store them in a three-ring binder. To record student progress, label each column with the activity, date, and objective, and then insert scores and brief comments.

Dawn Rainbowstar, The Colorado Springs School, Colorado Springs, CO

Journal Writing
Date April 17

Name	Score	Capitalization Comments	Score	Punctuation Comments	Score	Spelling Comments
Donta	✔	Work on proper nouns and ou/ow words.	✔+		✔	
David	✔	Work on capitalizing I, names of people, and beginnings of sentences.			✔-	Work on high-frequency words.
Jaida	✔+		✔-	Not putting end marks on sentences.	✔	

STICK TO IT!

This timesaving tip makes **taking anecdotal records** trouble free! Purchase sheets of address labels from an office supply store. Place several sheets on a clipboard and keep it at hand for observations. To record notes, write the date and the child's name or number on a label and then add information about his work. If one label is not enough, continue to the next. Later, peel the label and place it on a page in the child's work portfolio. Now notes are organized and ready for progress reports, conferences, or planning!

Karen Slattery, Marie of the Incarnation School
Bradford, Ontario, Canada

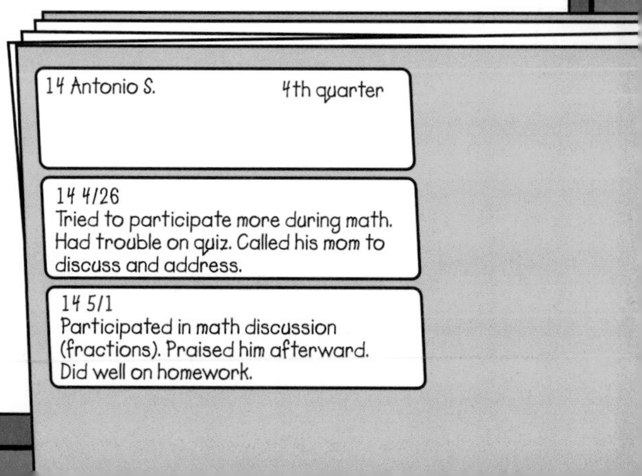
14 Antonio S. 4th quarter
14 4/26
Tried to participate more during math. Had trouble on quiz. Called his mom to discuss and address.
14 5/1
Participated in math discussion (fractions). Praised him afterward. Did well on homework.

It's a Wrap!
Celebrating the End of the School Year

Luisa Herrera
Luisa is a good reader. She has a nice smile.

Marcus Coleman
Marcus is really good at kickball. He also likes to help people.

YEAR-END COUNTDOWN

Give each child a **memento of the school year and create a simple display** at the same time! A few weeks before the end of school, gather a supply of 2" x 12" colorful paper strips and program each with a different child's name. Next, give each student a strip other than his own and have him write something complimentary about the person listed. Afterward, collect the strips and use them to create a paper chain. Post the chain in the classroom. Then, each day, detach a link from the chain and read its compliment aloud. Finally, give each child his link to take home as a school year souvenir!

Andrea Schoenbeck, Springville Elementary, Springville, IA

WHO IS THIS?

Find out how well students know their classmates with this **identification game**! In advance, make a class supply of the reproducible on page 310. Have each child answer the questions; then collect the papers and shuffle them. Over the next several days, select a few papers to read aloud to the class. Encourage students to use the clues in the responses to guess each child's identity. If they are correct, choose another paper and repeat the process. If they are incorrect, have the student reveal herself. Continue in this manner until each child's responses have been read aloud and identified.

Andrea Selking, Lantern Farms School, Fishers, IN

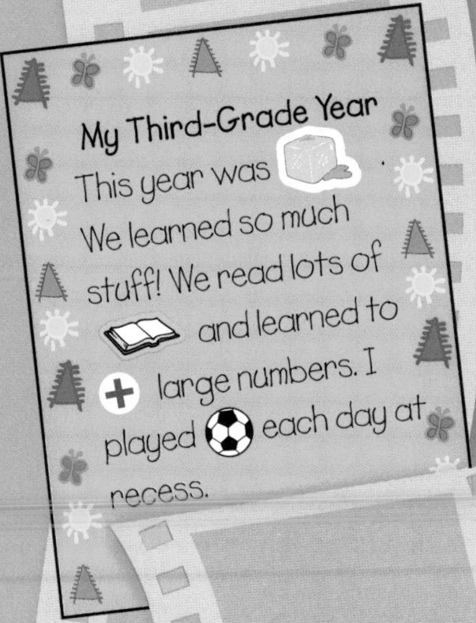
My Third-Grade Year
This year was [sticker]. We learned so much stuff! We read lots of [sticker] and learned to [sticker] large numbers. I played [sticker] each day at recess.

STICKER SUMMARIES

These rebus-style summaries create a **lasting memories** of the school year! Prepare by gathering a supply of stickers, including the following types: seasonal, sports, and school related. Cut the stickers apart and place several of each type in a snack-size resealable bag. Start by showing students on chart paper how to write a sentence and replace a word or words with a sticker. After completing several sentences, give each child a bag of stickers. Have the student write a brief summary of his school year on a scrap sheet of paper, inserting stickers when possible without affixing them to the page. After editing his first draft, he rewrites it on a sheet of colored construction paper, attaching stickers where desired. He titles his summary and adds a decorative border. After allowing students to share their writing, post the summaries on a display titled "That's Our Story and We're Sticking to It!"

adapted from an idea by Kimberly Fincher
New Madrid County R-1/Matthews Elementary, Matthews, MO

Name______________________________

All About Me

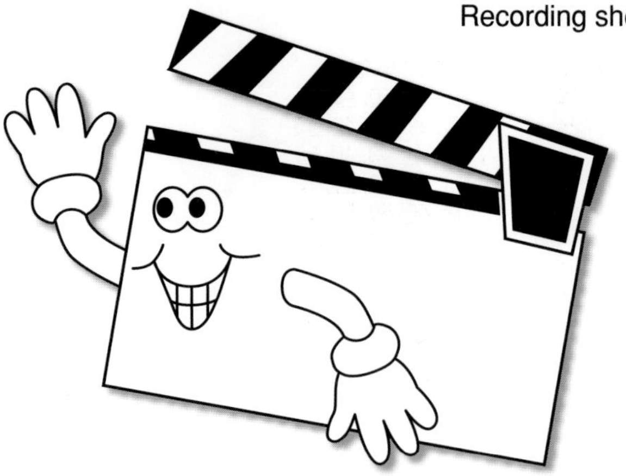

Answer each question.

What's your favorite subject?______________________________

What are three things you are good at? ______________________________

____

What do you do after school? ______________________________

____

Do you have any brothers or sisters? __________ If so, how many? __________

____

Do you have any pets? __________ If so, what are their names? __________

____

____

What is your favorite book? ______________________________

What's your favorite kind of music? ______________________________

What's your favorite movie or TV show? ______________________________

____

Do you play any sports? __________ If so, what are they? __________

____

What do you want to be when you grow up? ______________________________

____

 Note to the teacher: Use with "Who Is This?" on page 309.

Answer Keys

Page 83

A. 3, 5, 7, 9, 11, 13, 15, 17, 19, 21
B. 85, 80, 75, 70, 65, 60, 55, 50, 45, 40
C. 18, 21, 24, 27, 30, 33, 36, 39, 42, 45
D. 56, 54, 52, 50, 48, 46, 44, 42, 40, 38
E. 18, 24, 30, 36, 42, 48, 54, 60, 66, 72
F. 22, 26, 30, 34, 38, 42, 46, 50, 54, 58
G. 100, 90, 80, 70, 60, 50, 40, 30, 20, 10
H. 37, 42, 47, 52, 57, 62, 67, 72, 77, 82
I. 46, 43, 40, 37, 34, 31, 28, 25, 22, 19
J. 61, 65, 69, 73, 77, 81, 85, 89, 93, 97

HE USED A SAND DOLLAR!

Page 87

Order of numbers will vary.

odd numbers less than 40			even numbers between 30 and 70			odd numbers greater than 60		
5	11	19	32	42	48	61	63	65
21	27	35	50	58	64	73	77	89
	39			66			95	

Page 89

Nose	Accessory
coal	scarf
coal	mitten
coal	hat
carrot	scarf
carrot	mitten
carrot	hat
button	scarf
button	mitten
button	hat
stick	scarf
stick	mitten
stick	hat

Page 91

All gelts should be colored except 110.

A.	B.	C.
60	40	80
− 10	+ 40	− 60
50	80	20

D.	E.	F.
80	50	80
+ 20	+ 20	− 20
100	70	60

G.	H.
60	60
− 30	− 50
30	10

I.	J.
70	60
− 30	+ 30
40	90

Page 92

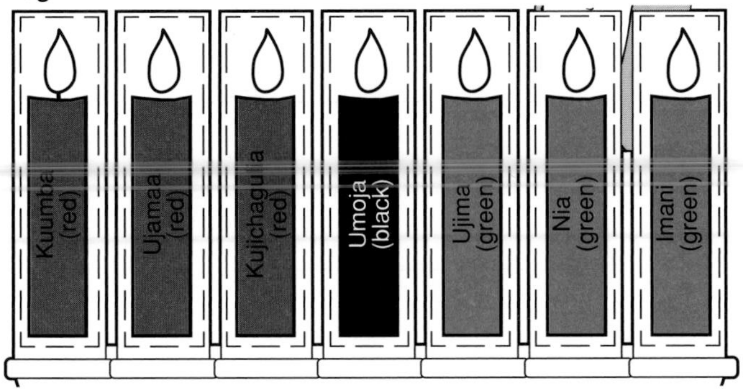

Kuumba (red)
Ujamaa (red)
Kujichagulia (red)
Umoja (black)
Ujima (green)
Nia (green)
Imani (green)

Page 97

1. turn
2. flip
3. turn
4. slide
5. flip
6. turn
7. slide
8. flip
9. slide

Page 137

The following sentences should be circled: 1, 3, 5, 8.
Sentences for the second part will vary.

Page 138

The following sentences should be circled: 2, 3, 7, 8, 10.

A. Ollie was our waitress.
She took our order.
B. I ordered chili.
It looked good.
C. Steve wanted soda.
I asked for water.
D. Ollie brought our food to the table.
It was hot.
E. I ate quickly.
Steve ate fast too.

Page 139

1. Did you get a sandwich?
2. I ate three burgers.
3. The fries here are good.
4. What did she order for dessert?
5. I like the cake better.
6. Our meal was great!

Page 155

1. Y. plays
2. S. practice
3. F. likes
4. A. rush
5. N. catches
6. T. clap
7. E. cheer
8. R. wins

They STAY NEAR the FANS!

Page 156

	Past	Present	Future
1. I went to the Bears game.	✓		
2. I bought a program when I got there.	✓		
3. Then I found my seat.	✓		
4. I see my favorite player over there!		✓	
5. I will try to get his autograph.			✓
6. I run to talk to him.		✓	
7. Then the game begins.		✓	
8. I watch the players make their shots.		✓	
9. Our team won the game!	✓		
10. I will go to another game soon!			✓

Page 160

1. I'm on my way to Orlando, Florida.
2. My friend Val is going to Los Angeles, California.
3. Vinnie is being sent to Honolulu, Hawaii.
4. Vera is being mailed to New York, New York.
5. Vickie is going to Myrtle Beach, South Carolina.
6. Van will arrive in Chicago, Illinois.
7. Vern is being mailed to Dallas, Texas.
8. Vanna is flying to Nome, Alaska.
9. Vic is going to Tucson, Arizona.
10. Vita is taking a train to Denver, Colorado.

Page 164

The transition words may vary for sentences 2 and 4 (see below). The remaining sentences should have the transition words shown.

1. First, I looked in the closet because I thought I put them there.
2. Then/Next, I looked under the bed.
3. Before looking any longer, I asked my sister.
4. Then/Next, I asked my mom.
5. After I asked my mom, I looked outside.
6. Finally, I found them in the yard!

Page 186

★	– 0	– 4	– 6	– 2	– 5	– 3	– 7	– 1
5	5	1	★	3	0	2	★	4
7	7	3	1	5	2	4	0	6
11	★	7	5	9	6	8	4	★
6	6	2	0	4	1	3	★	5
4	4	0	★	2	★	1	★	3
9	9	5	3	7	4	6	2	8
10	★	6	4	8	5	7	3	★
12	★	8	6	★	7	9	5	★
8	8	4	2	6	3	5	1	7

Page 190

C. 31 > S. 28 B. 18 < I. 81 E. 36 > G. 32

M. 19 < D. 29 F. 61 < O. 78 U. 21 < Y. 91

J. 15 < R. 17 H. 41 > Z. 33 P. 57 > Q. 43

T. 63 > V. 59 K. 80 < A. 89 N. 24 > W. 12

IN THE DICTIONARY!

Page 191

A. (294), 322, 428, 487, 506, 561

B. 755, 854, (898), 926, 971, 987

C. (548), 583, 616, 624, 632, 695

D. 234, 255, 289, 315, 347, (365)

Page 195

I. 90	U. 83	X. 616	K. 981
M. 921	N. 85	R. 680	P. 57
L. 93	O. 993	G. 658	A. 81
N. 909	U. 86	D. 606	

They're always ROUNDING UP!

Page 198

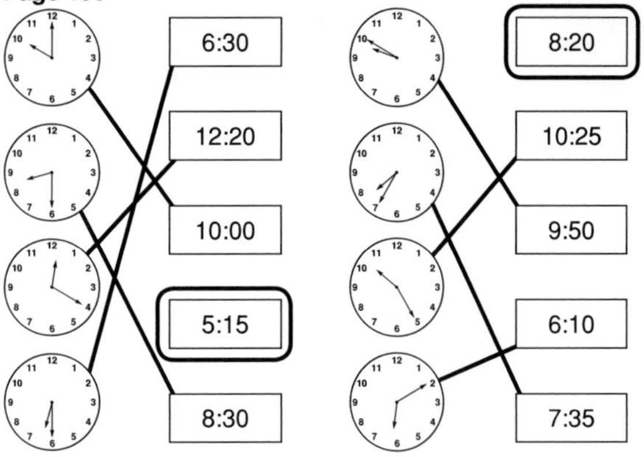
6:30
12:20
10:00
5:15
8:30
8:20
10:25
9:50
6:10
7:35

Bonus Box: 3 hours and 5 minutes.

Page 207

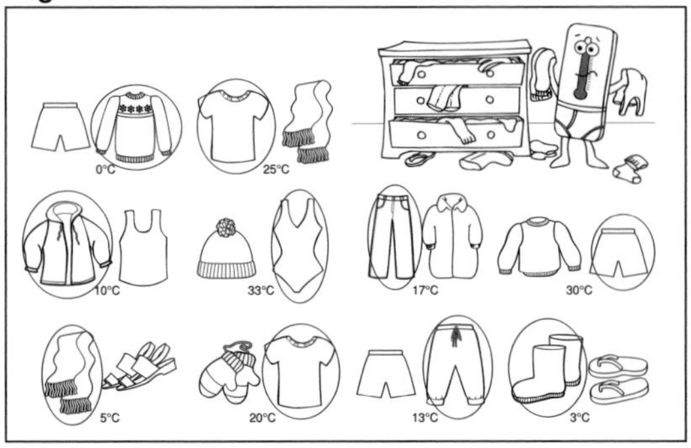
0°C
25°C
10°C
33°C
17°C
30°C
5°C
20°C
13°C
3°C

Page 213

	8:00	9:00	10:00	11:00	12:00	1:00
Sally Sphere		★				
Seth Square Pyramid				★		
Cole Cube						★
Rita Rectangular Prism					★	
Cindy Cylinder			★			
Connor Cone	★					

Page 216

A. $\frac{2}{5}$	F. $\frac{1}{3}$
B. $\frac{1}{4}$	G. $\frac{7}{8}$
C. $\frac{5}{7}$	H. $\frac{2}{4}$
D. $\frac{3}{8}$	I. $\frac{5}{6}$
E. $\frac{4}{6}$	J. $\frac{2}{3}$

Page 218

A. 119	G. 254
B. 151	H. 182
C. 193	I. 52
D. 67	J. 163
E. 159	K. 363
F. 550	L. 186

Page 221

A. 48, 50, 52, 54, 56, 58, 60, 62, 64
B. 17, 20, 23, 26, 29, 32, 35, 38, 41
C. 75, 65, 55, 45, 35, 25, 15, 5
D. 30, 35, 40, 45, 50, 55, 60, 65
E. 88, 85, 82, 79, 76, 73, 70, 67, 64
F. 80, 70, 60, 50, 40, 30, 20, 10
G. 55, 59, 63, 67, 71, 75, 79, 83, 87
H. 20, 18, 16, 14, 12, 10, 8, 6, 4
I. 27, 32, 37, 42, 47, 52, 57, 62, 67
J. 13, 17, 21, 25, 29, 33, 37, 41, 45

They MAKE THEM SPOTLESS!

Page 224

1. 109 carrots
2. 9 plants
3. 17 pounds
4. $130.95
5. 70 radishes
6. 5 hours and 20 minutes
7. 67 pounds
8. 36 pies
9. 7 days
10. 54 plants

Page 227

1. 264 carrots
2. 89 gallons of milk
3. 2 pounds
4. 42 roses
5. 40 pansies
6. 70 minutes
7. 78 heads of lettuce
8. 7 pies

Page 231

1. Week 5
2. 27 flags
3. 27 flags
4. Week 1
5. 6 flags
6. 15 flags
7. 48 flags
8. 9 flags

Page 232

	Striped Flag	Polka-Dot Flag	Starry Flag	Triangular Flag	Octagonal Flag
Ernie					★
Evan		★			
Erin			★		
Eva	★				
Ellie				★	

Page 244

Tug	Tug and Taz	Taz
CD	water	map
raisins	seeds	camera
whistle	hat	gum
compass	watch	journal
flashlight	shades	bandage

Page 257

				1 F	I	S	H				
			2 P	R	O	T	E	C	T		
			3 S	O	I	L					
				4 M	I	N	E	R	A	L	S
		5 C	O	T	T	O	N				
6 S	U	N	S	H	I	N	E				
		7 C	L	E	A	N	A	I	R		
		8 O	C	E	A	N	S				
			9 P	A	P	E	R				
10 W	A	T	E	R							
11 P	L	A	N	T	S						
			12 S	H	E	L	T	E	R		

They come <u>from the earth</u>!

Page 259

Food: bat, coyote, javelina, jackrabbit, pack rat
Shelter: elf owl, lizard, snake, spider
Both: ants, white-winged dove, Gila woodpecker

Page 266

1. goods
2. supply
3. needs
4. demand
5. producer
6. consumer
7. factory
8. service
9. wants
10. income

<u>FOLD IT IN HALF</u>!

Page 276

A. 6
B. 20
C. 5
D. 4
E. 300
F. 90
G. 10
H. 30
I. 200
J. 40
K. 900
L. 60
M. 700
N. 8
O. 600

The following pumpkins should not be colored: 50, 7.

Page 283

1. He wanted black people and white people to be treated equally.
2. They had separate schools and bathrooms. Black people didn't have equal seating on buses.
3. He solved problems peacefully.
4. Answers will vary.
5. c

Page 284

1. Atlanta, Georgia
2. 1947
3. b
4. 1983
5. Coretta Scott
6. 1963

Page 289

Order of answers will vary.

Ticket 1	Ticket 2	Total
$3.75	$4.25	$8.00
$3.75	$4.50	$8.25
$3.75	$4.75	$8.50
$3.75	$5.25	$9.00
$4.25	$4.50	$8.75
$4.25	$4.75	$9.00
$4.25	$5.25	$9.50
$4.50	$4.75	$9.25
$4.50	$5.25	$9.75
$4.75	$5.25	$10.00

Page 295

Card 1
orange, blue, red, pink, purple, yellow
Card 2
blue, purple, yellow, red, pink, orange
Card 3
red, pink, orange, yellow, purple, blue
Card 4
purple, orange, blue, yellow, pink, red

Page 296

Order of answers will vary.

friendly	faster	prettiest
slowly	smaller	largest
sweetly	dirtier	cleanest
quickly	shinier	tallest

Page 300

Order will vary.

dog's	brothers'
dancer's	girls'
children's	students'
Carrie's	cats'
Mom's	teachers'
author's	players'

Index

ISBN-13: 978-156234725-3
ISBN-10: 156234725-X
9 781562 347253